The Oracle8™ to Oracle8i Upgrade™ Cram Sheet

This Cram Sheet contains the distilled, key facts about new Oracle8i features to be tested in t exam. Review this information last thing before you enter the test room, paying special attenti to those areas where you feel you need the most review. You can transfer any of these facts on a blank sheet of paper before beginning the exam.

MIGRATIONS AND UPGRADES: ORACLE7 TO ORACLE8I

1. Oracle8i introduced a new Java-based Oracle software installer called the Universal Installer.
2. The Universal Installer provides two installation modes: interactive and silent. Use interactive mode for normal installations. Use silent mode for installations—such as installing the exact same database configuration at multiple sites—that require no user interaction.
3. You can use the Data Migration Assistant to migrate a 7.*x* database to Oracle8i. You can also migrate the database manually, use the Oracle Export/Import feature, or use SQL*Copy in SQL*Plus.
4. You can use the Data Migration Assistant to upgrade an 8.*x* database to Oracle8i. You can also upgrade the database manually, use the Oracle Export/Import feature, or use SQL*Copy in SQL*Plus.
5. Upgrade scripts are provided for manually upgrading an Oracle8 database to Oracle8i. (Some early versions of Oracle8 can't be directly upgraded to Oracle8i.)
6. Oracle has introduced a new SQL script, utlrp.sql, to allow you to recompile any PL/SQL packages invalidated by the migration.
7. The method used to install the migration utility in the Oracle7 ORACLE_HOME directory has changed. Now you use the Oracle migprep utility to copy the mig utility from the Oracle8i ORACLE_HOME directory to the Oracle7 ORACLE_HOME directory.

JAVA IN ORACLE8I

8. To install the JVM (Java Virtual Machine) in the Oracle8i database, you should run the initjvm.sql script.
9. The loadjava utility is used to load **Java** classes in the Oracle8i database.
10. The dropjava utility is used to remove **Java** classes from the Oracle8i database.
11. The **JAVA_POOL_SIZE** parameter, set in the init.ora file of the database, configures the JVM's memory pool.
12. The init.ora parameters **JAVA_SOFT_SESSIONSPACE _LIMIT** and **JAVA_MAX_SESSIONSPACE _SIZE** deter-mine the memory-usage limits for individual Java sessions.

AVAILABILITY AND RECOVERABILITY ENHANCEMENTS

13. Archived-redo-log multiplexing is done by using the **LOG_ARCHIVE_DEST_n** parameter in the database's init.ora file. This parameter supersedes the **LOG_ARCHIVE_DEST** parameter in Oracle8.
14. A stand by database can be kept in managed recovery mode, which allows the database to automatically apply the archive redo logs as they arrive from the primary database.
15. The LogMiner utility is used to analyze redo logs from Oracle8 and Oracle8i databases. You can create SQL statements that represent the redo required to re-create a SQL command, or the undo required to roll back a given SQL command.
16. Fast-start fault recovery in Oracle8i speeds up the instance recovery process in case of a crash.

SUMMARY MANAGEMENT

17. A materialized view is a new Oracle8i object that provides new functionality to speed up summary queries of large data sets. Unlike a traditional view, the materialized view is a real Oracle object that stores the result set in its own segment.

create resource plan directives; assign users to the resource consumer group; and specify a plan for the instance.

ARTITIONING TABLES AND INDEXES

3. Oracle8i provides three types of partitioned tables: range, hash, and composite.

9. Partitioned tables and indexes can be equipartitioned (the logical partitioning attributes are the same) or nonequipartitioned (the logical partitioning attributes are different). A partitioned table can have a maximum of 65,535 partitions.

. Index-organized tables (IOTs) can be partitioned in Oracle8i. IOT overflow segments (if created) will be equipartitioned with the IOT.

. Oracle8i now allows the partitioning of tables that contain LOBs. Each partition of a partitioned table that contains a LOB will have an equipartitioned LOB data segment and LOB index segment associated with it.

.. **LONG** and **LONG RAW** columns are not supported in partitioned tables.

3. There are two types of partitioned indexes: global and local. Global indexes allow you to define the partitions of the index and can be nonequipartitioned with the associated table. Global indexes are harder to manage because Oracle doesn't maintain the relationships between the index and the table when DDL operations are performed against the table. Thus, a global index, or one or more of its partitions, might become unusable and have to be rebuilt.

4. Local indexes must be equipartitioned with the associated table.

5. Secondary indexes can now be created for IOTs. Oracle8i provides logical row IDs to facilitate the creation of these indexes.

ARTITION MAINTENANCE OPERATIONS

76. The **ALTER TABLE...SPLIT PARTITION**, **DROP PARTITION**, and **MERGE PARTITIONS** commands are not supported when you're administering hash-partitioned tables.

77. The **ALTER TABLE ADD PARTITION** and **ALTER TABLE COALESCE PARTITION** commands can be used for administering hash-partitioned tables.

78. Certain operations can use **NOLOGGING** mode. These include: parallel **CREATE TABLE...AS SELECT** operations; **CREATE INDEX** operations; and **SPLIT**, **MOVE**, or **REBUILD PARTITION** operations; and direct-load insert operations.

79. Certain operations can put global partitioned indexes in an **UNUSABLE** state. These include certain types of imports and partitioned-table operations (**SPLIT**, **TRUNCATE**, or **DROP** on the associated table). Also, when you drop an index partition in a global index, the next highest partition (based on partition range) will be marked **UNUSABLE**. SQL*Loader direct loads can cause this as well.

80. Use the **ALTER INDEX REBUILD PARTITION** clause to rebuild the index partitions that are marked **UNUSABLE**.

MANAGEABILITY ENHANCEMENTS

81. You can now move a table between different tablespaces by using the **ALTER TABLE...MOVE** command. You can also specify new storage parameters for the table. DML is prohibited during a move operation on an ordinary table.

82. You can drop columns in tables by using the **ALTER TABLE...DROP COLUMN** command. An alternative is the **ALTER TABLE...SET UNUSED COLUMN** command, which makes the column no longer visible but retains the data. You can then use the **ALTER TABLE...DROP UNUSED COLUMNS** command to permanently remove the column data.

83. The **V$SESSION_LONGOPS** view helps you monitor long-running operations.

84. Oracle8i has two new constraint options: **RELY** and **NORELY. RELY** allows the DBA to tell Oracle that it should assume that the data is valid, and not enforce the constraint. **NORELY** (the default) causes the constraint to act as it always has dne..

RECOVERY MANAGER

85. RMAN recovery operations do not require the recovery catalog (unless you have lost the control file and no backup is available).

86. The new commands **CREATE CATALOG**, **UPDATE CATALOG**, and **DROP CATALOG** make it easier to maintain the recovery catalog.

87. The **DUPLICATE** command is used to create a database by using the backup of another.

88. You can create multiple copies of a backup piece.

89. Tablespace point-in-time recovery is supported by RMAN.

90. The performance views **V$BACKUP_SYNC_IO** and **V$BACKUP_ASYNC_IO** help you monitor RMAN backup performance.

b. Create the application context package.

c. Create a logon trigger to set the context at logon.

d. Create the context-checking package, which will return a predicate, which is appended to any SQL statement as an additional **WHERE** clause.

43. Deferred constraint enforcement allows you to delay enforcement of constraints until the end of a transaction.

44. The **ENFORCE** clause of the **ALTER TABLE** command can be used to enable a constraint without checking all existing records to ensure that they are valid.

OPTIMIZER AND QUERY IMPROVEMENTS

45. The **DBMS_STATS** package is provided for gathering more detailed statistics than those gathered by the **ANALYZE** command. Oracle8i also supports the export and import of statistics between schemas and even other databases.

46. The ability to save and reuse stored execution plans is introduced in Oracle8i. This capability provides much more stable execution plans in critical, tuned application code. The **OUTLN_PKG** package is provided to manage these stored plans.

47. The **OUTLN** schema contains two tables: **OL$** and **OL$HINTS**. These tables are used to store the outlines and the hints.

48. The SQL **ROLLUP** and **CUBE** operators are introduced in Oracle8i to help you create cross-tab reports. **ROLLUP** provides multiple levels of subtotals and grand totals, and **CUBE** creates subtotals for groupings of a result set.

49. Top-N SQL queries are used to return only a specific number of rows based on the results of a sorted subquery.

50. In a multiprocessor system, the init.ora parameter **PARALLEL_AUTOMATIC_EXECUTION=TRUE** can improve the performance of large-table scans and joins. This parameter can also aid performance during large index creations, large inserts, updates, deletes, and partitioned index scans.

TABLESPACE MANAGEMENT

51. Oracle8i offers two types of tablespace extent management: dictionary and local. Dictionary-managed tablespaces are the default; this is the same method Oracle has always used to manage tablespaces.

52. Locally managed tablespaces require less data-dictionary activity. This occurs because the extents are managed by using a bitmap that resides in each data file of the locally managed tablespace.

53. Extents in a locally managed tablespace are of two types: uniform or system managed.

54. When you create a locally managed tablespace, use the keyword **UNIFORM** in the **CREATE TABLESPACE** statement to specify that extent management should be uniform in size. The default extent size for **UNIFORM** sizing is 1MB. (This default can be changed in the **CREATE TABLE** statement.)

55. When you create a locally managed tablespace, use the keyword **AUTOALLOCATE** in the **CREATE TABLESPACE** statement to specify that extent management should be system managed. Oracle will determine the optimal extent size for each extent (64KB is the default).

56. Oracle8i introduced transportable tablespaces. Using the **DBMS_TTS** package and the Export/Import utility, you can move a tablespace from one database to another. Two new parameters for the Export utility—**TRANSPORT_TABLESPACE** and **TABLESPACES**—are required. Two new parameters for the Import utility—**TRANSPORT_TABLESPACE** and **DATAFILES**—are also required.

57. In Oracle8i, a tablespace can be made read-only while transactions are occurring in the database. If database DML or DDL activity is occurring in the tablespace, then it will go into transitional read-only mode until that activity is completed.

INDEXES AND INDEX-ORGANIZED TABLES

58. A function-based index is based on a function being applied to a column or columns in a table.

59. New parameters—**QUERY_REWRITE_ENABLED** and **QUERY_REWRITE_INTEGRITY**—must be correctly set to enable function-based indexes.

60. Indexes in Oracle8i can be built online while DML activity is occurring in the underlying table.

61. Additional secondary performance indexes are allowed with index-organized tables.

62. Descending-key indexes sort the columns of an index in descending order.

63. Reverse-key indexes reverse the bytes in the index columns, reducing index browning.

THE DATABASE RESOURCE MANAGER

64. The Database Resource Manager is used to manage system and database resources.

65. Resources that can be managed include:

    - Allocation of a percentage of CPUs to a group of users
    - Limitation of the degree of parallelism for groups of users

66. A resource plan is a plan for allocating system resources. A resource plan directive is used to assign a consumer group to a resource plan.

67. To use the Database Resource Manager: create a resource plan; create a resource consumer group;

18. Oracle8i can maintain some materialized views automatically on commit, but other views have to be refreshed on demand.
19. Materialized view logs track all changes to the view's underlying base table(s). This tracking helps to synchronize the materialized view with its underlying base table(s). Use the **CREATE**, **ALTER**, and **DROP MATERIALIZED VIEW LOG** commands to administer these objects.
20. Use the **CREATE MATERIALIZED VIEW** command to create a materialized view. You can alter a materialized view with the **ALTER MATERIALIZED VIEW** command, and drop it with the **DROP MATERIALIZED VIEW** command.
21. You must enable a materialized view for query rewrite by including the **ENABLE QUERY REWRITE** clause when you're using the **CREATE** or **ALTER MATERIALIZED VIEW** command. The query rewrite feature allows the Oracle optimizer to convert a SQL statement that contains columns from tables (or views in its FROM clause that are also contained in a given materialized view) to use the the materialized view instead.
22. To enable query rewrite, set the **QUERY_REWRITE_ENABLED** parameter in the init.ora file. The **QUERY_REWRITE_INTEGRITY** parameter defines the freshness that is required of a given view if it is to be considered for a query rewrite.
23. You can defer the initial build of the view when you create it; to do this, use the **BUILD DEFERRED** clause of the **CREATE MATERIALIZED VIEW** command.
24. Two refresh modes are available: **ON COMMIT** and **ON DEMAND**. The **ON COMMIT** mode allows the view to be updated when changes to the base tables are committed. This mode is allowed in only two cases: when the materialized view is built on a single table aggregate, and when the view is built on a join (no aggregation).
25. The **ON DEMAND** mode causes the view to not be updated, except when requested. You use the data warehouse refresh utility in the **DBMS_MVIEW** package to refresh materialized views.
26. Four refresh options are available: **COMPLETE**, **FAST**, **FORCE**, and **NEVER**. (Don't confuse refresh modes with refresh options.)
27. You can register an existing view as a materialized view by using the **ON PREBUILT TABLE** clause of the **CREATE MATERIALIZED VIEW** command.
28. Dimensions in Oracle8i define hierarchical structures that are present in different data sets in an Oracle database. These dimensions are used by the query rewrite feature to determine whether a materialized view can be used.
29. The **DBMS_OLAP** package is used to identify materialized view candidatesin a schema.

NET8

30. Client load balancing and failover.
31. Service naming is introduced in Net8 and Oracle8i. Service naming allows you to define a single service that is serviced by one or more databases.
32. Automated instance registration is a new feature of Oracle8i. New parameters can be added to the init.ora file to facilitate enhanced automated listener-registration features.

SQL*PLUS, PL/SQL, AND NLS

33. SQL*Plus now supports database administration commands formerly availablein Server Manager. These commands include **STARTUP**, **SHUTDOWN**, **RECOVER**, **SHOW SGA**, and **SHOW PARAMETERS**.
34. New trigger types available in Oracle8i include database and user events. Database events include startup, shutdown, and server errors. User events include user logons and logoffs of the database.
35. Two packages, **DBMS_TRACE** and **DBMS_PROFILER**, can be used to analyze application performance.
36. Support for dynamic SQL is enhanced with the addition of native dynamic SQL. Dynamic SQL reduces the coding previously required to use the **DBMS_SQL** package and reduces the need for the **DBMS_SQL** package.
37. The new invoker-rights model is now supported for PL/SQL stored programs. This model allows you to define whether the stored program should be called by using the object privileges of the invoker or of the definer (default).
38. Oracle8i supports autonomous transactions, a feature that allow a transaction to call a separate transaction that's independent of the calling transaction. The results of the autonomous transaction can be made immediately available to the calling transaction.

DATABASE SECURITY AND CONSTRAINTS

39. Fine-grained access control (FGAC) is a new Oracle8i feature that allows the implementation of row-level security on tables and views.
40. Benefits of FGAC include enhanced security, flexibility, transparency to the application, and scalability.
41. Typically, FGAC will use a context area. Contexts are global "storage" areas that are established upon user login. These areas can be used to store specific data that is unique to each user login. Use the **CREATE OR REPLACE CONTEXT** command to create a context.
42. The typical steps to create FGAC against a given table are:
    a. Do the initial setup (create the schema, tables, and so on).

Oracle8™ to Oracle8i™ Upgrade

Robert G. Freeman
Charles A. Pack

Oracle8™ to Oracle8i™ Upgrade Exam Cram

The Coriolis Group, LLC
14455 N. Hayden Road
Suite 220
Scottsdale, Arizona 85260

(480)483-0192
FAX (480)483-0193
www.coriolis.com

Library of Congress Cataloging-in-Publication Data
Freeman, Robert G., 1965-
Oracle8 to 8i upgrade exam cram/by Robert Freeman and Charles Pack.
p. cm.
Includes index.
ISBN 1-57610-737-X
1. Oracle (Computer file) 2. Application software--Development. I. Title: Oracle8 to 8i upgrade exam cram. II. Pack, Charles. III. Title.

QA76.76.D47.F74 2000
005.75'85--dc21 00-058925
CIP

President and CEO
Keith Weiskamp

Publisher
Steve Sayre

Acquisitions Editor
Jeff Kellum

Product Marketing Manager
Brett Woolley

Project Editor
Sybil Ihrig,
Helios Productions

Technical Reviewer
Peter Sharman

Production Coordinator
Kim Eoff

Cover Designer
Jesse Dunn

Layout Designer
April Nielsen

CD-ROM Developer
Michelle McConnell

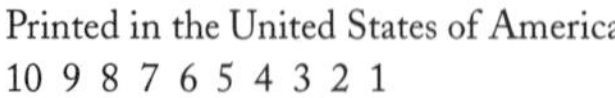

Printed in the United States of America
10 9 8 7 6 5 4 3 2 1

The Coriolis Group, LLC • 14455 North Hayden Road, Suite 220 • Scottsdale, Arizona 85260

ExamCram.com Connects You to the Ultimate Study Center!

Our goal has always been to provide you with the best study tools on the planet to help you achieve your certification in record time. Time is so valuable these days that none of us can afford to waste a second of it, especially when it comes to exam preparation.

Over the past few years, we've created an extensive line of *Exam Cram* and *Exam Prep* study guides, practice exams, and interactive training. To help you study even better, we have now created an e-learning and certification destination called **ExamCram.com**. (You can access the site at **www.examcram.com**.) Now, with every study product you purchase from us, you'll be connected to a large community of people like yourself who are actively studying for their certifications, developing their careers, seeking advice, and sharing their insights and stories.

I believe that the future is all about collaborative learning. Our **ExamCram.com** destination is our approach to creating a highly interactive, easily accessible collaborative environment, where you can take practice exams and discuss your experiences with others, sign up for features like "Questions of the Day," plan your certifications using our interactive planners, create your own personal study pages, and keep up with all of the latest study tips and techniques.

I hope that whatever study products you purchase from us—*Exam Cram* or *Exam Prep* study guides, *Personal Trainers*, *Personal Test Centers*, or one of our interactive Web courses—will make your studying fun and productive. Our commitment is to build the kind of learning tools that will allow you to study the way you want to, whenever you want to.

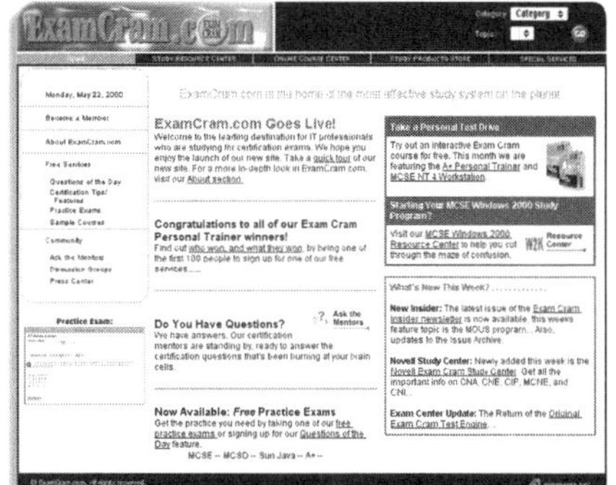

Visit ExamCram.com now to enhance your study program.

Help us continue to provide the very best certification study materials possible. Write us or email us at **learn@examcram.com** and let us know how our study products have helped you study. Tell us about new features that you'd like us to add. Send us a story about how we've helped you. We're listening!

Good luck with your certification exam and your career. Thank you for allowing us to help you achieve your goals.

Keith Weiskamp
President and CEO

To my patient wife and kids, who make my life go round.
To my friends, who when needed are always to be found.
To my parents, who put up with me through laughter and tears—
May my second book make it worth all those trying years.
—Robert G. Freeman

❧

To Peanut, and Jencie.
—Charles A. Pack

❧

About the Authors

Robert G. Freeman is an Oracle7, Oracle8, and Oracle8i Oracle Certified Professional with more than 9 years of Oracle database administration experience and more than 13 years of overall IT experience. He is the author of the *Oracle DBA 7.3 to 8 Cer1tification Upgrade Exam Cram* published by The Coriolis Group, and he has written various training courseware modules as well as university-level DBA training courseware. He has taught various Oracle DBA training classes and has presented at Oracle user group meetings. He currently resides in Jacksonville, Florida, where he keeps his co-worker and co-author Charles Pack in line, and where he lives with his wife, five kids, and Clifford the cat.

Charles A. Pack is an Oracle7, Oracle8, and Oracle8i Certified Professional DBA with more than 15 years of IT experience in operations, management, application development, and database administration. He holds a Bachelor of Science degree from Oklahoma State University, a Master's in Business Administration from The University of Oklahoma, and a Master's in Computer Science from Texas A&M University, Corpus Christi. He lives in Jacksonville, Florida, with his wonderful wife Donna. He is employed by CSX Technology, Inc. as a Senior Oracle DBA, and teaches Oracle DBA classes at Florida Community College, Jacksonville.

Acknowledgments

Thanks to everyone at Coriolis for all the hard work. Thanks to Acquisitions Editor Jeff Kellum, Managing Editor Paula Kmetz, Project Editor Sybil Ihrig who tried (in vain) to keep us on schedule, copy editor Catherine Oliver who made my English look more like it should, technical reviewer Pete Sharman who did a great job, Dan Fiverson for his technical help, and my co-author Charles Pack (who, fairly, I had to kick in the butt a few times).
Thanks to Joel and Mike for being my friends!

Thanks to Bob Just from Oracle, whom I failed to include in my acknowledgments in the 7.3 to 8 Upgrade guide. Bob is a great resource for the hard-to-find answers. Larry Ellison, if you are reading this, give that man a raise!
Thanks to Norman Thompson, Bill Sullivan, Tim Stippler, Bill "follow the change control" Barker, Maritza Gonzalez, Jay Jarboe, Yang Jiang, Richard McClain, and last (but certainly not least), Don Mongeon. All my friends and co-workers! Special thanks to Gunjan Nath and Nirupam Majumdar for taking the Oracle8i New Features for Administrators Beta exam!!!

Special thanks to Richard Basile and Mike Ault.

Thanks to Master Clark, Ms. Skutnik, Mr. Moraes, and Mr. Lindenmuth for making my kicks higher, my family closer, and giving my kids something to shoot for. ATA!

Finally, thanks to my wife Debbie, my five kids, Felicia, Sarah, Jacob, Jared, and Elizabeth, for all your support and love. Without you, my life would not be a whole. Thanks to my Dad and Ruth for putting up with me (and, as the Managing Editor Paula will tell you, I'm still a handful!)...

Finally, thanks to all of you who bought this book! Once you are certified, and even before, remember to go out and do some good!

—Robert G. Freeman

Thanks to Robert for asking me to share the responsibilities and rewards of writing this book, and for not using me as a karate demonstration. Thanks to the gang—Terri Severson, Bob Just, Jay Jarboe, Nirupam Majumdar, Gunjan Nath,

Don Mongeon, Maritza Gonzalez, Yang Jiang, John King, Bill Sullivan, Bill Barker, Tim Stippler, Rich McClain, and Charlie Crissman.

Extra-special buckets of thanks to Maury Jarrell—my mentor, for your technical review, friendship, and ever-present humor. Thanks to Bobby Everitt for your leadership, and Mike Towery, the world's most hilarious DBA, for throwing me into the Oracle world. Thanks to Jim Sirico and Keith Murphy of Oracle Corporation, for shining a light onto the Oracle tuning path. Thanks to Tim, Zach de la Rocha, Tom Morello, and Brad Wilk for inspiration; to my sister Natalie Lane and my brothers Mark Guerra, Mike King, and Rob Johnson for humoring me through my struggle.

And, of course, thanks to my parents Charlene (Sarge) and Gus (007)—who taught me the important things in life. I'm proud of you two!!! Most of all, thanks to my beautiful, wonderful, awesome wife Donna—the love of my life—who has always encouraged me and always been there for me, even when I worked on this book instead of playing in the Florida sun....

—Charles A. Pack

Contents at a Glance

Table of Contents

Chapter 9
Optimizer and Query Improvements 171

Chapter 10
Tablespace Management 193

Introduction

Welcome to *Oracle8 to Oracle8i Upgrade Exam Cram*! This book will help you get ready to take—and pass—the Oracle Certified Professional-Oracle8i: New Features for Administrators (OCP-DBA) certification exam. In this Introduction, we'll talk about Oracle's certification programs in general and about how the *Exam Cram* series can help you prepare for Oracle8i certification exams.

Oracle Exam Cram books help you understand and appreciate the subjects and materials you need to pass Oracle certification exams. The books are aimed strictly at test preparation and review. They do not teach you everything you need to know about a topic. Instead, we present and dissect the questions and problems that you're likely to encounter on a test.

Nevertheless, to completely prepare yourself for any Oracle test, we recommend that you begin by taking the Self-Assessment included in this book (immediately following this Introduction). This tool will help you evaluate your knowledge base against the requirements for an Oracle Certified Professional DBA (OCP-DBA) under both ideal and real circumstances.

Based on what you learn from that exercise, you might decide to begin your studies with some classroom training or by reading one of the many DBA guides available from Oracle and third-party vendors. We also strongly recommend that you install, configure, and fool around with the software or environment that you'll be tested on because nothing beats hands-on experience and familiarity when it comes to understanding the questions you're likely to encounter on a certification test. Book learning is essential, but hands-on experience is the best teacher of all.

The Oracle Certified Professional (OCP) Program

The Oracle8i: New Features for Administrators OCP exam is designed for two types of Oracle Certified Professionals who want to upgrade their OCP certification to include Oracle8i. The first group includes those who have taken and passed the Oracle7 OCP exams (which are now retired) and have since taken the

Oracle8: New Features for Administrators OCP exam. The Oracle8i: New Features for Administrators OCP exam is also designed for the DBA who has taken the Oracle8 OCP exam, which consists of five tests. A brief description of each test in the Oracle8 OCP exam series (shown in Table 1) follows:

- *Introduction to Oracle: SQL and PL/SQL (Exam 1Z0-001)*—Test 1 is the base test for the series. Knowledge tested in Test 1 is also used in all other tests in the DBA series. Besides testing knowledge of SQL and PL/SQL language constructs, syntax, and usage, Test 1 covers Data Definition Language (DDL), Data Manipulation Language (DML), and Data Control Language (DCL). Also covered in Test 1 are basic data modeling and database design.
- *Oracle8: Database Administration (Exam 1Z0-013)*—Test 2 deals with all levels of database administration in Oracle8 (primarily version 8.0.5 and later). Topics include architecture, startup and shutdown, database creation, management of database internal and external constructs (such as redo logs, rollback segments, and tablespaces), and all other Oracle structures. This test also covers database auditing, use of National Language Support (NLS) features, and use of SQL*Loader and other utilities.
- *Oracle8: Backup and Recovery (Exam 1Z0-015)*—Test 3 covers one of the most important tasks of the Oracle DBA's job: database backup and recovery operations. Test 3 tests your knowledge in backup and recovery methods, architecture as it relates to backup and recovery, backup methods, failure scenarios, recovery methodologies, archive logging, support by 24x7 shops, troubleshooting, and use of Oracle8's standby database features. The test also covers use of the Recovery Manager (RMAN) product from Oracle, new in Oracle8.
- *Oracle8: Performance Tuning (Exam 1Z0-014)*—Test 4 covers all aspects of tuning an Oracle8 database. Topics in both application and database tuning are covered. Test 4 tests your knowledge of the diagnosis of tuning problems, optimal database configuration, shared pool tuning, buffer cache tuning, Oracle block usage, tuning of rollback segments and redo mechanisms, monitoring and detection of lock contention, tuning of sorts, load optimization, and tuning in OLTP, DSS, and mixed environments.
- *Oracle8: Network Administration (Exam 1Z0-016)*—Test 5 covers all parts of the Net8 product: Net8, Oracle Names Server, the listener process, lsnrctl (the listener control utility), and the Net8 configuration files sqlnet.ora, tnsnames.ora, and listener.ora.

The exam this book is written to help you with is a bridge exam, designed to upgrade your existing Oracle8 certification to Oracle8i without having to take

Table 1 Oracle8 OCP-DBA Requirements

All 5 of these tests are required	
Exam 1Z0-001	Introduction to Oracle: SQL and PL/SQL
Exam 1Z0-013	Oracle8: Database Administration
Exam 1Z0-014	Oracle8: Performance Tuning
Exam 1Z0-015	Oracle8: Backup and Recovery
Exam 1Z0-016	Oracle8: Network Administration

If you are currently an OCP certified in Oracle7.3, you need take only the upgrade exam (Oracle8: New Features for Administrators, Exam 1Z0-010) to be certified in Oracle8. If you have passed Introduction to Oracle: SQL and PL/SQL during your pursuit of Oracle7.3 certification, you do not need to retake it for Oracle8 certification.

the entire set of Oracle8i OCP exams. To obtain an Oracle8i certification, an individual must meet one of the following criteria:

- Have passed the five Oracle8i OCP certification exams.
- Have passed the five Oracle8 OCP certification exams and also passed the Oracle8 to 8i certification bridge exam.
- Have passed the four Oracle 7.3 certification exams (which are no longer offered) and have taken the Oracle 7.3 to 8 certification bridge exam folowed by the Oracle8 to 8i certification bridge exam.

You don't have to take these tests in any particular order, but you must complete the set in order to receive your Oracle8i certification. As of this writing, you can even take the Oracle8i: New Features for Administrators exam before you have completed your Oracle8 OCP exams, but you won't get your Oracle8i certificate until you have completed the Oracle8 OCP exams. If you already have your Oracle7.3 certification, you'll need to take one additional exam—Oracle8: New Features for Administrators (Exam 1Z0-010)—to be able to take the Oracle8i: New Features for Administrators exam (Exam 1Z0-020). In fact, Coriolis has a great book to help you with that very exam!

It's not uncommon for many individuals to find that they must take the test more than once to pass. In fact, Oracle8i is rich with so many new features that it's hard to know what to prepare for. That's the primary goal of the *Exam Cram* series: to make it possible, given proper study and preparation, to pass all of the OCP-DBA tests on the first try.

Finally, certification is an ongoing activity. When an Oracle version becomes obsolete, OCP-DBAs (and other OCPs) typically have a six-month time frame in which they can become recertified on current product versions. (If you don't get recertified within the specified time period, your certification becomes invalid.) Because technology keeps changing and new products continually supplant old ones, this should come as no surprise.

The best place to keep tabs on the OCP program and its various certifications is on the Oracle Web site. The current root URL for the OCP program is at **http://education.oracle.com/certification**. Oracle's certification Web site changes frequently, so if this URL doesn't work, try using the Search tool on Oracle's site (**www.oracle.com**) with either "OCP" or the quoted phrase "Oracle Certified Professional Program" as the search string. This will help you find the latest and most accurate information about the company's certification programs.

Taking a Certification Exam

Alas, testing is not free. You'll be charged $125 for each test you take, whether you pass or fail. In the United States and Canada, tests are administered by Prometric. Prometric can be reached at 1-800-891-3926, any time from 7:00 A.M. to 6:00 P.M. Central Time, Monday through Friday. If you can't get through at this number, try 1-612-896-7000 or 1-612-820-5707.

Sometimes Oracle offers beta copies of an exam at a reduced price. Before you sign up for the exam, make sure you check Oracle's Web site (**www.oracle.com**) to see whether a beta exam is available. Be forewarned: the betas can be brutal; they're typically four times the length of the standard exam and contain about 240 questions rather than the standard 60. So make sure the monetary savings are worth the extra test-taking time and stress. Also keep in mind that with beta exams, your results aren't available immediately. For example, those who took the Oracle8i beta exam during the summer of 2000 had to wait 8 to 12 weeks for results. On the positive side, though, those beta exams cost only $25.

To schedule an exam, call at least one day in advance. To cancel or reschedule an exam, you must call at least one day before the scheduled test time (or you might be charged the $125 fee). When calling Prometric, please have the following information ready for the telesales staffer who handles your call:

- Your name, organization, and mailing address.
- The name of the exam you want to take.
- A method of payment. (The most convenient approach is to supply a valid credit card number with sufficient available credit. Otherwise, payments by check, money order, or purchase order must be received before a test can be scheduled. If the latter methods are required, ask your order-taker for more details.)

An appointment confirmation will be sent to you by mail if you register more than five days before an exam, or it will be sent by fax if you register less than five days before the exam. A Candidate Agreement letter, which you must sign to take the examination, will also be provided.

On the day of the test, plan to arrive at least 15 minutes before the scheduled time slot. You must supply two forms of identification, one of which must be a photo ID.

All exams are completely closed book. In fact, you will not be permitted to take anything with you into the testing area. We suggest that, just before the test, you review the most critical information about it. (*Exam Cram* books provide a brief reference—The Cram Sheet, located inside the front of this book—that lists the essential information from the book in distilled form.) You will have some time to compose yourself, to mentally review this critical information, and even to take a sample orientation exam before you begin the real thing. We suggest that you take the orientation test before taking your first exam; the exams are all more or less identical in layout, behavior, and controls, so you probably won't need to do this more than once.

When you complete an Oracle8 certification exam, the testing software will tell you whether you've passed or failed. Results are organized into several topical areas. Whether you pass or fail, we suggest that you ask for—and keep—the detailed report that the test administrator prints for you. You can use this report to help you prepare for another go-round, if necessary, and even if you pass, the report shows areas you might need to review to keep your edge. If you need to retake an exam, you'll have to call Prometric, schedule a new test date, and pay another $125.

Tracking OCP Status

Oracle generates transcripts listing the exams you have passed and your corresponding test scores. After you pass the exam covered in this book, you'll be certified as an Oracle8i DBA. Official certification normally takes anywhere from four to six weeks (generally within 30 days), so don't expect to get your credentials overnight. Once certified, you will receive a package with a Welcome Kit that contains a number of elements:

- An OCP-DBA certificate, suitable for framing.
- A cool, credit-card-sized OCP-DBA ID card.
- A license agreement to use the OCP logo. After the OCP license agreement is sent to Oracle and you receive your packet of logo information, the license agreement allows you to use the logo for advertisements, promotions, documents, letterhead, business cards, and so on. An OCP logo sheet, which includes camera-ready artwork, comes with the license.

How to Prepare for an Exam

At a minimum, preparing for the Oracle8i: New Features OCP-DBA exam requires that you obtain and study the following materials:

- The Oracle8 Server version 8.1.5 (or later) Documentation Set on CD-ROM.
- The exam preparation materials, practice tests, and self-assessment exams on the Oracle certification page (**http://education.oracle.com/certification**). Find the materials, download them, and use them!
- This *Exam Cram* book. It's the first and last thing you should read before taking the exam. Also, check out **ExamCram.com** for study tips, practice exams, and more.

In addition, you'll probably find any or all of the following materials useful in your quest for Oracle8i DBA expertise:

- *OCP resource kits*—Oracle Corporation has a CD-ROM with example questions and materials to help with the exam; generally, you can get these for free by requesting them from your Oracle representative. They have also been offered free for the taking at most Oracle conventions, such as IOUGA-Alive! and Oracle Open World.
- *Classroom training*—Oracle, TUSC, LearningTree, and many other vendors offer classroom- and computer-based training material that you will find useful as you prepare for the exam. But a word of warning: These classes are fairly expensive (in the range of $300 per day of training). However, they do offer a condensed form of learning to help you brush up on your Oracle knowledge. The tests are closely tied to the classroom training provided by Oracle, so we suggest taking at least the introductory classes to get the Oracle-specific (and classroom-specific) terminology under your belt.
- *Other publications*—You'll find direct references to other publications and resources in this book, and there's no shortage of materials available about Oracle8i DBA topics. To help you sift through some of the publications out there, we end each chapter with a "Need to Know More?" section that provides pointers to more complete and exhaustive resources covering the chapter's subject matter. This section tells you where to look for further details.
- *MetaLink and Oracle Technet Web sites*—These Web sites provide Oracle support from Oracle itself. MetaLink is available for all Oracle support customers. There you have access to bug reports, you can open TARs, and you can participate in forums. MetaLink is an official Oracle site that sells Oracle products and contains the most current Oracle documentation versions.

- *The Oracle KnowledgeBase, PL/SQL Developer, and other products*—These are online references from RevealNet, Inc., a provider of Oracle and database online reference material. These online references provide instant lookup on thousands of database and developmental topics and are an invaluable resource for study and learning about Oracle. Demo copies can be downloaded from **www.revealnet.com**. Also available at the RevealNet Web site are the DBA and PL/SQL Pipelines—online discussion groups where you can obtain expert information from Oracle DBAs worldwide. (The authors of this book often frequent the site, too.) The costs of these applications run about $400 each (current pricing is available on the Web site) and are worth every cent.

These required and recommended materials represent a nonpareil collection of sources and resources for Oracle8 DBA topics and software. In the section that follows, we explain how this book works and give you some good reasons why this book should also be on your list of required and recommended materials.

About This Book

Each topical *Exam Cram* chapter follows a regular structure, along with graphical cues about especially important or useful material. Here's the structure of a typical chapter:

- *Opening hotlists*—Each chapter begins with lists of the terms, tools, and techniques that you must learn and understand before you can be fully conversant with the chapter's subject matter. We follow the hotlists with one or two introductory paragraphs to set the stage for the rest of the chapter.

- *Topical coverage*—After the opening hotlists, each chapter covers a series of topics related to the chapter's subject. Throughout this section, we highlight material most likely to appear on a test by using a special Exam Alert layout, like this:

This is what an Exam Alert looks like. Normally, an Exam Alert stresses concepts, terms, software, or activities that will most likely appear in one or more certification test questions. For that reason, any information found offset in Exam Alert format is worthy of unusual attentiveness on your part. Indeed, most of the facts appearing in The Cram Sheet appear as Exam Alerts within the text.

Even if material isn't flagged as an Exam Alert, *all* the contents of this book are associated, at least tangentially, to something test-related. This book is tightly focused for quick test preparation, so you'll find that what appears in the meat of each chapter is critical knowledge.

We have also provided tips that will help build a better foundation of data administration knowledge. Although the information might not be on the exam, it is highly relevant and will help you become a better test-taker.

This is how tips are formatted. Keep your eyes open for these, and you'll become an Oracle8i guru in no time!

- *Practice questions*—A section at the end of each chapter presents a series of mock test questions and explanations of both correct and incorrect answers. We also try to point out especially tricky questions by using a special icon, like this:

  Ordinarily, this icon flags the presence of an especially devious question, if not an outright trick question. Trick questions are calculated to "trap" you if you don't read them carefully, and more than once at that. Although they're not ubiquitous, such questions make regular appearances in the Oracle8 exams. That's why exam questions are as much about reading comprehension as they are about knowing DBA material inside out and backward.

- *Details and resources*—Every chapter ends with a section titled "Need to Know More?". This section provides direct pointers to Oracle and third-party resources that offer further details on the chapter's subject matter. In addition, this section tries to rate the quality and thoroughness of each topic's coverage. If you find a resource you like in this collection, use it, but don't feel compelled to use all these resources. On the other hand, we recommend only resources we use on a regular basis, so none of our recommendations will be a waste of your time or money.

The bulk of the book follows this chapter structure slavishly, but there are a few other elements that we would like to point out. Chapter 17 includes a sample test that provides a good review of the material presented throughout the book to ensure that you're ready for the exam. Chapter 18 provides an answer key to the sample test. In addition, you'll find a handy glossary and an index.

Finally, look for The Cram Sheet, which appears inside the front of this *Exam Cram* book. This Cram Sheet is a valuable tool that represents a condensed and compiled collection of facts, figures, and tips that we think you should memorize before taking the test. Because you can dump this information out of your head onto a piece of paper before answering any exam questions, you can master this information by brute force—you need to remember it only long enough to write it down when you walk into the test room. You might even want to look at it in the car or in the lobby of the testing center just before you walk in to take the test.

How to Use This Book

In case you're prepping for a first-time test, we've structured the topics in this book to build on one another. Therefore, some topics in later chapters make more sense after you've read earlier chapters. That's why we suggest that you read this book from front to back for your initial test preparation.

If you need to brush up on a topic or you have to bone up for a second try, use the index or table of contents to go straight to the topics and questions that you need to study. Beyond the tests, we think you'll find this book useful as a tightly focused reference to some of the most important aspects of topics associated with being a DBA, as implemented under Oracle8i.

Given all the book's elements and its specialized focus, we've tried to create a tool that you can use to prepare for—and pass—the Oracle OCP-DBA set of examinations. Please share your feedback on the book with us, especially if you have ideas about how we can improve it for future test-takers. We'll consider everything you say carefully, and we will try to respond to all suggestions. You can reach us via email: Robert Freeman at **dbaoracle@aol.com** or Charles Pack at **charlesapack@csx.com**. Or you can send your questions or comments to **learn@examcram.com**. Please remember to include the title of the book in your message; otherwise, we'll be forced to guess which book of ours you're making a suggestion about. Also, be sure to check out the Web pages at **www.examcram.com**, where you'll find information updates, commentary, and certification information.

Thanks, and enjoy the book!

Self-Assessment

We've included a Self-Assessment in this *Exam Cram* to help you evaluate your readiness to tackle the Oracle Certified Professional-Oracle8i: New Features for Administrators (OCP-DBA) certification exam. This Self-Assessment should also help you understand what you need in order to master the topic of this book—namely, Exam 1Z0-020, "Oracle8i: New Features for Administrators." But before you tackle this Self-Assessment, let's talk about the concerns you may face when pursuing an Oracle8i OCP-DBA certification and about what an ideal Oracle8i OCP-DBA candidate might look like.

Oracle8i OCP-DBAs in the Real World

In the next section, we describe an ideal Oracle8i OCP-DBA candidate, knowing full well that only a few actual candidates meet this ideal. In fact, our description of that ideal candidate might seem downright scary. But take heart; although the requirements to upgrade to an Oracle8i OCP-DBA may seem pretty formidable, they are by no means impossible to meet. However, you should be keenly aware that it does take time, requires some expense, and consumes a substantial effort.

You can get all the real-world motivation you need from knowing that many others have gone before you. You can follow in their footsteps. If you're willing to tackle the process seriously and do what it takes to obtain the necessary experience and knowledge, you can take—and pass—the Oracle8i upgrade certification test. The same, of course, is true for other Oracle certifications, including:

- *Oracle8 and Oracle8i OCP-DBA*—These exams require five core tests each.
- *Application Developer, Oracle Developer Rel 1 OCP*—This is aimed at software developers and requires five exams.
- *Application Developer, Oracle Developer Rel 2 OCP*—This is aimed at software developers and requires five exams.
- *Oracle Database Operators OCP*—This is aimed at database operators and requires only one exam.
- *Oracle Java Technology Certification OCP*—This is aimed at Java developers and requires five exams.

The Ideal Oracle8i OCP-DBA Upgrade Candidate

Just to give you some idea of what an ideal Oracle8i Upgrade OCP-DBA candidate is like, here are some relevant statistics about the background and experience such an individual might have. Don't worry if you don't meet these qualifications (or if you don't even come close), because this world is far from ideal, and where you fall short is simply where you'll have more work to do. The ideal candidate will have:

- Academic or professional training in relational databases, Structured Query Language (SQL), performance tuning, backup and recovery, and Net8 administration
- Three-plus years of professional database administration experience, including experience installing and upgrading Oracle executables, creating and tuning databases, troubleshooting connection problems, creating user accounts, and managing backup and recovery scenarios

We believe that well under half of all certification candidates meet these requirements. In fact, most probably meet less than half of these requirements (at least when they begin the certification process). But, because all those who have their certifications already survived this ordeal, you can survive it, too—especially if you heed what this Self-Assessment can tell you about what you already know and what you need to learn.

Put Yourself to the Test

The following series of questions and observations is designed to help you figure out how much work you'll face in pursuing Oracle certification and what kinds of resources you can consult on your quest. Be absolutely honest in your answers, or you'll end up wasting money on exams you're not ready to take. There are no right or wrong answers, only steps along the path to certification. Only you can decide where you really belong in the broad spectrum of aspiring candidates.

Two things should be clear from the outset, however:

- Even a modest background in computer science will be helpful.
- Hands-on experience with Oracle products and technologies is an essential ingredient to certification success.

Educational Background

1. Have you ever taken any computer-related classes? [Yes or No]

   If Yes, proceed to question 2; if No, proceed to question 4.

2. Have you taken any classes on relational databases? [Yes or No]

   If Yes, you'll probably be able to handle Oracle's architecture and network administration discussions. If you're rusty, brush up on the basic concepts of databases and networks. If the answer is No, consider some basic reading in this area. We strongly recommend a good Oracle database administration book, such as *Oracle8i Administration and Management* by Michael Ault (Wiley, 2000). Or, if this title doesn't appeal to you, check out reviews for other, similar titles at your favorite online bookstore.

3. Have you taken any networking concepts or technologies classes? [Yes or No]

   If Yes, you'll probably be able to handle Oracle's networking terminology, concepts, and technologies (but brace yourself for frequent departures from normal usage). If you're rusty, brush up on basic networking concepts and terminology. If your answer is No, you might want to check out the Oracle Technet Web site (**http://technet.oracle.com**) and read some of the white papers on Net8. If you have access to the Oracle MetaLink Web site or the Technet Web site, download the *Oracle Net8 Administration* manual.

4. Have you done any reading on relational databases or networks? [Yes or No]

   If Yes, review the requirements from questions 2 and 3. If you meet those, move on to the next section, "Hands-on Experience." If you answered No, consult the recommended reading for both topics. This kind of strong background will be of great help in preparing you for the Oracle exams.

Hands-on Experience

Another important key to success on all of the Oracle tests is hands-on experience. If we leave you with only one realization after you take this Self-Assessment, it should be that there's no substitute for time spent installing, configuring, and using the various Oracle products upon which you'll be tested repeatedly and in depth.

5. Have you installed, configured, and worked with Oracle8i? [Yes or No]

   If Yes, make sure that you have a well-rounded understanding of the wealth of new features in the Oracle8i database product.

You can download the candidate certification guide, objectives, practice exams, and other information about Oracle exams from the company's Training and Certification page on the Web at **http://education.oracle.com/certification**.

If you haven't worked with Oracle, you must obtain a copy of Oracle8i or Personal Oracle8i. Of course, if you have not worked with Oracle, you likely have not taken the prerequisite five Oracle8 exams that you'll need to take before you can upgrade your certification with the Oracle8i: New Features for Administrators OCP exam.

For any and all of these Oracle exams, the candidate guides for the topics involved are a good study resource. You can download them free from the Oracle Web site (**http://education.oracle.com**). You can also download information on purchasing additional practice tests.

If you have the funds or your employer will pay your way, consider taking a class at an Oracle training and education center.

Before you even think about taking any Oracle exam, make sure you've spent enough time with Oracle8i to understand how it can be installed and configured, how to maintain such an installation, and how to troubleshoot that software when things go wrong. This will help you in the exam—as well as in real life.

Testing Your Exam-Readiness

Whether you attend a formal class on a specific topic to get ready for an exam or use written materials to study on your own, some preparation for the Oracle certification exams is essential. At $125 a try, pass or fail, you want to do everything you can to pass on your first try. That's where studying comes in.

We have included in this book several practice exam questions for each chapter and a sample test, so if you don't score well on the chapter questions, you can study more and then tackle the sample test at the end of the book. If you don't earn a score of at least 80 percent after this test, you'll want to investigate other practice test resources.

For any given subject, consider taking a class if you've tackled self-study materials, taken the test, and failed anyway. If you can afford the privilege, the opportunity to interact with an instructor and fellow students can make all the difference in the world. For information about Oracle classes, visit the Training and Certification page at **http://education.oracle.com**.

If you can't afford to take a class, visit the Training and Certification page anyway because it also includes free practice exams that you can download. Even if you can't afford to spend much, you should still invest in some low-cost practice exams from commercial vendors because they can help you assess your readiness to pass a test better than any other tool.

6. Have you taken a practice exam on your chosen test subject? [Yes or No]

   If Yes—and you scored 80 percent or better—you're probably ready to tackle the real thing. If your score isn't above that crucial threshold, keep at it until you break that barrier. If you answered No, obtain all the free and low-budget practice tests you can find (or afford), and get to work. Keep at it until you can comfortably break the passing threshold.

There is no better way to assess your test-readiness than to take a good practice exam and pass with a score of 80 percent or better. When we're preparing, we shoot for 85-plus percent just to leave room for the "weirdness factor" that sometimes shows up on Oracle exams.

Assessing Your Readiness for Exam 1Z0-020

In addition to the general exam-readiness information in the previous section, other resources are available to help you prepare for the Oracle8i: New Features for Administrators exam. For starters, visit the RevealNet pipeline (**www.revealnet.com**) or **http://technet.oracle.com**. These are great places to ask questions and get good answers or simply to observe the questions that others ask (along with the answers, of course).

Oracle exam mavens also recommend checking the Oracle Knowledge Base from RevealNet. You can get information on purchasing the RevealNet software at **www.revealnet.com**.

For Introduction to Oracle: SQL and PL/SQL preparation in particular, we'd also like to recommend that you check out one or more of these books as you prepare to take the exam:

- Ault, Michael. *Oracle8i Administration and Management.* Wiley, 2000.
- David Austin, Megh Thakkar, and Kurt Lysy. *Migrating to Oracle8i.* Sams Publishing, 2000.
- Scherer, Douglas, et al. *Oracle8i Tips & Techniques.* Oracle Press, 1999.

Stop by your favorite bookstore or online bookseller to check out one or more of these books.

One last note: We want to stress the importance of hands-on experience in the context of the Oracle8i: New Features for Administrators exam. As you review the material for this exam, you'll realize that hands-on experience with Oracle8i commands, tools, and utilities is invaluable.

Onward, through the Fog!

Once you've assessed your readiness, undertaken the right background studies, obtained the hands-on experience that will help you understand the products and technologies at work, and reviewed the many sources of information to help you prepare for a test, you'll be ready to take a round of practice tests. When your scores come back high enough to get you through the exam, you're ready to go after the real thing. If you follow this assessment regime, you'll know not only what you need to study, but also when you're ready to make a test date at Prometric. Good luck!

Oracle OCP Certification Exams

Terms you'll need to understand:

✓ Radio button

✓ Checkbox

✓ Exhibit

✓ Multiple-choice question formats

✓ Careful reading

✓ Process of elimination

Techniques you'll need to master:

✓ Assessing your exam-readiness

✓ Preparing to take a certification exam

✓ Practicing (to make perfect)

✓ Making the best use of the testing software

✓ Budgeting your time

✓ Saving the hardest questions until last

✓ Guessing (as a last resort)

As experiences go, test-taking is not something that most people anticipate eagerly, no matter how well they're prepared. In most cases, familiarity helps ameliorate test anxiety. In plain English, this means that you probably won't be as nervous when you take your fourth or fifth Oracle certification exam as you will be when you take your first one.

But no matter whether it's your first test or your tenth, understanding the exam-taking particulars (how much time to spend on questions, the setting you'll be in, and so on) and the testing software will help you concentrate on the material rather than on the environment. Likewise, mastering a few basic test-taking skills should help you recognize—and perhaps even outfox—some of the tricks and gotchas you're bound to find in some of the Oracle test questions.

In this chapter, we'll explain the testing environment and software, as well as describe some proven test-taking strategies you should be able to use to your advantage.

Assessing Exam-Readiness

Before you take any Oracle exam, we strongly recommend that you take the Self-Assessment included with this book (it appears just before this chapter, in fact). This will help you compare your knowledge base to the requirements for obtaining an OCP, and it will also help you identify parts of your background or experience that might need improvement, enhancement, or further learning. If you get the right set of basics under your belt, obtaining Oracle certification will be that much easier.

After you've gone through the Self-Assessment, you can remedy those topical areas where your background or experience might not measure up to an ideal certification candidate. But you can also tackle subject matter for individual tests at the same time, so you can continue making progress while you're catching up in some areas.

After you've worked through an *Exam Cram*, have read the supplementary materials, and have taken the practice test at the end of the book, you'll have a pretty clear idea of when you should be ready to take the real exam. Although we strongly recommend that you keep practicing until your scores top the 80 percent mark, 85 percent would be a better goal to give yourself some margin for error in a real exam situation (where stress will play more of a role than when you practice). When you hit that point, you should be ready to go. But if you get through the practice exam in this book without attaining that score, you should keep taking practice tests and studying the materials until you get there. You'll find more information about other practice test vendors in the Self-Assessment, along with even more pointers on how to study and prepare. But now, on to the exam itself!

The Testing Situation

When you arrive at the Prometric Testing Center where you scheduled your test, you'll need to sign in with a test coordinator. He or she will ask you to produce two forms of identification, one of which must be a photo ID. Once you've signed in and your time slot arrives, you'll be asked to leave any books, bags, or other items you brought with you, and you'll be escorted into a closed room. Typically, that room will be furnished with anywhere from one to half a dozen computers, and each workstation is separated from the others by dividers designed to keep you from seeing what's happening on someone else's computer.

You'll be furnished with a pen or pencil and a blank sheet of paper or, in some cases, an erasable plastic sheet and an erasable felt-tip pen. You're allowed to write down any information you want on this sheet, and you can write stuff on both sides of the page. We suggest that you memorize as much as possible of the material that appears on The Cram Sheet (inside the front of this book), and then write that information down on the blank sheet as soon as you sit down in front of the test machine. You can refer to the sheet any time you like during the test, but you'll have to surrender it when you leave the room.

Most test rooms feature a wall with a large window. This allows the test coordinator to monitor the room, to prevent test-takers from talking to one another, and to observe anything out of the ordinary that might go on. The test coordinator will have loaded the Oracle certification test you've signed up for, and you'll be permitted to start as soon as you're seated in front of the machine.

All Oracle certification exams permit you to take up to a certain maximum amount of time (usually 90 minutes) to complete the test. (The test itself will tell you, and it maintains an on-screen counter/clock so that you can check the time remaining any time you like.) Each exam consists of between 50 and 70 questions, randomly selected from a pool of questions.

The passing score varies per exam and the questions selected. For the Oracle8i: New Features OCP-DBA exam, the passing score is 60%.

All Oracle certification exams are computer generated and use a multiple-choice format. Although this might sound easy, the questions are constructed not just to check your mastery of basic facts and figures about Oracle8iDBA topics, but also to require you to evaluate one or more sets of circumstances or requirements. Often, you'll be asked to give more than one answer to a question; likewise, you may be asked to select the best or most effective solution to a problem from a range of choices, all of which technically are correct. The tests are quite an adventure, and they involve real thinking. This book will show you what to expect and how to deal with the problems, puzzles, and predicaments you're likely to find on the tests—in particular, Exam 1Z0-020, Oracle8i: New Features for Administrators.

Test Layout and Design

A typical test question is depicted in Question 1. It's a multiple-choice question that requires you to select a single correct answer. Following the question is a brief summary of each potential answer and why it was either right or wrong.

Question 1

You issue this SQL*Plus command:

```
SAVE my_file REPLACE
```

What task was accomplished?

- ❍ a. A new file was created.
- ❍ b. An existing file was replaced.
- ❍ c. The command was continued to the next line of the SQL prompt.
- ❍ d. No task was accomplished because a file extension was not designated.

Answer b is correct. The **SAVE** command has only one option: **REPLACE**. **SAVE** without **REPLACE** requires that the file not exist; **SAVE** with **REPLACE** replaces an existing file. No file extension is required; the default is .sql. Answer a is incorrect because the **REPLACE** option is specified. With just a **SAVE**, a new file is created; with a **SAVE...REPLACE**, an existing file is replaced. Answer c is incorrect because the continuation of a line is done automatically when you press the Return key. Answer d is incorrect because if a suffix isn't specified, a default one is added.

This sample question corresponds closely to those you'll see on Oracle certification tests. To select the correct answer during the test, you would position the cursor over the radio button next to answer b and click the mouse to select that particular choice. The only difference between the certification test and this question is that the real questions are not immediately followed by the answers.

Next, we'll examine a question for which one or more answers are possible. This type of question provides checkboxes, rather than radio buttons, for marking all appropriate selections.

Question 2

Which three ways can the SQL buffer be terminated?

- ❑ a. Enter a slash (/).
- ❑ b. Press Return (or Enter) once.
- ❑ c. Enter an asterisk (*).
- ❑ d. Enter a semicolon (;).
- ❑ e. Press Return (or Enter) twice.
- ❑ f. Press Esc twice.

Answers a, d, and e are correct. A slash (/) is usually used for terminating PL/SQL blocks, procedures, and functions, but it can also be used for SQL commands. A semicolon (;) is generally used for terminating SQL commands. Pressing the Return key (or the Enter key on many keyboards) twice in succession will also tell the buffer that your command is complete, but will not execute it. Most of the time, the slash or semicolon will also result in execution of the previous command (except within a PL/SQL block); a subsequent entry of the slash, the semicolon, or an "r" (short for **run**) will be required to execute the command(s) terminated with a double Return.

For this type of question, one or more answers must be selected to answer the question correctly. For Question 2, you would have to position the cursor over the checkboxes next to items a, d, and e to obtain credit for a correct answer.

These two basic types of questions can appear in many forms. They constitute the foundation on which all the Oracle certification exam questions rest. More complex questions may include so-called "exhibits," which are usually tables or data-content layouts of one form or another. You'll be expected to use the information displayed in the exhibit to guide your answer to the question.

Other questions involving exhibits may use charts or diagrams to help document a workplace scenario that you'll be asked to troubleshoot or configure. Paying careful attention to such exhibits is the key to success—be prepared to toggle between the picture and the question as you work. Often, both are complex enough that you might not be able to remember all of either one.

Using Oracle's Test Software Effectively

A well-known test-taking principle is to read over the entire test from start to finish first, but to answer only those questions that you feel absolutely sure of on the first pass. On subsequent passes, you can dive into more complex questions, knowing how many such questions you have to deal with.

Fortunately, Oracle test software makes this approach easy to implement. At the bottom of each question, you'll find a checkbox that permits you to mark that question for a later visit. (Note that marking questions makes review easier, but you can return to any question by clicking the Forward and Back buttons repeatedly until you get to the question.) As you read each question, if you answer only those you're sure of and mark for review those that you're not, you can keep going through a decreasing list of open questions as you knock the trickier ones off in order.

There's at least one potential benefit to reading the test completely before answering the trickier questions: Sometimes, you find information in later questions that sheds more light on earlier ones. Other times, information you read in later questions might jog your memory about Oracle8i DBA facts, figures, or behavior that also will help with earlier questions. Either way, you'll come out ahead if you defer those questions about which you're not absolutely sure of the answer(s).

Keep working on the questions until you are absolutely sure of all your answers or until you know you'll run out of time. If there are still unanswered questions, you'll want to zip through them and guess. A blank answer guarantees no credit for a question, and a guess has at least a chance of being correct. (Oracle scores blank answers and incorrect answers as equally wrong.)

At the very end of your test period, you're better off guessing than leaving questions blank or unanswered.

Taking Testing Seriously

The most important advice we can give you about taking any Oracle test is this: Read each question carefully. Some questions are deliberately ambiguous; some use double negatives; others use terminology in incredibly precise ways. We've taken numerous practice tests and real tests, and in nearly every test we've missed at least one question because we didn't read it closely or carefully enough.

Here are some suggestions on how to deal with the tendency to jump to an answer too quickly:

- Make sure you read every word in the question. If you find yourself jumping ahead impatiently, go back and start over.
- As you read, try to restate the question in your own terms. If you can do this, you should be able to pick the correct answer(s) much more easily.
- When returning to a question after your initial read-through, reread every word—otherwise, the mind falls quickly into a rut. Sometimes seeing a question afresh after turning your attention elsewhere lets you see something you missed before, but the strong tendency is to see what you've seen before. Try to avoid that tendency at all costs.
- If you return to a question more than twice, try to articulate to yourself what you don't understand about the question, why the answers don't appear to make sense, or what appears to be missing. If you chew on the subject for a while, your subconscious might provide the details that are lacking, or you may notice a "trick" that will point to the right answer.

Above all, try to deal with each question by thinking through what you know about being an Oracle8i DBA—utilities, characteristics, behaviors, facts, and figures involved. By reviewing what you know (and what you've written down on your information sheet), you'll often recall or understand things sufficiently to determine the answer to the question.

Question-Handling Strategies

Based on the tests we've taken, a couple of interesting trends in the answers have become apparent. For those questions that take only a single answer, usually two or three of the answers will be obviously incorrect, and two of the answers will be plausible. But, of course, only one can be correct. Unless the answer leaps out at you (and if it does, reread the question to look for a trick; sometimes those are the ones you're most likely to get wrong), begin the process of answering by eliminating those answers that are obviously wrong.

Things to look for in the "obviously wrong" category include spurious command choices or table or view names, nonexistent software or command options, and terminology you've never seen before. If you've done your homework for a test, no valid information should be completely new to you. In that case, unfamiliar or bizarre terminology probably indicates a totally bogus answer. As long as you're sure what's right, it's easy to eliminate what's wrong.

Numerous questions assume that the default behavior of a particular Oracle utility (such as SQL*Plus or SQL*Loader) is in effect. It's essential, therefore, to know and understand the default settings for the SQL*Plus, SQL*Loader, and Server Manager utilities. If you know the defaults and understand what they mean, this knowledge will help you cut through many Gordian knots.

Likewise, when dealing with questions that require multiple answers, you must know and select all of the correct options to get credit. This, too, qualifies as an example of why careful reading is so important.

As you work your way through the test, another counter that Oracle thankfully provides will come in handy—the number of questions completed and questions outstanding. Budget your time by making sure that you've completed one-fourth of the questions one-quarter of the way through the test period, and check again three-quarters of the way through.

If you're not through after 85 minutes, use the last five minutes to guess your way through the remaining questions. Remember, guesses are potentially more valuable than blank answers, because blanks are always wrong, but a guess might turn out to be right. If you haven't a clue with any of the remaining questions, pick answers at random, or choose all a's, b's, and so on. The important thing is to submit a test for scoring that has an answer for every question.

Mastering the Inner Game

In the final analysis, knowledge breeds confidence, and confidence breeds success. If you study the materials in this book carefully and review all of the questions at the end of each chapter, you should be aware of those areas where additional studying is required.

Next, follow up by reading some or all of the materials recommended in the "Need to Know More?" section at the end of each chapter. The idea is to become familiar enough with the concepts and situations that you find in the sample questions to be able to reason your way through similar situations on a real test. If you know the material, you have every right to be confident that you can pass the test.

Once you've worked your way through the book, take the practice test in Chapter 17. The test will provide a reality check and will help you identify areas you need to study further. Before scheduling a real test, make sure you follow up and review materials related to the questions you missed. Only when you've covered all the ground and feel comfortable with the whole scope of the practice test should you take a real test.

If you take the practice test (Chapter 17) and don't score at least 85 percent correct, you'll want to practice further. At a minimum, download the practice tests and the self-assessment tests from the Oracle Education Web site's download page (its location appears in the next section). If you're more ambitious or better funded, you might want to purchase a practice test from one of the third-party vendors that offer them.

Armed with the information in this book and with the determination to augment your knowledge, you should be able to pass the certification exam. But if you don't work at it, you'll spend the test fee more than once before you finally do pass. If you prepare seriously, the execution should go flawlessly. Good luck!

Additional Resources

By far, the best source of information about Oracle certification tests comes from Oracle itself. Because its products and technologies—and the tests that go with them—change frequently, the best place to go for exam-related information is online.

If you haven't already visited the Oracle certification pages, do so right now. As we're writing this chapter, the certification home page resides at **http://education.oracle.com/certification/** (see Figure 1.1).

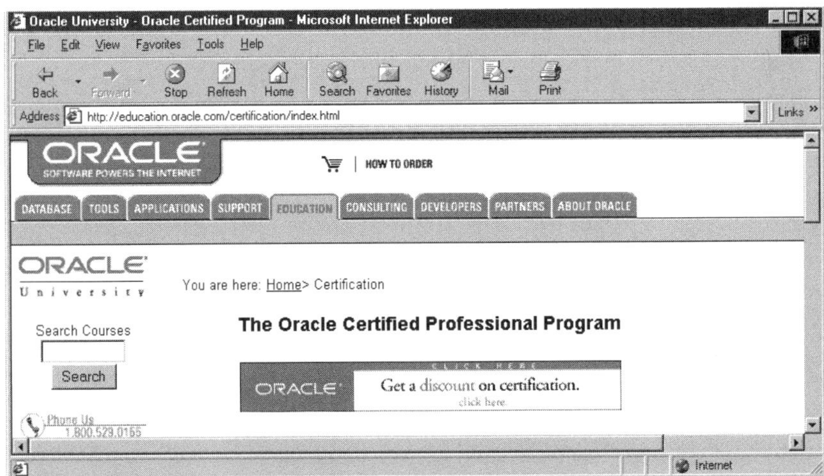

Figure 1.1 The Oracle certification page should be your starting point for further investigation of the most current exam and preparation information.

Note: It might not be there by the time you read this, or it might have been replaced by something new and different, because things change regularly on the Oracle site. Should this happen, please read the section titled "Coping with Change on the Web," later in this chapter.

The menu options in the left column of the page point to the most important sources of information in the certification pages. Here's what to check out:

- *FAQs*—Frequently Asked Questions; yours may get answered here.
- *What's New*—Any new tests will be described here.
- *Test Information*—This detailed section provides many jump points to detailed test descriptions for the several OCP certifications.
- *Practice Tests*—This section is a source for practice tests.
- *Test Registration*—This section provides information for phone registration and a link to the Prometric Web page for online registration. Also, this section provides a list of testing sites outside the USA.
- *Candidate Agreements*—Just what are you agreeing to be by becoming Oracle certified?
- *OCP Logo*—After you receive your certification, you can go to this page to download OCP graphics.
- *Oracle Partners*—This link provides information about test discounts and other offers for Oracle Partner companies.

Of course, these are just the high points of what's available in the Oracle certification pages. As you browse through them—and we strongly recommend that you do—you'll probably find other things we didn't mention here that are every bit as interesting and compelling.

Coping with Change on the Web

Sooner or later, all the specifics we've shared with you about the Oracle certification pages, and all the other Web-based resources mentioned throughout the rest of this book, will go stale or be replaced by newer information. In some cases, the URLs you find here might lead you to their replacements; in other cases, the URLs will go nowhere, leaving you with the dreaded "404 File not found" error message.

When that happens, please don't give up. There's always a way to find what you want on the Web—if you're willing to invest some time and energy. To begin with, most large or complex Web sites—and Oracle's qualifies on both counts—offer a search engine. As long as you can get to Oracle's home page (and we're sure that it will stay at **www.oracle.com** for a long while yet), you can use this tool to help you find what you need.

The more particular or focused you can make a search request, the more likely it is that the results will include information you can use. For instance, you can search the string "training and certification" to produce a lot of data about the subject in general, but if you're looking for the Preparation Guide for the Oracle DBA tests, you'll be more likely to get there quickly if you use a search string such as this:

```
"DBA" AND "preparation guide"
```

Likewise, if you want to find the training and certification downloads, try a search string such as this one:

```
"training and certification" AND "download page"
```

Finally, don't be afraid to use general search tools such as **www.search.com**, **www.altavista.com**, or **www.excite.com** to search for related information. Even though Oracle offers the best information about its certification exams online, there are plenty of third-party sources of information, training, and assistance in this area that don't have to follow a party line like Oracle does. The bottom line is this: If you can't find something where the book says it lives, start looking around. If worse comes to worst, you can always email us! We just might have a clue. Our email addresses are **dbaoracle@aol.com** and **charlesapack@yahoo.com**.

2

Installing, Configuring, and Migrating to Oracle8i

Terms you'll need to understand:

- ✓ Universal Installer
- ✓ Silent-mode installation
- ✓ Database Configuration Assistant
- ✓ Oracle Software Packager
- ✓ Migration
- ✓ Upgrade
- ✓ Data Migration Assistant

Techniques you'll need to master:

- ✓ Using the features of the Universal Installer
- ✓ Performing a silent-mode installation
- ✓ Describing how the installer uses Oracle Optimal Flexible Architecture (OFA)
- ✓ Knowing and understanding the features of the Database Configuration Assistant
- ✓ Migrating and upgrading databases to Oracle8i

This chapter deals with the many changes that have been made to the Oracle8i installation process and with what you'll be expected to know about it in the Oracle8i Oracle Certified Professional (OCP) Upgrade exam. Oracle has introduced a whole new installer for 8i—we will discuss this installer, including its new features, in this chapter. We will also review the new features of the Database Configuration Assistant and the Oracle Software Packager as we cover these areas. Finally, the methods of migrating or upgrading previous Oracle database versions to Oracle8i will also be discussed, as will configuration issues related to migrating or upgrading to Oracle8i.

The Oracle Universal Installer

In previous versions of Oracle, a character-based installer was available on Unix platforms (among others), and a graphical-based installer was available for Windows platforms. For Oracle8i, Oracle decided to standardize on one single software installer package called the *Oracle Universal Installer*.

Based on Java, the Oracle Universal Installer provides a common graphical front end for Oracle8i Relational Database Management System (RDBMS) software installations, as well as installations of products packaged by the Oracle Software Packager. (For details, see "Oracle Software Packager" later in this chapter.) As a result of the introduction of the Universal Installer, the character-based installation program that you might be more familiar with is no longer available. Because the method of running the Universal Installer is different for each platform, refer to the *Oracle8i Installation Manual* for more information regarding your specific platform type.

The features of the Oracle Universal Installer include the following:

- The Universal Installer provides a common interface for all Oracle RDBMS installations.
- Automatic dependency resolution is supported.
- Support for multiple ORACLE_HOME locations is provided.
- Silent-mode installs are supported (see details later in this chapter).
- Through the Oracle Software Packager, customized installation routines of additional, third-party products are supported as well. (For more details, see the section on the Oracle Software Packager later in this chapter.)

Note: Support for multiple CDs and compression is expected in a later release.

Be certain to concentrate heavily on the common elements of the Universal Installer. Although it's important to know about platform-specific issues, you don't need to worry about them for the exam.

Because the Universal Installer is Java based, you have to run the server installation from a Java-based client. An alternative to the client-based graphical installation program is the use of the *silent-mode installation*. The silent-mode installation uses a response file that contains all the information the installer needs to provide an automated installation on the Oracle RDBMS software without any user interaction. In this section, we'll look at Universal Installer first. Following that, we'll look at the silent-mode method of installing the RDBMS software, and finally, we'll do example installs using both methods.

Installing the Oracle RDBMS Software with the Universal Installer

As noted before, the Universal Installer is a Java-based product and therefore requires the use of the Java Runtime Environment (JRE). Several tools are available that can provide the JRE if you are doing, for example, a Unix installation on an NT client. The screen captures you'll see in this chapter were generated on a Windows NT PC using ReflectionX. The Oracle RDBMS installation was done on a Sun Solaris machine.

Note: Following are the names of the programs that you'll want to use to start the Universal Installer. On NT, it's simply setup.exe, located in the \install\win32 directory of the CD-ROM from which you are installing. On Unix, it's RunInstaller, which is in the root directory of the 8.1.5 CD.

The Universal Installer has a point-and-click interface and is very user friendly. Figure 2.1 provides an example of the look and feel of the Universal Installer. As you can see from the figure, the Installer is a graphical application with almost a wizard feel to it. Also, at the bottom of the figure, note that the Installer indicates where it's keeping a log of the installation processes. It's a good idea to note the location of this log file for future reference should some problem with the installed database software appear later.

The installation process itself remains generally the same as it was in previous versions of Oracle with the character-based installer. You identify the ORACLE_HOME and ORACLE_BASE locations either by setting the correct environment variables or after opening the Installer itself. The Installer then leads you through the various steps of the installation, giving you the option of

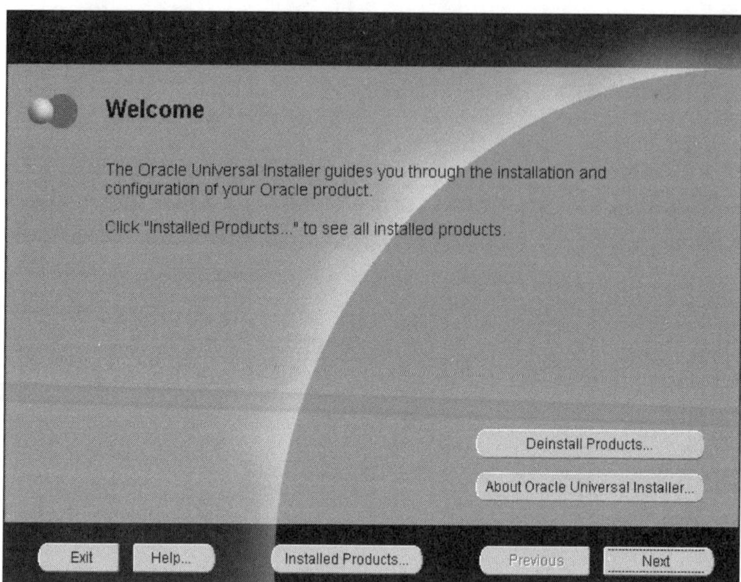

Figure 2.1 Sample screen from the Oracle Universal Installer program.

loading the server software, loading the client software, or selecting the specific software you wish to load through a custom installation. When you use the Universal Installer, you might also have the option to create a starter database, depending on which installation configuration you select. If you choose this option, then the Installer will start the Oracle Database Configuration Assistant along with the NET8 Configuration Assistant after the RDBMS software has been installed.

Oracle8i requires its own ORACLE_HOME directory, and you cannot install the software over any existing version of Oracle. Thus, if you are low on available hard-drive space, you'll have to remove the previous version of the Oracle RDBMS before you can install Oracle8i. You can, of course, load Oracle8i into its own ORACLE_HOME directory, separate from any other ORACLE_HOME directory, if you have the space available. This allows you to run one database in Oracle8i and other databases on different versions of the RDBMS software at the same time.

Installing the Oracle RDBMS Software with the Silent-Mode Installer

Sometimes you might want to use the Oracle Universal Installer (to install the Oracle RDBMS database software on a group of networked servers, for example) without requiring a user response to any prompts and without needing to use the graphical capabilities of the universal installer. This is a case when you might consider using the silent-mode installation method supported by the Universal Installer. Note that on Unix, although the installation itself is silent, the installer still requires an Xwindows connection to the client, even if the Installer is running in silent mode. Of course, this isn't an issue if you're using the Installer on NT.

When doing a silent-mode installation of the Oracle RDBMS software, you use a response file (see Listing 2.1) that will be used by the Universal Installer in silent mode. The response file provides the information that the Universal Installer needs to properly install the RDBMS software. Before you do the silent-mode installation, you modify the response file so that the settings, such as ORACLE_HOME, reflect the settings you want the Installer to use.

Listing 2.1 Example of response file used to do a silent-mode installation.

```
####################################################################
## This is a sample response file                                 ##
## Before you run, make sure these are set properly:              ##
##  1) UNIX_GROUP_NAME                                            ##
##  2) ORACLE_HOME && ORACLE_HOME_NAME                            ##
##  3) s_GlobalDBName                                             ##
##  4) s_dbSid                                                    ##
##  5) s_mountPoint                                               ##
##                                                                ##
##  ALSO, MAKE SURE /var/opt/oracle/oraInst.loc EXISTS.           ##
##  TYPICAL ENTRY IN "oraInst.loc" LOOKS LIKE -                   ##
##  inventory_loc=/home/dba/oraInventory                          ##
##  BASICALLY, WHEREVER INVENTORY NEEDS TO BE LOCATED.            ##
##                                                                ##
##  AT THE END OF SILENT INSTALL LOOK UP THE FOLLOWING LOGS:      ##
##  - oraInventory/logs/installActions.log                        ##
##    (for $ORACLE_HOME/root.sh execution, etc.)                  ##
##  - /tmp/silentInstall.log                                      ##
##                                                                ##
####################################################################
[General]
RESPONSEFILE_VERSION=1.0.0.0.0
[Session]
#This entry is not used on Windows platforms
UNIX_GROUP_NAME;String;Used in Dialog
#Group that the current user is part of, for ownership of the
#installation files.
UNIX_GROUP_NAME="dba"
#FROM_LOCATION;String;Used in Dialog
#Full path for the products.jar file.
#Replace the X: with the drive letter of your CD-ROM device.
FROM_LOCATION="X:\stage\products.jar"
```

```
#ORACLE_HOME;String;Used in Dialog
#Enter the path to your oracle home.  Replace the drive letter and
#optionally alter the home path.
ORACLE_HOME="c:\Oracle\Ora81500"
#ORACLE_HOME_NAME;String;Used in Dialog
#Enter the name of this oracle home.  The name will be used to
# identify this home.
ORACLE_HOME_NAME="OraHome81500"
#TOPLEVEL_COMPONENT;StringList;Used in Dialog
#Choices: "oracle.server", "8.1.5.0.0"
TOPLEVEL_COMPONENT={"oracle.server", "8.1.5.0.0"}
#SHOW_COMPONENT_LOCATIONS_PAGE;Boolean;Used in Dialog
#Some components are flexible in where they are installed,
# although all have default locations. Set this to FALSE
# if you want to accept the default locations
# and not show this page.
SHOW_COMPONENT_LOCATIONS_PAGE=false
#SHOW_SUMMARY_PAGE;Boolean;Used in Dialog <---------------
#MUST be <false> for "silent" install
SHOW_SUMMARY_PAGE=false
#SHOW_INSTALL_PROGRESS_PAGE;Boolean;Used in Dialog <--------------
#MUST be <false> for "silent" install
SHOW_INSTALL_PROGRESS_PAGE=false
#SHOW_REQUIRED_CONFIG_TOOL_PAGE;Boolean;Used in Dialog
SHOW_REQUIRED_CONFIG_TOOL_PAGE=false
#SHOW_OPTIONAL_CONFIG_TOOL_PAGE;Boolean;Used in Dialog
SHOW_OPTIONAL_CONFIG_TOOL_PAGE=false
#SHOW_END_SESSION_PAGE;Boolean;Used in Dialog <---------------
#MUST be <false> for "silent" install
SHOW_END_SESSION_PAGE=false
[oracle.server_8.1.5.0.0]
#INSTALL_TYPE;String;Used in Dialog
# Minimal - Optional pre-configured DB (b_createDB), Networking
# services, Server utilities
# Typical - Pre-configured starter DB, Licensable options and
#         Cartridges, Networking services, Server utilities
INSTALL_TYPE="Typical"
[oracle.rdbms_8.1.5.0.0]
#OPTIONAL_CONFIG_TOOLS;StringList
#OPTIONAL_CONFIG_TOOLS={"dbassist"}  OR OPTIONAL_CONFIG_TOOLS=
#{"Oracle Database Configuration Assistant"}
#s_GlobalDBName;String;Used in Dialog
#This is the name of the database which will be created
#as part of the typical install.
#You should modify this string to use an appropriate name.
s_GlobalDBName="robert.us.business.com "
```

```
#This entry not needed for Windows installation.
#s_mountPoint;String;Used in Dialog
#Database file location: directory for datafiles, control files,
# redo logs
#s_mountPoint="/ora01/oracle/test8i"
#s_dbSid;String;Used in Dialog
#Value for ORACLE_SID. Change this to an appropriate SID.
s_dbSid="TEST8i"
#b_createDB;Boolean
#Relevant only in MINIMAL, set to TRUE if you want a starter
#database, set to FALSE if not.
#b_createDB=false
```

You should clearly understand the purpose of the silent-mode installation and in what cases (such as when installing Oracle databases at multiple sites without requiring user interaction) you would use it.

Performing a Silent-Mode Installation

To execute a silent-mode installation, follow these steps:

1. Make a copy of one of the two Oracle-provided response files (typical815.rsp or custom815.rsp) somewhere on your hard drive so you can edit the file. The response file can be found in the /response directory of the Oracle installation media. Generally, if you choose to edit the response file, you should use the custom815.rsp file. Also, you should rename the edited file so it's clear that changes have been made.

2. After you have copied the file, edit the contents of the file as required. In particular, you might want to change the ORACLE_HOME directory into which the software will load, the Unix group name, and so on.

3. After you have customized the response file, use the Universal Installer to begin the RDBMS software load, and use the **-responsefile** parameter to define the location of the response file you have just customized. Other, optional parameters include the **-silent** parameter, which causes output for the installation process to be sent to a log file called silentinstall.log. This log file will be located in a directory that is specified by a user environment defined by the **temp** variable. As always, confirm this by checking the user-specific documentation for your platforms. Finally, the **-nowelcome** parameter suppresses the welcome screen when the installer begins its operation.

Oracle Flexible Architecture and the Oracle Universal Installer

The Oracle Optimal Flexible Architecture (OFA) recommendations suggest directory names and placement of the Oracle RDBMS software on your system. Oracle strongly suggests that you follow the OFA guidelines when you're installing the Oracle database product as well as when you're creating Oracle databases. In addition, this standard defines the recommended placement of database data files on your system. Oracle strongly suggests the use of OFA for the following reasons:

- OFA allows for the organization of large amounts of complicated software and data on disks in a way that helps avoid bottlenecks and poor performance. For example, OFA defines a file structure that allows for different versions of the Oracle RDBMS software to be installed on the same machine.
- OFA facilitates maintenance tasks, such as backups of software and data.
- OFA contains design flexibility, allowing for easily managed and administered database growth.
- OFA is scalable.
- OFA helps reduce resource contention and helps remove fragmentation of free space in the data dictionary and elsewhere.
- In OFA the file system is organized to simplify locating specific database datafiles, and adding database datafiles as the database grows.
- OFA defines naming conventions for database files and directories, thus making them easier to distinguish between instances on a single system.

As an experienced DBA, you should already be very aware of the OFA standards. If you are not, you should refer to the Oracle8i documentation and refresh your memory regarding OFA and its implementation.

The Oracle Database Configuration Assistant

For a long time, the ability to create databases has been the mystery that has made the DBA seem like such a wise old sage. More than one poor beginning DBA who has ventured into the SQL reference guide and looked at the **CREATE DATABASE** statement has surely thrown the book out the window and decided to become a Java programmer. Fear not—if you're a beginning DBA, you'll benefit from one of Oracle's newer tools, the *Oracle Database Configuration Assistant.*

Although many people might not often use the Oracle Database Configuration Assistant, it's still important for you to know about it.

Using the Database Configuration Assistant to Create a Database

Oracle has introduced the Database Configuration Assistant to help the DBA create databases. You can use this tool when you install the Oracle database software as well as after the software has been installed. The Database Configuration Assistant will start automatically when you install the Oracle8i RDBMS soft ware if you choose an option that will cause the starter database to be installed.

If you choose not to install the starter database, and you want to use the Database Configuration Assistant later to create a database, you may do so by simply running the Assistant by whatever method your platform supports.

To start the Database Configuration Assistant on NT, open the Start menu and choose Programs|Oracle815|Database Administration|Database Configuration Assistant. On Unix, the command to start the Database Configuration Assistant from a Unix prompt is **dbassist**. You must be running Xwindows in order to run the Database Configuration Assistant on Unix.

The Database Configuration Assistant provides several features for the database administrator. These features provide the following benefits:

- Using the Default option, you can create an Oracle database based on a set of predefined defaults.
- Using the Custom option, you can create more customized Oracle databases through a wizard-like interface.
- The Database Configuration Assistant creates the appropriate configuration files based on the type of database you choose to configure—for example, an Online Transaction Processing (OLTP) System, a decision support system (DSS), or hybrid database.
- You can save the database-creation steps to a batch file to be used later.

When using the Custom configuration option of the Database Configuration Assistant, you are prompted for a great deal more database creation information. For example, you provide information about the tablespaces you want created, how much space you want the tablespaces to be created with, and where you want the tablespace data files to reside. You'll also be prompted for information on redo log size, control files and location, rollback segment creation, and various database configuration settings, such as SGA sizing. After you've provided this information, the Database Configuration Assistant will create the database for you, or you can save the creation commands to a batch file that you can run later.

The Database Configuration Assistant can be customized with your own database setup configuration. Then, you can package a complete installation process that requires no user interaction. An example of one of the screens from the Oracle Database Configuration Assistant is provided in Figure 2.2.

The Oracle Software Packager

The Oracle Software Packager (OSP) is used to package products into components that can be installed by the Oracle Universal Installer. When you use OSP, you define the installation characteristics and installation requirements of a component (for example, the presence of other software components, such as the RDBMS software). OSP then verifies the component and stages it for release.

OSP contains three wizards to facilitate these operations:

- *The Component Wizard*—Used to specify the properties of the components to be installed later by the Universal Installer. These components are placed in a component definition file. Properties might include files to be copied and the directories to copy them to, dependencies that products have, variables, installation types, and actions.

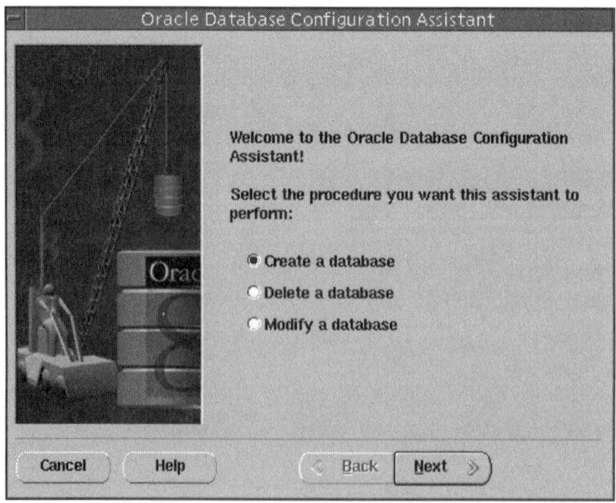

Figure 2.2 Sample screen from the Oracle Database Configuration Assistant.

- *The Verify Wizard*—Used to verify the component definition file.
- *The Staging Wizard*—Used to move the component definition file from the development area to the installation area, such as a CD-ROM, file server, or other medium.

The OSP can be customized to allow a developer to create Java classes to add to the predefined library of actions, queries, and dialogs. This feature allows the developer to customize the installation process or tasks as needed for the installation of the product.

Before you can use the OSP, you must have a Java Development Kit (JDK) installed.

Migrating or Upgrading the Database

If you already have an Oracle database that you want to change to an Oracle8i database, you'll be either migrating the database or upgrading the database, depending on the version of Oracle the database currently uses. If you are moving from an Oracle7.x database to Oracle8i, you'll be *migrating the database*. If you are moving from an Oracle8 database to Oracle8i, you'll be *upgrading the software*.

You have several options for migrating a database. You can use the Oracle Data Migration Assistant (which has a graphical user interface), the Oracle Migration utility (a command-line utility), the Oracle Export and Import utilities, the SQL*Plus **COPY** command, or the SQL **CREATE TABLE AS SELECT** command. When you upgrade a database, you can do so manually or use the Data Migration Assistant.

In this section, we'll discuss:

- Actions you'll need to take before upgrading or migrating the database (see "Before the Upgrade or Migration Occurs")
- Migration from an Oracle7.x database to Oracle8i (see "Migrating from Oracle7 to Oracle8i")
- Upgrading from an Oracle8 database to Oracle8i (see "Upgrading from Oracle8 to Oracle8i")
- Various supported methods of moving data from a pre-Oracle8i database into a fresh Oracle8i database (see "Alternative Methods of Moving Your Database to Oracle8i")

- Post-migration issues you'll need to deal with (see "After the Upgrade or Migration Is Complete")
- Several configuration changes that have to be considered (see "Configuration Issues When Converting to Oracle8i")

Before the Upgrade or Migration Occurs

To ensure a trouble-free conversion, Oracle suggests that you take several actions before you begin the upgrade or migration of your Oracle database to Oracle8i. Some of these actions are required only if you are migrating the database. When this is the case, we will note this specifically. Here are the steps you should take to prepare for upgrading or migrating your database:

1. Prepare for the conversion of the database.
   - Become familiar with the features of the Oracle8i database.
   - If you are migrating, decide which method to use. (See "Alternative Methods of Moving Your Database to Oracle8i" for more information on the advantages and disadvantages of the different migration methods available.) If you are upgrading, determine whether you want to do the upgrade manually or use the Migration Assistant.
   - Determine the system resources required for the conversion.
   - Create a plan for the conversion process.
   - Plan your recovery strategy—what you'll need to do if the conversion process runs into problems and needs to be canceled.
2. Test the conversion process by performing a test migration on a database other than the production database. Conduct this test in an environment as close to the production environment as possible. Run your test on this platform and validate the results.
3. Test the converted test database.
4. Prepare and preserve the production database. Schedule the outage time required to do the conversion. Perform full backups of the current production database. If time allows (and database size allows), do an export of the database as well. Test your backup to make sure it's recoverable.
5. Check the block size of the Oracle7 database. Oracle8i requires a minimum block size of 2K. Check the database you are converting, and ensure that it has a minimum block size of 2K. (Migration only)

6. Make sure the procedural option is installed. You can determine this by checking the SQL*Plus banner when starting SQL*Plus. (Migration only)
7. In the Oracle7 database to be converted, check the **SYSTEM** tablespace for available disk space for the larger Oracle8i control files, following the guidelines for your operating system. Also make sure that the **SYSTEM** rollback segment is large enough, that the **MAXEXTENTS** are set as high as possible, and that the **SYSTEM** rollback segment doesn't have **OPTIMAL** set. You should also check the space available where the control files will be located. (Migration only)
8. Check all schema names and ensure that none is called **MIGRATE** (Migration only) or **OUTLN**. Make sure that there isn't a role called **MIGRATE** or **OUTLN**. If either of these names is used, you'll need to remove it for the migration to take place. **MIGRATE** is created to give the migration program a working schema for the re-creation of the Oracle8i data dictionary. **MIGRATE** is a temporary user account, which will be dropped after the migration. **OUTLN** is created to provide a schema in which to store plans for a new feature in Oracle8i called *plan stability*. (See Chapter 9 for more on plan stability.)
9. Certain **init.ora** parameters need to be modified during the period of the migration. These include:

   - **job_queue_processes** should be set to 0.

Note: The Oracle conversion documentation suggests commenting out this value, but other sources suggest setting the value to 0. We suggest setting the value to 0.

   - The **large_pool_size** parameter should be commented out in most cases.
   - **db_domain** should be set correctly because Oracle no longer applies a default value to this parameter. Generally you can add the **db_domain** parameter with a **.world** value.
   - **ifile** parameter files should be checked for all the parameters shown above. Be aware of the possibility of duplicate parameters in various **ifile** parameter files.

10. Resolve all pending transactions with users (for example, sessions that have not committed their transactions yet). Check **dba_2pc_transactions** for any possible unresolved distributed transactions, and resolve them appropriately. (Migration only)
11. Make sure that **two_task** is or isn't set—whichever is required by your operating system (OS). If you are not using the **US7ASCII** character set,

check that the **ORA_NLS33** environment is set to $ORACLE_HOME/ocommon/nls/admin/data. (Migration only)

12. Check that all tablespaces and data files in the database to be migrated are **online, offline normal**, or **available.** Refer to the **V$RECOVER_FILE** view to make sure that no data files require recovery. If data files do require recovery, you must take steps to correct the situation. (Migration only)

Migrating from Oracle7 to Oracle8i

If you are familiar with Oracle8, then you should already understand the migration process from Oracle7. In this section, we will review the migration process and discuss the most significant change in this process. We will also review a new tool available in Oracle8i, the Data Migration Assistant.

Using the Migration Utility

When you're using the Oracle8i Migration utility, the basic migration process consists of several steps (provided next). For details on the Migration utility, see the next section. For more details on the steps in the migration process, see the *Oracle8i Migration Guide*. In the list that follows, for steps that are new in Oracle8i, we've added "(New in Oracle8i)" so that you can better understand the differences between the Oracle8 and Oracle8i migration processes.

Note: This isn't intended to be an all-encompassing list of every action to take when you're migrating a database to Orace8i. The Oracle8i Migration Guide *is a large book. This list addresses higher-level tasks and, in particular, concentrates on the differences between the Oracle8 migration process and the Oracle8i migration process. This list doesn't address additional steps that are required for parallel server environments.*

The steps required for the migration process include the following:

1. Install the Oracle8i software.
2. Check the status of the last backup, and ensure that it was successful.
3. Using the new Oracle8i Migration utility, prepare the Oracle7 database environment for the migration processes. (New in Oracle8i) The Migration utility will copy the software from the Oracle7 **ORACLE_HOME** to the Oracle8i **ORACLE_HOME** that is needed for the migration.
4. Shut down the database normally. Do *not* use **SHUTDOWN ABORT**.
5. While you're still set for the Oracle7 environment, run the Migration utility with the parameter **check_only=true**. (More information on the Migration Utility, which is used to migrate the database to Oracle8i, is

provided later in this section.) This step will determine whether sufficient space is available for the creation of the Oracle8i data dictionary. Review the output from the execution of this step to ensure that sufficient space is available.

6. Run the Migration Utility: **mig spool=\"/tmp/oracle/migrate/migrate_001.lst\"** (note the \ [escape] before the quotation marks). Check the spool file for any errors.
7. Make sure that the utility created the *convert file* called convSID.dbf in the **$ORACLE_HOME**/dbs directory. The convert file is a database data file created by the Migration utility, and is used when you issue to **ALTER DATABASE CONVERT;** command (in step 13). The convert file contains various types of information, including control file information, that is used during the initial conversion of the database after it has been restarted under the Oracle8i database software.
8. If time allows, perform another backup before finishing the migration to Oracle8.
9. Change the environment for the new Oracle8 home.
10. Copy the init.ora file of the database from the Oracle7 ORACLE_HOME/dbs directory to the Oracle8i ORACLE_HOME/dbs directory. Adjust the file for any new Oracle8i database settings you might want to take advantage of. Change the **compatible** parameter and other parameters as needed. (For more information on issues you should consider when changing the init.ora file, see "Configuration Issues When Converting to Oracle8i," later in this chapter.)
11. Rename the existing control files for the old Oracle7 database. New ones will be created.
12. Copy the converted dbf file from the Oracle7 $ORACLE_HOME directory to the Oracle8 ORACLE_HOME directory. If you have a password file, move it to the Oracle8 environment.
13. Start Server Manager, and issue the **CONNECT INTERNAL** and **STARTUP NOMOUNT** commands. *Do not start the database in any other mode.* Then, to convert the database, issue the **ALTER DATABASE CONVERT** command.
14. Open the new Oracle8 database. Issue the **ALTER DATABASE OPEN RESETLOGS** command.

15. Spool the output to a text file, and run the u0703040.sql script. If you are running advanced replication, run the catrep.sql and r0703040.sql scripts, in that order. Run the utlrp.sql script to recompile any PL/SQL packages invalidated by the migration. (New in Oracle8i)
16. Shut down the database by using the **normal** or **immediate** option. Do *not* perform a **SHUTDOWN ABORT** at this point, or corruption may occur.
17. Start up the database again.

A lot can go wrong in a migration. Issues can also arise after the migration that might require reversion to the previous version of Oracle. We strongly suggest that you do multiple backups both before and after the migration process.

Using the Migration Preparation Utility (migprep)

If you have done any Oracle8 migrations, you'll remember that you had to install the Migration utility (mig) in the Oracle7 ORACLE_HOME directory by using the installer. For Oracle8i, Oracle simplified this step by providing the migprep utility. Now the Migration utility is loaded in the Oracle8i ORACLE_HOME directory when you install the Oracle8i RDBMS software. You use the migprep utility to copy the software needed to do the migration to the ORACLE_HOME directory (or directories) of the database(s) on which you'll run the Migration utility.

The syntax of the migprep utility is pretty simple, as shown here:

```
migprep [oracle8i_oracle_home] [oracle7_oracle_home]
```

When you run the migprep utility, you need to specify the location of the ORACLE_HOME directory for the Oracle8i software and the ORACLE_HOME directory of the Oracle7 database you are migrating from. Following is an example of the use of the migprep utility:

```
migprep /ora01/oracle/product/8.1.5 /ora01/oracle/product/7.3.4.4
```

Using the mig Utility

As stated earlier in this chapter, you use the mig utility (mig) to convert the Oracle7 data dictionary into an Oracle8i data dictionary. The Migration utility has changed little since its last incarnation in Oracle8, but let's review the parameters of the Migration utility.

As with earlier versions of Oracle8, the Migration utility is executed from the Oracle7 ORACLE_HOME directory with the Oracle7 environment set.

The mig utility has several parameters that add to its versatility in the process of migrating to Oracle8i. Some versions of the mig utility may have additional parameters that are platform specific; refer to your platform-specific documentation for these parameters (which won't show up on the exam). Table 2.1 lists the valid parameters for the mig utility and defines the purpose of these parameters.

At the end of the migration process, the mig utility creates a convertSID.ora file in the $ORACLE_HOME /dbs directory of the Oracle7 database you are converting. This file will be used during the migration process to Oracle8i.

Table 2.1 Parameters of the Oracle Migration (mig) utility.

Parameter Name	Description
check_only	When this parameter is **TRUE**, the Migration utility will only perform the space check calculations to ensure that enough **SYSTEM** tablespace space is available for the migration; the utility won't perform the migration. The default value for this parameter is **FALSE**.
dbname	Specifies the name of the database to migrate. Optional.
multiplier	Defines the initial size of the Oracle8i **i_file#_block#** index relative to the Oracle7 **i_file#_block#** index. With a default value of 15, the result is the creation of an index in the Oracle8i data dictionary that is 1.5 times larger than the index in the Oracle7 data dictionary. In certain migration situations, this converted index can run out of space. This parameter solves this problem.
new_dbname	Specifies a new name for the migrated database. Optional.
nls_nchar	Defines the National Language Standard (NLS) character for the Oracle8i database. If no option is used, the Migration utility defaults to the existing Oracle7 database character set.
no_space_check	Tells the migration program not to do the space check that is typically done on the data dictionary. Defaults to **FALSE** and is mutually exclusive with the **check_only** parameter defined earlier.
pfile	Defines the name of the init.ora initialization file. The default is the init.ora file for the database.
spool	Defines the output file name for a spool file that will contain all messages generated by the Migration utility during its run.

Using the Data Migration Assistant

Oracle has provided a wizard called the Data Migration Assistant to assist with the migration process from Oracle7 to Oracle8i. The Data Migration Assistant replaces many of the manual steps required by the Migration utility with a single, smooth point-and-click operation. The Data Migration Assistant also will upgrade an Oracle8 database to Oracle8i, another benefit of the utility. An example of one of the screens of the Data Migration Assistant is shown in Figure 2.3.

As with any simplification, there is the loss of some flexibility in the process, and this is true with the Data Migration Assistant. Primarily missing from the Data Migration Assistant are the command-line options of the Migration utility. Thus, certain migration scenarios (such as one that requires the use of the **multiplier** parameter) negate the use of the Data Migration Assistant. In addition, the Data Migration Assistant won't migrate databases at 7.1 and earlier levels. The Data Migration Assistant also requires the use of SQL*Net version 2. Check your operating system documentation for specific information on this. For more comparisons of the various migration methods, including the Data Migration Assistant, see "Alternative Methods of Moving Your Database to Oracle8i," later in this chapter.

Following are the steps for using the Data Migration Assistant to migrate a database:

1. Install the Oracle8i software.
2. Check the status of the last backup, and ensure that it was successful.

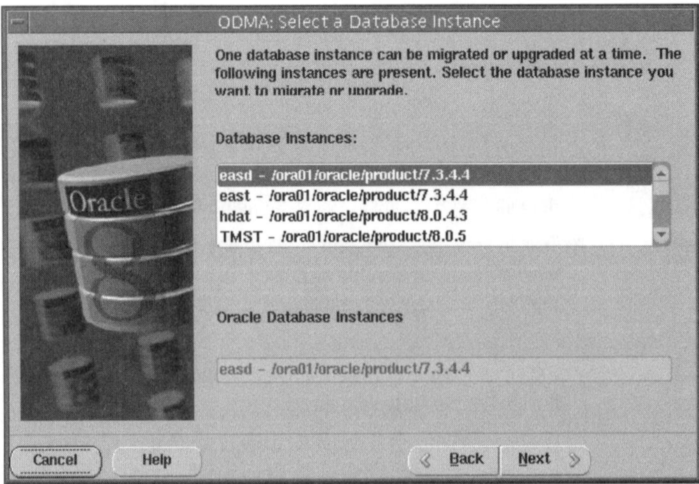

Figure 2.3 Sample screen from the Oracle Data Migration Assistant.

3. Remove any obsolete Oracle7 init.ora parameters before using the Data Migration Assistant.
4. Shut down the database normally. Do *not* use **SHUTDOWN ABORT**.
5. Remove any parameters from the init.ora that are not compatible with Oracle8i.
6. Perform any platform-specific pre-migration operations.
7. Following the operating-system-specific documentation, start the Data Migration Assistant. Follow the prompts as it completes the migration, and carefully check all prompts, checkboxes, and dialog boxes for the correct values. During its execution, the Data Migration Assistant will:
   - Shut down the database.
   - Review the requirements for using the program.
   - Allow you to select the database you want to migrate, its password, and its parameter file. The Data Migration Assistant will move the parameter file to the new Oracle8i location.
   - Allow you the option of moving data files to a new location.
   - Allow you the final option to back up the database.
   - Give you the option to set an NLS character set for the new Oracle8i database.
   - Proceed with the migration.
   - Offer to modify the listener.ora configuration for you. (See "Configuration Issues When Converting to Oracle8i.")

The Oracle Data Migration Assistant can be run from the Start menu in NT (choose Start|Oracle8150|Migration Utilities|Data Migration Assistant). From Unix, run the **odma** executable.

8. After the migration is complete, open the database with the **STARTUP RESTRICT** command. Check that the database comes up OK.
9. Run the utlrp.sql script to recompile any PL/SQL packages invalidated by the migration.

10. In the database, perform any specific migration tasks required by any options you may have loaded (such as Advanced Replication).
11. Do a final SHUTDOWN IMMEDIATE, and then start up the database again.

Abandoning the Migration

In most cases, it's possible to abandon the migration to Oracle8i as long as the ALTER DATABASE CONVERT command has not been executed. When you want to abandon the migration before this point, follow these steps:

1. Make sure the environment is set to the Oracle7 environment for the database.
2. Start the Oracle database by using Server Manager.
3. Drop the user called MIGRATE by using the DROP USER MIGRATE CASCADE command.
4. Rerun the version 7 catalog.sql and catproc.sql scripts.
5. Run any additional scripts that may be required based on the products you have installed.

Note: If you are using the Data Migration Assistant, it's possible that the ALTER DATABASE CONVERT command may have been run before you chose to abandon the migration. In this case, a full recovery of the Oracle7 database will be required if you choose to abandon the migration. The Oracle Migration Manual *provides steps to downgrade the Oracle8i database. Refer to this manual if you need to downgrade an Oracle8i database that you have already migrated or upgraded.*

Upgrading from Oracle8 to Oracle8i

If you are already running on a previous version of Oracle8, good for you. Obviously, you have already seen some of the new benefits of Oracle8 and are no doubt ready to upgrade your 8.0 database to 8i. In this section, we'll look at valid upgrade paths and discuss how to upgrade to Oracle8i.

Upgrade Paths to Oracle8i from Previous Versions of Oracle8

Following is a table that lists the supported upgrade paths from previous versions of Oracle8 to Oracle8i. With some older versions of Oracle8, direct upgrade to Oracle8i isn't supported. In these cases, you might have to upgrade these databases to versions that can be directly upgraded to Oracle8i. Table 2.2 lists the releases and the upgrade paths from those releases to Oracle8i.

Table 2.2 Upgrade paths to Oracle8i.

Old Release	Upgrade Process
8.0.1	You cannot do a direct upgrade from this version. You must first upgrade to release 8.0.2, followed by an upgrade to release 8.0.5, followed by an upgrade to Oracle8i.
8.0.2	You cannot do a direct upgrade from this version. You must first upgrade to release 8.0.5, followed by an upgrade to Oracle8i.
8.0.3	You can do a direct upgrade to Oracle8i.
8.0.4	You can do a direct upgrade to Oracle8i.
8.0.4S	You cannot do a direct upgrade from this version. You must first upgrade to release 8.0.5, followed by an upgrade to Oracle8i.
8.0.5	You can do a direct upgrade to Oracle8i.
8.1.1	Upgrading from this version isn't supported by Oracle. (You can use Export/Import instead.)
8.1.2	Upgrading from this version isn't supported by Oracle.
8.1.3	You can do a direct upgrade to Oracle8i.
8.1.4	You can do a direct upgrade to Oracle8i.

Manual Upgrade to Oracle8i

This section will provide you with the details of doing a manual Oracle8i upgrade from a supported, upgradable version of Oracle8. You should first have completed the tasks—all those not marked "(Migration only)"—listed in "Before the Upgrade or Migration Occurs," earlier in this chapter.

Manually upgrading an Oracle8 database to Oracle8i isn't terribly complex. Generally, you complete the following steps to perform the upgrade. As always, check your platform-specific documentation, and make sure you perform any supplementary steps required for additional products you may have installed.

Following are the steps for upgrading an Oracle8 database to Oracle8i:

1. Start Server Manager and connect to the database (**CONNECT INTERNAL**).
2. Shut down the database (**SHUTDOWN IMMEDIATE**).
3. Copy the password and init.ora files from the old ORACLE_HOME directory to the new 8i ORACLE_HOME directory. Adjust the init.ora file for any new Oracle8i settings you want to use, and make sure your environment is set up for the new Oracle8i environment (i.e., ORACLE_HOME, PATH, and so on.)

4. Start up the database in **RESTRICTED** mode.
5. Using Table 2.3, run the script file designated to upgrade your version of the database to Oracle8i. These scripts will be located in the $ORACLE_HOME/rdbms directory.
6. Perform any specific upgrade tasks required by additional products you may be using (such as Advanced Replication).
7. After the script is complete, issue a **SHUTDOWN IMMEDIATE** command. Restart the database, which is now upgraded.

Using the Data Migration Assistant

You can use the Oracle Data Migration Assistant to upgrade your Oracle8 database. If you select an Oracle8 database from the Select A Database Instance screen, the Data Migration Assistant will proceed to upgrade your Oracle8 database.

After the Upgrade

After you have finished the upgrade, you should review the upgrade guide for your operating system to ensure that there are no additional steps that you need to take. Also review the guide for any optional product upgrade requirements. Finally, review the section titled "After the Upgrade or Migration Is Complete," later in this chapter, for some post-upgrade to-do's.

Alternative Methods of Moving Your Database to Oracle8i

In addition to the Data Migration Assistant, there are alternative methods to migrating or upgrading an Oracle database (version 7 or 8) to Oracle8i. These alternative methods include using the Oracle Export/Import utility, using the SQL*Plus **COPY** command, or using the SQL **CREATE TABLE AS SELECT** command to move data from the old database to the new database. Tables 2.4 and 2.5 provide a quick summary of the advantages and disadvantages of each method.

Table 2.3 Script files used to manually upgrade Oracle8 databases to Oracle8i.

Version 8 Release	Script to Use to Upgrade to 8i
8.0.3	u0800030.sql
8.0.4	u0800040.sql
8.0.5	u0800050.sql
8.1.3	u0801030.sql
8.1.4	u0801040.sql

Table 2.4 Advantages of Oracle-supported migration methodologies.

Method Used	Factors to Consider for Use
Migration utility	Migrates v7 Oracle databases.
	Generally, if errors occur, just correct them and restart the Migration utility.
	Is generally as fast as or faster than other methods.
	Requires fewer system resources than other methods.
	Moves the entire database with relative ease.
	Migration time is generally not affected by database size.
	Migration time is reduced significantly; useful for 24x7 operations to reducc outagc for Oracle8i migration to a minimum.
Data Migration Assistant	Migrates v7 Oracle databases or upgrades v8 databases to 8i.
	Is generally as fast as or faster than other methods.
	Provides a wizard-like interface for the migration processes.
	"One-stop" migration; little additional work is required.
	Requires fewer system resources than other methods.
	Moves the entire database with relative ease.
	Migration time is generally not affected by database size.
	Migration time is reduced significantly; useful for 24x7 operations to reduce outage for Oracle8i migration to a minimum.
Export/Import utility	Converts Oracle6 and Oracle7 databases.
	Allows more selective migration of objects.
	Keeps the old Oracle7 database available.
	Can be used to defragment existing database objects.
	Can be used to migrate across different hardware platforms.
SQL*Plus **COPY** or SQL **CREATE TABLE AS SELECT** command	Allows conversion of Oracle6 and Oracle7 databases.
	Allows more selective migration of objects.
	Keeps the old Oracle7 database available.
	Can be used to defragment existing database objects.
	Can be used to migrate across different hardware platforms.

Table 2.5 Disadvantages of Oracle-supported migration methodologies.

Method Used	Factors to Consider Against Use
Migration utility	Doesn't migrate pre-Oracle7.x databases.
	Doesn't upgrade Oracle8 databases.
	Cannot migrate specific objects.
	Doesn't allow you to maintain the old Oracle7 database.
	Cannot be used to migrate across different hardware platforms.
Migration Assistant	Doesn't migrate pre-Oracle7.x databases.
	Migration or upgrade failures can require recovery of the Oracle7 database before you can rerun the conversion routine.
	Less flexible than the Migration utility.
	Cannot migrate specific objects.
	Doesn't allow you to maintain the old Oracle7 database.
	Cannot be used to migrate across different hardware platforms.
Export/Import utility	Requires more system resources to run two databases.
	Requires much more time and disk space generally than does the Migration utility.
SQL*Plus **COPY** or SQL **CREATE TABLE AS SELECT** command	Requires more system resources to run two databases.
	Requires much more time and disk space generally than does the Migration utility.

After the Upgrade or Migration Is Complete

After you have converted your database, whether by migration or upgrade, you should complete all post-conversion tasks. Some tasks are specific to just the migration of the database, and these are identified for you in the following procedure. Of course, you should have reviewed your operating system documentation before starting the update or migration for specific issues with your platform, but following are some general items to complete:

1. Change any backup and administration scripts to reflect the new Oracle8i database. Back up the new Oracle8i database. (Exporting the database might also be advisable.)
2. Run your test plan and validate the results.
3. Review the new Oracle8i features (by reading the rest of this book). For the new Oracle8i features you want to take advantage of, make any changes to the init.ora and listener.ora files as described later in this chapter in

"Configuration Issues When Converting to Oracle8i" and throughout the book. In the init.ora file, make sure you reset the settings that you changed for the benefit of the conversion (**JOB_QUEUE_PROCESSES** and **LARGE_POOL_SIZE**).

4. Check the SQL*Net net connection with the client. Make sure all the networking to the database works properly.
5. Run the utlconst.sql script to check for bad date constraints. Run the test plan and then validate the results. (Migration only)
6. You might need to rebuild certain bitmap indexes that might have become unusable as a result of the migration. (Migration only)
7. Change the password for the **OUTLN** user for security purposes.
8. Perform any platform-specific post-migration operations.

Configuration Issues When Converting to Oracle8i

Oracle8i is rich with a host of new features. This book will be covering many of them as we prepare you for the Oracle8i OCP upgrade exam. This section introduces a couple of new settings that you may want to consider using initially when upgrading to 8i. In addition, this section provides a list of all the changed parameters and renamed parameters.

New Settings to Consider

One of the initial setting changes to consider in the init.ora file revolves around the listener processes. Oracle8i changes the way the database interacts with the listener. Now when the database goes up or down, it will register itself with the listener associated with that database. This feature entails some optional init.ora configuration changes. The Data Migration Assistant will even offer to make these changes for you.

Also, consider changing the **compatible** parameter in the init.ora file to 8.1.5.0. This will allow you to take advantage of the new Oracle8i features. If you do not set this parameter, you won't be able to use 8i features. Note that with Oracle8i, you cannot set this parameter to anything less than 8.0.0.

If you set the database compatibility level and later wish to reduce the value, you'll need to refer to the migration document for specific instructions on performing this task. Reducing the compatibility level requires some DBA intervention, particularly making sure that the database isn't using any features that are allowed only by the higher compatibility settings and using the **ALTER DATABASE RESET COMPATIBILITY** command.

New, Obsolete, and Renamed Parameters

Tables 2.6 and 2.7 list all new and renamed parameters for Oracle8i. Refer to these tables when determining if you have your init.ora file set up correctly for Oracle8i. Oracle has removed many parameters in 8i, so you should carefully check your database before migrating or upgrading. If you don't change obsolete or renamed parameters, Oracle8i will generally just warn you that they are obsolete by sending an error message to Server Manager or SQL*Plus and then logging the error message in the alert log file. Regardless of this error, the database will open and the configuration parameter will be ignored.

Table 2.6 New parameters in Oracle8i.

db_block_checking	ent_domain_name
fast_start_io_target	fast_start_parallel_rollback
hs_autoregister	instance_name
java_pool_size	log_archive_dest_n
log_archive_dest_state_n	log_archive_max_processes
nls_comp	nls_dual_currency
parallel_automatic_tuning	parallel_server_instances
parallel_threads_per_cpu	plsql_load_without_recompile
query_rewrite_enabled	query_rewrite_integrity
resource_manager_plan	service_names
sort_multiblock_read_count	standby_archive_dest

Table 2.7 Renamed parameters in Oracle8i.

Old Parameter Name (Version)	New Parameter Name (Version)
mview_rewrite_enabled (8.1.3)	**query_rewrite_enabled** (8.1.4)
rewrite_integrity (8.1.3)	**query_rewrite_integrity** (8.1.4)
nls_union_currency (8.1.4)	**nls_dual_currency** (8.1.5)
parallel_transaction_recovery (In 8.1.4)	**rewrite**
fast_start_parallel_rollback (in 8.1.5)	**rewrite**

Practice Questions

Question 1

When you perform a migration from Oracle7 to Oracle8i, what two new users are created in the database? [Choose two]

- ❑ a. **MIGRATE**
- ❑ b. **SYS-MIG**
- ❑ c. **OUTLN**
- ❑ d. **PLAN**
- ❑ e. **CONFIGURE**

Answers a and c are correct. **MIGRATE** is a temporary user created for the purpose of giving the migration program a working schema. **OUTLN** is created for the purpose of providing a schema to store plans for plan stability, a new feature in Oracle8i. (See Chapter 9 for more on plan stability.) The other answers are incorrect because they do not list users that are created during the migration process.

Question 2

What is the best method to use to install identical databases without user interaction being required?

- ❍ a. Use the Universal Installer in **no_response_mode**.
- ❍ b. Use the Universal Installer in silent mode.
- ❍ c. Create a custom installation package with the Oracle Software Packager.
- ❍ d. Use the Universal Installer, clicking on the Silent Mode button on the welcome screen.
- ❍ e. Use the character-based installer in silent mode.

Answer b is correct. Use the silent-mode installation option of the Universal Installer. Answer a is incorrect because the option isn't called **no_response_mode**. Answer c is incorrect, though you might be fooled into selecting this answer because you know that the Software Packager is used to create custom installation types for the Universal Installer; thus, this is a trick question. This answer isn't the best one, however, because the silent-mode installation is designed for the task asked in the question. Answer d is incorrect because there is no Silent Mode button on the welcome screen. Finally, answer e is incorrect because there is no longer a character-based installer in Oracle8i.

Question 3

Which step is required before you migrate or upgrade a database to Oracle8i?

- ❍ a. Shut down the database and make init.ora changes.
- ❍ b. Back up the database.
- ❍ c. Check for the user **MIGRATE** in the database and remove if it's present.
- ❍ d. Check for the user **OUTLN** in the database and remove if it's present.
- ❍ e. Issue a **SHUTDOWN ABORT** command on the database to remove all users before the migration or upgrade.

Answer b is correct, back up the database. You should back up the Oracle database before migrating or upgrading it. Answer a is incorrect because changes to the init.ora file might not be required, though you should check it. Answers c and d are incorrect because during an upgrade, the **MIGRATE** user is never created, and the **OUTLN** user might legitimately exist (for example, if you're migrating between 8.1.4 and 8.1.5). Answer e is incorrect because you should never do a **SHUTDOWN ABORT** before doing a migration or an upgrade of the database.

Question 4

If you currently have an Oracle6 database, and you want to use the Migration utility to upgrade it to Oracle8i, what actions must you take first?

- ❍ a. Use the Data Migration Assistant.
- ❍ b. You must first upgrade the Oracle6 database to Oracle7 and then migrate the database to Oracle8i.
- ❍ c. Use the Migration utility to upgrade the database to Oracle8i.
- ❍ d. Export the Oracle6 database, and then import it into a new Oracle8i database; this is the only supported method.
- ❍ e. You cannot migrate an Oracle6 database.

Answer b is correct. You must first upgrade an Oracle6 database to a version of the Oracle7 database that is supported by the Migration utility. Answer a is incorrect because the Data Migration Assistant won't migrate an Oracle6 database. Answer c is incorrect because the Migration utility won't migrate an Oracle6 database, either. Answer d is incorrect because there are other supported methods of migration to Oracle8i besides Import and Export. Answer e is incorrect because Oracle does provide migration paths from Oracle6 to Oracle8i.

Question 5

A graphical method of migrating an Oracle7 database is provided by Oracle through the ____________________.

The correct answer is the Oracle Migration Assistant.

Question 6

What will happen if you start the Oracle8i database with an obsolete 7.3 parameter?

- ❍ a. The database won't start, and an error will be generated but not logged to the alert log.
- ❍ b. The database won't start, and an error will be logged to the alert log but won't be displayed on the Server Manager screen.
- ❍ c. The database will start, and an error will be logged to the alert log.
- ❍ d. The database will start, using the obsolete 7.3 parameter, with no error being logged.
- ❍ e. The database will crash when you attempt the first operation on it.

Answer c is correct. If you attempt to start the Oracle8i database with an obsolete 7.3 parameter, an error will be recorded in the alert log, but the database will open normally, ignoring the obsolete parameter. Answer a is incorrect because the error is logged to the alert log. Answer b is incorrect because the database will indeed start. Answer d is incorrect because the error will be logged. Answer e is incorrect because the database won't crash (at least, not because of an obsolete parameter).

Question 7

Which of the following isn't a valid method of migrating to Oracle8i?

❍ a. Using the Migration utility

❍ b. Using the Data Migration Assistant

❍ c. Using Export/Import

❍ d. Using the Database Configuration Assistant

❍ e. Using **CREATE TABLE AS SELECT** commands from SQL*Plus

Answer d is correct. The Database Configuration Assistant is a wizard used to help create Oracle databases; it isn't used in the process of migrating a database to Oracle8i. Answers a, b, c, and e are all valid methods of migrating to or from Oracle7 to Oracle8i.

Question 8

Which isn't a feature of the Oracle Universal Installer?

❍ a. It provides a silent-mode installation option.

❍ b. It provides a Java-, character-, or silent-based method of operation.

❍ c. It provides a common installer for all Oracle products.

❍ d. It provides support for multiple ORACLE_HOME directories.

❍ e. It provides automatic dependency resolution.

Answer b is correct. Although the Oracle Universal Installer does include Java mode and silent mode methods of operation, it doesn't include a character-based installer. Answers a, c, d, and e are features of the Oracle Universal Installer and thus are incorrect answers for this question.

Question 9

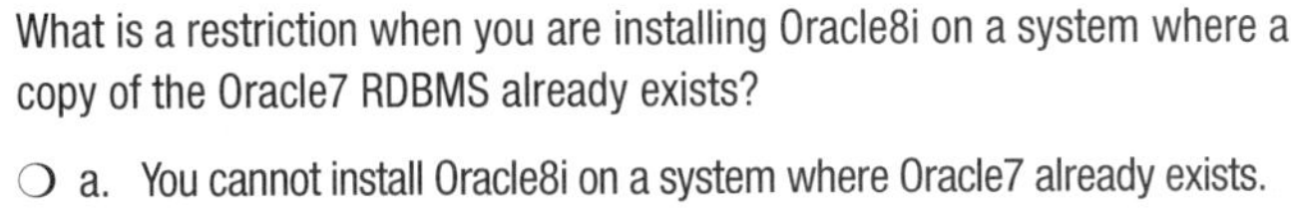

What is a restriction when you are installing Oracle8i on a system where a copy of the Oracle7 RDBMS already exists?

- ❍ a. You cannot install Oracle8i on a system where Oracle7 already exists.
- ❍ b. You must install Oracle8i in the same ORACLE_HOME directory as the Oracle7 software.
- ❍ c. You must install the Oracle8i software in an ORACLE_HOME directory that is different from the Oracle7 ORACLE_HOME directory.
- ❍ d. You must shut down all Oracle7 databases before you install the Oracle8i software.
- ❍ e. You must first remove the Oracle7 database software before you can install Oracle8i software.

Answer c is correct. You must install the Oracle8i software in an **ORACLE_HOME** directory other than the one that the Oracle7 software resides in. Answer a is incorrect because you can install Oracle8i on a system where Oracle7 already exists. Answer b is incorrect because you must not install the Oracle8i RDBMS software in the same **ORACLE_HOME** directory as the Oracle7 software. Answer d is incorrect because you do not have to shut down the Oracle7 databases to install the Oracle8i software. Finally, answer e is incorrect because you do not have to remove the Oracle7 database software before you install the Oracle8i software.

Question 10

Migration from Oracle7 to Oracle8i increases disk space requirements in which area?

- ❍ a. SGA
- ❍ b. Sort area
- ❍ c. Data dictionary
- ❍ d. Sort extent pool
- ❍ e. Database buffer cache
- ❍ f. None of the above

Answer c is correct. Additional space in the **SYSTEM** tablespace is required to accommodate the size increase of the Oracle8 data dictionary. Answer a is incorrect because the SGA size is controlled by the init.ora file and there are no disk-space requirements associated with it in regards to the upgrade. Answer b is incorrect for the same reason that answer a is wrong. Answer d is incorrect because the sort extent pool isn't affected by the migration. Answer e is incorrect because the database buffer cache is a memory area and isn't stored on disk. Answer f is incorrect because there is a correct answer to this question.

Need to Know More?

Ault, Mike. *Oracle8i Administration and Management.* Wiley Computer Publishing, 2000. ISBN 0-471-35453-8. This classic is upgraded for Oracle8i and is as good as ever. Includes installation, conversion, and migration topics that are worth reading.

Austin, David, Meghraj Thakkar, and Kurt Lysy. *Migrating to Oracle8i.* Sams Publishing, 2000. ISBN 0-672-31577-7. This book covers everything you wanted to know about installing, migrating, or upgrading to Oracle8i, but were afraid to ask. The definitive guide on this topic.

Oracle's documentation is good reference material. Oracle has numerous guides available on CD or in hardcover. In particular, the Oracle8I migration guide relates to the material in this chapter.

support.oracle.com is Oracle's Metalink Web site and is a wonderful resource if you have Oracle metals support (Gold or Silver support plan).

www.revealnet.com is a wonderful site with Oracle tips for DBAs and PL/SQL developers. You might want to check out some of the products they offer as well, like the Oracle KnowedgeBase.

Java in the Database

Terms you'll need to understand:

- ✓ Java
- ✓ Java virtual machine (JVM)
- ✓ **DBMS_JAVA** package
- ✓ **JAVA_SHARED_POOL** parameter
- ✓ JServer
- ✓ JPublisher (Beta)
- ✓ JDeveloper
- ✓ SQLJ (Embedded SQL in Java)
- ✓ Java Database Connectivity (JDBC)
- ✓ Java stored procedure
- ✓ loadjava and dropjava utilities
- ✓ Enterprise JavaBeans (EJBs)
- ✓ Common Object Request Broker Architecture (CORBA)

Techniques you'll need to master:

- ✓ Installing the JServer Environment
- ✓ Managing Java security with database roles
- ✓ Using the various methods to access Oracle with Java
- ✓ Writing a simple Java stored procedure and loading it in the database
- ✓ Publishing a Java stored procedure
- ✓ Executing a Java stored procedure from PL/SQL and SQL
- ✓ Using SQL and PL/SQL from Java

In this chapter, we'll present the core information about the new Java-related features of Oracle8i. We'll discuss the Java virtual machine (JVM) and how to install it in the database. The new Java-specific init.ora parameters, views, and packages are also presented in this chapter. We'll discuss JDBC, SQLJ, and supported methods to connect to the JVM, and we'll work through the steps necessary to create and execute a small Java stored procedure.

Oracle Java Components

Possibly the most exciting new feature of Oracle8i is the extended support for Java and the incorporation of a highly optimized JVM within the database server. As a DBA preparing to migrate or upgrade to Oracle8i and preparing to take the OCP upgrade exam, you'll need to possess a cursory knowledge of Java, understand the different methods of using Java with the database, understand the mechanics of loading and calling Java stored procedures, and, what's most important, understand that Java will play a significant role in your future as an Oracle8i DBA.

This isn't a Java tutorial, nor is it an Oracle Java language reference. The exam doesn't test your skills as a Java developer but instead tests your basic understanding of Oracle's integrated approach to using Java with the database. If you're cramming for this exam, don't stop to read a 4-inch-thick Java book. Do that *after* you pass the exam.

The Java Virtual Machine (JVM)

The Java Virtual Machine includes these major components:

- *SQLJ Translator*—Allows developers to write programs containing both Java and SQL.
- *Object Memory Management*—Allocates and frees memory in standard chunks called object memories. Object memory can be specialized by indicating how it is to be garbage collected, whether it has any preinitialized state associated with it, and whether it's transactional in nature.
- *Memory Manager/Garbage Collector*—Has been optimized for the Oracle database environment. It automatically manages the Java VM's memory heaps, allocating and collecting object memories efficiently.
- *Java Class Loader*—Provides users with the ability to interchange—both import and export—Java binaries between the Oracle VM and other systems using the standard ".class" format and in a compressed form. The Java VM provides an embedded Java class loader that locates, loads, and initializes local DBMS-stored Java classes (in Java binary or native compiled form), in

response to requests generated by the runtime. Java classes must be loaded into the database.

- *Bytecode Compiler*—Translates standard Java programs into standard Java .class binary representations.
- *Interpretation/run-time*—Executes standard Java binaries. The interpreter is a 100% implementation of standard Java, including advanced features such as Java threads and exceptions.
- *Native Compilation*—Increases the execution performance of Java programs to near compiled C-language levels. This is done by generating specialized C programs which are compiled into dynamic load libraries.
- *Library Manager*—Manages Java programs. It maps Java namespaces to database schemas.
- *Standard Libraries*—Are supported by the Oracle Java VM, including all of the standard libraries that are part of the core Java API specification—java.lang, java.io, java.net, java.math, and java.util.

The Java interpreters and compilers are based on the JDK 1.1.6 standards.

With Oracle8i, a Java language processor is included in the database—much like the PL/SQL language processor is included in the database engine. The Oracle JVM goes by the name *JServer*, and it's optimized for Oracle database functionality. JServer is scalable, stable, and standard, and it promises high performance because it's built into the database. With JServer, you can load and execute standard Java applications within the database, and you can create and run Java stored procedures. A JDBC driver and a SQLJ translator are also included so that you can create Java applications within the database to access Oracle data. However, you can't use the Java Abstract Windowing Toolkit (AWT) within the database. The JServer Accelerator native compiler is available with Oracle8i release 8.1.6.

init.ora Parameters That Affect JVM Performance

Before you install the JVM, it's important that you become familiar with the new init.ora parameters for Java. Two of these parameters are configured for you if you create a starter database when you install the server software. If you created your database independently of the software installation, check the parameters and associated values before attempting to install the JVM. The following init.ora parameters determine memory pool size in the System Global Area (SGA):

- The parameter **SHARED_POOL_SIZE** is set to 15MB in the starter database. This memory is used when the JVM is installed and when Java classes are loaded.

- The parameter **JAVA_POOL_SIZE** is set to 20MB in the starter database. This memory is used by shared in-memory Java classes and methods. You can adjust the size of this parameter as needed. If you don't plan to use Java in your database, set this value to 0.

The following init.ora settings place limits on per-session memory usage:

- The parameter **JAVA_SOFT_SESSIONSPACE_LIMIT** isn't included in the starter database init.ora file, and the default value is 0. Oracle documentation states that the default value is 1MB. A trace file is created when this value is exceeded by a Java session.
- The parameter **JAVA_MAX_SESSIONSPACE_SIZE** is also initially set to 0 and isn't included in the starter database's init.ora file. Again, documentation states that the default is 4GB.The session is killed when it exceeds this value.

Install the JServer Environment

If you installed Oracle8i and created the starter database (see Chapter 2), then Java is already installed and enabled in the database. If, however, you have created an Oracle8i database separate from the server-software installation process, you'll need to be aware of the following before you run the script to load the Java classes and start the JVM:

- The JVM objects are loaded in the **SYS** schema.
- The JVM includes over 4,000 classes.
- To install the JVM, the minimum size for the **SYSTEM** tablespace is 150MB.
- The init.ora parameter **SHARED_POOL_SIZE** should be 15728640 or greater.
- The init.ora parameter **JAVA_POOL_SIZE** should be 20971520 or greater.
- To install the JVM, run the script ORACLE_HOME/javavm/install/initjvm.sql.

The DBMS_JAVA Package

The package **DBMS_JAVA** is created when you run the initjvm.sql script. The corresponding Java class name for **DBMS_JAVA** is **DbmsJava**. **DBMS_JAVA** provides SQL and PL/SQL access to the JVM. The procedures and functions available in this package will probably increase in number with future releases of Oracle8i. Features of **DBMS_JAVA** include the following:

- The procedure **LONGNAME** displays the full Java class name—useful if the class name is more than 30 characters.

- The DBA can view, set, and reset JVM compiler options with the function **get_compiler_option** and the procedures **SET_COMPILER_OPTION** and **RESET_COMPILER_OPTION**.
- The DBA or developer can make calls to **DBMS_OUTPUT** from Java code.

Java Security and New Java Roles

The JVM includes support for Java security. When the JVM is started, the Java class SecurityManager is invoked. Oracle implements Java security through database roles that can be granted or revoked just like other roles. Users don't require the assignment of a Java security role to execute Java applications that affect only their own sessions. Additional privileges require the assignment of the new roles. The new roles in Oracle8i that are specifically for Java application security are:

- **Javauserpriv**—Allows interaction with the external environment, such as reading or writing to an OS file. This role has restrictions similar to those of the PL/SQL **file_io** package.
- **Javasyspriv**—Allows the user to create OS files.
- **Javadebugpriv**—Allows the user to debug Java code in the database by running the debugging agent. Access to debugging is provided through **dbms_java.start_debug** and **dbms_java.stop_debug**. This debugging agent is provided but not supported.

If an application fails due to insufficient privileges, then a **java.lang.SecurityException** will be thrown. You can't replace the Java system classes created by the installation script initjvm.sql. Classes in packages that contain system classes can be created only in the **SYS** schema. Please be very careful about whom you grant these roles to. The ability to read, write, and create files on a server file system can be very dangerous.

JDBC

Oracle8i has improved support for Java Database Connectivity (JDBC). JDBC is a JavaSoft standard for writing applications that communicate with relational databases. Oracle provides JDBC drivers that are used to access a relational database from a Java application. Oracle has three types of JDBC drivers:

- *Server*—The server driver runs inside the database and allows Java stored procedures to access the data in the database. The server driver is built into the database when you install the JVM.

- *Oracle Call Interface (OCI)*—The OCI driver converts JDBC calls to OCI calls. The OCI driver is useful for middle-tier to database connectivity. The OCI driver requires a client setup.
- *Thin*—The thin driver is small and easily downloaded to a client computer for direct connection to an Oracle database. The thin driver requires no client setup and is great for small applets running over the Internet.

SQLJ

SQLJ is an American National Standards Institute (ANSI) standard for embedding static SQL statements in Java code. Using SQLJ is an alternative to writing JDBC code. The SQLJ translator is conceptually similar to the Oracle Pro* language precompilers. The SQLJ translator converts SQLJ statements into standard JDBC calls. Oracle delivers both server and client SQLJ translators. Later in this chapter, we'll walk through the steps necessary to convert Java-SQLJ source code into a Java stored procedure.

For information about SQLJ and the SQLJ ANSI standard, visit these Web sites: **www.sqlj.org** and **www.nssn.org**.

Developing Oracle Applications with Java

Oracle provides us with three Java methodologies to develop applications in the database: Java stored procedures, Enterprise JavaBeans (EJBs), and Common Object Request Broker Architecture (CORBA). Java stored procedures work closely with database triggers, functions, and procedures. The Java stored procedures method allows you to move Java applications into the database, execute them with the JVM, and return values to PL/SQL programs. Enterprise JavaBeans is a standard for 100 percent Java distributed applications. To support CORBA, Oracle8i has an Object Request Broker (ORB) in the database, allowing Internet Inter-ORB Protocol (IIOP) communication with distributed objects in any language, including Java. Java-implemented CORBA server and EJB applications require that you use the multithreaded server (MTS) configuration.

For information about CORBA, visit the Web site **www.omg.org**. For information about Enterprise JavaBeans, visit the Web site **http://developer.java.sun.com/developer/technicalArticles/Beans/EJBEntity/index.html**.

Java Stored Procedures

Probably the quickest way to begin using Java in the Oracle8i database is with Java stored procedures. You can quickly create small Java applications, load them into the database, and call them as you would a PL/SQL procedure. Some noteworthy benefits of Java stored procedures are as follows:

- Java stored procedures provide improved application performance.
- They provide centralized enforcement of business rules.
- They are part of the SQLJ standard.
- The Java language is an alternative and complement to PL/SQL.

The latest Java Development Kit (JDK) can be downloaded from **http://java.sun.com**.

Write the Java Code and Load It in the Database

If you're not already a savvy Java developer, you'll need to first understand the different types of Java files. Java source code files have the .java extension and are simple text files. Java source code is compiled into portable bytecode files that have the extension .class. Java .class and resource files can be compressed and combined into archive files, which end with the .jar extension. You can load the following types of Java files into the database:

- Source code (and then compile it using the database bytecode compiler)
- Compiled code (.class or .jar files)
- Resource files, such as images

You can use two methods to load Java files into the database. One method is to run the Oracle loadjava utility from the command line. Because loadjava simplifies the process, we'll refer to it in the following sections. The other method is to execute the **CREATE JAVA** DDL statement from SQL*Plus. This requires the following steps:

1. Write the code, using your favorite text editor or Integrated Development Environment (IDE).
2. Load the code into a BLOB or LOB with the **CREATE JAVA** statement.
3. Manually resolve any external references.

Using loadjava

The **loadjava** utility can load .class, .java, and .jar files, and it automates all of the steps required in the **CREATE JAVA** method. If you haven't already created the **CREATE$JAVA$LOB$TABLE** and **JAVA$CLASS$MD5$TABLE** tables in the target schema, loadjava will do so for you. In a normal JDK environment, the Java class loader is responsible for dynamic class loading from disk when a program is executed. The loadjava utility accomplishes a similar task by placing the application into a schema, where it's dynamically loaded when the program is called. Figure 3.1 illustrates the basic steps in the loadjava process.

Write the Code

You can use any text editor to develop Java source code. For a more sophisticated Java program, you might want to use an IDE such as Oracle JDeveloper.

Compile the Source Code

To compile the source code, you'll need to install the JDK or an IDE such as JDeveloper. Compile the source code to bytecode at the command line with your Sun JDK or within an IDE.

Load the Bytecode File into the Database

The next step is to load the bytecode file into the database by using the loadjava utility. See Listing 3.1 for the loadjava syntax. You can also create a per-schema database table called **JAVA$OPTIONS** to hold persistent compiler settings, but override them with the loadjava options.

Listing 3.1 Syntax for the loadjava utility.

```
Loadjava {-user | -u} username/password[@database]
[-option_name -option_name...] filename filename...

loadjava Help
loadjava {-help | -h}
```

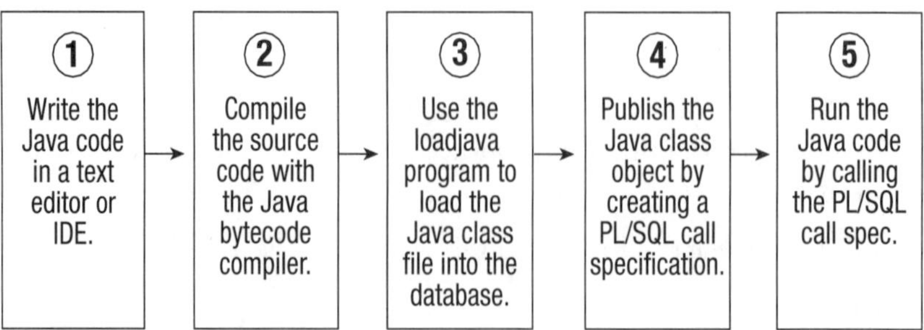

Figure 3.1 Steps in the loadjava process.

Publish the Java Stored Procedure

Now that the code is loaded into the database, you'll need to write a call specification to call the Java stored procedure. The call specification is simply a PL/SQL function, trigger, or procedure that refers to the Java app. Refer to Listing 3.2 for the correct format of a call specification.

Listing 3.2 The syntax for a PL/SQL call specification.

```
CREATE [OR REPLACE]
{ PROCEDURE procedure_name [(param[, param]...)]
| FUNCTION function_name [(param[, param]...)] RETURN sql_type}
[AUTHID {DEFINER | CURRENT_USER}]
[PARALLEL_ENABLE]
[DETERMINISTIC]
{IS | AS} LANGUAGE JAVA
NAME 'method_fullname (java_type_fullname[,
java_type_fullname]...)
[return java_type_fullname]';
```

Methods to Access the Java Stored Procedure

Once you've created the stored procedure and call spec, you'll probably want to test the function before you hand it over to your users. To access the Java stored procedure from a SQL*Plus session, you can use any of the following three methods:

- Write a query to call the function.
- Use the CALL statement.
- Call the Java stored procedure from a PL/SQL block.

Where Is My Java Stored Procedure?

The loadjava utility uses the built-in package **LOADLOBS** to load Java files into a **BLOB** column in the table **CREATE$JAVA$LOB$TABLE** in the schema passed on the command line. The loadjava utility then uses **CREATE JAVA** to load the Java files into database schema objects. You can use the function **dbms_java.longname** to get the full Java class name if it's longer than 30 characters. The DBA can pin the call specification in the shared pool using the DBMS_SHARED_POOL.KEEP procedure.

Drop a Java Stored Procedure

The utility program dropjava is used to remove Java stored procedures from the database. If you dropped the Java stored procedure, and you created a call specification for it, you might consider dropping the call spec at this point. If you attempt to execute the call specification, it will fail. Refer to Listing 3.3 for the dropjava syntax.

Listing 3.3 Syntax for the dropjava utility.

```
dropjava {-user | -u} username/password[@database]
[-option_name -option_name ...] filename filename...
```

Those are the basic steps to write, compile, load, call, and drop a simple Java stored procedure in the Oracle database.

Using SQL and PL/SQL in a SQLJ Application

The SQLJ standard is designed so that programming static SQL statements in Java code won't be overly difficult for the developer. As with the Oracle Pro* precompilers, the code is modified to include standard data types and calls before it's sent to the compiler and converted into binary form. SQLJ programming is well covered in other texts, so we'll only introduce the topic here.

These are the basic steps to create a SQLJ Java application that executes a simple SQL statement, providing the developer with an alternative to pure PL/SQL stored procedures:

1. Write the Java code, and include a simple SQL call, indicated by the **#sql** prefix:

   ```
   #sql newGreet={ select olamondo() from dual };
   ```

2. Translate it at the command prompt:

   ```
   %sqlj -user=scott/tiger@jdbc:oracle:thin:@host1:1521:orcl
   MyGreet.sqlj
   ```

3. Create a .jar file for the above app.
4. Load the .jar file into the database by using the loadjava utility, as shown in the previous exercise, "Load the Bytecode File into the Database."
5. Create the PL/SQL call specification for the Java app, as shown in the previous example.
6. Call the PL/SQL call specification, as shown in the previous example.

Enterprise JavaBeans (EJB)

Enterprise JavaBeans is a JavaSoft methodology for writing 100% Java server-side applications that interact with other Java applications in a distributed environment.

Each bean can be written for a discrete purpose, such as a server-side business logic component. The Oracle8i JServer includes support for the following:

- The EJB 1.0 standard
- Session beans only
- Remote Method Invocation (RMI) transport protocol for EJBs

Common Object Request Broker Architecture (CORBA)

The CORBA model was designed before Java became available. CORBA is a component-based model that allows applications built in diverse languages running on diverse platforms to communicate with each other. You can develop CORBA Java applications and run them in the JVM. CORBA objects can interact with EJBs and Java stored procedures, and vice versa.

You can develop CORBA applications with SQLJ. You'll need to be familiar with the following CORBA terms:

- *Interface Definition Language (IDL)*—This is the common language specification in which client interfaces are developed.
- *Internet Inter-Orb Protocol (IIOP)*—This transport mechanism, running over TCP/IP, provides a common software bus for handling communication between CORBA objects.
- *Object Request Broker (ORB)*—The ORB is the program that processes requests between objects.

JServer runs the VisiBroker ORB and IIOP for Java version 3.2 by Inprise.

Practice Questions

Question 1

For which of the following tiers can the developer create Java applications in the Oracle architecture? [Choose three]

- ❑ a. Client-side GUI apps
- ❑ b. Middle-tier business-logic server apps
- ❑ c. Database stored procedures
- ❑ d. OS-level applications to manipulate the Oracle SGA

Answers a, b, and c are correct. Oracle's strategy is to integrate Java development for the client, the middle tier, and the database. The developer can use Oracle's JDeveloper to create GUI client applications that use Java built-in classes, create middle-tier applications that replace the business logic in old COBOL programs, and create Java stored procedures that deliver optimal access to Oracle data. Answer d is incorrect because Oracle doesn't encourage you to write your own OS-level utilities that mess with the SGA.

Question 2

Which one of the following actions will load the HelloWorld.class file into the database?

- ❍ a. **CREATE JAVA PACKAGE HelloWorld AS LANGUAGE JAVA USING HelloWorld.class;**
- ❍ b. **loadjava -u scott/tiger@jellyfish:blue:1521 -v -t HelloWorld.class**
- ❍ c. **CREATE PACKAGE scott.HelloWorld AS SELECT * FROM JAVA FILE 'c:\orant\JavaCode\src\HelloWorld.class';**
- ❍ d. **INSERT INTO sys.DBMS_JAVA SELECT * FROM BFILE 'c:\orant\JavaCode\src\HelloWorld.class'**

Answer b is correct. The loadjava utility will load and resolve the Java class. In this example, the class will be loaded into SCOTT's schema in the "blue" database on the "jellyfish" server, using port 1521. Some of the terms in answer a might look correct, but it will return the error message "ORA-00905: missing keyword". You could use **CREATE JAVA** instead of the loadjava utility to load

Java code into the database, but answer a simply uses the wrong syntax. Answer c is incorrect because it will fail with compilation errors. Answer d is incorrect because it will fail and return the error message "ORA-00933: SQL command not properly ended".

Question 3

You want to create a small Java stored procedure. Before you can call the Java application with a PL/SQL code block, you must complete which of the following steps? [Choose three]

- ❑ a. Create public synonyms for the Java code.
- ❑ b. Write the Java code.
- ❑ c. Load and resolve the Java code.
- ❑ d. Publish the Java code.
- ❑ e. Grant privileges on the Java code to **PUBLIC**.

Answers b, c, and d are correct. If somebody else wrote the Java code, that still counts. The Java application can be loaded and resolved with the loadjava utility. You publish the Java application by creating a PL/SQL code specification. Answers a and e might be necessary to make your code available to other schemas in the database, but won't be necessary for you to execute the Java stored procedure.

Question 4

Support for which of the following Java virtual machine features is not included in JServer? [Choose one]

- ❍ a. CORBA.
- ❍ b. Java Stored Procedures.
- ❍ c. Enterprise Java Beans.
- ❍ d. The Abstract Windowing Toolkit.

Answer d is correct; support for the Java Abstract Windowing Toolkit (AWT) isn't supported in Oracle's JServer JVM. Each of the other features is supported in JServer.

Question 5

Which one of the following isn't a supported methodology for developing Java applications in the Oracle8i database?

- ❍ a. CORBA
- ❍ b. Pro*Java
- ❍ c. Enterprise JavaBeans
- ❍ d. Java stored procedures

Answer b isn't a supported mechanism for developing Java applications in the Oracle database. Although you might be familiar with Pro*C, Pro*COBOL, and Pro*Ada, Pro*Java isn't an Oracle product. Oracle8i supports CORBA, Enterprise JavaBeans, and Java stored procedures development methodologies.

Question 6

Which of the following init.ora parameters will affect the performance of Java in the database? [Choose two]

- ❑ a. **SHARED_POOL_SIZE**
- ❑ b. **DB_BLOCK_BUFFERS**
- ❑ c. **JAVA_PACKAGE_THRESHOLD**
- ❑ d. **SHARED_JAVA_SIZE**
- ❑ e. **JAVA_POOL_SIZE**

Answers a and e are correct. The **SHARED_POOL_SIZE** parameter is important when you're installing the Java components, creating call specifications, and loading classes, and the **JAVA_POOL_SIZE** parameter is important when Java code is being executed. The DBA needs to size the shared pool based on Java requirements as well as on requirements for SQL and PL/SQL objects. Answer b is incorrect because it doesn't directly affect Java performance but does affect query performance. Answers c and d are incorrect because they are not valid init.ora parameters.

Question 7

A trace file is created when a user's "session-duration Java state" exceeds the value of which init.ora parameter?

- ❍ a. **SHARED_JAVA_SIZE**
- ❍ b. **JAVA_MAX_SESSIONSPACE_SIZE**
- ❍ c. **JAVA_SOFT_SESSIONSPACE_LIMIT**

Answer c is correct. By creating a trace file, the instance is sending you a warning that you might have memory usage problems in your Java code. Answer a is incorrect because it's not a valid init.ora parameter. Answer b is incorrect because the session is killed if the application exceeds the value of JAVA_MAX_SESSIONSPACE_SIZE.

Question 8

You are user SCOTT. Which of the following Oracle-provided views will show the Java classes that belong to you? [Choose two]

- ❑ a. **USER_JAVA_OBJECTS**
- ❑ b. **DBA_OBJECTS**
- ❑ c. **ALL_OBJECTS**
- ❑ d. **USER_OBJECTS**
- ❑ e. **JAVASNM**
- ❑ f. **USER_JAVA_CLASSES**

Answers c and d are correct. The ALL_OBJECTS view will show your objects and the objects to which you've been granted access. The USER_OBJECTS view will show the objects that you own. The column OBJECT_TYPE will indicate whether the object is a JAVA CLASS or JAVA RESOURCE. Answer b is incorrect because, by default, user SCOTT can't see the DBA_OBJECTS view. Answer e is incorrect because the JAVASNM view contains the built-in Java class names, not your Java classes. Answers a and f are incorrect because the views USER_JAVA_OBJECTS and USER_JAVA_CLASSES are not Oracle-provided views.

Question 9

By default, the Java virtual machine classes are installed into which schema?

- ❍ a. **SYSTEM**
- ❍ b. **SCOTT**
- ❍ c. **SYS**
- ❍ d. **JAVASYS**

Answer c is correct. The initjvm.sql script loads the Java classes and creates the JVM in the **SYS** schema. Answer a is incorrect because the objects are created in the **SYSTEM** tablespace, not in the **SYSTEM** schema. Answer b is incorrect because, by default, no Java classes are installed in the **SCOTT** schema. Answer d is incorrect because the **JAVASYS** schema isn't a default Oracle schema.

Question 10

The DBA needs to print the full Java name of all the Java objects in a schema. To accomplish this, the DBA can use the Oracle-supplied ____________________ function.

The correct answer is **dbms_java.longname**. The full name of a Java schema object is stored in the **object_name** column of **DBA_**, **ALL_**, and **USER_OBJECTS**; however, if the name is longer than 30 characters, the **shortname** is stored. The function **DBMS_JAVA.LONGNAME** accepts the Oracle Java object name and returns the full Java object name.

Need to Know More?

Morisseau-Leroy, Nirva, editor. *Oracle8i SQLJ Programming*. Oracle Press, 1999. ISBN 0-07-212160-2. The definitive book on SQLJ programming. The exam doesn't go into the kind of detail presented in the book; however, the book is an excellent resource.

Scherer, Douglas, et al. *Oracle8i Tips & Techniques*. Oracle Press, 1999. ISBN 0-07-212103-3. This book has several good chapters on Oracle8i and Java. Chapter 2 describes the architecture in detail. Chapter 9 focuses on SQLJ and JDBC programming. Chapter 10 looks at Enterprise JavaBeans. Chapters 2 and 9 cover everything you need for the Java part of the exam.

The following documents are on the distribution media for your Oracle server software, and they can be downloaded from the Oracle Technet Web site: **http://technet.oracle.com**. If you don't already have an account, get one.

Harris, Steven G. *Oracle8i Java Developer's Guide* (Part No. A64682-01). Oracle Corporation, 1999.

Pfaeffle, Thomas. *Oracle8i JPublisher User's Guide* (Part No. A68027-01). Oracle Corporation, 1999.

Portfolio, Tom. *Oracle8i Java Stored Procedures Developer's Guide* (Part No. A64686-01). Oracle Corporation, 1999.

Smith, Tim and Bill Courington. *Oracle8i Enterprise JavaBeans and CORBA Developer's Guide* (Part No. A64683-01). Oracle Corporation, 1999.

Understanding the Oracle8i Internet File System (iFS) Option (Oracle white paper). Oracle Corporation, 1999.

Wright, Brian. *SQLJ Developer's Guide and Reference* (Part No. A64684-01). Oracle Corporation, 1999.

Availability and Recoverability Enhancements

Terms you'll need to understand:

- ✓ Duplex and multiplex archived redo logs
- ✓ **LOG_ARCHIVE_DEST_*n*** parameter
- ✓ Standby database managed recovery
- ✓ Read-only database
- ✓ Suspend and resume database I/O
- ✓ LogMiner utility
- ✓ Fast-start fault recovery
- ✓ **DBMS_REPAIR** package

Techniques you'll need to master:

- ✓ Configuring multiple destinations for archived redo logs
- ✓ Configuring a standby database for managed recovery mode
- ✓ Configuring a standby database for read-only operations
- ✓ Suspending and then resuming database I/O
- ✓ Using LogMiner to analyze redo-log entries
- ✓ Configuring fast-start recovery from a database failure
- ✓ Detecting and repairing corrupt data blocks

In this chapter we'll explain miscellaneous availability and recoverability enhancements. This chapter looks at diverse features that improve Oracle8i's ability to prevent a database failure and to recover from a database failure. Duplexed or multiplexed archived redo logs improve your chances of recovering a database in case of a failure. The standby database feature has been improved in Oracle8i; now you can use the standby database for read-only operations. With the **ALTER SYSTEM SUSPEND** command, you can now suspend database I/O without shutting down the database. LogMiner is a new utility that allows you to analyze redo-log entries and investigate transactions. Fast-start fault recovery allows for faster startup following a database crash. The **DBMS_REPAIR** package can be used to detect and repair corrupt data blocks.

Duplex and Multiplex Archived Redo Logs

Oracle8 allowed you to archive redo logs to two destinations by using the **LOG_ARCHIVE_DUPLEX_DEST** init.ora parameters. **LOG_ARCHIVE_DEST** indicates the primary destination, and **LOG_ARCHIVE_DUPLEX_DEST** indicates a local secondary destination. This option is still available, but Oracle8i offers an improvement with multiplexed archived redo logs. Whereas duplex archived redo logs allow for a local secondary destination for the logs, multiplex archived redo logs allow up to five destinations, one of which can be a remote system.

You can either use duplexed archived redo logs, by setting a value for **LOG_ARCHIVE_DUPLEX_DEST**, or use multiplexed archived redo logs, by setting values for **LOG_ARCHIVE_DEST_*n***. Duplex and multiplexed archived redo logs are mutually exclusive.

Set the init.ora parameter **LOG_ARCHIVE_DEST_*n*** (where ***n*** is an integer value between 1 and 5) to enable multiplexing. You can configure either a local disk destination or a standby database on a separate server. Use the keyword **LOCATION** to specify a file system, or use the keyword **SERVICE** to indicate a Net8 service name. See Listing 4.1 for **LOG_ARCHIVE_DEST_*n*** syntax, and Listing 4.2 for sample init.ora parameter settings. Here's a brief description of the keywords for the **LOG_ARCHIVE_DEST_*n*** parameter:

- **SERVICE** followed by a valid service name from the tnsnames.ora file indicates that a standby database will process the archived redo logs. Net8, using IPC or TCP, will transmit the archived redo log automatically.
- **LOCATION** (the destination) is a local file system.

- MANDATORY indicates that the redo log file can't be reused unless archiving to the specified destination succeeds.
- OPTIONAL indicates that the redo log file can be reused even if archiving to the specified destination fails. If a failure occurs and the optional redo-log-file location cannot be written to, an error message will be written to the alert log, and database processing will continue. If the number of multiplexed redo logs written is greater than or equal to LOG_ARCHIVE_MIN_SUCCEED _DEST, then the redo log file is marked for reuse. The value of REOPEN specifies the interval in seconds following a failure before a retry is attempted.

Listing 4.1 Syntax of the LOG_ARCHIVE_DEST parameter.

```
LOG_ARCHIVE_DEST_n =    ("null_string" | SERVICE=tnsnames-service |
                        LOCATION=directory-spec)[MANDATORY |
                        OPTIONAL][REOPEN=integer]
```

Listing 4.2 Configuring the instance for muliplexed archived redo logs.

```
LOG_ARCHIVE_DEST_1 = 'LOCATION=/ora01/oracle/arc/'
LOG_ARCHIVE_DEST_2 = 'LOCATION=/ora02/oracle/arc/'
LOG_ARCHIVE_DEST_3 = 'SERVICE=standby1'
```

The LOG_ARCHIVE_DEST_STATE_*n* parameter (where *n* is an integer from 1 to 5) can be either ENABLE or DEFER. ENABLE indicates that Oracle can use the destination; DEFER tells Oracle to not write to the destination. You can query the V$ARCHIVE_DEST view for details on multiple destinations for archived redo logs.

You dynamically defer archived-redo-log creation to a mandatory location by issuing the command **ALTER SYSTEM LOG_ARCHIVE_DEST_STATE_*n* = DEFER**. Be sure to know this when preparing for the exam.

The STANDBY_ARCHIVE_DEST parameter is set in the standby database init.ora file. This parameter specifies the destination for archived redo logs sent from the primary instance. It is the counterpart of LOG_ARCHIVE_DEST_*n* = 'SERVICE=standby1'.

Specify multiple archive processes (**ARC*n***) to alleviate **LGWR** (log writer) bottlenecks due to multiple destination archiving. This information is important for the exam.

Standby Database Enhancements

In Oracle8, the standby database feature allowed the manual copying and application of archived redo logs to the standby database. In Oracle8i, the two major enhancements to standby databases are the automatic transfer and application of redo logs and the ability to use the standby database as a read-only database.

Managed Recovery Mode

In Oracle8i, the new automated standby database feature means that the archived redo logs can be automatically transferred and applied. You don't have to create scripts or batch jobs to copy redo logs from the primary database to the standby database. Oracle8i does this for you. The standby database is kept in *managed recovery mode,* which means it will wait for an archived log file to arrive from the primary database and then will apply it to the standby database.

The command that takes a mounted database and places it in managed recovery mode is **RECOVER MANAGED STANDBY DATABASE**. The optional **TIMEOUT=*n*** clause indicates the number of minutes that the standby database will wait for an archived redo log before sustained recovery mode is canceled. You can manually cancel the managed-recovery-mode operation by issuing the **RECOVER MANAGED STANDBY DATABASE CANCEL** command. If you **CANCEL** the operation with the **IMMEDIATE** option, Oracle will stop managed recovery before reading the next block from the redo log file or opening the next redo log file. Without the **IMMEDIATE** option, Oracle waits for managed recovery to apply the current redo log file and then terminates the recovery operation.

Archived redo logs are transmitted by the **ARC*n*** background process of the primary database to the standby database. The tnsnames.ora file on the primary database and the listener.ora file on the standby database must have the correct service name. Each **ARC*n*** process creates a corresponding **RFS** (Remote File Server) process on the standby server. The **RFS** process is responsible for managing incoming archived redo logs and for updating the control file on the standby database. As mentioned in the previous section, the standby database init.ora parameter **STANDBY_ARCHIVE_DEST** determines where the RFS processes look for the archived redo logs to apply. The parameter **LOG_ARCHIVE_FORMAT** determines the file names to look for.

Remember, each **ARC*n*** process creates a corresponding **RFS** process on the standby server.

Read-Only Databases

Read-only mode and managed recovery mode are mutually exclusive. You can make a standby database available for queries but not for update by starting the database in read-only mode. To open a standby database in read-only mode, cancel the recovery and issue the command **ALTER DATABASE OPEN READ ONLY**. When the database is in read-only mode, no database writes occur, except to temporary segments if sort operations occur. Also, while the database is in read-only mode, archived redo logs are not applied. You can continue copying the files from the primary site, but you cannot apply the logs to the standby database until you return to a recovery mode: either manual or managed. You can return to a recovery mode by first clearing all read-only sessions and then issuing the command **RECOVER [MANAGED] STANDBY DATABASE**. At this point, the **RFS** processes will begin to apply all redo logs that have queued up since managed recovery mode was cancelled.

Note: Temporary segments are the only segments written in a read-only database.

Database SUSPEND/RESUME

The **ALTER SYSTEM SUSPEND** statement suspends all I/O and queries, and prevents new locks and I/O. This statement enables you to make copies of the database files without I/O interference and without instance shutdown. To cancel the **SUSPEND** operation and resume I/O, issue the **ALTER SYSTEM RESUME** command.

The **SUSPEND** and **RESUME** options are useful in a mirrored disk environment when you want to split the mirror and copy files for a backup. By issuing the **SUSPEND** command, you cease I/O activity on the database, and then you can split the mirror.

Redo Log Analysis with LogMiner

The Oracle8i LogMiner utility allows you to read the log files and:

- Analyze data access patterns.
- Track changes made by a user, and see the "before" and "after" data.
- Determine when a logical corruption occurred in the database.
- Perform historical and trend analysis.

LogMiner reads the redo logs and converts the entries into SQL statements that are visible only to the current session in the **V$LOGMNR_CONTENTS** view. LogMiner creates one row in the **V$LOGMNR_CONTENTS** view for each redo record (SQL statement) from the redo logs. The **SQL_REDO** column shows the reconstructed original SQL statement; the **SQL_UNDO** column shows the SQL statement to reverse the original SQL statement. See Listing 4.3 for a sample from the **V$LOGMNR_CONTENTS** view.

Listing 4.3 Excerpt from the V$LOGMNR_CONTENTS view.

```
SELECT sql_redo, sql_undo FROM v$logmnr_contents
WHERE username = 'TRAINMAN' AND tablename = 'TRAIN_MAINT'
/

SQL_REDO                            SQL_UNDO
--------                            --------
delete * from TRAIN_MAINT           insert into
                                    TRAIN_MAINT(TRAIN#,
                                    MAINT_DIV)
where MAINT_DIV# < 100;             values (101843, 75);
```

LogMiner has limitations, of course. The analyzing database must be Oracle8i, but LogMiner can analyze redo logs from Oracle8 databases. The source database must have the same database character set and hardware platform as the analyzing database. You must use a PL/SQL package to create a dictionary file that translates object IDs into actual object names. LogMiner does not support operations on chained rows, index-organized tables, cluster tables or indexes, or non-scalar data types. Also, only the session that generates the LogMiner records can view them in **V$LOGMNR_CONTENTS**, and the records go away when the session ends. It's not recommended that you use LogMiner for database auditing or for performing point-in-time recovery.

Using LogMiner

You can run the procedure **DBMS_LOGMNR_D.BUILD** on the originating database to create a dictionary file that translates object IDs to actual object names. Make sure you have set the init.ora parameter **UTL_FILE_DIR** to a valid file location, or the dictionary file creation will fail. See Listing 4.4 for an example dictionary file session. Without the dictionary file, your queries will contain object IDs, not object names.

To create the dictionary file for an Oracle8 database, run the Oracle8i-supplied script $ORACLE_HOME/rdbms/admin/dbmslogmnrd.sql for 8.1.5, or $ORACLE_HOME/rdbms/admin/dbmslmd.sql for 8.1.6.

Listing 4.4 Creating a LogMiner dictionary.

```
exec dbms_logmnr_d.build(
dictionary_filename =>'test1_dictionary.ora',
dictionary_location => '/ora01/logs');
```

Your next step is to specify log files that you want to analyze. With the analyzing database up and running, execute the PL/SQL procedure **DBMS_LOGMNR.ADD _LOGFILE**. See Listing 4.5 for a sample run. Create a new list of logs with the **NEW** enumerated constant. Add a log file with the **ADDFILE** keyword, and remove a log file with the **REMOVEFILE** enumerated constant.

Listing 4.5 Adding and removing log files for analysis.

```
exec dbms_logmnr.add_logfile(
LogFileName => '/ora01/logs/test1_2208.arc',
Options => dbms_logmnr.NEW);

exec dbms_logmnr.add_logfile(
LogFileName => '/ora01/logs/test1_2209.arc',
Options => dbms_logmnr.ADDFILE);

exec dbms_logmnr.add_logfile(
LogFileName => '/ora01/logs/test1_2208.arc',
Options => dbms_logmnr.REMOVEFILE);

Exec dbms_logmnr.end_logmnr;
```

Now for the fun part—analyzing the log files that you have just specified. Use the PL/SQL procedure **DBMS_LOGMNR.START_LOGMNR** to populate the **V$LOGMNR_CONTENTS** view. If you don't include the dictionary file, the SQL REDO and SQL UNDO columns won't be populated. You can specify start and end times, or start and end SCNs (system change number) to narrow the range of log entries that you want to analyze. See Listing 4.6 for an example.

Listing 4.6 Populating the V$LOGMNR_CONTENTS view.

```
execute dbms_logmnr.start_logmnr(
DictFileName => '/ora01/test1_dictionary.ora',
StartScn => 99845,
EndScn => 101134);
```

Once the **V$LOGMNR_CONTENTS** view is populated, simply query the view to begin analyzing.

No other session can see the records generated by your LogMiner session. When you exit from your LogMiner session, your entries will be deleted from the **V$LOGMNR_CONTENTS** view. If you want to keep the contents for a future session, you must copy the rows to another table before you exit.

Fast-Start Fault Recovery

Oracle8i introduces *fast-start fault recovery,* designed to minimize downtime following a system crash. The three components of fast-start recovery are fast-start checkpointing, on-demand rollback, and parallel rollback.

Fast-Start Checkpointing

During instance recovery, Oracle8i reads the redo logs to see what has been changed, and reads data blocks to decide whether or not to apply changes. Fast-start checkpointing allows you to configure an upper limit on the number of I/O operations that Oracle will perform during instance recovery. The dynamically configurable init.ora parameter **FAST_START_IO_TARGET** specifies the maximum number of data blocks Oracle will process during instance recovery. A small value means that fewer blocks require recovery, so recovery performance is improved. However, normal processing suffers because **DBW*n*** is busier: the frequency of buffer writes to disk will increase as **DBW*n*** advances the checkpoint to keep up with the **FAST_START_IO_TARGET** parameter. Since **DBW*n*** writes dirty buffers to disk more frequently, the buffer cache will have fewer dirty buffers in it when a crash occurs; therefore, recovery time will be quicker because there are fewer data blocks to recover by applying redo logs.

Oracle8i ensures that the target checkpoint position doesn't lag behind the end of the redo log by more than 90 percent of the size of the smallest redo log.

The **V$INSTANCE_RECOVERY** view shows recovery information based on the value of **FAST_START_IO_TARGET**. The **FAST_START_IO_TARGET_REDO_BLKS** column indicates the number of redo blocks that need to be recovered to meet **FAST_START_IO_TARGET**.

If you have set **TIMED_STATISTICS=TRUE**, the **AVGIOTIM** column in the **V$FILESTAT** view will show average I/O time statistics that you can use to determine the optimal value for **FAST_START_IO_TARGET**.

Fast-Start On-Demand Rollback

During instance recovery, Oracle8i rolls forward and then rolls back uncommitted transactions. In previous Oracle versions, users were blocked until the entire rollback was completed. With fast-start on-demand rollback, new transactions can start as soon as the roll-forward phase is finished—they don't have to wait for complete rollback of a dead transaction. Oracle automatically rolls back whatever changes are necessary to complete a transaction, and then rolls back the remainder of the dead transaction in the background. There are no init.ora parameters or commands associated with this feature.

Fast-Start Parallel Rollback

In Oracle8i fast-start parallel recovery, **SMON** coordinates parallel transaction rollback, reducing the amount of time required for recovery. Inter-transaction recovery occurs when each recovery process rolls back a separate transaction. Intra-transaction recovery occurs when a single transaction is divided among several processes. When **SMON** discovers that the amount of time required to recover in parallel is less than the time required to recovery serially, fast-start parallel recovery is invoked.

The init.ora parameter **FAST_START_PARALLEL_ROLLBACK** controls the number of processes used for transaction recovery. This parameter has three possible values:

- FALSE—Do not use fast-start parallel rollback.
- LOW—CPU_COUNT * 2 is the maximum number of recovery servers.
- HIGH—CPU_COUNT * 4 is the maximum number of recovery servers.

The **V$FAST_START_SERVERS** view shows information about fast-start parallel rollback recovery processes. The **V$FAST_START_TRANSACTIONS** view shows the transaction recovery process.

Corrupt Block Detection and Repair

Oracle has four methods for detecting corruption. The **ANALYZE** command with the **VALIDATE STRUCTURE** option can be used to verify the structure of a table, index, or cluster, and to confirm that a table and its indexes are in sync. The external **DB_VERIFY** utility (**dbv** in Unix) is used to validate blocks in data files that are offline. The init.ora parameter **DB_BLOCK_CHECKING=TRUE** forces verification when a block is changed, and any errors detected are written to the alert log. New to Oracle8i, the **DBMS_REPAIR** package gives you the ability to detect corrupt blocks in tables, partitions, and indexes. You can detect and report corrupt blocks to a repair table, make the object usable, and then repair the blocks and rebuild lost data. During the repair, data might be lost and logical inconsistencies might be introduced; therefore, it is important that you understand the significance of the data before making repair decisions.

DBMS_REPAIR Procedures

The procedures in the **DBMS_REPAIR** package are used to discover, repair, or ignore corrupt blocks. These procedures are also used to rebuild freelists, report on orphaned indexes, and perform administrative tasks on corrupt blocks.

- ADMIN_TABLES—Grants administrative privileges such as the ability to delete rows and drop objects. Use this procedure to create a repair table.
- CHECK_OBJECT—Detects corrupt blocks in an object, and reports the corruptions and fixes to the repair table.
- FIX_CORRUPT_BLOCKS—Fixes corrupt blocks based on data gathered with CHECK_OBJECT.
- SKIP_CORRUPT_BLOCKS—Indicates whether to ignore blocks marked corrupt during table or index scans, or to write an ORA-1578 error message to the alert log when a marked corrupt block is read.
- REBUILD_FREELISTS—Rebuilds the object's freelists if they are corrupt.
- DUMP_ORPHAN_KEYS—Lists the index keys that point to rows in corrupt data blocks.

Using the DBMS_REPAIR Package

Once you have determined that **DBMS_REPAIR** is the preferred option over **DB_VERIFY**, **ANALYZE**, and **DB_BLOCK_CHECKING**, the process is pretty straightforward. Use the **ADMIN_TABLES** procedure to create a repair table; use the **CHECK_OBJECT** procedure to determine if an object has a corrupt block; then query the repair table for results. You might now determine that it's best to drop the object and recover the data from a logical backup or another data source. If the corrupt object is an index, or if executing **DUMP_ORPHAN_KEYS** indicates errors, you will need to drop the index and build it again, or use the **ALTER INDEX...REBUILD** command to rebuild it.

The **FIX_CORRUPT_BLOCKS** procedure has potential problems: referential integrity problems might arise; or reinserting rows might cause triggers to fire and data will be duplicated. After you use **FIX_CORRUPT_BLOCKS**, make sure that referential integrity constraints are still valid by disabling and then enabling them.

Limitations of DBMS_REPAIR

Tables with LOBS, nested tables, and **VARRAY**s can be analyzed and fixed with **DBMS_REPAIR**, but out-of line columns are ignored. Index-organized tables and LOB indexes aren't supported. The **CHECK_OBJECT** procedure doesn't support clusters. The **DUMP_ORPHAN_KEYS** procedure doesn't work with bitmap indexes or function-based indexes; also, it only processes keys up to 3,950 bytes long.

Practice Questions

Question 1

Which of the following views is populated in a LogMiner session?

- ❍ a. **V$LOGMINER_ENTRIES**
- ❍ b. **V$LOGMNR_CONTENTS**
- ❍ c. **V$LOGMINER_CONTENTS**
- ❍ d. **V$LOGMNR_ENTRIES**
- ❍ e. **V$LOGMNR_REDO**

Answer b is correct. **V$LOGMNR_CONTENTS** is used to view the records in a LogMiner session. Each redo entry in a redo log file corresponds to one row in the **V$LOGMNR_CONTENTS** view. The **SQL_REDO** column corresponds to the redo log entry; the **SQL_UNDO** column indicates what you would execute to undo the change. No other sessions can see the current session's contents in the view. When the current session goes away, the **V$LOGMNR_CONTENTS** view is cleared. Answers a, c, d, and e are incorrect because they are not valid views.

Question 2

You can ignore corrupt blocks with the ________________ procedure in the **DBMS_REPAIR** package.

Answer: **SKIP_CORRUPT_BLOCKS**. The **SKIP_CORRUPT_BLOCKS** procedure is used to ignore blocks in indexes or tables that have been marked corrupt by the **FIX_CORRUPT_BLOCKS** procedure. Skipping corrupt blocks can give inconsistent results, for example, when rows are chained.

Question 3

What is the maximum number of remote archived-redo-log destinations, and of total archived-redo-log destinations?

- ❍ a. 2,5
- ❍ b. 0,5
- ❍ c. 1,5
- ❍ d. 0,2

Answer c is correct. The maximum number of remote archived-redo-log destinations is one, and the total number of archived-redo-log destinations is five. Set the init.ora parameter **LOG_ARCHIVE_DEST_*n***, where *n* is an integer 1 through 5, to a local file system with the **LOCAL** keyword for local archived-redo-log multiplexing, or use a valid TNS service name with the **SERVICE** keyword to automatically transmit the archived redo logs to a remote system.

Question 4

Which is the correct syntax to place a mounted database in automatic recovery mode? [Choose two]

- ❑ a. **RECOVER MANAGED STANDBY DATABASE**
- ❑ b. **RECOVER STANDBY DATABASE MANAGED RECOVERY MODE**
- ❑ c. **RECOVER MANAGED STANDBY DATABASE TIMEOUT=60**
- ❑ d. **RECOVER AUTOMATIC STANDBY DATABASE**
- ❑ e. **RECOVER AUTOMATIC STANDBY DATABASE TIMEOUT=60**

Answers a and c are correct. The command **RECOVER MANAGED STANDBY DATABASE** places the standby database in automatic (managed) recovery mode. Archive redo logs will be applied as they arrive in the **STANDBY_ARCHIVE_DEST** directory. Answers d and e are incorrect because the **AUTOMATIC** keyword is not valid. Answer b is incorrect because the syntax is not correct.

Question 5

Use the **ALTER SYSTEM** __________ command to stop all I/O in the database. [Fill in the blank]

Answer: **SUSPEND**. When the instance is in **SUSPEND** mode, no I/O occurs in the database. No new queries are allowed. You can't switch log files. To resume database I/O, enter the command **ALTER SYSTEM RESUME**. While the database is in suspended mode, you can copy data files and control files, or split a mirror in a disk-mirroring environment. This might be the only way to split a mirror without an instance shutdown.

Question 6

Which of the following are valid tools to detect corruption in the database? [Choose two]

- ❑ a. **DBMS_REPAIR**
- ❑ b. **ANALYZE...VALIDATE SCHEMA**
- ❑ c. **ANALYZE...VALIDATE STRUCTURE**
- ❑ d. **DBMS_CORRUPT_BLOCK**
- ❑ e. **DBMS_BLOCK_CHECKING**

Answers a and c are correct. Use the **DBMS_REPAIR** package to detect block corruption in a table, cluster, or index. **DBMS_REPAIR** reports block corruption to a repair table, and has procedures for checking, fixing, and skipping corrupt blocks. It also allows you to rebuild object freelists and detect orphaned index keys. Use **ANALYZE...VALIDATE STRUCTURE** to verify that indexes are synchronized with their base table. You can also use **DBVERIFY** to detect corruption in offline data files, or set the init.ora parameter **DB_BLOCK_CHECKING=TRUE** to detect corruption as a block is written. Answer b is incorrect because the **SCHEMA** keyword is not allowed. Answers d and e are not valid packages or init.ora parameters.

Question 7

Which of the following options for the **LOG_ARCHIVE_DEST_*n*** init.ora parameter will prevent a redo log from being overwritten if the write to the archived-redo-log destination fails?

- ❍ a. **REOPEN**
- ❍ b. **DEFER**
- ❍ c. **OPTIONAL**
- ❍ d. **MANDATORY**
- ❍ e. **LOCATION**

Answer d is correct. The **MANDATORY** keyword indicates that the write to the target must succeed, or the online redo log file will not be overwritten. Answer a is incorrect because **REOPEN** is a modifier of the **MANDATORY** or

OPTIONAL keyword, indicating when an attempt will be made to write to the archived-redo-log destination. Answer b is incorrect because **DEFER** is an option for the **LOG_ARCHIVE_DEST_STATE_*n*** parameter. Answer c is incorrect because **OPTIONAL** indicates that if the write to the archived-redo-log destination fails, it's all right to overwrite the online redo log. Answer e is incorrect because the **LOCATION** keyword indicates the local file-system destination for the archived redo logs.

Question 8

A standby database in read-only mode is useful for which of the following operations?

- ❍ a. End-user reporting that is synchronized with the primary database
- ❍ b. Batch updates, corrupt block repair, and table reorganizations before exporting back to the primary database
- ❍ c. Running reports that are current with the primary database up to the point when the standby database was placed in read-only mode
- ❍ d. Immediate failover from the primary database in a high-availability scenario
- ❍ e. Running LogMiner sessions

Answer c is correct. A read-only database can be used only for running select queries and reporting. The only allowed write activity on a read-only database is to the temporary sort segments. In a read-only standby database environment, specifically one that was in managed recovery mode, the database is current up to the point that recovery was canceled and the database was placed in read-only mode. Answer a is incorrect because while the database is in read-only mode, archived redo logs are not applied; therefore, the read-only standby database is not synchronized with the primary database. Answer b is incorrect because the specified activities require writes to the read-only database. Answer d is incorrect for the same reason that a is incorrect; a high-availability system needs the most recent archived redo logs applied quickly. It cannot wait for the read-only database to process a backlog of log files. Answer e is incorrect because a LogMiner session writes data to the database.

Question 9

Which of these views is the best place to get information to determine the optimal setting for **FAST_START_IO_TARGET**?

❍ a. **V$FILE_STAT**

❍ b. **V$FILESTAT**

❍ c. **V$FAST_START_IO**

❍ d. **V$FAST_START_SERVERS**

Answer b is correct. The **AVGIOTIM** column in the **V$FILESTAT** view shows average I/O time statistics that you can use to determine the optimal value for FAST_START_IO_TARGET. Answer a is incorrect because it is not a valid view name. Answer c is incorrect because **V$FAST_START_IO** is not a valid view name. Answer d is incorrect because **V$FAST_START_SERVERS** shows information about fast-start parallel recovery processes.

Question 10

Which of the following are valid settings for the init.ora parameter **FAST_START_PARALLEL_ROLLBACK**? [Choose two]

❑ a. **FALSE**

❑ b. **TRUE**

❑ c. **LOW**

❑ d. **MEDIUM**

❑ e. **QUICK**

Answers a and c are correct. **FALSE** tells Oracle8i to not use fast-start parallel rollback. **LOW** tells Oracle8i to use a maximum of **CPU_COUNT** * 2 recovery server processes. Answers b, d, and e are not valid settings. The other valid setting is **HIGH**, which tells Oracle8i to use a maximum of **CPU_COUNT** * 4 recovery server processes.

Need to Know More?

Austin, David, Meghraj Thakkar, and Kurt Lysy. *Migrating to Oracle8i*. Sams Publishing, 2000. ISBN 0-672-31577-7. See Chapter 32 for a fine discussion on LogMiner.

The following documents are on the distribution media for your Oracle Server software, and they can be downloaded from the Oracle Technet Web site: **http://technet.oracle.com**.

Baylis, Ruth and Paul Lane. *Getting to Know Oracle8i* (Part No. A68020-01). Oracle Corporation, 1999. Introduction to each of the topics presented in this chapter.

Cyran, Michele. *Oracle8i Supplied Packages Reference* (Part No. A68001-01). Oracle Corporation, 1999. See the **DBMS_REPAIR** and **DBMS_LOGMNR** chapters.

Dialeris, Connie, Joyce Fee, and Lance Ashdown. *Oracle 8i Backup and Recovery Guide* (Part No. A67773-01). Oracle Corporation, 1999. See the chapter on operating system backups for the specifics of **SUSPEND/RESUME** in a mirrored environment.

Durbin, Jason. *Oracle8i Reference* (Part No. A67790-01). Oracle Corporation, 1999. See Chapter 1 for details about the **LOG_ARCHIVE _DEST** parameters.

Fee, Joyce. *Oracle8i Administrator's Guide* (Part No. A67772-01). Oracle Corporation, 1999. See Chapter 19 for the guide to corrupt block detection and repair.

In addition to being available on the Oracle server installation CD, the documents just listed (all but the book listed first) can be downloaded from **http://technet.oracle.com**.

Summary Management

Terms you'll need to understand:

- ✓ Summary management
- ✓ Dimension table
- ✓ Fact table
- ✓ Materialized view
- ✓ Refresh mode
- ✓ Refresh option
- ✓ Query rewrite
- ✓ Dimension

Techniques you'll need to master:

- ✓ Using Oracle8i summary management features
- ✓ Creating, altering, and dropping materialized view logs
- ✓ Creating, altering, and dropping materialized views
- ✓ Creating, altering, and dropping dimensions
- ✓ Determining which Oracle-supplied packages are available to manage materialized views

Summary management is a new Oracle8i feature that allows for the storage of aggregate or summary data from both fact tables and dimension tables. This chapter reviews the things you need to know about this new feature to pass the Oracle8i OCP Upgrade Exam. We'll discuss why summary management is needed and how its component features or tools are used. One new feature added in Oracle8i for addressing summary management is the materialized view. We'll discuss what a materialized view is and how to create, drop, alter, and refresh these views. Later in this chapter, we'll discuss the query rewrite option and dimensions. Finally, we'll look at the Oracle packages associated with materialized views.

Summary Management in Oracle8i

In this chapter, we'll look at Oracle8i's new summary management features. The Oracle8i OCP exam contains several questions about these new features of which you should be aware. This chapter takes a detailed look at what summary management is and provides an overview of its features.

Why Summary Management?

Data warehouses collect data from various enterprise databases, providing a historical repository of information. Generally, the data from the enterprise systems will be loaded into the warehouse on a regular basis—perhaps daily, weekly, or monthly. The data can then be manipulated by load programs as it's moved into various warehouse tables.

Data stored in warehouses is generally stored in two types of tables. The first type of table is the dimension table. *Dimension tables,* also often known as *reference* tables or *lookup* tables, contain specific information about an entity. For example, a dimension table called **PLANE** could contain facts on each aircraft in an airline, such as the plane's registration number, type, purchase date, and home base.

The second type of table is generally called a *fact table.* A fact table contains detailed information that is related to one or more dimension tables. Continuing our example, we could have a **REVENUE** fact table containing the various revenues generated by the airline. This **REVENUE** table might include relationships to the **PLANE** dimension table (because the plane generates revenue) and might include other dimension tables, such as **SCHEDULE, LOCATION, PASSENGERS**, and so on. When these relationships are demonstrated in an entity relationship diagram (ERD), they often resemble a star; consequently, these are known as *star schemas*. An example of the star schema we'll be using in the examples in this chapter is shown in Figure 5.1.

After the data is loaded in the warehouse, users and applications will issue queries against this data. These queries might request summaries of the detail data at

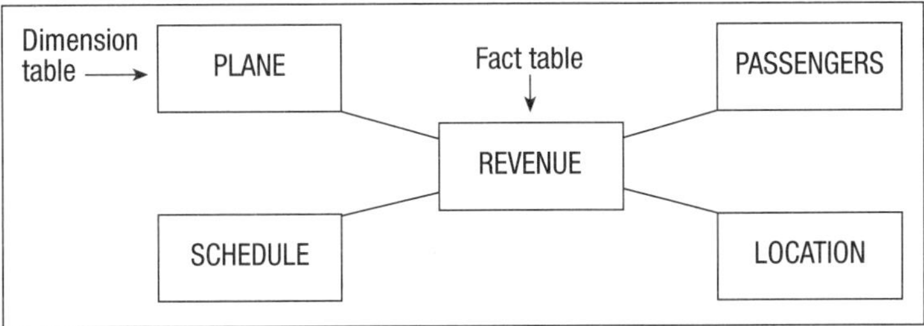

Figure 5.1 The type of star schema used in most examples in this chapter.

some higher level (roll up) or request specific detailed data that is a subset of the summary data (drill down). For example, a user of flight revenue data might want to summarize daily sales by departure location, time of day, or length of flight. These types of queries can typically run a long time and consume significant system resources.

Because of the constraints associated with running these queries against the entire table (or against several tables with a join), data-warehouse designers often design a separate set of tables to store commonly summarized data sets. This technique allows the user to have a set of precalculated tables from which to query known data summaries. Unfortunately, these types of tables will often require high maintenance and might take a great deal of time to rebuild whenever new data is loaded into the warehouse.

Overview of Summary Management Features

Recognizing the need for a database that can better handle these summary requirements, Oracle8i introduced summary management features that simplify the management of these aggregate tables. Summary management in Oracle consists of four basic features. These features include:

- An object known as a *materialized view* that allows the DBA to define various summaries and dimensions.
- The ability to refresh the materialized views in a scheduled manner that is uncomplicated and easy to manage.
- The ability to transparently rewrite a user query to use the materialized view rather than the table. This ability requires that the DBA enable a feature known as *query rewrite* and define a new Oracle8i object known as a *dimension*.
- A utility program—run by the DBA or database architect—that can recommend the creation, removal, or retention of these materialized views. This program is provided by Oracle in the form of the **DBMS_MVIEW** package.

In the following sections of this chapter, we'll discuss each of these features.

Materialized Views

As part of Oracle8i's new summary management feature, Oracle has introduced a new Oracle8i database object called a *materialized view*. Materialized views are used for several purposes in Oracle8i, including:

- Summary management for data warehouses
- Distributed computing (formerly known as *snapshots*)
- Mobile computing

For the purposes of the OCP exam, you need to be concerned with only the first bulleted item: materialized views for data warehouses, or *summary management*.

Why Use Materialized Views?

When used for summary management, materialized views provide new functionality to speed up summary queries of large data sets; materialized views accomplish this by calculating summaries, forming joins, and storing the results in the database. Oracle8i can maintain materialized views for you automatically, keeping the data in it as current as you need it to be. This maintenance often requires the use of a *materialized view log*, depending on your needs (see "Managing Materialized View Logs," later in this chapter).

So, why are materialized views such a big deal? Imagine, if you will, that you are an airline executive; you have a data warehouse that contains a fact table with the revenue of every flight (and, according to our ERD, every passenger, location, and so on) for the past three years. Even if the correct columns of this fact table were indexed, should there be a need to summarize revenue by some period or dimension—say, by month or for specific passenger groups—this operation could take a lot of time to complete. Imagine what would happen if many users needed this same kind of summary data, and imagine that many of these users were poor SQL coders.

Consider the impact on a system if 10 users executed a statement such as:

```
SELECT SUM(xyz) FROM revenue WHERE date_of_sale
BETWEEN ('01-JAN-00','31-MAR-00')
```

What if the **date_of_sale** column were not indexed? What if users started doing even more complex queries or wanted to drill down further—to find, say, the total revenue from first-class passengers on flights from New York to Las Vegas, that stopped in Detroit, and that ran on every Tuesday?

With a *materialized view*, we can create a view on this table that contains various summary information and that is updated when the related fact table is updated.

If we do our homework correctly, we can even push the optimizer into using the view instead of using the table, invisibly, without users ever knowing it. Because the optimizer can recognize that the materialized view is there (if we have set up everything correctly), the materialized view can be transparent to users.

So, we have established that the fact table will likely benefit from a materialized view. The first step is to create a materialized view log on that table. (Actually, the first step might be to analyze the table with a package to determine if it is indeed a candidate for a materialized view, but we'll discuss that in more detail later in this chapter; see "Packages for Managing Materialized Views.")

You should clearly understand the benefits of summary management and materialized views for the Oracle8i upgrade exam.

Managing Materialized View Logs

If you are familiar with Oracle snapshots, then you know what a *snapshot log* is; a *materialized view log* is exactly the same. It's simply a record of every change that takes place in a given table. The materialized view log is then used to update the materialized views associated with that table. The materialized view log is used to update the materialized view during a process called a *fast refresh*, which we'll discuss in greater detail later in this chapter. (Note that a materialized view log can't be built on a view, whereas a materialized view can.)

You're not required to create a materialized view log. The log simply enables the materialized view to be updated with the fast refresh method. In a fast refresh, the materialized view is updated based solely on the delta changes that take place in the table associated with that view. If there isn't a materialized view log for the table, then full refreshes of the materialized view will have to be scheduled. The result of a full refresh is that the data presented in the materialized view will temporarily be unavailable during the refresh process (the view will have no data). The full refresh process will take more time and more system resources than will a fast refresh. Finally, if you are going to create a materialized view that is based on a join of several tables, then you should create a materialized view log for each table associated with that join. This will allow the materialized view to be updated properly using the fast refresh method.

You should understand the purpose of a materialized view log for the Oracle8i upgrade exam.

Creating Materialized View Logs

To create a materialized view log, you use the **CREATE MATERIALIZED VIEW LOG SQL** statement. You must own the table that you want to create the log on, and you must have the **CREATE TABLE** privilege. If you don't own the table, then you must have the **CREATE ANY TABLE** and **COMMENT ANY TABLE** privileges. You must also have **SELECT** privileges on the table on which the log will be built, or you must have the **SELECT ANY TABLE** privilege. Also note that the **CREATE SNAPSHOT LOG** and **CREATE MATERIALIZED VIEW LOG** commands are interchangeable.

When you're creating a materialized view log, it can be partitioned, and it can have **STORAGE** and **TABLESPACE** clauses as well. Also, the materialized view log can be based on either the associated table's primary key or the **ROWID** of the rows in the table.

An example of the use of the **CREATE MATERIALIZED VIEW LOG** statement is shown here:

```
CREATE MATERIALIZED VIEW LOG ON flight_fact
   PCTFREE 5
   TABLESPACE fact_tbs
   STORAGE (INITIAL 10K NEXT 10K);
```

Because of the length and variety of options available with the command, please review the *Oracle8i SQL Reference* guide for the complete syntax of this command. Also, certain nondefault options must be used in certain cases to ensure that fast refreshes are possible. One example of this is the use of the **INCLUDING NEW VALUES** clause when your materialized view contains joins. For more information on the different combinations of views that can be created and on the requirements for fast refresh of these views, see "Managing Materialized Views," later in this chapter.

Dropping Materialized View Logs

To drop a materialized view log, use the **DROP MATERIALIZED VIEW LOG SQL** command. For you to drop the materialized view log, it must be in your own schema or you must have the **DROP ANY TABLE** privilege. The following shows an example of this command:

```
DROP MATERIALIZED VIEW LOG ON flight_fact;
```

Altering Materialized View Logs

You can alter several attributes of materialized view logs with the **ALTER MATERIALIZED VIEW LOG** command. Again, this command is quite lengthy, and you should refer to the *Oracle8i SQL Reference* guide for the command syntax, detailed information, and specific restrictions. To alter a materialized view log, you must own the table with which the log is associated or you must have **SELECT** privileges on the table. An example of the **ALTER MATERIALIZED VIEW LOG** command is shown here:

```
ALTER MATERIALIZED VIEW LOG ON flight_fact
   ADD PRIMARY KEY;
```

Managing Materialized Views

Materialized views are created using the **CREATE MATERIALIZED VIEW** SQL command (more on that shortly). Just like tables, materialized views can be partitioned, built using the **NOLOGGING** command, queried in parallel, and so on. Refer to the *Oracle8i SQL Reference* guide for information on specific creation issues.

When you create the materialized view, you use a **SELECT** statement to define the column composition of the materialized view, much as you do for a regular view. This query can contain several joins, but these joins cannot be to remote databases if you want to take advantage of query rewrite or the warehouse refresh facility. Tables, views, inline views, subqueries, and other materialized views are all allowed in a materialized view. Unlike a regular view, a materialized view is a real physical object in the database. The view stores rows of data, so space and indexing considerations must be taken into account when the materialized view is created.

When you define a materialized view, you can use the **BUILD IMMEDIATE** clause to instruct Oracle to build the view and populate it immediately. If you want to defer the data population of the view due to system or time constraints, use the **BUILD DEFERRED** clause.

If you want to use the view for query rewrite, then you'll need to use the **ENABLE QUERY REWRITE** clause when creating the view. Note that query rewrite is disabled by default, so you'll need to use the **ALTER MATERIALIZED VIEW** command to enable it if you create the view without the **ENABLE QUERY REWRITE** clause. Also note that there are several restrictions to doing query rewrite that you'll need to consider when creating a materialized view (see "Query Rewrite," later in this chapter).

Of course, after you create your materialized view, the first time someone changes one of the underlying (or master) tables associated with the view, the view will no longer be consistent with the master table. To avoid this problem, you define the refresh method that the materialized view should take. When you're determining the refresh method, you need to consider two issues: which refresh mode to use and how to execute the refresh.

Refresh Modes and Refreshing the Materialized View

The *refresh mode* of a materialized view defines when the materialized view will be refreshed. There are two modes: refresh **ON COMMIT** and refresh **ON DEMAND**. When you refresh using the **ON COMMIT** mode, a commit operation performed on the underlying master table will cause the associated materialized view date to be refreshed. You can use the **ON COMMIT** refresh mode in only these cases:

- The materialized view is created on a single table aggregate.
- The materialized view is created on a join.

Use the **ON DEMAND** refresh mode when you can't use the **ON COMMIT** mode or when you want to have greater control over when the view is updated. The refresh of the materialized view is executed through the use of the **DBMS_MVIEW** package (discussed later in this chapter). Using the **ON DEMAND** refresh mode also means that you can take advantage of what Oracle calls the *warehouse refresh facility* (which is basically represented in the **DBMS_MVIEW** package). The warehouse refresh facility provides a means to refresh views entirely or just with the addition of detail data.

You should clearly understand the different refresh modes and how they work. Also make sure that you're clear on the refresh options associated with materialized views.

After you decide when the materialized view should be refreshed, you must decide which *refresh option* to use:

- *complete*—Refreshes the entire materialized view based on its defining query. This results in all rows in the table disappearing as the table is refreshed. If the init.ora setting **atomic_refresh** is set to **FALSE**, then the **complete** refresh option is the same as the **FORCE** refresh option.
- *fast*—Updates the materialized view by modifying only the data that has been changed since the last refresh. If, for whatever reason, the refresh fails, an error message is logged, and user intervention will have to occur before the view will be further refreshed. The **fast** refresh option has several restrictions, which we'll discuss in a moment.
- *force*—Determines whether a **fast** refresh is possible and, if so, executes that method of refreshing the materialized view. If the **fast** method of refresh isn't possible, then Oracle will use the **complete** refresh option to refresh the materialized view.

- *never*—Suppresses the refresh of the materialized view.
- *always*—Causes an unconditional complete refresh to occur on the materialized view.

As we just mentioned, the **fast** refresh option has a number of restrictions. First, it should be noted that Oracle divides materialized views into three main classes:

- *Join; no aggregation*—A materialized view based on a query that performs either an inner or an outer join and contains no aggregation functions.
- *Single table; no join*—A materialized view based on a single table, with aggregation and no join criteria.
- *Join and aggregation*—A materialized view that contains both aggregation and joins.

These three classes and the nature of the materialized view query itself determine whether a **fast** refresh of the view is possible. For the purposes of the OCP exam, you won't need to have the long lists of requirements for fast refresh memorized. You should refer to the list of requirements in the Oracle documentation if you are creating materialized views on which you want to use the **fast** refresh option.

Oracle 8.1.5.0 has some bugs with materialized views and fast refresh. If you can't get fast refresh to work for you, find the 8.1.5.1 patch set or the new 8.1.6 release.

Many rules must be followed if you want to do warehouse incremental refreshes with the **DBMS_MVIEW** package. These rules depend on which of the three classes the materialized view belongs to (join, no aggregation; single table, no join; or join and aggregation). You should review these rules in the Oracle documentation. Again, the OCP exam won't expect you to have all these rules memorized.

Creating Materialized Views

To create a materialized view, you use the **CREATE MATERIALIZED VIEW** command. Refer to the *Oracle8i SQL Reference* guide for detailed information on the various options available for this command. To create a materialized view, you use the **SELECT** command, and you can use any number of joins.

Make sure that you understand the basic syntax needed to create a materialized view.

In Listing 5.1, we'll create a materialized view using a join between the **FLIGHT_FACT** fact table and the **REVENUE_DETAIL** and **FLIGHT_FROM_TO_DETAIL** dimension tables. This materialized view will enable us to quickly determine a specific flight's revenue for a specific revenue type. This particular materialized view will use the warehouse refresh package, **DBMS_MVIEW**, which we'll discuss later in this chapter. Finally, don't forget to **ANALYZE** your materialized view.

Listing 5.1 Example of creating a materialized view.

```
CREATE MATERIALIZED VIEW airline_revenue_mv
PCTFREE 0
TABLESPACE m_views
STORAGE (INITIAL 100K NEXT 100K PCTINCREASE 0)
PARALLEL
BUILD IMMEDIATE
REFRESH COMPLETE ON DEMAND
ENABLE QUERY REWRITE
AS
SELECT a.flight_num, c.from_city, c.to_city, a.revenue_key,
SUM(revenue_amt)
FROM flight_fact a, revenue_detail b, flight_from_to_detail c
WHERE a.revenue_key=b.revenue_key
AND a.from_to_key=c.from_to_key
GROUP BY a.flight_num, c.from_city, c.to_city,a.revenue_key;
```

If you get an error message when you try to create the materialized view, you should check permissions on the associated tables. You must have direct grants to the objects that you want to create materialized views on. If your permissions are through roles, your attempt to create the view will fail.

Dropping Materialized Views

To drop a materialized view, use the **DROP MATERIALIZED VIEW** command. For you to drop a materialized view, it must exist in your own schema, or you must have the **DROP ANY MATERIALIZED VIEW** privilege. You'll also need to have privileges to drop the internal tables, indexes, and views associated with the materialized view (**DROP TABLE**, **DROP VIEW**, and **DROP INDEX**). Here's an example of the **DROP MATERIALIZED VIEW** command:

```
DROP MATERIALIZED VIEW airline_revenue_mv;
```

Altering Materialized Views

There are a few alterations you can make to a materialized view. These include:

- Physical attributes (**PCTFREE**, **PCTUSED**)
- **STORAGE** clauses
- Partitioning
- **PARALLEL** clauses
- **LOGGING** and **NOLOGGING** attributes
- **LOB** storage clauses
- Recompiling the view
- Enabling or disabling query rewrite on the view

The materialized view must be in your schema, or you must have the **ALTER ANY MATERIALIZED VIEW** privilege. To enable query rewrite for a materialized view, you must have the following privileges:

- If all the master tables of the materialized view are in your schema, you must have the **QUERY REWRITE** privilege.
- If any of the master tables are in another schema, you must have the **GLOBAL QUERY REWRITE** privilege.
- If the materialized view is in another schema, both you and the owner of that schema must have the **QUERY REWRITE** privilege.

Here's an example of using the **ALTER MATERIALIZED VIEW** command:

```
ALTER MATERIALIZED VIEW airline_revenue_mv
STORAGE (next 50m);
```

Registering an Existing Table as a Materialized View

You might have already created an entity similar to a materialized view in your data warehouse. If so, no doubt you have triggers and stored code all over the place to mimic the refresh process. Converting these tables to materialized views can also provide the ability to do query rewrites.

To help you with moving these tables to materialized views, Oracle has included an option in the **CREATE MATERIALIZED VIEW** command that will turn an existing table into a materialized view. To do this, you use the **CREATE MATERIALIZED VIEW** command, naming the materialized view the same as the table to be converted. You then use the **ON PREBUILT TABLE** keyword, which indicates that the materialized view will be built on an existing table. After you've done this, the table can be updated, and the query rewrite feature can be enabled with the restriction that the **QUERY_REWRITE_INTEGRITY** parameter must be set to **TRUSTED**.

Listing 5.2 provides an example of creating a materialized view from an existing table. In this example, we have created a table that summarizes flight revenue by date and flight number. Suppose that we created the table in an Oracle8 database and that, after we installed Oracle8i, we wanted to convert this table to a materialized view. We do this by using the following **CREATE MATERIALIZED VIEW** command.

Listing 5.2 Using an existing table to build a materialized view.

```
CREATE TABLE revenue_by_flight
TABLESPACE fact_tbs
STORAGE (INITIAL 10k NEXT 10k)
AS
SELECT flight_date, flight_num, SUM(a.revenue_amt) revenue_amt
FROM flight_fact a
GROUP BY flight_date, flight_num;

CREATE MATERIALIZED VIEW revenue_by_flight
ON prebuilt table
ENABLE query rewrite
AS
SELECT flight_date, flight_num, sum(a.revenue_amt) revenue_amt
FROM flight_fact a
GROUP BY flight_date, flight_num;
```

Database Parameters That Affect Materialized Views

Several database parameters affect the use of materialized views. These parameters affect the ability of a materialized view to be updated, the ability of query rewrite to work properly, and the circumstances in which a query can be rewritten to use the materialized view. Table 5.1 lists these parameters and their impact on materialized views.

Query Rewrite

Associated with materialized views is a feature known as query rewrite. *Query rewrite* is the ability of the Oracle optimizer to convert a user-issued SQL statement containing tables and views into a statement using defined materialized views. This modification of the SQL isn't seen by the user unless the user is generating an explain plan of the current session. Because query rewrite is an internal process of the optimizer, the materialized views can be added and dropped without affecting user code unless the code directly accesses the materialized view.

Make sure you understand what query rewrite is and what parameters affect query rewrite.

How Oracle Does Query Rewrite

Before doing a query rewrite, Oracle checks the issued SQL to see if it's a candidate for query rewrite. If the SQL isn't a candidate, then the query isn't rewritten and the base tables are used. Oracle uses two methods to determine whether it can rewrite a query to use a materialized view. These methods are:

- Checking the query's SQL text to see if it matches the materialized view's SQL text
- Comparing join conditions, data columns, grouping columns, and aggregate functions of the SQL text

If Oracle determines that it can rewrite the query, then it will determine which materialized view it should use (if more than one fits the bill), and it will optimize the query to use that materialized view. After the query is rewritten, the optimizer will again determine if a further rewrite of the query is possible. When this process is completed and the query can be rewritten no more, Oracle checks the cost of the rewritten query against the cost of the original query and determines which plan to execute based on cost.

Table 5.1 Init.ora parameters and materialized views.

Parameter Name	Description
JOB_QUEUE_PROCESSES	The number of scheduled jobs that can be run concurrently. This affects how many refreshes of materialized views can be run concurrently.
JOB_QUEUE_INTERVAL	The number of seconds between which the job scheduler checks for new jobs to execute.
OPTIMIZER_MODE	To take advantage of query rewrite, must be set to **CHOOSE**, **FIRST_ROWS**, or **ALL_ROWS**.
QUERY_REWRITE_ENABLED	Must be set to **TRUE** to enable query rewrite.
QUERY_REWRITE_INTEGRITY	Set to **ENFORCED**, **TRUSTED**, or **STALE_TOLERATED**. Determines how fresh a materialized view must be to be used by query rewrite. (See the "Query Rewrite" section.)
COMPATIBLE	Must be set to 8.1 or higher.

Note: You must be using cost-based optimization for the optimizer to decide to rewrite a query. This also implies that you should analyze your tables so the optimizer can determine the cost of each possible plan and properly optimize the SQL query.

Parameters Affecting Query Rewrite

There are several ways that you can affect the optimizer's logic in rewriting a query. First, using the **QUERY_REWRITE_ENABLED** parameter, you can enable or disable the ability of the entire database to do query rewrites.

The **QUERY_REWRITE_INTEGRITY** parameter determines the "freshness" that is required of a materialized view. The options for this parameter are:

- ENFORCED—The default setting for the **QUERY_REWRITE_INTEGRITY** parameter, this setting tells the optimizer to use only materialized views that contain fresh data. This setting also instructs the optimizer to use relationships that are based on enforced constraints (foreign key, **NOT NULL**).
- TRUSTED—In this mode, the optimizer trusts that the data in the materialized views is correct and the relationships are correct. The optimizer also trusts declared but not enforced relationships and constraints, and it will use relationships specified by dimensions.
- STALE_TOLERATED—In this mode, the optimizer trusts that the data in the materialized views is correct even if the views aren't current. This mode offers the greatest flexibility in terms of rewrite capabilities but with the risk of returning incorrect results.

The safest level of rewrite integrity is **ENFORCED**. This setting guarantees that no data returned by the materialized view will be out of sync with a similar query against the base tables of the materialized view.

Using the **ALTER SESSION** command, you can enable or disable query rewrite and change the integrity setting at the session level. Following are two examples of the use of the **ALTER SESSION** command for this purpose:

```
ALTER SESSION SET QUERY_REWRITE_ENABLED=TRUE;
ALTER SESSION SET QUERY_REWRITE_INTEGRITY=STALE_TOLERATED;
```

Oracle also allows you to embed hints into SQL queries to disable query rewrite or to attempt to force a rewrite using a materialized view. These hints are **NOREWRITE** and **REWRITE**. Also, note that query rewrite must be enabled on the materialized view when it's created. If the view isn't enabled for query rewrite, the optimizer won't select it as a candidate for rewrite when optimizing SQL statements.

Privileges Needed for Query Rewrites

You must have certain privileges to do query rewrites. These privileges are based, not on the materialized view, but rather on the privileges granted on the view's underlying base tables. The **GRANT REWRITE** privilege allows you to enable rewrite on materialized views in your own schema, but only if all tables in the materialized view are contained in your schema. If you need to grant rewrite privileges to objects in other schemas, you need to use the **GRANT GLOBAL REWRITE** privilege.

Dimensions

Dimensions are an optional feature associated with materialized views. The use of dimensions makes query rewrite much more flexible. A *dimension* is an Oracle object that stores hierarchical information about your data. This information is used by the optimizer as it determines whether it can rewrite your query to use a materialized view.

The Purpose of Dimensions

Data in a data warehouse typically represents various hierarchical structures. One example would be the time relationship of data, which might be of the form of decade, year, quarter, month, week, day, hour, and so on. These types of relationships generally are used in data warehouse queries to roll up or drill down to more or less detail as needed. Oracle8i has introduced an object called a *dimension* that allows you to define these relationships in tables. Oracle then uses these dimension relationship definitions to more effectively rewrite queries and to determine if a materialized view can best be used.

Although Oracle can rewrite queries without the presence of dimensions, the definition of dimensions makes the query rewrite process much more versatile. The use of dimensions allows the query rewrite to move beyond SQL checking of the query's **SELECT** clause and its join conditions in the **WHERE** clause; with dimensions, the query rewrite can look at the summary grouping and also other operations.

When you create a dimension, you define the various components of the dimension and then the various hierarchies of the dimension. For example, if you created a table with columns for the number of landing cycles that an aircraft might go through (one cycle represents a single landing), you might create a table called **LANDING_CYCLES**, and in it, you might create columns for **year**, **quarter**, **month**, **week**, **day**, and **date_of_landing**. These columns would be the components, or levels, of the hierarchy; the order in which they appear would constitute the hierarchy itself.

Managing Dimensions

Several new Oracle8i SQL statements are available to manage the creation, removal, and altering of dimensions. In this section, we'll look at these statements, including the **CREATE DIMENSION**, **DROP DIMENSION**, and **ALTER DIMENSION** statements.

Creating Dimensions

To create a dimension, use the **CREATE DIMENSION** statement. You must have the **CREATE DIMENSION** privilege if you are going to create the dimension in your own schema, or the **CREATE ANY DIMENSION** privilege if you are going to create it in someone else's schema. Additionally, you must have the **SELECT** privilege for the objects you refer to in the dimension.

When you create a dimension, you can assign one or more table columns to that dimension in the **LEVEL** section of the **CREATE DIMENSION** command. You can also assign one table (a normalized dimension) or multiple tables (a denormalized dimension) to a dimension. If you assign multiple tables to a dimension, the columns in the various tables need to be joined by foreign-key relationships and should also be constrained as **NOT NULL**. The dimension can also consist of one or more hierarchies that represent the hierarchy relationships of the data shown in the **LEVEL** section.

Listing 5.3 provides an example of the **CREATE DIMENSION** command. Here, the dimension is derived from a retailer. We start out with the company as a whole, then move down to region and then to store. Within the stores, the retailer has departments (women's apparel) that products belong to. In each department, a product belongs to a class (jeans). Each product then is assigned to a style (black jeans) and finally to the UPC, which defines the actual individual product (black jeans, size 4).

In the **CREATE DIMENSION** statement in Listing 5.3, note the use of the **ATTRIBUTE** clause. This clause indicates that the specific column listed (for example, style) also determines another column's attribute. Thus, in the example below, the **style** column also determines the value in a column called **color**. Note that the **color** column must also exist in the same table. Note also that, in the **LEVEL** section, we begin with the most granular column and work our way up the hierarchy.

Listing 5.3 Example of the CREATE DIMENSION command.

```
CREATE DIMENSION dim_clothes
LEVEL upc                       IS     retail_tab.upc
LEVEL style                     IS     retail_tab.style
```

```
LEVEL class                IS     retail_tab.class
LEVEL department           IS     retail_tab.department
LEVEL store                IS     retail_tab.store
LEVEL region               IS     retail_tab.region
LEVEL company              IS     retail_tab.company
HIERARCHY sales_rollup (
Upc            CHILD OF
Style          CHILD OF
Class          CHILD OF
Department     CHILD OF
Store          CHILD OF
Region         CHILD OF
Company)
ATTRIBUTE style            DETERMINES (color)
ATTRIBUTE UPC              DETERMINES (item_size) ;
```

In essence, then, with the **CREATE DIMENSION** command, what we have done is defined the roll-up and drill-down relationships for the optimizer. Because the user might start looking at the department level for sales trends, we have defined for the optimizer the drill-down path from the department level. Thus, as queries are executed, the optimizer will have information that might let it rewrite the query using a materialized view that represents the appropriate level in the hierarchy.

Dropping Dimensions

To drop a dimension, you use the **DROP DIMENSION** command. The dimension to be dropped must be in your own schema, or you must have the **DROP ANY DIMENSION** privilege. Here's an example of the command:

```
DROP DIMENSION dim_clothes;
```

Altering Dimensions

With the **ALTER DIMENSION** command, you can add or drop hierarchies, attributes, and levels for an existing **DIMENSION**. The **ALTER DIMENSION** command also allows you to recompile a dimension if it becomes invalidated (as with the dropping or re-creation of the table on which the dimension depends). The dimension must be in your schema, or you must have the **ALTER ANY DIMENSION** privilege. Following is an example of an **ALTER DIMENSION** command:

```
ALTER DIMENSION dim_clothes
ADD ATTRIBUTE store DETERMINES sales_quota;
```

Validating Dimensions

The DBMS_OLAP package (see the next section) includes a procedure called DBMS_OLAP.VALIDATE_DIMENSION. This procedure is used to validate the relationships defined in a dimension. This is important because if the relationships in a dimension are incorrect, query results might also be incorrect.

Packages for Managing Materialized Views

Oracle provides two new packages to help you use the new summary management features of 8i. In this section, we'll review the DBMS_MVIEW package and the DBMS_OLAP package.

The packages that Oracle provides for management of materialized views are important to understand. You should generally be aware of the functions and procedures available with each package, and how they work with materialized views.

The DBMS_MVIEW Package

The DBMS_MVIEW package is used to manage materialized views and provide fast warehouse refresh capabilities on materialized views. To use the fast warehouse refresh facility in DBMS_MVIEW, you must define the materialized-view refresh as ON DEMAND.

The DBMS_MVIEW package consists of different functions:

- DBMS_MVIEW.REFRESH—Used to refresh one or more materialized views. This function takes nine parameters (four of which always remain the same and are covered together in the list that follows). These parameters, listed in the order they appear in the function, are:
  - The list of materialized views (comma delimited) to be updated
  - The refresh method to use (A-always, F-fast, ?-Force, C-Complete)
  - The rollback segment to use, or NULL
  - Continue the refresh job on other views if an error occurs refreshing a single view (TRUE or FALSE)
  - In all cases, there are four parameters that will always need to be set to FALSE,0,0,0

    - Atomic refresh (**TRUE**—warehouse refresh isn't used—or **FALSE**—each refresh operation is performed in its own transaction)

- **DBMS_MVIEW.REFRESH_ALL_MVIEWS**—Used to refresh all materialized views. If any materialized view fails to refresh, this fact, and the number of failures, are returned in the first parameter. This function takes five parameters:

    - The number of failures
    - The refresh method to use (A-always, F-fast, ?-Force, C-Complete)
    - The rollback segment to use, or **NULL**
    - Continue after errors (**TRUE** or **FALSE**)
    - Atomic refresh (**TRUE**—warehouse refresh isn't used—or **FALSE**—each refresh operation is performed in its own transaction)

- **DBMS_MVIEW.REFRESH_DEPENDENT**—Used to refresh all table-based materialized views that depend on specific tables. Thus, if you add data to a specific table on which a materialized view is built, only the materialized views affected by that table will be updated. This function takes six parameters:

    - The number of failures
    - Comma-delimited list of tables upon which the refresh can depend; all materialized views based on these tables will be refreshed (you can also pass in a PL/SQL table of type **DBMS_UTILITY.UNCL_ARRAY**, in which each element is the name of a table)
    - The refresh method to use (A-always, F-fast, ?-Force, C-Complete)
    - The rollback segment to use, or **NULL**
    - Continue after errors (**TRUE** or **FALSE**)
    - Atomic refresh (**TRUE**—warehouse refresh isn't used—or **FALSE**—each refresh operation is performed in its own transaction)

These procedures also create a log file if the **UTL_FILE_DIR** parameter is set correctly. You can rename this log file by using the **DBMS_OLAP.SET_LOGFILE_NAME** package (see the next section). See *Oracle8i Tuning* in the Oracle documentation for the specific parameters for these functions. Following is an example of the use of these packages:

```
Exec dbms_mview.refresh('airline_mv','A','',TRUE,FALSE,  -
0,0,0,FALSE);
```

The DBMS_OLAP Package

To help the DBA determine which materialized views should be created within a schema, Oracle provides a package that can do materialized view analysis and advisory functions. The name of this package is **DBMS_OLAP**, and it's also known as the *summary advisor*. With the summary advisor, you can:

- Estimate the size of a materialized view
- Have materialized views recommended to you
- Report the use of existing materialized views based on collected workload

When the summary advisor is executed, it populates a table with its results (with the exception of size estimation, which doesn't populate any tables with results), and the values in this table can be queried at a later date. In order to use the summary advisor, you must have first analyzed the tables that you want the summary advisor to report on. In addition, you must define dimensions on the various tables.

The functions used to recommend views are:

- **DBMS_OLAP.RECOMMEND_MV**—This function uses the data-dictionary statistics associated with the object but no workload statistics. Based on these statistics, it builds recommendations. This function takes four parameters:
  - Fact table names, or **NULL** to analyze all fact tables
  - Maximum storage that can be used for a materialized view
  - A list of materialized views to retain
  - A number between 1 and 100 that defines the percentage of materialized views that must be retained
- **DBMS_OLAP.RECOMMEND_MV_W**—This function uses both data-dictionary statistics and workload statistics. The parameters for this function are the same as for the **RECOMMEND_MV** function.

An example call to the package might look like this:

```
DBMS_OLAP.RECOMMEND_MV('AIRLINE_FACT',10000,'',10)
```

The results from the run of the package can be found in the table **MVIEWS$_RECOMMENDATIONS**. You can query this table directly with your own SQL code, or you can use a SQL script called sadvdemo.sql (located in $ORACLE_HOME/rdbms/demo/summgmt) to query the contents of the table, and then use the **DEMO_SUMADV.PRETTYPRINT_RECOMMENDATIONS** package to format the output for printing.

An additional procedure provided in the **DBMS_OLAP** package is the **EVALUATE_UTILIZATION_W** procedure. This procedure takes no parameters. It will output to the **MVIEW$EVALUATIONS** table a report providing the following information:

- The owner and name of the materialized view
- The rank of the view, in descending order based on the view's benefit-to-cost ratio
- The size of the view in bytes
- The number of times the view has appeared in the workload
- A comparative number that represents the cumulative benefit of the view

The **DBMS_OLAP.VALIDATE_DIMENSION** procedure is provided to validate created dimensions. When run, this procedure validates the dimension, populating a table called **MVIEW$_EXCEPTIONS**; this table shows the owner, table, relationship, and invalid **ROWID** of the row in the table that violates the integrity of the dimension. The parameters of the procedure are:

- The name of the dimension.
- The name of the schema that owns the dimension.
- A **TRUE/FALSE** value indicating if all rows of the tables in the dimension should be validated (**TRUE**) or if only new rows should be validated (**FALSE**).
- A **TRUE/FALSE** value indicating whether Oracle should check all columns defined in the levels of the dimension to ensure that they don't contain NULL values. If set to **FALSE**, the procedure won't check for **NULL**s.

The **DBMS_OLAP.ESTIMATE_SIZE** procedure can be used to determine how much space a materialized view will take. This procedure takes four arguments. The first two are the proposed name of the materialized view and the SQL statement that will be associated with the materialized view. The second two arguments are returned from the procedure and are the number of rows and number of bytes that the procedure will require.

Finally, note that some of the procedures in the **DBMS_OLAP** package (**RECOMMEND_MV** and **RECOMMEND_MV_W**) take some setup before they can be run. You must set up your listener.ora and tnsnames.ora files to properly handle external procedure calls, and you must add some Oracle trace settings to the database configuration file. This isn't covered in the Oracle8i OCP exam, so please refer to your Oracle documentation to prepare for the use of the **DBMS_OLAP** package.

Materialized Views and the Data Dictionary

You need to be aware of several new administrative views associated with materialized views. Table 5.2 provides a summary of these administrative views and a quick description of their contents.

You should understand the use of the various data dictionary views in relation to materialized views.

There are also new views used for the administration of dimensions. These views are described in Table 5.3.

Table 5.2 Administrative views used to manage materialized views.

View Name	Description
ALL_REFRESH_DEPENDENCIES	Contains all tables on which materialized views depend for refresh. There is no **DBA*** view of this name.
DBA_MVIEW_AGGREGATES	Provides information on materialized-view aggregate functions.
DBA_MVIEW_ANALYSIS	Provides information about materialized views that support query rewrite.
DBA_MVIEW_DETAIL_RELATIONS	Provides information on all objects referred to in a materialized view.
DBA_MVIEW_JOINS	Provides information on joins used in materialized views.
DBA_MVIEW_KEYS	Provides information on relationships, with additional detail related to **DBA_MVIEW_DETAIL_RELATIONS**.

Table 5.3 Administrative views used to manage dimensions.	
View Name	**Description**
DBA_DIMENSIONS	Provides information on dimensions that have been created.
DBA_DIM_LEVELS	Provides information on levels in a dimension.
DBA_DIM_LEVEL_KEY	Provides information about the columns defined in a dimension level.
DBA_DIM_HIERARCHIES	Provides information about the hierarchies within a dimension.
DBA_DIM_CHILD_OF	Provides information about the hierarchical relationship between various levels in a dimension.
DBA_DIM_JOIN_KEY	Provides information about the join between dimension tables if more than one table is used in a dimension.
DBA_DIM_ATTRIBUTES	Provides information about the relationship between dimension levels and any dependent columns.

Practice Questions

Question 1

What are two types of tables in a data warehouse? [Choose two]

- ❑ a. Fact
- ❑ b. Profile
- ❑ c. Determinate
- ❑ d. Dimension
- ❑ e. Join

Answers a and d are correct. Answers b, c, and e are incorrect because these aren't tables used in data warehouse terminology.

Question 2

Which of the following is not a benefit of a materialized view?

- ❍ a. It can provide calculated and current summaries of various data contained in a table.
- ❍ b. User queries can be redirected to use the view without the user knowing it.
- ❍ c. A materialized view can reduce the time needed to complete a user's query.
- ❍ d. A materialized view takes up no space in the database except for the space in the data dictionary required to maintain it.
- ❍ e. Oracle provides packages to assist with the management of materialized views.

Answer d is correct. This is a trick question because if you were not clear on the physical nature of a materialized view, you might mistakenly think that it's like a regular view. Because a regular view doesn't require any database storage to speak of, answer d might sound tempting. Answers a, b, c, and e are all incorrect answers because they are all benefits of materialized views.

Question 3

Which of the following is not a valid refresh method for a materialized view?

- ❍ a. **COMPLETE**
- ❍ b. **FORCE**
- ❍ c. **NEVER**
- ❍ d. **FAST**
- ❍ e. **IMMEDIATE**

Answer c is correct. There isn't an **IMMEDIATE** refresh method for a materialized view. Answers a, b, c, and d are all valid refresh methods for a materialized view, though they might not all be available based on the view's construction.

Question 4

Which package contains functions that can be used to execute a warehouse refresh on a materialized view?

- ❍ a. **DBMS_OLAP**
- ❍ b. **DBMS_MVIEW**
- ❍ c. **DBMS_REFRESH**
- ❍ d. **DBMS_WHSE**
- ❍ e. **DBMS_JOB**

Answer b is correct. The **DBMS_MVIEW** package contains several functions, including functions you can use to do a warehouse refresh of materialized tables. Answer a is incorrect because the **DBMS_OLAP** package is used for analyzing tables and views in terms of performance and possible candidates for materialized view construction. Answers c and d are incorrect because they aren't valid packages in Oracle8i. Answer e is incorrect because although it's a valid package in Oracle8i, it isn't used for warehouse refresh.

Question 5

Fill in the missing keyword in this statement if this materialized view is to be created on a table that has already been built.

```
CREATE MATERIALIZED VIEW revenue_by_flight
ON ____________ TABLE
ENABLE QUERY REWRITE
AS
SELECT flight_date, flight_num,
SUM(a.revenue_amt) revenue_amt
FROM flight_fact a
GROUP BY flight_date, flight_num;
```

PREBUILT is the correct answer. If you want to create a materialized view on a table that has already been built (and presumably contains data), you use the **ON PREBUILT TABLE** clause to tell Oracle that the table already exists.

Question 6

Which of the following is not provided by the summary advisor?

- ❍ a. Space-usage estimate for proposed materialized views
- ❍ b. Usage statistics on existing materialized views
- ❍ c. Recommendations for new materialized views
- ❍ d. Report of user-access privileges for materialized views
- ❍ e. Storage of the summary advisor's results in a table for later review

Answer d is correct. The summary advisor doesn't provide any user-access privilege information for the DBA to use. Answers a, b, c, and e are all features of the summary advisor.

Question 7

Which of the following init.ora parameters needs to be set for materialized views to be updated properly?

❍ a. **JOB_QUEUE_COUNT**

❍ b. **JOB_QUEUE_ASSIGNMENT**

❍ c. **JOB_QUEUE_ORDER**

❍ d. **JOB_QUEUE_TIMEOUT**

❍ e. **JOB_QUEUE_INTERVAL**

Answer e is correct. The **JOB_QUEUE_INTERVAL** parameter in the init.ora file should be set correctly so the job scheduler will start at the correct interval to check for a pending warehouse refresh job. Answers a, b, c, and d are all incorrect because they aren't valid parameter settings. This is a trick question because answer d was a valid parameter in a previous version of Oracle.

Question 8

What kind of object stores hierarchical information about columns in one or more tables?

❍ a. Relational view

❍ b. Materialized view

❍ c. Dimension

❍ d. Object view

❍ e. The Oracle data dictionary

Answer c is correct. A dimension is used to store hierarchical information about columns in one or more tables so that the optimizer can use that information for query rewrite. Answers a, b, d, and e are all incorrect because these don't store hierarchical information.

Question 9

Which is not an Oracle-supplied package associated with materialized views?

- ❍ a. **DBMS_OLAP**
- ❍ b. **DBMS_MVIEW**
- ❍ c. **DEMO_SUMADV**
- ❍ d. **DBMS_UTILITY**
- ❍ e. **DBMS_DDL**

Answer e is correct. **DBMS_DDL** isn't used to manage or create materialized views. Answer a is incorrect because the **DBMS_OLAP** package is used to recommend materialized views and other functions. Answer b is incorrect because **DBMS_MVIEW** is used to refresh materialized views. Answer c is incorrect because **DEMO_SUMADV** is used to print the results of runs of some of the procedures of the **DBMS_OLAP** package. Answer d is incorrect because **DBMS_UTILITY** contains a PL/SQL table that can be used with some of the procedures in **DBMS_MVIEW**.

Question 10

In which case is a materialized view a candidate for use?

- ❍ a. You have small and infrequently used tables.
- ❍ b. You have large tables that are used for OLAP (Online Analytical Processing) transactions.
- ❍ c. You have large fact tables that are related to smaller lookup tables that are often subjects of queries that summarize data.
- ❍ d. You have small but high-volume tables that require lots of summaries of the data in them.
- ❍ e. You want a quick lookup of a row and you know the key of that row.

Answer c is correct. A materialized view is used primarily when you have a large table with detail information (a fact table) and smaller lookup tables (dimension tables). When the fact and dimension tables are often used together to create summaries of the data contained in those tables, materialized views might be helpful. Answers a, b, d, and e are incorrect because a materialized view is generally not useful in these cases.

Need to Know More?

Ault, Michael. *Oracle8i Administration and Management.* Wiley Computer Publishing, 2000. ISBN 0-471-35453-8. A classic upgraded for Oracle8i and as good as ever. Includes sections on materialized views and dimensions.

Oracle's documentation is good reference material. Oracle has numerous guides available on CD or in hard cover. In particular, the *Oracle8i Tuning Guide* has several chapters on materialized views.

Schierer, Douglas, William Gaynor, Jr., Arlene Valentinsen, and Xerxes Cursetjee. *Oracle8i Tips and Techniques: Real-World Approaches to Maximizing Oracle8i's Web-Enabled Database Server.* Oracle Press/Osborne/McGraw-Hill, 2000. ISBN 0-07-212103-3. This book is a very good Oracle8i reference. It contains a good introduction to materialized views, although it leaves out some of the detail (detail that's not needed for the OCP exam).

www.revealnet.com is a wonderful site with Oracle tips for DBAs and PL/SQL developers. The Oracle Administration Knowledge Base is a great help for DBAs wanting to master Oracle.

support.oracle.com is Oracle's Metalink Web site, a wonderful resource if you have Oracle Metals support (Oracle's "Gold" and "Silver" technical support offerings).

New Features of Net8

Terms you'll need to understand:

- ✓ Advanced Security Option (ASO)
- ✓ Service names
- ✓ Load balancing
- ✓ Failover

Techniques you'll need to master:

- ✓ Configuring and using automated instance registration
- ✓ Enabling load balancing on Oracle
- ✓ Implementing client failover

Oracle8i introduces new Net8 features that administrators should be aware of. These Net8 features are designed to help you make your databases more available and easier to manage. In this chapter, we'll review these new features, which are covered on your OCP exam.

New Features of Net8

Among the smaller subject areas of the Oracle8i OCP upgrade exam, in terms of the total number of questions on the test, are new Net8 enhancements. These include Oracle security changes in Net8, plus various connectivity and management features, such as service naming, automated instance registration, failover, and connection load balancing.

Net8 Security Solutions

In version 8, Oracle combined several security products into one product called the Advanced Networking Option (ANO). In Oracle8i, this product has been renamed to Oracle Advanced Security Option (ASO). ASO sits on top of Net8, delivering various security solutions to the Oracle network. ASO also integrates industry-standard encryption, authentication, and remote access.

In ASO, Oracle has expanded the choice of security solutions with the availability of SSL (Secure Sockets Layer), which is an industry-standard protocol for securing network connections, and RADIUS (Remote Authentication Dial-In User Service) protocol adapters, which provide an industry standard for remote authentication and controlled access to networks.

Oracle also introduces its Integrated Security and Directory Services (ISDS). In Beta with the first 8i release, this service provides several benefits, including:

- Single sign-on to multiple services in the enterprise
- Single enterprise user accounts, instead of multiple accounts per user
- Reduced costs and administrative burdens through single-station user administration
- A well-integrated, standards-based public key infrastructure

ISDS also incorporates various components, such as:

- *Oracle Wallet Manager*—A tool that is used to manage an Oracle wallet, which is a user's set of credentials used to authenticate a user to multiple services. This tool allows a user to access various services through one password without needing to have those services store and manage local passwords.

- *Certificate of Authority*—A tool that allows users to obtain certificates from any X509V3 Certificate Authority.
- *Oracle Internet Directory (OID)*—An LDAPv3-compliant directory. Oracle allows the storing of wallets in the OID.

Service Naming

Oracle8i introduces *service naming* to allow configuration of multiple services that reside in a single database. Before Oracle8i, a system identifier (SID) defined in Net8 was related to a single instance rather than to a database. Because of this, a database could not have more than one service or replication of data among databases.

Because a database can contain several services, the system identifier has been replaced with a *service-name* identifier. Thus, the parameters **SERVICE_NAME** and **INSTANCE_NAME** now should be set in the init.ora file of your 8.1.5 database and should replace the **ORACLE_SID** parameter in your tnsnames.ora file. (If you just have one instance listening on a single service, then you don't need to include the **INSTANCE_NAME** parameter in the tnsnames.ora file.) Note that Net8 is backward compatible with SQL*Net Version 2 parameter settings, so you usually won't have to change anything if you choose not to.

A service name allows clients to access:

- An entire service through the service name
- An instance of a database (just as a SID did before) through the instance name

Remember that the **SERVICE_NAME** and **INSTANCE_NAME** parameters replace the **ORACLE_SID** parameters used previously in the tnsnames.ora file. **ORACLE_SID** is still available for backward compatibility. To prepare for the OCP exam, clearly understand how this part of Net8 has changed.

Service naming can include multiple services provided by a single database or services that span multiple databases. A service can also be implemented as multiple database instances.

To implement service naming, Oracle has introduced two new instance ini.ora parameters: **SERVICE_NAME** and **INSTANCE_NAME**. The definitions of these parameters follow:

- **SERVICE_NAME**—This parameter allows clients to access services as a whole. A service name can span instances and nodes.

- INSTANCE_NAME—This parameter allows clients to access an instance of a database. It is essentially the same as the SID in previous Oracle versions.

Note: In previous versions of Oracle, an alias for a connect descriptor was SERVICE_NAME. This alias has been changed to NET_SERVICE_NAME.

You should clearly understand the new parameters, **INSTANCE_NAME** and **SERVICE_NAME,** before you take your OCP exam.

Automatic Instance Registration

Another feature added in Oracle8i is the ability of an instance to register itself automatically with the listener at startup. Before Oracle8i, an instance had to be configured via the listener.ora file. Now Oracle provides automated instance registration with the associated listener. Database instance registration enables load balancing and failover features as well.

When started, the database will register itself with the default listener without any additional configuration requirements. If you use multiple listener configurations, then you'll need to add some additional parameters to the init.ora file for that instance. Configuration for listeners other than the default listener will require the inclusion of the SERVICE_NAME and LOCAL_LISTENER optional parameters in the init.ora file of the instance you want registered. Note that the LOCAL_LISTENER parameter also overrides the MTS_LOCAL_LISTENER and MTS_MULTIPLE_LISTENERS parameters, which are obsolete in Oracle8i. An example of these init.ora settings is shown in Listing 6.1.

Listing 6.1 Configuring an instance's init.ora file for a listener other than the default listener.

```
DB_NAME = DING
INSTANCE_NAME = DING
SERVICE_NAMES = ( DING )
LOCAL_LISTENER = "(ADDRESS_LIST = (Address = (Protocol =
TCP)(Host=Mulder_one)(Port=1525))(Address=(Protocol = IPC)
(Key=DING)))"
DB_FILES = 255
DB_BLOCK_SIZE = 8192
DB_BLOCK_BUFFERS = 10000
SHARED_POOL_SIZE = 25600000
PROCESSES = 300
```

If you use multiple listeners, you'll need to modify your init.ora file, or you'll find your database registering itself with both the listener you have defined for it and the default listener.

Client and Connection Load Balancing

Load balancing, first offered in Oracle7.3, is improved in Net8. Net8 provides both client and connection load balancing. *Client load balancing* allows a client to randomly choose between listener services for connect requests, thus reducing the load on databases, dispatchers, and listeners across the network. This reduces the likelihood of a single resource being overburdened. To enable client load balancing, you must configure multiple listener addresses for each net service name, and you must use the **LOAD_BALANCE** parameter in the tnsnames.ora file. If the service selected is not available, the client will be connected to the other service, essentially providing failover.

An example of a tnsnames.ora file configured for client load balancing is shown in Listing 6.2.

Listing 6.2 A tnsnames.ora file set up for client load balancing.

```
reports=
 (DESCRIPTION=
  (LOAD_BALANCE=on)
  (ADDRESS=
      (PROTOCOL=tcp)
      (HOST=report01-pc)
      (Port=1521)
  )
  (Address=
       (PROTOCOL=tcp)
       (HOST=report02-pc)
       (PORT=1521)
  )
  (CONNECT_DATA=
    (SERVICE_NAME=reports.com)
  )
 )
```

Connection load balancing is available only in a multithreaded server (MTS) environment and is further made available by Net8's new, automated database-instance registration enables connection load balancing. The listener facilitates load balancing by balancing the number of active connections between the various instances and dispatchers for the same service. Load balancing allows listeners to decide where to route a connection based on how many connections a dispatcher already has and how loaded the nodes of the instance are. Connection load balancing also has the effect of providing connect time failover, which we'll discuss in the next section.

Remember, there are two kinds of load balancing: connection and client. Make sure you understand how each of these types of load balancing occurs.

Failover

Failover occurs if a connection can't be made to one database, and the connection is automatically rerouted to another database by Oracle. By itself, Net8 provides *connect time failover*, also known as *static failover*. Oracle also provides runtime failover with the Oracle8i Oracle Call Interface (OCI), but that's beyond the scope of this book.

Net8 connect time failover is facilitated through the setup of the service name in the tnsnames.ora file. After defining the service name, you use the **DESCRIPTION_LIST** keyword followed by the description of the primary and then secondary servers. When a connection attempt is made, the server will first attempt to connect to the primary database server. If that server is not available, the client will connect to the secondary server. Listing 6.3 provides an example of a tnsnames.ora set up for static failover.

Listing 6.3 A tnsnames.ora file set up for static failover.

```
db01.world=
     (DESCRIPTION_LIST =
        (DESCRIPTION =
           (ADDRESS =
             ( PROTOCOL = TCP )
             ( HOST = gargoyle )
             ( PORT = 1521 )
            )
           ( CONNECT_DATA = (SID = wing1))
        )
        (DESCRIPTION =
           (ADDRESS =
             ( PROTOCOL = TCP )
             ( HOST = vampire )
             ( PORT = 1521 )
            )
           ( CONNECT_DATA = (SID = wing2))
        ) )
```

Other Net8 Enhancements

An improvement in the Oracle connectivity world is that client connections can now be established without requiring Net8 be installed on the client. Now you can use various non-Net and Java protocols to connect to an Oracle database by configuring connections via the Java option.

Java-Based Connections

Java-based connections are supported via three methods, namely:

- Java stored procedures, which can establish both dedicated and shared server connections to the Oracle8i server
- Enterprise JavaBeans, which can establish MTS connections to Oracle8i
- CORBA (Common Object Request Broker Architecture) servers, which can also connect to Oracle8i through MTS

Oracle has modified the Network and Presentation layers (OSI level 6), as well as the session layer to accommodate these new connection types. Additional configuration of the database might be required to enable these new communications options. Finally, Net8 provides support for level-2 ODBC-compliant drivers. Refer to the *Oracle8i Net8 Administrator's Guide* for more information on these options if you require their use in your database.

Connection Manager

Introduced in Net8, the Connection Manager product provides several features, including:

- Multiprotocol support, which can be useful in connecting legacy systems to the Internet
- Network access control in an Internet environment
- Support for connection pooling and multiplexing

Connection Pooling and Multiplexing

Finally, you should be aware of two additional Net8 enhancements: connection pooling and multiplexing. Both of these options require the use of MTS and the Connection Manager.

Connection pooling is a method of allowing a large number of user sessions to share a single physical connection to a database. This feature can be helpful if you have many users who connect to the database and remain connected for a long period of time with infrequent database activity. (You should not consider connection pooling in a high-volume database environment.)

Multiplexing allows a database to support a large number of users who are constantly active at the same time. The users will share a common physical connection to the database. With multiplexing, the queries of several users will be combined into one large packet sent to the database. The packet will be disassembled, the queries will be executed, and the results will be assembled into a packet and returned to the Connection Manager for disassembly and rerouting to the user.

Practice Questions

Question 1

Which is not a new or enhanced feature of Net8?

- ❍ a. LSNRCTL interface improvements
- ❍ b. Client and connection load balancing
- ❍ c. The ability of non-Net8 protocols to connect to the database
- ❍ d. Automated database registration
- ❍ e. Service naming

Answer a is correct. Though there have been several enhancements in Net8, the interface of the Listener Control Utility (LSNRCTL) has not changed. Answer b is incorrect because client and connection load balancing is a new Net8 feature. Answer c is incorrect because the ability to use non-Net8 protocols is a new feature of Net8 in Oracle8i. Answers d and e are incorrect because automated database registration and service naming are also new features of Net8 in Oracle8i.

Question 2

Which two parameters in an instance's init.ora file are associated with automated instance registration? [Choose two]

- ❑ a. **INSTANCE_NAME**
- ❑ b. **SERVICE**
- ❑ c. **SERVICE_NAME**
- ❑ d. **MTS_MULTIPLE_LISTENERS**
- ❑ e. **NET8_NAME**

Answers a and c are correct. You use the **INSTANCE_NAME** and **SERVICE_NAME** parameters along with the **LOCAL_LISTENER** parameter to set up automated instance registration with the correct Net8 listener. Answer b is incorrect because this is not a valid parameter. Answer d is incorrect because this is a discontinued parameter in Oracle8i. Answer e is incorrect because it is not a valid parameter.

Question 3

What parameter do you use to configure load balancing in the tnsnames.ora file?

❍ a. **BALANCE**

❍ b. **LOAD_CONFIGURE**

❍ c. **LOAD_MEASURE**

❍ d. **LOAD_DISTRIBUTE**

❍ e. **LOAD_BALANCE**

Answer e is correct. You include the LOAD_BALANCE parameter in the tnsnames.ora file to tell Oracle that it should balance the load for the service to the databases listed. Answers a, b, c, and d are all incorrect because they are not valid Net8 parameters.

Question 4

The process of selecting a database to attach to so that it properly distributes the connections is called ____________________.

The correct answer is *load balancing*. You can use Net8 load balancing to distribute connections to databases to reduce the burden on one specific system.

Question 5

Which two parameters have replaced the SID descriptor in the tnsnames.ora file?

❑ a. **SERVICE_NAME**

❑ b. **SID_IDENTIFIER**

❑ c. **INSTANCE_NAME**

❑ d. **CONNECTION_TYPE**

❑ e. **SERVICE_TYPE**

Answers a and c are correct. You use the **INSTANCE_NAME** and **SERVICE_NAME** parameters in the tnsnames.ora file to allow a database to have more than one service associated with it. Answers b, d, and e are incorrect because they are not valid parameters.

Question 6

The two new init.ora parameters introduced to support service naming are [Choose two]:

- ❑ a. **SERVICE_NAME**
- ❑ b. **DB_NAME**
- ❑ c. **DB_SERVICE**
- ❑ d. **DB_INSTANCE**
- ❑ e. **INSTANCE_NAME**

Answers a and e are correct. Both **SERVICE_NAME** and **INSTANCE_NAME** are new init.ora parameters used to configure an Oracle database to support service naming. Answer b is incorrect because **DB_NAME** is not a new parameter and doesn't support service naming directly. Answers c and d are incorrect because they aren't valid init.ora parameters.

Question 7

When a client is set up for client load balancing, if the service selected is not available, what will be the default action?

- ❍ a. An error will be reported.
- ❍ b. The client will wait five seconds and retry the connection.
- ❍ c. The client will failover and attempt to connect to a different service.
- ❍ d. The client will prompt the user for an alternate service name.
- ❍ e. Client load balancing is not available in Net8.

Answer c is correct. When the client is set up for load balancing, a service will be randomly selected by the client software. If that service is not available, the client will failover and select another service. Answer a is incorrect unless all services have been cycled through. Answer b is incorrect because the client will not wait and then try again. Answer d is incorrect because the client will not prompt for another service name. Answer e is incorrect because load balancing is available in Net8.

Question 8

What Oracle8i feature facilitates both client load balancing and failover?

- ❍ a. MTS
- ❍ b. The Advanced Security Option
- ❍ c. Automated instance registration
- ❍ d. New init.ora settings
- ❍ e. Service naming

Answer c is correct. Automated instance registration in Net8 facilitates both client load balancing and failover. Answer a is incorrect because MTS is not required to use these features. Answer b is incorrect because ASO is not required to use these features. Answer d is incorrect because, although there are new init.ora settings to facilitate automated instance registration, there are not any that facilitate failover or load balancing specifically. Answer e is incorrect because service naming does not facilitate load balancing, but rather names a service.

Need to Know More?

As always, Oracle's documentation is good reference material. Oracle has numerous guides available on CD or in hardcover. The *Oracle8i Application Developers Guide* contains chapters on Advanced Queuing. The *NET8 Administrators Guide* contains a wealth of information on Net8 features.

Ault, Michael. *Oracle8i Administration and Management*. Wiley Computer Publishing, 2000. ISBN 0-471-35453-8. This classic has been upgraded for Oracle8i and is as good as ever.

Austin, David, Meghraj Thakkar, and Kurt Lysy. *Migrating to Oracle8i*. Sams Publishing, 2000. ISBN 0-672-31577-7. Good coverage of new Net8 features and Advanced Queuing. This book is quickly becoming one of my favorite references for Oracle8i new features.

Feuerstein, Steven. *Oracle PL/SQL Programming Guide to Oracle8i Features*. O'Reilly and Associates, Inc. 1999. ISBN 1-56592-675-7. A very good reference for new Oracle8i features. In particular, this book covers new Net8 and Advanced Queuing features very well.

www.revealnet.com is a wonderful site with Oracle tips for DBAs and PL/SQL developers. The knowledge base is a good Oracle reference for DBAs.

support.oracle.com is Oracle's Metalink Web site, a wonderful resource if you have Oracle metals support.

SQL*Plus, PL/SQL, and National Language Support

Terms you'll need to understand:

- ✓ SQL*Plus
- ✓ Server Manager
- ✓ Database and user event triggers
- ✓ **SERVERERROR** database operation
- ✓ **DBMS_PROFILER** package
- ✓ **DBMS_TRACE** package
- ✓ Native dynamic SQL
- ✓ Invoker-rights routines
- ✓ Bulk binds
- ✓ **NOCOPY** compiler hint
- ✓ Autonomous transaction
- ✓ **NLS_DUAL_CURRENCY** parameter
- ✓ **NLS_COMP** parameter
- ✓ **NATIONAL_CHARACTER_SET** clause
- ✓ **NCHAR**, **NCLOB**, and **NVARCHAR2** data types

Techniques you'll need to master:

- ✓ Migrating from Server Manager to SQL*Plus for database administration
- ✓ Using PL/SQL for database and user event triggers
- ✓ Using new PL/SQL built-in packages for monitoring application performance
- ✓ Using PL/SQL language enhancements for improved performance
- ✓ Calling autonomous transactions from within a PL/SQL block
- ✓ Using National Language Support (NLS) enhancements

This chapter focuses on the shift from Server Manager to SQL*Plus for command-line database administration, on PL/SQL enhancements, and on National Language Support changes. We'll cover the move to SQL*Plus in detail because you'll need it when Server Manager is no longer available. Our coverage of the PL/SQL enhancements is pretty light because there are so many and we don't want to swamp you with the details. With the NLS changes, we'll demonstrate the new commands and parameters and refresh your memory on the NLS data types.

SQL*Plus Enhancements

The command-line Server Manager utility is included in Oracle8i, but Oracle Corporation plans to omit it in future releases. The database administration commands that were unique to Server Manager have been added to SQL*Plus, so you can begin using SQL*Plus exclusively now. However, some syntax changes must be made in your Server Manager scripts before you migrate them to SQL*Plus. Oracle recommends that you migrate your Server Manager scripts to SQL*Plus as soon as possible.

Migrating Server Manager Scripts to SQL*Plus

Scripts written specifically for Server Manager might have some syntax components that don't work in SQL*Plus. There's no utility program that converts the syntax for you. For your scripts to work properly in SQL*Plus, you must make the following changes:

- When you're using the **CREATE TYPE** and **CREATE LIBRARY** stored procedures, write the slash (/) on a new line.
- Remove any blank lines within SQL statements.
- Use a double dash (--) instead of a pound sign (#) to indicate a comment line.
- Use the hyphen (-) as a continuation character for long SQL*Plus commands.
- Use the **SET ESCAPE** (-) command whenever the ampersand (&) is being used as a literal in a SQL statement. Otherwise, the ampersand will be treated as a substitution variable.

For more information on SQL script changes, see the *SQL*Plus User's Guide and Reference, Appendix B, "Release Enhancements."*

New SQL*Plus Commands for Database Administration

SQL*Plus has traditionally been used by the DBA and everybody else for report writing, whereas Server Manager was reserved for startups, shutdowns, recovery, and archive logging operations. Because Server Manager will be replaced by SQL*Plus, Oracle added the necessary commands to SQL*Plus:

- STARTUP—Starts an Oracle instance.
- SHUTDOWN—Shuts down an Oracle instance.
- RECOVER—Performs media recovery for the database, data files, or tablespaces.
- ARCHIVE LOG—Allows archive logging operations, such as **LIST**, **NEXT**, **ALL**, **START**, and **STOP**.
- CONNECT AS—Allows a user with **SYSOPER** or **SYSDBA** privileges to make privileged connections.
- SET AUTORECOVERY ON|OFF—Specifies whether to use the default archived redo logs during recovery.
- SET DESCRIBE—Specifies the depth to which objects can be described.
- SET INSTANCE—Changes the default instance for the session.
- SET LOGSOURCE—Specifies the location from which log files will be retrieved during recovery.
- SET SQLBLANKLINES ON|OFF—Allows blank lines in SQL statements.
- SHOW PARAMETER(S)—Displays parameters that match a passed value; for example, **show parameter log** displays the value of each initialization parameter that has the string **log** in its name.
- SHOW SGA—Displays SGA memory usage by area, in bytes.

Figure 7.1 illustrates how you can use SQL*Plus to shut down and start up an Oracle8i instance.

PL/SQL Enhancements

With the release of Oracle8i, PL/SQL has been enhanced in several significant ways. Triggers have been expanded to handle database events and user events. The packages **DBMS_PROFILER** and **DMBS_TRACE** have been added to

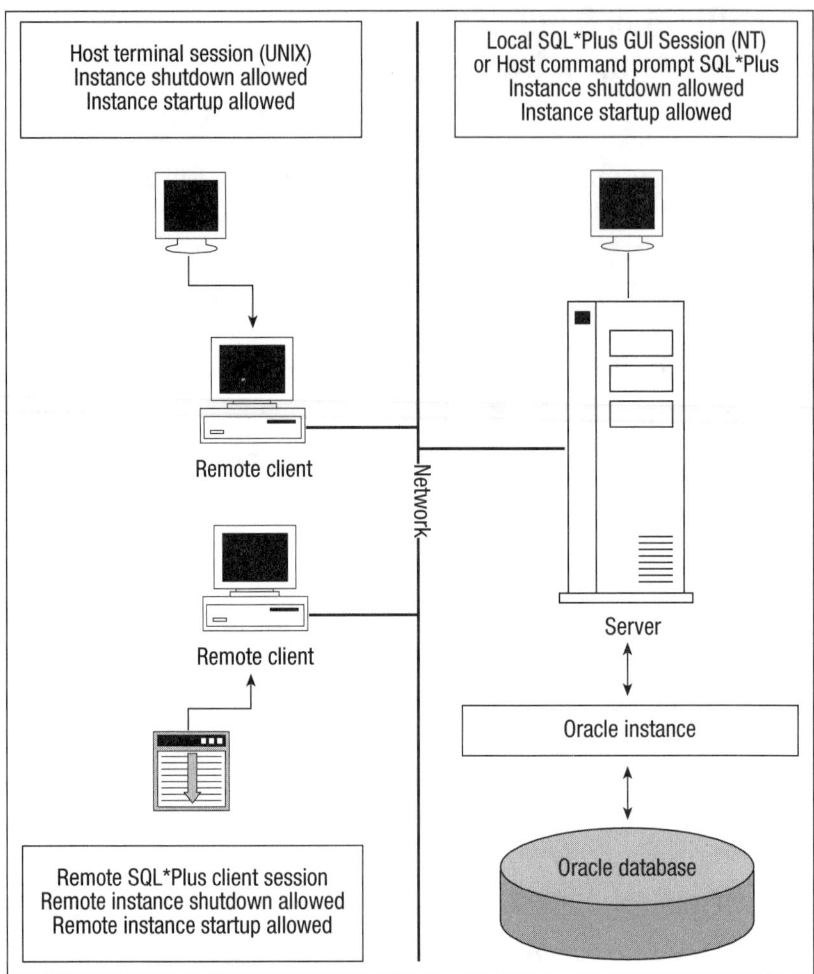

Figure 7.1 Oracle8i SQL*Plus instance shutdown and startup.

help with application performance tuning. Native dynamic SQL has been added to PL/SQL with the **EXECUTE IMMEDIATE** command. Bulk binds and the **NOCOPY** command have been added to improve performance. Also, autonomous transactions can be called from a PL/SQL block.

In Oracle8i, you can create triggers to be fired on any of the following:

- DML (Data Manipulation Language) statements—**INSERT, UPDATE,** and **DELETE (as in previous versions of Oracle that supported triggers).**
- DDL (Data Definition Language) statements (new to Oracle8i)—**CREATE, ALTER,** and **DROP.**

- Database operations (new to Oracle8i)—**STARTUP**, **SHUTDOWN**, and **SERVERERROR**.
- User events (new to Oracle8i)—when users log on and log off.

Database Event Triggers

In Oracle8i, triggers support system and other data events on **DATABASE** and **SCHEMA**. Database triggers fire each time the event occurs in the database. Database events include:

- **STARTUP**—A trigger is fired just after the database is opened.
- **SHUTDOWN**—A trigger is fired just before the database is shut down.
- **SERVERERROR**—A trigger is fired when a specific **ERRNO** occurs, or for all errors if no **ERRNO** is specified.

User (Client) Event Triggers

You can create triggers that fire when an object is created, altered, or dropped, or during logon and logoff. For example, a trigger created to fire **AFTER ALTER** will fire after an object is modified, and an **AFTER DROP** trigger will be fired when an object is dropped.

The DBMS_PROFILER Package

The **DBMS_PROFILER** package is used to monitor the performance of any user-defined function, procedure, or package. When executed, this package collects execution times and iterations for PL/SQL programs. To create the **DBMS_PROFILER** package and associated tables, execute the Unix scripts $ORACLE_HOME/rdbms/admin/profload.sql and proftab.sql, or the NT scripts $ORACLE_HOME\rdbms\admin\profload.sql and proftab.sql. The proftab.sql script builds the tables **PLSQL_PROFILER_RUNS**, **PLSQL_PROFILER_UNITS**, and **PLSQL_PROFILE_DATA**, and builds the sequence **PLSQL_PROFILE_RUNNUMBER**. The **DBMS_PROFILER** package contains the following procedures and functions:

- **FLUSH_DATA** function—Flushes data collected for the session to the **PLSQL_PROFILE** tables.
- **GET_VERSION** procedure—Returns the major and minor versions of the **DBMS_PROFILER** API.
- **INTERNAL_VERSION_CHECK** function—Verifies that the version of **DBMS_PROFILER** and the database version are compatible. Zero means that all is well.

- **START_PROFILER** function—Starts the profiler data collection in the current session. Accepts a comment of type **VARCHAR2** as input.
- **STOP_PROFILER** function—Stops the profiler data collection in the current session. Flushes data collected up to this point in the session and indicates the end of the run.

To begin profiling in a SQL*Plus session for a fictitious profile called **my_test**, simply enter **SELECT DBMS_PROFILER.START_PROFILER('my_test') FROM DUAL;**. Then execute a few PL/SQL programs, such as **DBMS_OUTPUT.PUT_LINE('noise')**, or execute some of your own PL/SQL. When you're through collecting data, enter **SELECT DBMS_PROFILER.STOP_PROFILER FROM DUAL;**. To make sense out of the data in the **PLSQL_PROFILER** tables, execute the script $ORACLE_HOME/plsql/demo/profsum.sql for Unix or $ORACLE_HOME\plsql\demo\profsum.sql for NT.

Profsum.sql calls profrep.sql without referring to a directory path. You might need to change directories to the $ORACLE_HOME/plsql/demo (Unix) or $ORACLE_HOME\plsql\demo\ (NT) directory before running the script, or modify the call to profrep.sql in the profsum.sql script to include the path.

The script profrep.sql creates four views: **PLSQL_PROFILER_GRAND_TOTAL, PLSQL_PROFILER_LINES_CROSS_RUN, PLSQL_PROFILER_UNITS_CROSS_RUN,** and **PLSQL_PROFILER_NOTEXEC _LINES.** The script also creates the package **PROF_REPORT_UTILITIES,** which supports the profiler reporting process. The output from profrep.sql goes to a text file called profsum.out in the current directory.

For an excellent description of the **DBMS_PROFILER** package and interpreting the profsum.out report, see Chapter 8 of the book *Oracle8i Tips and Techniques* by Douglas Scherer, et al.

The DBMS_TRACE Package

This new built-in package, created by either the $ORACLE_HOME/rdbms/admin/dbmspbt.sql for Unix or the $ORACLE_HOME\rdbms\admin\dbmspbt.sql for NT script during instance creation, allows you to perform runtime debugging on PL/SQL applications and dump the results to a trace file. To run

DBMS_TRACE, you must have a dedicated (non-MTS) connection to the database. You can include the debugging option when you compile a PL/SQL application or alter the session to allow tracing. See Listing 7.1 for the commands to enable debugging. There are four levels of debugging:

- Call Level 1: Trace all routine calls.
- Call Level 2: Trace only enabled routine calls.
- Exception Level 1: Trace all exceptions.
- Exception Level 2: Trace only exceptions for enabled routines.

Listing 7.1 Enabling PL/SQL runtime debugging.

```
ALTER SESSION SET PLSQL_DEBUG=TRUE|FALSE;
ALTER [PROCEDURE|FUNCTION|PACKAGE BODY] <routine_name>
COMPILE DEBUG;
```

DBMS_TRACE includes three procedures to manage PL/SQL runtime debugging. They are:

- SET_PLSQL_TRACE(n)—Where **n** is an integer value in the set {1,2,4,8}. See Table 7.1 for details.
- CLEAR_PLSQL_TRACE—Executing this procedure ends debugging for the session.
- PLSQL_TRACE_VERSION—Executing this procedure displays the version of DBMS_TRACE installed.

Native Dynamic SQL

In versions before Oracle8i, you could create and execute dynamic SQL by using the DBMS_SQL package. In Oracle8i, you can use the EXECUTE IMMEDIATE statement instead. It requires less coding to accomplish the same results, and it requires fewer steps by the PL/SQL processor.

Table 7.1 Integer values for the SET_PLSQL_TRACE procedure.

What to Trace	Value
Trace all routine calls	1
Trace only enabled routine calls	2
Trace all exceptions	4
Trace only exceptions for enabled routines	8

Invoker-Rights Routines

In previous versions of Oracle, PL/SQL code is resolved with the privileges of the definer of the code; hence the term *definer-rights routines*. In Oracle8i, you can create *invoker-rights routines:* routines that are executed with the privileges of the invoker. Use the **AUTHID CURRENT_USER** clause when you're creating programs if you want the invoker's rights to be used. The default value for **AUTHID** is **DEFINER**, which is the same as definer-rights behavior. When **AUTHID** is **CURRENT_USER**, references to tables that aren't fully qualified are resolved in the invoker's schema. External references to other PL/SQL functions and procedures are resolved in the definer's schema.

Triggers are always definer-rights routines.

The **AUTHID** value for a package applies to all routines within the package.

Bulk Binds

New to Oracle8i, bulk binding of SQL statements reduces overhead by sending multiple statements to the server in one bundle. The **FORALL** clause instructs the PL/SQL processor to bind all of the input collections in the statement and then send them to the SQL processor all at once. The **BULK COLLECT** clause is similar in function to **FORALL**, except for output collection.

The NOCOPY Compiler Hint

When you're using **IN**, **IN-OUT**, or **OUT** parameters in a procedure or function, you can use the **NOCOPY** compiler hint to ask the compiler to refer to the memory locations of the actual parameters, instead of referring to copies of the parameters. Doing this can save significant amounts of time because there's less activity copying values to and from memory locations. The syntax for the **NOCOPY** hint is shown in Listing 7.2.

Listing 7.2 Using the NOCOPY PL/SQL compiler hint.

```
CREATE OR REPLACE PROCEDURE MY_GOOFY_PROCEDURE
(o_goofball OUT NOCOPY varchar2,
io_goofball IN OUT NOCOPY varchar2)
...
```

For detailed examples of **NOCOPY**, bulk binds, invoker-rights routines, and all the new PL/SQL features, see Chapter 8 of the book *Oracle8i Tips and Techniques* by Douglas Scherer, et al.

Autonomous Transactions

Simply put, an autonomous transaction (AT) is called from within another transaction. For simplicity, we'll refer to the calling transaction as the main transaction or MT. The AT feature allows the developer to suspend the MT, call a PL/SQL object that has independent transactions, then return to the MT. The AT can be nested to any level, and when an AT is committed the results are visible to the MT and everybody else. However, an AT does not see changes made in the MT, and a commit or rollback in an AT does not affect the outcome of the MT.

You define an autonomous transaction with the PL/SQL pragma AUTONOMOUS_TRANSACTION. The pragma should be coded at the top of the declarative section. See Listing 7.3 for an example of how to define an AT.

An Autonomous Transaction can be defined by using the pragma directive in the following PL/SQL routines: triggers, top-level anonymous PL/SQL blocks, methods of a SQL object type, and in local, stand-alone, and packaged functions and procedures.

Listing 7.3 Defining an Autonomous Transaction.

```
CREATE OR REPLACE PACKAGE BODY Build_Train AS
       FUNCTION Add_Car (Car_nbr integer) RETURN REAL IS
       PRAGMA AUTONOMOUS_TRANSACTION;
       BEGIN --add code here
       END;
END Banking;
```

National Language Support (NLS) Enhancements

Oracle8i includes support for additional character sets and includes new NLS-related commands and init.ora parameters. For a list of newly supported character sets, see your *Oracle8i National Language Support Guide, Appendix A, "Locale Data."* In this section, we'll detail the new parameters, describe the commands that you can use to change the national language for the instance and the session, and describe the different NLS (National Language Support) data types.

Init.ora and Session Parameters

You can view the current NLS parameters for the instance by executing **SHOW PARAMETER nls** in SQL*Plus, or you can see the current session values by querying the **V$NLS_PARAMETERS** view. The parameters **NLS_CURRENCY**, **NLS_DUAL_CURRENCY**, and **NLS_COMP** are new or enhanced in Oracle8i. Also, NLS time parameters have been added since Oracle 8.0.x: **NLS_TIME_FORMAT**, **NLS_TIMESTAMP_FORMAT**, **NLS_TZ_FORMAT**, and **NLS_TIMESTAMP_TZ_FORMAT**.

NLS_CURRENCY

When this parameter is set, it will override the **NLS_CURRENCY** default for the **NLS_TERRITORY**. When set to **EURO**, it supports the new euro currency.

NLS_DUAL_CURRENCY

With release 8.1.5, the parameter **NLS_DUAL_CURRENCY** specifies the dual currency symbol to use. This is a 10-character string parameter, which can be set for the instance or for a session. When you specify the number format "U" with the **TO_CHAR** or **TO_NUMBER** functions, the **NLS_DUAL_CURRENCY** symbol will replace the "U" in the format mask.

NLS_COMP

New to 8.1, the **NLS_COMP** parameter is used for linguistics comparison (ordering). The options for **NLS_COMP** are **BINARY** or **ANSI**. The default value uses the **BINARY** value of the string for sorting. Linguistics sorting sequences are used by the comparison operators when the parameter's value is set to **ANSI**. Linguistics sorting uses the ordering of the NLS alphabet to determine the sort order.

NLS_TIME Parameters

New to Oracle8i, NLS time parameters can be configured for the session and the instance. NLS time parameters control the format of time and timestamp display masks. Each of the four NLS time parameters has a unique combination of date, time, and time-zone masks:

- NLS_TIME_FORMAT—Includes the hour, minute, and seconds.
- NLS_TIMESTAMP_FORMAT—Similar to NLS_TIME_FORMAT, except prefixed with a date mask.
- NLS_TIME_TZ_FORMAT—Similar to NLS_TIME_FORMAT, except suffixed with the time-zone hour and minute.
- NLS_TIMESTAMP_TZ_FORMAT—Similar to NLS_TIMESTAMP_FORMAT, except suffixed with the time-zone hour and minute.

Information on NLS time parameters is sparse, to put it nicely. If you have discovered interesting things about the NLS time parameters that Oracle hasn't documented, please feel free to share your findings with the Oracle community.

NLS Commands

When creating a new database, you have the option of specifying the NLS character set in the **CREATE DATABASE** command by using the **NATIONAL _CHARACTER_SET** clause. If you don't specify the national character set when creating a database, it defaults to the database character set. See Listing 7.4 for the syntax to alter the national character set for the database or the current session.

After the database has been created, you can alter the character set; however, the old character set must be a strict subset of the new one.

Listing 7.4 The syntax for the ALTER DATABASE and ALTER SESSION commands.

```
ALTER DATABASE [<db_name>] CHARACTER SET <new_character_set>;
ALTER DATABASE [<db_name>] NATIONAL CHARACTER SET
<new_NCHAR_character_set>;

ALTER SESSION SET <nls_parameter> = <value>;
```

NLS Data Types

The national character set stores data in **NCHAR**, **NVARCHAR2**, and **NCLOB** data types. These data types aren't new to Oracle8i. Using these data types is almost as easy as using the regular data types. Simply create columns with these data types as you would with **CHAR**, **VARCHAR2**, and **CLOB**. When you insert data into the NLS column or use the **WHERE** clause to select data from an NLS column, precede the string with the 'N' character. See Listing 7.5 for an example of using an NLS column.

NCHAR

NCHAR is a fixed-length character-string data type, similar to **CHAR**. An **NCHAR** column can have a maximum of 2,000 characters.

NVARCHAR2

NVARCHAR2 is a variable-length character-string data type, similar to **VARCHAR2**. An **NVARCHAR2** column can have a maximum of 4,000 characters.

NCLOB

NCLOB is an internal **LOB** similar to **CLOB**, except that the data is in the national character set. An **NCLOB** is by definition a fixed-width data type. You don't specify the column size when you create an **NCLOB** column in a table. Multiple **NCLOB** columns are allowed in a table, and they can be stored in separate tablespaces. **NCLOB** objects have a maximum length of 4,000 bytes inline, and a maximum of 4GB using an additional tablespace.

Listing 7.5 The syntax for using an NLS data type column.

```
INSERT INTO EMP
(emp_id, emp_name)
VALUES
(1,N'Charles Pack');

SELECT * FROM EMP
WHERE EMP_NAME LIKE N'Charles Pack';
```

Practice Questions

Question 1

Which of the following statements about NLS data types is correct?

❍ a. **NVARCHAR2** and **NCHAR** are fixed-width character data types.

❍ b. **NCHAR** and **NCLOB** are fixed-width character data types.

❍ c. All **NCLOB** data is stored inline.

❍ d. All **NCLOB** data is stored out-of-line.

❍ e. **NVARCHAR2** has a maximum size of 2 terabytes.

Answer b is correct. NCHAR and NCLOB are fixed-width character data types. Answer a is incorrect because NVARCHAR2 is variable-width. Answers c and d are incorrect because up to 4K of NCLOB data is stored inline, and additional data, up to 4GB, is stored out-of-line. Answer e is incorrect because NVARCHAR2 has a maximum size of 4,000 bytes.

Question 2

Use the built-in package _____ to debug PL/SQL routines during runtime. [Fill in the blank]

The DBMS_TRACE package is used to debug PL/SQL routines during runtime.

Question 3

Oracle recommends that you convert your Server Manager scripts to SQL*Plus scripts as soon as possible for what reason?

❍ a. SQL*Plus is more efficient.

❍ b. Oracle plans to omit Server Manager in a future release.

❍ c. Server Manager has too many bugs.

❍ d. Server Manager syntax will change to SQL*Plus syntax in the next release of 8i.

Answer b is correct. Oracle Corporation has announced that it intends to drop the command-line Server Manager utility from a future release of the database software.

Question 4

In Oracle8i, for what additional types of actions can triggers be written? [Choose three]

- ❑ a. Database events such as startup and shutdown
- ❑ b. User events such as logon and logoff
- ❑ c. DDL actions such as **DROP TABLE** and **CREATE TABLE**
- ❑ d. Database control statements such as **ARCHIVE LOG NEXT**

Answers a, b, and c are correct. Oracle8i supports database and user event triggers, as well as triggers on DDL statements. Answer d is incorrect because triggers aren't supported for Data Control Language (DCL) statements.

Question 5

Which NLS parameter is used to control sort ordering and comparison operations?

- ❍ a. **NLS_SORT_ORDER**
- ❍ b. **NLS_COMP**
- ❍ c. **NLS_COMPARE**
- ❍ d. **NLS_ORDER**
- ❍ e. **NLS_NCHAR**

Answer b is correct. The **NLS_COMP** parameter has two possible values: **BINARY** (default) and **ANSI**. Setting **NLS_COMP** to **BINARY** causes sort ordering and comparisons to occur based on the binary value of the variables. Setting it to **ANSI** causes an alphabetic or linguistics sort-order precedence. Answers a, c, and d are incorrect because they aren't valid NLS parameters: **NLS_SORT_ORDER** and **NLS_COMPARE** are very similar to actual NLS parameters, but they aren't legitimate. Answer e is incorrect because **NLS_NCHAR** specifies the character set for national character set data in a client application. If it isn't specified, the database character set is used.

Question 6

Which of the following NLS parameters are used to support the euro? [Choose two]

- ❑ a. **NLS_ECU_CURRENCY**
- ❑ b. **NLS_DUAL_CURRENCY**
- ❑ c. **NLS_EURO_CURRENCY**
- ❑ d. **NLS_CURRENCY**
- ❑ e. **NLS_CURRENCY_TYPE**

Answers b and d are correct. NLS_DUAL_CURRENCY specifies the dual currency symbol to use, which may be the euro. NLS_CURRENCY can be set to override the existing value set when NLS_TERRITORY is set. Answers a, c, and e are incorrect because they don't exist.

Question 7

The _______ package is used to track the performance of PL/SQL routines by writing timing information to database tables. [Fill in the blank]

The DBMS_PROFILER package allows you to measure the performance of PL/SQL routines. Data is written to the PLSQL_PROFILER_RUNS, PLSQL_PROFILER_DATA, and PLSQL_PROFILER_UNITS tables.

Question 8

Which of the following are valid SQL*Plus commands in Oracle8i? [Choose three]

- ❑ a. **SHUTDOWN**
- ❑ b. **STARTUP FORCE**
- ❑ c. **ARCHIVE LOG OFF**
- ❑ d. **SHOW PARAMETER nls**
- ❑ e. **DISPLAY SGA**

Answers a, b, and d are correct. In Oracle8i, you can SHUTDOWN and STARTUP the database from a SQL*Plus session. SHOW PARAMETER is also a valid SQL*Plus command. Answer c is incorrect because the correct syntax is **ARCHIVE LOG STOP**. Answer e is incorrect because the correct syntax is SHOW SGA.

Question 9

Which of the following are valid trigger types? [Choose two]

- ❑ a. **AFTER SHUTDOWN**
- ❑ b. **BEFORE STARTUP**
- ❑ c. **ON SERVERERROR**
- ❑ d. **AFTER STARTUP**

Answers c and d are correct. Answer c is correct because you can create a trigger that will fire when a specific server-error number is encountered, or for all server errors if no error number is specified. Answer d is correct because you can create a trigger that will fire immediately after database startup. Answer a is incorrect because the database is down, so no trigger can fire. Answer b is incorrect because the database isn't up yet, so no trigger can fire.

Question 10

Which of the following statements is true?

- ❍ a. The pound (#) sign is used for comments in SQL*Plus.
- ❍ b. The ampersand (&) is a substitution variable in Server Manager.
- ❍ c. The slash (/) sign is used as a continuation character in SQL*Plus.
- ❍ d. The slash (/) must be written on a new line when you use the **CREATE TYPE** and **CREATE LIBRARY** stored procedures.
- ❍ e. SQL*Plus will ignore blank lines in SQL statements, just like Server Manager does.

Answer d is correct. Answer a is incorrect because the double dash (--) is used for comments in SQL*Plus. Answer b is incorrect because the ampersand (&) is used as a substitution variable in SQL*Plus, not in Server Manager. Answer c is incorrect because the slash (/) tells the SQL*Plus engine to process the SQL statement just typed in. Answer e is incorrect because SQL*Plus doesn't ignore blank lines in SQL statements, but Server Manager does.

Need to Know More?

Austin, David, Meghraj Thakkar, and Kurt Lysy. *Migrating to Oracle8i*. Sams Publishing, 2000. ISBN 0-672-31577-7. See Chapters 10, 11, and 32 for further information on SQL*Plus and PL/SQL compatibility, upgrading Server Manager scripts, and miscellaneous enhancements.

Scherer, Douglas, William Gaynor Jr., Arlene Valentinsen, and Xerxes Cursetjee. *Oracle8i Tips and Techniques*. Oracle Press, 1999. ISBN 0-07-212103-3. See Chapter 8 for practical and detailed examples of the new PL/SQL features.

The following documents are on the distribution media for your Oracle server software, and they can be downloaded from the Oracle Technet Web site: **http://technet.oracle.com**.

Lane, Paul and Gail Yamanaka. *Oracle8i National Language Support Guide* (Part No. A67789-01). Oracle Corporation, 1999.

Rovitto, Frank. *SQL*Plus User's Guide and Reference* (Part No. A66736-01). Oracle Corporation, 1999.

Portfolio, Tom. *PL/SQL*Plus User's Guide and Reference* (Part No. A67842-01). Oracle Corporation, 1999.

8

Using New Oracle8i Database Security Features and Constraint Types

Terms you'll need to understand:

- ✓ Profiles
- ✓ Fine-grained access control (FGAC)
- ✓ Security policies
- ✓ Context
- ✓ Predicate
- ✓ Application context
- ✓ Context-checking package
- ✓ Context variable

Techniques you'll need to master:

- ✓ Setting up and using Oracle password management
- ✓ Setting up and using Oracle fine-grained access control
- ✓ Setting up and using the new Oracle8i constraint features

This chapter covers several security features in the Oracle8i database product. These security features include password management, first introduced in Oracle8, and row-level security as implemented with fine-grained access control. Following a discussion of security, we'll look at new constraint types introduced in Oracle8i.

User Password Management

With version 8, Oracle introduced several new security features. These features made Oracle8 much more secure and introduced features that database administrators (DBAs) have wanted to have at their disposal for years. The *Candidate Guide* for Oracle8i indicates that you should be familiar with these features. Therefore, we'll briefly review these security features. We'll also review password management, which allows you to configure user accounts to force password changes and to disable passwords after a certain number of failed login attempts. In addition, you can control how passwords are used by not allowing the reuse of passwords and by requiring that a certain number of characters and numbers be used in the password. We'll conclude the discussion by looking at setting a custom **PASSWORD VERIFY** function.

Although it's listed in the 8i OCP *Candidate Guide* as of this writing, user password management isn't an area that you'll need to "cram" particularly hard for. It's included here, as are any topics that Oracle included in the *Candidate Guide,* because it's possible that an exam question will appear on the topic. Note that from Oracle8 to Oracle8i, nothing has changed regarding user password management.

Profile Management and Security

Oracle8 uses *profiles* to manage password security. In the profiles, you establish the criteria for various password functions. You then assign profiles to users, and those users must meet the password criteria established for that profile. This section reviews what profiles are and then looks at the new profile settings available in Oracle8.

Using Profiles

As an Oracle DBA, you should already be familiar with profiles. *Profiles* are used to enforce certain restrictions (such as maximum idle time or CPU time) on users. After you create the profile, you assign the profile to the user, enforcing the profile's constraints upon the user. As of Oracle8, the **CREATE PROFILE** command includes elements that allow the DBA to set password security restrictions.

You can look at profiles and how they are defined in the system by examining the **DBA_PROFILES** table. Listing 8.1 shows a partial list of the **DBA_PROFILES** view and one profile's entries. Oracle8 introduced several new profile **resource_names** associated with password security; in Listing 8.1, these are in boldface for easier reference.

Listing 8.1 Using the DBA_PROFILES view to display settings.

```
SQL> select * from dba_profiles
  2  order by profile;

PROFILE    RESOURCE_NAME                   RESOURCE LIMIT
------   ---------------------           -------- ----------
DEFAULT    COMPOSITE_LIMIT                 KERNEL   UNLIMITED
DEFAULT    SESSIONS_PER_USER               KERNEL   UNLIMITED
DEFAULT    FAILED_LOGIN_ATTEMPTS           PASSWORD UNLIMITED
DEFAULT    PASSWORD_LIFE_TIME              PASSWORD UNLIMITED
DEFAULT    PASSWORD_REUSE_TIME             PASSWORD UNLIMITED
DEFAULT    PASSWORD_REUSE_MAX              PASSWORD UNLIMITED
DEFAULT    PASSWORD_VERIFY_FUNCTION        PASSWORD UNLIMITED
DEFAULT    PASSWORD_LOCK_TIME              PASSWORD UNLIMITED
DEFAULT    PASSWORD_GRACE_TIME             PASSWORD UNLIMITED
DEFAULT    IDLE_TIME                       KERNEL   UNLIMITED
DEFAULT    PRIVATE_SGA                     KERNEL   UNLIMITED
DEFAULT    CONNECT_TIME                    KERNEL   UNLIMITED
DEFAULT    LOGICAL_READS_PER_CALL          KERNEL   UNLIMITED
DEFAULT    LOGICAL_READS_PER_SESSION       KERNEL   UNLIMITED
DEFAULT    CPU_PER_CALL                    KERNEL   UNLIMITED
DEFAULT    CPU_PER_SESSION                 KERNEL   UNLIMITED
```

New Security Profile Settings

Oracle8 introduced security concepts that were new to Oracle but familiar to many other organizations in the computing world. Responding to requests for Oracle password security, Oracle Corporation introduced the following options in Oracle8:

- *Account locking*—Allows DBAs to lock and unlock an account at will.
- *Password aging*—Allows DBAs to set passwords to expire after a certain amount of time, forcing the user to change passwords with some regularity.
- *Password expiration*—Allows DBAs to set passwords to expire after a certain number of unsuccessful login attempts and to have the account unlock after some predetermined time.

- *Password history*—Keeps track of previous passwords used over a specified time and prevents their reuse during that time interval. Generally used to help make passwords more secure.
- *Custom password-authentication routines*—Force users to create passwords that are more secure. As an administrator, you can introduce controls that will force users to create passwords of a specific length, a certain number of characters and numbers, and so on. Doing this can make Oracle8 passwords much more secure than Oracle7 passwords.

When a database is created, the **DEFAULT** profile doesn't have defaults assigned for the password settings; they are all unlimited. You can set the **DEFAULT** profile by doing one of the following:

- Altering the default profile and changing the password profile settings to the default settings that you want to use.
- Running the Oracle-supplied script utlpwdmg.sql (included in the ORACLE_HOME/rdbms/admin directory on Unix). When you run this script, it sets up default password settings for the new password parameters. The script also loads a sample user-defined password-authentication PL/SQL script. Review this file and run it if it suits your purpose.

Password-Related Profile Settings

Oracle introduced several new profile settings associated with the new security features in Oracle8. These profile settings revolve around the users and their passwords. The new profile settings for Oracle8 are:

- FAILED_LOGIN_ATTEMPTS—Specifies the number of failed login attempts that can be tried before Oracle locks out an account.
- PASSWORD_GRACE_TIME—Specifies the amount of time a user has to change his or her password after the password expires.
- PASSWORD_LIFE_TIME—Specifies how long a user's password can be used if a user is assigned to this profile. After the time has passed, the password expires and the user cannot sign onto the system. To delay the password expiration, use the **PASSWORD_GRACE_TIME** parameter.
- PASSWORD_LOCK_TIME—Specifies how long an account will remain locked out if the number of failed attempts, as defined by **FAILED_LOGIN_ATTEMPTS**, is exceeded.
- PASSWORD_REUSE_MAX—Specifies the number of times a password has to be changed before an old password can be reused. If this parameter is set, the **PASSWORD_REUSE_TIME** parameter must be set to **unlimited**.

- PASSWORD_REUSE_TIME—Specifies the number of days before a password can be reused.
- PASSWORD_VERIFY_FUNCTION—Specifies the user-defined PL/SQL function that is called to control the complexity of the password. (For details, see "The **PASSWORD VERIFY** Function" later in this chapter.)

Locking Users Out and Letting Them Back In

When users are locked out by password management, they have two ways to get back in: They can wait for the amount of time set in **PASSWORD_LOCK_TIME** to pass, or they can ask the DBA to unlock their accounts. DBAs can use the **ALTER USER UNLOCK** command to unlock locked accounts. Also, DBAs can now use the **ALTER USER LOCK** command to lock out user accounts.

Oracle8i also allows DBAs to expire passwords, forcing users to change their passwords before they can get back into the system. This feature is useful if you want to force a whole group of users to change their passwords. (Of course, make sure that you provide some way for them to change their passwords.)

Finally, you can create a user account with an expired password. When you expire passwords by using the **CREATE USER** or **ALTER USER** command, the **PASSWORD_GRACE_TIME** setting has no effect. You must reset a user's password when the user wants to access the account, or provide a method for users to reset their own passwords (if that is desirable).

Dictionary Changes for Security

Of course, the additional security added in Oracle8 has required some changes in the views that DBAs use to determine the status of accounts. The **DBA_USERS** view has a new column called **account_status**, along with several new status codes associated with the new column. These codes are:

- OPEN—The user can access the account.
- EXPIRED—The account password has expired.
- EXPIRED(GRACE)—An account has expired but is still accessible because of the **PASSWORD_GRACE_TIME** setting.
- LOCKED—The account is locked out.
- LOCKED(GRACE)—The account is locked out after **PASSWORD_GRACE_TIME** has expired.
- LOCKED(TIMED)—The account is locked out after **PASSWORD_LOCK_TIME** has been activated (for example, after multiple sign-on failures).

The **account_status** column can even display multiple status codes, such as EXPIRED(GRACE) and LOCKED(TIMED). Other new columns include **lock_date**, which indicates when the account was locked out, and **expiry_date**, which indicates when the password will expire.

The **DBA_PROFILES** table has been changed to display the new profile options available since Oracle8. The **resource_type** column has been added to distinguish between password and kernel resource settings.

Finally, there's new view, **USER_PASSWORD_LIMITS**, which shows the password limits applied to a specific user. This view allows you to see which password limits the DBA has established for all userids. Note that there's no related **DBA_** or **ALL_** views for this view.

The PASSWORD VERIFY Function

As already noted, Oracle allows you to define a custom **PASSWORD VERIFY** function. The function can have any name, so you can actually have multiple **VERIFY** functions if you want. The **SYS** role must own this function in order for it to be used to validate passwords. Listing 8.2 defines this function.

Listing 8.2 Defining the PASSWORD VERIFY function.

```
CREATE OR REPLACE FUNCTION sys.name_your_verify_function_here
( user_id           IN            VARCHAR2(30),
  new_password      IN            VARCHAR2(30),
  old_password      IN            VARCHAR2(30)
)
RETURN BOOLEAN;
```

Fine-Grained Access Control

Fine-grained access control (FGAC) is a new feature introduced in Oracle8i. It allows the implementation of row-level security on tables and views. Row-level security provides a more granular level of security than was previously available in Oracle. In this section, we'll address fine-grained access control and what you should know about it before taking the Oracle8i OCP exam.

There are lots of new terms related to the implementation of FGAC, and this feature can seem quite complex at first. We suggest that as you read this section, you use an 8i database to implement the examples we show. After you run through the examples once or twice, you'll have no problem understanding how FGAC works.

You'll need to be familiar with FGAC. You should know what it's used for and how it's set up. You should also know what an application context is and how it's set up.

Basics of Fine-Grained Access Control

Before we get into the details about FGAC, we'll provide an overview of some of its benefits and related terminology. Some of the benefits of FGAC include:

- *Enhanced security*—The policies set with the use of FGAC are stored on the server and cannot be bypassed by client software.
- *Flexibility*—Dynamic and complex security policies can be enforced with the use of FGAC. This is because FGAC is dynamic in nature and allows the DBA to create powerful security protocols based on multiple critera. Based on the various security criteria that are defined, final access decisions don't need to be made until run time.
- *Transparency*—Changes in security policies can be made without requiring changes in application code.
- *Scalability*—The SQL statements used are parsed, optimized, and stored in the shared pool, making them available to other users.

Before we begin our discussion, you'll need to know the following terms:

- *Security policies*—A rule or set of rules that should be followed when a script or script set determines whether a particular user should have access to a specific row or set of rows of data in a table. Using FGAC, Oracle enforces security policies within the database itself. The enforcement of these policies—being native to the database rather than to an application—provide greater security, simplicity, and flexibility.
- *Context (application context)*—A holding area for information that's useful to have easily available. You use the **CREATE OR REPLACE CONTEXT** command to create a context. You then can use the **DBMS_SYSTEM.SET_CONTEXT** command to set different variables, and you can use the **SYS_CONTEXT** command to retrieve these variables. Oracle also makes several default variables available.
- *Application security*—The attachment of privileges and roles to an application such that users won't be able to misuse the roles or privileges when they're not using the application.
- *Predicate*—Additional SQL syntax (to be added to a SQL statement), which restricts the rows returned by the SQL statement. The predicate is at the heart of enforcing the security policy.

Using the various features just described, we can implement FGAC within the Oracle8i database.

Using Fine-Grained Access Control

Let's start learning how to use FGAC. In this section, we'll use an example to demonstrate the power of FGAC. This example consists of a table called **HR** that contains a list of employees. Employees can see their own data. Members of the Human Resources (HR) department can see all the data. We'll then create a security policy that gives HR users access to all rows in the table but otherwise restricts access to just the row of the employee querying against the table.

Learning by Example

As an example of implementing a security policy using FGAC, we'll follow these steps:

1. Create the object-owning schema (in our example, **HR_OWN**) and database objects (in our example, a table called **HR**) that will require FGAC. Then create schemas for users who will need to access the tables: create a schema (**HR_USER**) for HR users to sign into to access the table; and create two employee schemas (**EMPL_USER1** and **EMPL_USER2**). Note that we're creating separate schemas for the owner of the object and for the users who will access the object.

2. Use the **CREATE OR REPLACE CONTEXT** command to create a context. Then create an application context package called **EMP_SECUR**. This package and the use of Oracle's application context facilities are optional, but because the OCP exam might have questions about using contexts, we'll use them here.

   The context package will be called as each user signs into the database. This package will assign the users to one of these three security levels:

   - READ
   - ALL
   - NONE

   and this status will be saved to a context variable. This context variable will be used later, when the user accesses the secured table, to determine what access the user should have to the table.

3. Create a client-event login trigger that will call the context package we created in Step 2. This is when the context of the user is set. (See Chapter 7 for details on system and client database event triggers, new to Oracle8i.)

4. Create a context-checking package. This package will be called any time DML is executed against the HR table for which we're creating the security

policy. When the context-checking package is ready, all we need do is use the **DBMS_RLS.ADD_POLICY** package to add the security policy to Oracle. After this is done, the database will ensure that the context-checking package is always called when the table is accessed.

Example, Step 1—Initial Setup

In this first step, we'll establish the environment that we're going to use for our FGAC example. We need to create the table with the employee information and then create two schemas, one for the HR department and one for an employee. Listing 8.3 provides the code used to execute these setup steps. All of this code should be familiar to DBAs taking the Oracle8i upgrade exam, so we'll leave comments to a minimum.

Listing 8.3 Creating the user and tables used in this FGAC example.

```
DROP USER hr_own CASCADE;
DROP USER hr_user;
DROP USER empl_user1;
DROP USER empl_user2;

CREATE USER hr_own IDENTIFIED BY hr_own
DEFAULT TABLESPACE users
TEMPORARY TABLESPACE temp
QUOTA UNLIMITED ON users;

CREATE USER hr_user IDENTIFIED BY hr_user
DEFAULT TABLESPACE users
TEMPORARY TABLESPACE temp;

CREATE USER empl_user1 IDENTIFIED BY empl_user1
DEFAULT TABLESPACE users
TEMPORARY TABLESPACE temp;

CREATE USER empl_user2 IDENTIFIED BY empl_user2
DEFAULT TABLESPACE users
TEMPORARY TABLESPACE temp;

GRANT CONNECT TO hr_own;
GRANT CREATE PUBLIC SYNONYM TO hr_own;
GRANT CONNECT TO hr_user;
GRANT CONNECT TO empl_user1;
GRANT CONNECT TO empl_user2;
GRANT CREATE PROCEDURE TO hr_own;

CONNECT hr_own/hr_own
CREATE TABLE hr
```

```
( empl_id                     NUMBER  NOT NULL,
  user_id                     VARCHAR2(30) NOT NULL,
  last_name                   VARCHAR2(30),
  first_name                  VARCHAR2(30),
  middle_name                 VARCHAR2(30),
  social_security_number      VARCHAR2(11),
  address                     VARCHAR2(30),
  city                        VARCHAR2(30),
  state                       VARCHAR2(2),
  zip                         VARCHAR2(20),
  country                     VARCHAR2(30),
  hire_date                   date,
  leave_date                  date
)
TABLESPACE users
STORAGE (INITIAL 10k NEXT 10k PCTINCREASE 0);
GRANT SELECT ON hr_own.hr TO empl_user1;
GRANT SELECT ON hr_own.hr TO empl_user2;
GRANT SELECT, INSERT, UPDATE, DELETE ON hr_own.hr TO hr_user;
```

Example, Step 2—Create the Application Context Package

Now that we have the schemas in place, we need to create the application context package. This package will be used to set each user's context variables. It will be called when a user logs in via a new Oracle8i trigger called a *login trigger*. Let's first look at the code (shown in Listing 8.4) and then analyze what it's doing.

Listing 8.4 Code for the application context package.

```
/* We need to create a context. Think of it as a storage area for
information for a given session. We can write and read from this
storage area. This context will be used in the package we are
getting ready to create next. Create this package connected
as system.*/

CREATE OR REPLACE CONTEXT cont_tab_hr
USING system.hr_context_pkg_01;

/* Now we need to create the application context package */
CREATE OR REPLACE PACKAGE HR_CONTEXT_PKG_01
AUTHID DEFINER AS
/* Note the AUTHID DEFINER is new syntax.
See Chapter 7 for more on this */
PROCEDURE GET_HR_CONTEXT(p_usern IN VARCHAR2);
END;
/
```

```
CREATE OR REPLACE PACKAGE BODY HR_CONTEXT_PKG_01 AS
hr_function   VARCHAR2(4):='NONE';
PROCEDURE GET_HR_CONTEXT(p_usern IN VARCHAR2) IS
BEGIN
     /* The p_usern variable will come in from the trigger that
        will call this package */
     IF p_usern = 'HR_OWN'
     THEN
          hr_function:='ALL';
     ELSIF p_usern = 'HR_USER'
     THEN
          hr_function:='ALL';
     ELSIF p_usern = 'EMPL_USER1' or p_usern = 'EMPL_USER2'
     THEN
          hr_function:='READ';
     ELSE
          hr_function:='NONE';
     END IF;
     /* Here, we are setting the application context. Note that
        the name of the context is cont_tab_hr,
        and the two variables we set in this
        context are hr_function and hr_who. */
     DBMS_SESSION.SET_CONTEXT('cont_tab_hr' -
          ,'hr_function',hr_function);
     DBMS_SESSION.SET_CONTEXT('cont_tab_hr','hr_who',p_usern);
END get_hr_context;
END hr_context_pkg_01;
/
DROP PUBLIC SYNONYM hr_context_pkg_01;
CREATE PUBLIC SYNONYM hr_context_pkg_01 for
system.hr_context_pkg_01;
GRANT EXECUTE ON hr_context_pkg_01 TO sys;
```

Using Context Namespaces

Let's look more closely at Listing 8.4. Note the **CREATE OR REPLACE CONTEXT** command at the beginning of the listing. It is with this command that we create a context namespace. A *context* is a set of application-defined attributes that validates and secures an application. The **CREATE OR REPLACE CONTEXT** command is used to associate the created context with a PL/SQL package that contains routines to set the various context variables. We can see in Listing 8.4 the **CREATE OR REPLACE CONTEXT** command creating a context namespace called **cont_tab_hr**. In this statement, we assign the package **system.hr_context_pkg_01** to the context, and that package will be used to populate variables in the context (which we see later in Listing 8.4).

Once the Context namespace is created (the name of the context being defined in the **CREATE OR REPLACE CONTEXT** command), you use the package assigned to the context to set values of various variables by means of the **DBMS _SESSION.SET_CONTEXT** procedure. As you will see shortly, typically this process executes when the user logs in by use of a logon event trigger. Certain session information will then be saved that can be reused later by the application. In our example case, we save the value of a variable called **hr_function** to one of three values—READ, ALL, or NONE—depending on the value of the **p_usern**.

Note that the context package associated with the context takes one input variable, which we have called **p_usern**. This variable, which contains the userid of the user logging on to the database, is passed in by the trigger, which will be created in the next step. With this userid, we then determine the security level of the user and set the **hr_function** variable in the **cont_tab_hr** context appropriately. The correct security level (READ, ALL, or NONE) is then stored in the context area via the **DBMS_SESSION.SET_CONTEXT** procedure. This information will be used later in our example to determine whether the user has access to specific rows of data. Note the syntax of the **DBMS_SESSION.SET_CONTEXT** procedure:

```
PROCEDURE DBMS_SESSIOIN.SET_CONTEXT
(context_name         VARCHAR2,
 context_variable     VARCHAR2,
 value                VARCHAR2 );
```

In this procedure, *context_name* is the name of the context namespace that was created with the **CREATE OR REPLACE CONTEXT** command. In our example, the context name would be **cont_tab_hr**. The second parameter is the **context_variable**, which is the variable name. There can be multiple variables assigned to one context namespace (for example, the name for a table, the name of a user, the date, security level, session information, or any number of other items). This context variable name will then be associated with the data stored in the value parameter.

Note that in the sample code, we allow only three users (EMPL_USER, HR_USER, and HR_OWN) any kind of access to the HR tables. By virtue of the constructed PL/SQL if statement, all other users are excluded from access to the table altogether.

Be sure you are clear about what a context is before taking the 8i upgrade exam!

Example, Step 3—Set the Context at Login

Back to setting up the context at login: When you created the package above, you might have wondered when and where it gets called. We gave you some insight into the answer to this question when we stated that we could create a login event trigger that would call the package. Oracle8i provides a new trigger type, called an *event trigger*, that we can call on (see Chapter 7). Using a login event trigger, we'll execute our package when any user signs in. This login event trigger will first get the username and then call the package we created, setting the context that we'll need if we query on the **HR** table.

When we create the trigger, we'll use the **SYS_CONTEXT** command to set the **username** variable. We'll then call the package **GET_HR_CONTEXT**, which we created in Step 1, sending the package the username of the user who has logged on.

Listing 8.5 provides the login trigger that we'll need to call the application context package that we created in Step 1.

Listing 8.5 Creating the login trigger.

```
CREATE OR REPLACE TRIGGER tr_hr_context
AFTER LOGON ON DATABASE
DECLARE
username VARCHAR2(30);
BEGIN
    username:=SYS_CONTEXT('USERENV','SESSION_USER');
    SYSTEM.HR_CONTEXT_PKG_01.GET_HR_CONTEXT(username);
EXCEPTION
WHEN OTHERS THEN
NULL;
END;
/
```

Let's step back from everything for a moment. You might be asking, at this point, how this relates to controlling access to the data in a table. Think of FGAC as being implemented in two parts. The first part, described here, is determining who the user is and, upon login, determining what rights the user has to certain rows in a given table.

The first part is actually optional. You could check access privileges in the code that we'll write in the next step, and then you wouldn't need to use contexts or login triggers. Using contexts can simplify your code, however. Using contexts can also reduce overhead and performance hits that might be required if you use other methods to constantly check a user's security level. Plus, contexts might also be covered in the OCP exam.

Now let's proceed to the second part, which occurs when the table is accessed through some action (**SELECT**, **INSERT**, **UPDATE**, or **DELETE**) . We'll create another package, and we'll register it with the database as a security policy. After these items have been completed, the FGAC policy will have been created and will be invoked each time the **HR** table is accessed.

Example, Step 4—Create the Context-Checking Package

There are two kinds of context packages. One is the *application context package,* which was created in Step 2 of our example. The second is the *context-checking package,* which checks the context and sets the predicate that will be attached to the SQL statement. If we decided not to use contexts, then this package would have to determine the user ID each time it ran, and this could affect performance.

In this context-checking package, we define the predicate to be appended to the SQL statement being issued against the table that this package is assigned to. The predicate acts much like a **WHERE** clause, limiting the rows that can be returned by the user. Because this predicate is generated within the database, the user will get the same rows back whether the user is logging in through an application or through some *ad hoc* query tool, such as SQL*Plus. This has the benefit of making the data much more secure.

Note that the function contained in the context-checking package (**fu_hr_check,** shown in Listing 8.6), is written to take two parameters: the schema name and the name of the object being accessed. Even if you are not using these in your code, you must include them in the definitions.

Listing 8.6 contains the context package that we have created to enforce the sample security policy.

Listing 8.6 The context-checking package.

```
CREATE OR REPLACE PACKAGE hr_auth_pkg_01
AUTHID DEFINER AS
FUNCTION fu_hr_check(p_schema VARCHAR2, p_name VARCHAR2)
RETURN VARCHAR2;
/* Oracle requires this function to accept the two variables.
   The database will call this package every time you access the
   table. This occurs after the DBA registers the package, as
   shown later in this package. */
PRAGMA RESTRICT_REFERENCES(fu_hr_check, WNDS);
END;
/
CREATE OR REPLACE PACKAGE BODY hr_auth_pkg_01 AS
FUNCTION fu_hr_check(p_schema  VARCHAR2, p_name VARCHAR2)
RETURN VARCHAR2 AS
```

```
v_predicate VARCHAR2(2000);
v_context   VARCHAR2(30);
v_usern     VARCHAR2(30);
BEGIN
     /* Using the SYS_CONTEXT function, we'll retrieve the
        context variables we saved earlier at login. */
     v_context:=SYS_CONTEXT('cont_tab_hr','hr_function');
     v_usern:=SYS_CONTEXT('cont_tab_hr','hr_who');

     /* Now, based on the context set earlier, we'll set the
        predicate that will be used to restrict access to the
        tables. */
     IF v_context = 'ALL'
     THEN
          v_predicate:=NULL;
     ELSIF v_context = 'READ'
     THEN
          v_predicate:=' user_id = '''||v_usern||'''';
     ELSIF v_context = 'NONE'
     THEN
          v_predicate:=' 1=2';
     ELSE
          v_predicate:=' 1=2';
     END IF;
    /* Return the predicate. This predicate will be attached to
       the SQL statement, much like a WHERE clause. */
    RETURN v_predicate;
END fu_hr_check;
END hr_auth_pkg_01;
/

BEGIN
    /* Use the DBMS_RLS.ADD_POLICY procedure to register the
       security policy with the database. This effectively enables
       the security policy. */
    DBMS_RLS.ADD_POLICY('HR_OWN','HR','HR_POLICY_01','SYSTEM',
    'hr_auth_pkg_01.fu_hr_check','SELECT,INSERT,UPDATE,DELETE');
END;
/
```

In the listing, notice that we read the two context variables with the **SYS_CONTEXT** function that we saved earlier in the application context package. We then created the predicate that will be used to restrict the rows according to the stated security policy. Now, using the **DBMS_RLS.ADD_POLICY** procedure, we register the security policy with the database. Note that you can add multiple security policies to a given table, and in this way you can implement very robust (albeit complicated) security policies within the database. Also note that security policies can be based on different statement types, such as **INSERT** and **UPDATE**. The definition of this procedure is shown in Listing 8.7 along with the **DBMS_RLS.DROP_POLICY** procedure, which is used to drop a security policy.

Listing 8.7 The DBMS_RLS package.

```
procedure DBMS_RLS.ADD_POLICY
(object_schema     IN  VARCHAR2, -- Schema of object to be secured
 object_name       IN  VARCHAR2, -- Object name policy applies to.
 policy_name       IN  VARCHAR2, -- Name assigned to the policy.
 function_schema   IN  VARCHAR2, -- Function that enforced the
                                    policy.
 policy_schema     IN  VARCHAR2, -- Schema that owns the procedure.
-- statement_types for Types of statements that policy applies
-- to (INSERT,
-- UPDATE, DELETE, SELECT)
 statement_types   IN  VARCHAR2,
-- update_check optional for INSERTS and UPDATES to check the
-- policy against
-- the value after the UPDATE or INSERT is performed.
 update_check      IN  BOOLEAN,
 ENABLE            IN  BOOLEAN);

procedure DBMS_RLS.DROP_POLICY
(object_schema     IN  ARCHAR2,  -- Schema of object to be secured
 object_name       IN  VARCHAR2, -- Object name policy applies to.
 policy_name       IN  VARCHAR2) -- Name assigned to the policy.
```

Example—The Results

So, let's look at the results of FGAC in action. We'll add a row to the **HR** table, and then we'll have the different accounts (**HR_USER**, **EMPL_USER1**, and **EMPL_USER2**). We have created a record for **EMPL_USER1**. Thus, as we would expect when **HR_USER** and **EMPL_USER1 SELECT** from the table, they can see the record, but **EMPL_USER2** cannot. Listing 8.8 shows the result of our use of FGAC.

Listing 8.8 A query against the HR table.

```
SQL> connect empl_user1
SQL> INSERT INTO empl_user1 (empl_id, user_id, last_name)
values(1,'EMPL_USER1','test');
SQL> connect hr_own
SQL> select empl_id, user_id, last_name from hr_own.hr;
```

```
   EMPL_ID USER_ID                        LAST_NAME
---------- ------------------------------ ---------------------
         1 EMPL_USER1                     test
SQL> connect empl_user1
SQL> select empl_id, user_id, last_name from hr_own.hr;
   EMPL_ID USER_ID                        LAST_NAME
---------- ------------------------------ ---------------------
         1 EMPL_USER1                     test
SQL> connect empl_user2
SQL> select empl_id, user_id, last_name from hr_own.hr;
no rows selected
```

Constraint Changes in Oracle 8 and 8i

In this section, we'll briefly discuss two subjects related to constraints and listed in the Oracle8 to 8i upgrade *Candidate Guide* as possibly being on the OCP exam. The first subject involves changes in constraint checking and enforcement introduced in Oracle8. The second subject is the introduction of the ability to use nonunique indexes to enforce primary keys and unique constraints.

Deferred Constraint Enforcement

In Oracle8, Oracle introduced two new options related to constraint checking. The first new option is called *deferred constraint enforcement*. The second option allows you to enable a constraint without checking all the records to ensure their validity.

Deferred constraint enforcement allows you to delay enforcement of a constraint or set of constraints until the end of a transaction. Before the introduction of deferred constraint enforcement, Oracle checked the constraint after each statement and then failed a statement if the constraint was violated. Now, with deferred constraint enforcement, these checks can be delayed until the end of the transaction. This feature allows you to change objects that previously might have required disabling of constraints.

To support this new constraint option, Oracle added new syntax. When you define the constraint, you can define it as **DEFERRABLE**. This allows the user to set the constraint to be deferred during a transaction. In addition, when you define the constraint, its initial state is set to be either **DEFERRED** or **IMMEDIATE**. If the constraint is set to **DEFERRED**, then the constraint will have a deferred status automatically and the user won't need to take any actions to use it as such. If the constraint is set to **IMMEDIATE**, then the user will need to use the **ALTER SESSION** command to set the constraints to **DEFERRED** status. Listing 8.9 shows an example of creating a deferred constraint.

Listing 8.9 Creating a deferred constraint.

```
ALTER TABLE dependents
ADD CONSTRAINT fk_emp_dep
FOREIGN KEY (emp_no)
REFERENCES employee(emp_no)
DEFERRABLE INITIALLY DEFERRED;
```

Enabling Constraints without Enforcement

Also introduced in Oracle8 is the ability to enable a constraint without checking all the existing records to ensure that they are valid. To enable this feature, you use the **ENFORCE** clause of the **ALTER TABLE** command. When a constraint is enabled with the **ENFORCE** clause, all new changes to the table with which the constraint is associated will be validated, but existing rows won't be validated. This feature can significantly reduce the time required to validate constraints on large tables. See listing 8.10 for an example of the **ENFORCE** clause.

Listing 8.10 Using the ENFORCE clause.

```
ALTER TABLE dependents
CONSTRAINT fk_emp_dep ENFORCE;
```

Other Oracle8i Constraint Enhancements

In Oracle8i, you can modify the attributes of existing constraints by using the **ALTER TABLE** command with the **MODIFY CONSTRAINT** clause. There are several restrictions on how and when you can modify a constraint. In the following example, we assume that you have created a table called **MYTABLE** with a primary constraint called **pk_01_testme** with the **USING INDEX** clause. Now you want to recreate the index on the primary key constraint in a different tablespace every time it's re-enabled. To do so, you can disable the index and then issue the SQL statement shown in Listing 8.11.

Listing 8.11 Moving an existing primary key index to a new tablespace.

```
ALTER TABLE mytable
MODIFY CONSTRAINT pk_01_testme
USING INDEX
TABLESPACE new_tbs
ENABLE;
```

You can also use the **RELY/NORELY** flag to indicate whether a constraint should be enabled but not enforced. The **RELY** feature is generally used only with materialized views because, depending on the **QUERY_REWRITE_INTEGRITY** mode that is enabled, the query rewrite facility can use the constraint, enforced or not, to determine join information. (See more about query re-write in Chapter 5, "Summary Management.") Listing 8.12 gives an example of the uses of the RELY/ NORELY clauses.

Listing 8.12 Using the RELY/NORELY clauses.

```
ALTER TABLE dependents
ALTER CONSTRAINT fk_emp_dep NORELY;
ALTER TABLE dependents
ALTER CONSTRAINT fk_emp_dep RELY;
```

Oracle has also added some options to the ALTER TABLE...MODIFY CONSTRAINT command such that you can disable a constraint, thus dropping its index, while keeping the constraint valid. To disable the constraint and keep it valid, use the ALTER TABLE...MODIFY CONSTRAINT DISABLE VALIDATE command. This feature can be used when you're moving data from a nonpartitioned table to a partitioned table. To save space during the move operation, no other SQL statements can be executed on the table. Note that if the partition key doesn't coincide with the primary key of the table being moved, additional full-table-scan operations might be performed, and the benefits of dropping the index might be negated.

Practice Questions

Question 1

What is the purpose of fine-grained access control?

❍ a. FGAC provides additional user password security.

❍ b. FGAC allows a single user to sign into multiple schemas at once.

❍ c. FGAC provides row-level security at the database level for applications.

❍ d. FGAC improves the performance of some long-running queries.

❍ e. FGAC is a new constraint type that allows you to drop indexes on primary and unique key indexes and still have them continue to validate entries.

Answer c is correct. FGAC provides database-controlled, row-level security for applications. This moves security inside the database, making it more secure. Answers a, b, d, and e are incorrect because these are not the purposes of FGAC.

Question 2

When you're using contexts in association with FGAC, what facilitates the setting of the specific user context information, such as the user's security level, when the user connects to the database?

❍ a. A client login event trigger.

❍ b. An event trigger on the table for which you want to establish FGAC control.

❍ c. A trigger on the **SYS.AUD$** table.

❍ d. The application must set this information before connecting to the database.

❍ e. The client application must set this information after connecting to the database.

Answer a is correct. If you use contexts to store user information, the logical way to do this is to use a client login event trigger. Answers b and c are incorrect because they are not the most efficient way to set user context information. Answers d and e are incorrect because the use of FGAC is designed to remove any need to create client or application code for the additional security provided by FGAC.

Question 3

Which of the following is not an available security feature in Oracle8i?

- ❍ a. User account locking
- ❍ b. User password aging
- ❍ c. Custom password-validation routines
- ❍ d. Password reuse history restrictions
- ❍ e. Oracle-generated passwords

Answer e is correct. Oracle doesn't provide a facility that allows it to generate passwords for users automatically, though you could certainly build a package that would perform this operation. Answers a, b, c, and d are all incorrect because they are security features in Oracle8i.

Question 4

Which Oracle database feature allows row-level security of data within a table?

- ❍ a. User account access management
- ❍ b. Fine-grained access control
- ❍ c. Oracle row-level security option
- ❍ d. Oracle security services
- ❍ e. The **SECURITY IS** option of the **CREATE TABLE** and **ALTER TABLE** statements

Answer b is correct. Answers a, c, d, and e are incorrect because they are not valid security options in Oracle.

Question 5

To implement fine-grained access control, Oracle will assign a ______________ to the end of a SQL statement. [Fill in the blank]

The correct answer is a *predicate*. A predicate is assigned to the end of the SQL statement before the SQL is executed. This predicate is much like a **WHERE** clause in that it limits the rows returned by the statement. The predicate is established by the presence of one or more security policies set for a table.

Question 6

Which of the following is a benefit of fine-grained access control?

- ❍ a. It allows row-level security at the application level.
- ❍ b. It allows row-level security at the database level.
- ❍ c. It provides additional features for user password management.
- ❍ d. It allows applications to store application code in the database.
- ❍ e. All of the above.

Answer b is correct. Fine-grained access control allows row-level security at the database level. This allows database DBAs and designers to control user access to specific rows regardless of the way the user connects to the database. Answer a is incorrect. This is a trick question because you might choose answer a, thinking that FGAC allows row-level security at the application level. But it's the fact that the FGAC security model is divorced from the application that makes FGAC such a versatile and powerful feature in Oracle8i. Answer c is incorrect because FGAC has no relationship to user password management. Answer d is incorrect because FGAC doesn't have anything to do with storing application code in the database. Answer e is incorrect because only answer b is correct.

Question 7

What will be the result after this statement is executed in a PL/SQL block?

```
DBMS_SESSION.SET_CONTEXT('cont_tab_hr', -
'hr_function',hr_stuff);
```

- ❍ a. This statement will establish a context variable called **cont_tab_hr**.
- ❍ b. This statement will establish a context variable in the context **cont_tab_hr**. The context variable is called **hr_stuff**.
- ❍ c. This statement will establish a context variable called **cont_tab_hr** in a context called **hr_function**. The value **hr_function** will be placed within the context variable.
- ❍ d. This statement will create the context variable **hr_function** and populate the context variable **hr_stuff** with the value in the parameter **HR_FUNCTION**.
- ❍ e. This statement will create a context variable called **hr_function** and populate it with the value contained in the variable **hr_stuff** within the previously created context **cont_tab_hr**.

Answer e is correct. This procedure will create or set a variable called **hr_function** in the context called **cont_tab_hr**. The value of the parameter HR_STUFF will be stored in that context variable. Answer a is incorrect because the SET_CONTEXT procedure doesn't create contexts. Answer b is incorrect because the statement won't establish the context **cont_tab_hr**. The context must be created using the CREATE OR REPLACE CONTEXT command. Answer c is incorrect because, again, the SET_CONTEXT procedure doesn't create contexts. Answer d is incorrect because **hr_stuff** is the variable and **hr_function** is the name of the context variable.

Question 8

What will occur if the following statement processes normally, without error?

```
DBMS_RLS.ADD_POLICY('HR_OWN','HR', -
'HR_POLICY_01','SYSTEM',
'hr_auth_pkg_01.fu_hr_check','SELECT,INSERT');
```

❍ a. A security policy called **HR_OWN** will be established on DML statements on the **HR_POLICY_01** table that is owned by **HR**. The procedure **FU_HR_CHECK** will be called to manage this security policy.

❍ b. A security policy called **HR_POLICY_01** will be created on the **HR_OWN.HR** table. The policy will be managed by the package **FU_HR_CHECK** and will occur on all DML statements.

❍ c. A security policy called **HR_POLICY_01** will be created on the **HR_OWN.HR** table. The policy will be managed by the package **FU_HR_CHECK** and will occur on **SELECT** and **INSERT** statements.

❍ d. This statement will fail because the **FU_HR_CHECK** procedure isn't owned by **SYS**.

❍ e. This statement will fail because security policies must be established for all DML actions (**SELECT**, **INSERT**, **UPDATE**, and **DELETE**).

Answer c is correct. The DBMS_RLS.ADD_POLICY statement is used to add a security policy to the system. In this example, it will add a security policy called HR_POLICY_01 on a table called HR_OWN.HR. The procedure FU_HR_CHECK will be used to enforce the policy, and this policy will be enforced only on SELECT and INSERT statements. Answer a is incorrect because the policy isn't called HR_OWN, and the table the policy is on isn't called HR_POLICY_01.

Answer b is incorrect because this policy will be enforced only on **SELECT** and **INSERT** statements. Answer d is incorrect because the procedure called to manage the policy doesn't have to be owned by **SYS**. Answer e is incorrect because policies can be established for one activity, multiple activities, or all DML activities.

Question 9

When you create a context-checking package, which parameters must be included when you create the PL/SQL function?

- ❍ a. The object-owning schema and the object number found in **DBA_OBJECTS**.
- ❍ b. The name of the user accessing the table and the name of the table being accessed.
- ❍ c. The schema name and the name of the table being accessed.
- ❍ d. The name of the schema making the access, the name of the schema the table resides in, and the name of the table.
- ❍ e. No parameters are required in the function.

Answer c is correct. The schema name and the name of the table being accessed must be included as a parameter of the function. Answer a is incorrect because the object name is required, not the object number. Answer b is incorrect because the name of the user accessing the table isn't required, but the name of the table's schema is. Answer d is incorrect because the name of the user making the access isn't required. Answer e is incorrect because parameters are required in the FGAC function.

Question 10

What will be the result of the following code?

```
ALTER TABLE mytable
DISABLE PRIMARY KEY;

ALTER TABLE mytable
MODIFY CONSTRAINT pk_01_testme
USING INDEX
TABLESPACE new_tbs
ENABLE;
```

- ❍ a. The table **MYTABLE** will have its primary key index dropped and recreated, moving the table to a new tablespace.
- ❍ b. The first statement will succeed. The second statement will fail due to a syntax error.
- ❍ c. The first statement will disable the primary key but not drop the primary key index. The second statement will fail because the primary key index was not dropped by using the **DROP INDEX** command.
- ❍ d. The table **MYTABLE** will have its primary key index dropped and recreated using a system default name, and the new primary key index will be moved to a new tablespace.
- ❍ e. The syntax of both statements is incorrect.

Answer a is correct. The table **MYTABLE** will have its primary key index dropped when the **DISABLE PRIMARY KEY** statement is issued. When the second statement is issued, the primary key index will be recreated, and a new tablespace will be used. Answer b is incorrect because the second statement is a valid statement. Answer c is incorrect because the second statement won't fail. You don't need to drop the primary key index after disabling it because this occurs automatically. Answer d is incorrect because the index will maintain the name originally assigned to it. Answer e is incorrect because the syntax of both statements is valid.

Need to Know More?

Ault, Michael. *Oracle8i Administration and Management.* Wiley Computer Publishing, 2000. ISBN 0-471-35453-8. This classic has been upgraded for Oracle8i. Includes installation, conversion, and migration topics that are worth reading.

Austin, David, Meghraj Thakkar, and Kurt Lysy. *Migrating to Oracle8i.* Sams Publishing, 2000. ISBN 0-672-31577-7. This book covers everything you wanted to know about installing, migrating, or upgrading to Oracle8i but were afraid to ask. The definitive guide on this topic.

Oracle's documentation is good reference material. Oracle has numerous guides available on CD or in hardcover. The *Concepts Guide* contains a great deal of information on FGAC and other security issues. The *Supplied Packages Guide* provides references to the various packages used in FGAC.

www.revealnet.com is a wonderful site with Oracle tips for DBAs and PL/SQL developers. Check out the DBAPipeline for questions and answers about FGAC and other security issues and questions about the OCP exam!

oracle.support.com is Oracle's Metalink Web site, a wonderful resource if you have Oracle Metals support.

Optimizer and Query Improvements

Terms you'll need to understand:

- ✓ **DBMS_STATS** package
- ✓ Stored plans
- ✓ **CREATE_STORED_OUTLINES** parameter
- ✓ **USE_STORED_OUTLINES** parameter
- ✓ **OUTLN_PKG** package
- ✓ **OL$** table, **OL$HINTS** table, **DBA_OUTLINES** view, **DBA_OUTLINE_HINTS** view
- ✓ **ROLLUP** operator
- ✓ **CUBE** operator
- ✓ **GROUPING** function
- ✓ Top-N SQL queries
- ✓ **TRIM** function
- ✓ **SORT_MULTIBLOCK_READ_COUNT** parameter
- ✓ Automatic parallel execution

Techniques you'll need to master:

- ✓ Using **DBMS_STATS** to create more sophisticated statistics
- ✓ Creating, modifying, and using stored plans
- ✓ Enabling stored plans for an instance or a session
- ✓ Creating a cross-tabular report by using aggregate functions
- ✓ Creating a Top-N SQL query and understanding what makes it unique
- ✓ Performing string manipulations with the **TRIM** function
- ✓ Using the new sort processing options in Oracle8i
- ✓ Configuring for automatic parallel execution

This chapter focuses on new features that improve query performance when you're using the cost-based optimizer (CBO). We'll introduce the **DBMS_STATS** package, which generates sophisticated statistics about the objects in a database. We'll discuss how to create and use stored plans—a new feature that stabilizes query performance by using a specific execution plan (with hints) for a matching query. Oracle8i provides two new aggregate operators, which are designed to improve OLAP (Online Analytical Processing) query performance, and a new **ORDER BY** subquery, which allows the creation of Top-N queries. The ANSI-standard TRIM function has been added, as well as new sort processing options that improve sort-to-disk performance. We'll also explain automatic parallel execution.

The DBMS_STATS Package

The **DBMS_STATS** package is used to generate and manage statistics for the CBO (cost-based optimizer). If you plan to use the CBO, use **DBMS_STATS** instead of the **ANALYZE** command. The statistics are more accurate and run automatically in parallel, and **ANALYZE** cannot replace statistics generated by **DBMS_STATS**. The **DBMS_STATS** package can also back up and restore statistics, store them in a database schema table instead of the data dictionary, and copy statistics for use in another database.

Gathering Statistics

Statistics can be gathered at the database, schema, or table/index level by using the **GATHER_DATABASE_STATS**, **GATHER_SCHEMA_STATS**, **GATHER_TABLE_STATS**, or **GATHER_INDEX_STATS** procedures. You can specify the degree of parallelism, the type of sampling (random block sampling or the default random row sampling), the percentage of rows or blocks to sample, and the granularity for partitioned tables. With the **STATTAB** parameter, the DBA can specify a schema table for storing the statistics. The DBA can gather statistics for all objects in the schema or database, for only those tables with no statistics (empty), or for only those tables with stale statistics.

Backing Up and Recovering Statistics

To back up data dictionary statistics to a non-data dictionary table, create a schema table with the **DBMS_STATS.CREATE_STAT_TABLE** procedure, and then execute the **DBMS_STATS.EXPORT_SCHEMA_STATS** procedure. The **EXPORT_SCHEMA_STATS** procedure copies data dictionary statistics to a schema table. When this is complete and you're rolling along in production, you might inadvertently gather statistics that cause less-than-optimal performance. To return to the original statistics, execute the **DBMS_STATS.IMPORT_SCHEMA_STATS** procedure, referring to the **STATTAB** parameter and schema where you stored the original statistics. The **IMPORT_SCHEMA _STATS** procedure populates the data dictionary tables with the schema-stored statistics.

Copying Statistics Between Databases

To copy statistics between databases, first back up your statistics, as described earlier. Then copy the table to another database via a database link, or with the Export and Import utilities. When the table is populated at the target, use the **DBMS_STATS.IMPORT_SCHEMA_STATS** procedure. It's that simple. Figure 9.1 illustrates how to export and import statistics.

Optimizer Plan Equivalence and Stored Plans

Have you ever been frustrated by the cost-based optimizer when it changes execution plans for reasons that you're not aware of? You can stabilize the cost-based optimizer's choices by creating stored execution plans. When you create an Oracle8i database, the **OUTLN** user is created for you. The **OUTLN** schema has two tables: **OL$**, which stores the outline name, SQL text, category, and creation timestamp for the outline; and the **OL$HINTS** table, which stores hints.

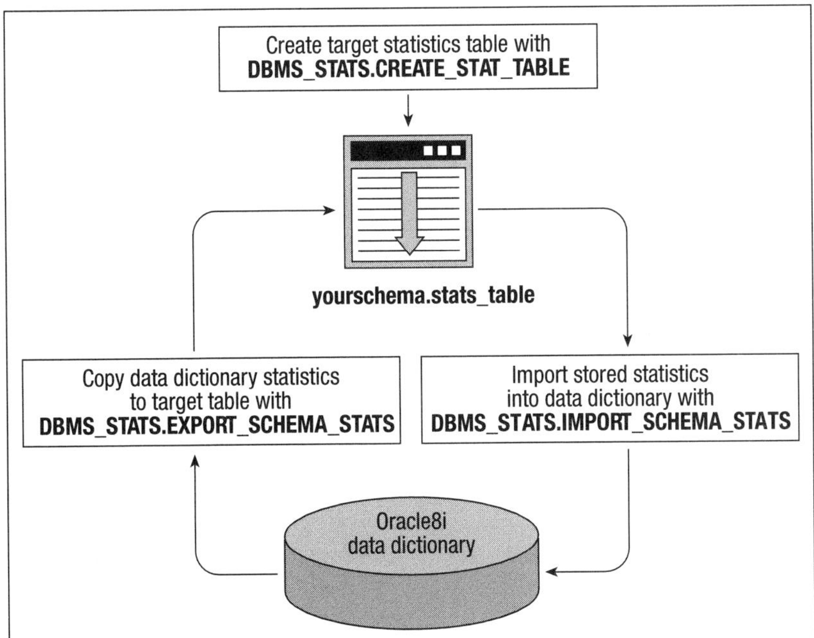

Figure 9.1 Backing up and restoring statistics in Oracle8i.

You can query the **DBA_OUTLINES** and **DBA_OUTLINE_HINTS** views to see the stored plans. Creating and using a stored outline will ensure that the cost-based optimizer uses an execution plan of your choice, but the SQL text must match the stored-outline SQL exactly.

You'll hear the term "Plan Stability" when referring to Optimizer Plan Equivalence, and the term "Stored Outlines" is synonymous with Stored Plans.

Creating Stored Outlines

Stored outlines are created by session or by instance and are collected dynamically. The DBA sets the parameters interactively in SQL*Plus. The general steps for creating stored execution plans are as follows:

1. Issue the command: **ALTER SYSTEM|SESSION SET CREATE _STORED_OUTLINES=TRUE**. If you need to create multiple categories, replace **TRUE** with a unique alpha identifier, such as **SCOTTS_OLTP**.
2. Execute the queries for which you want to store plans.
3. Issue the command: **ALTER SYSTEM|SESSION SET CREATE _STORED_OUTLINES=FALSE** to disable capturing.

Note that **CREATE_STORED_OUTLINES** is set dynamically—it's not a valid startup parameter in the init.ora file. If you attempt to set its value in the init.ora file, the database won't open.

You can also create a stored outline for an individual SQL statement by using the **CREATE OR REPLACE OUTLINE** statement. Simply provide names for the outline and category, and then enter the SQL statement. See Listing 9.1 for an example.

Listing 9.1 Creating a stored outline for an individual SQL statement.

```
CREATE OR REPLACE OUTLINE scotts_emp
FOR CATEGORY scott
ON
SELECT * FROM SCOTT.EMP
WHERE EMPNO =7900;
```

Using Stored Outlines

Using stored outlines is as simple as creating stored outlines, and is also done dynamically. If you want all the sessions to utilize the stored outlines, then **ALTER SYSTEM SET USE_STORED_OUTLINES=TRUE|named**

_category will do it. If you want only your session to use stored outlines, then use **ALTER SESSION SET USE_STORED_OUTLINES=TRUE|named _category**. If you want to return to *not* using stored outlines, use **ALTER SYSTEM|SESSION SET USE_STORED_OUTLINES=FALSE**. As with **CREATE_STORED _OUTLINES, USE_STORED_OUTLINES** isn't a valid init.ora parameter.

Altering Stored Outlines

The DBA can rename a category, rename a stored outline, or rebuild a stored outline by using the **ALTER OUTLINE** statement. See Listing 9.2 for the options.

Listing 9.2 Altering a stored outline for an individual SQL statement.

```
ALTER OUTLINE <outline_name> {REBUILD|RENAME TO <new_outline_name> |
CHANGE CATEGORY TO <new_category_name>};

ALTER OUTLINE SCOTTS_EMP RENAME TO SCOTTS_EMP_PK;
ALTER OUTLINE SCOTTS_EMP_PK CHANGE CATEGORY TO SCOTTS;
ALTER OUTLINE SCOTTS_EMP_PK REBUILD;
```

Using the OUTLN_PKG Package

The DBA can use the **OUTLN_PKG** package to manage stored outlines. The **OUTLN_PKG** package is created automatically from the script $ORACLE_HOME\rdbms\bin\dbmsol.sql (unix) or $ORACLE_HOME/rdbms/bin/dbmsol.sql (NT) when you build an Oracle8i database. The procedure **UPDATE_BY_CAT** is used to move stored outlines to a different category. The procedure **DROP_BY_CAT** will drop all stored outlines for a single category. The procedure **DROP_UNUSED** drops all outlines that have never been used.

Why Use Stored Outlines?

Very simply, if you're using the cost-based optimizer (CBO), stored outlines allow you to test various hints to determine the optimal performance and then force the CBO to use the best execution plan. For hybrid systems—systems that are a combination of OLTP (Online Transaction Processing), DSS (decision support system), or DWHSE (data warehouse)—you can schedule a batch job to set the use of the default outline or a named category. That means that you can have multiple categories for the same SQL query. The query text must match the stored outline *exactly* (this is similar to comparing cursors in the shared pool). If you query the **OUTLN.OL$** table, you'll see that each row has a unique signature and hash value. You can copy or export/import the **OL$** and **OL$HINTS** tables to another database and test the effects of a changed execution plan.

You must use the cost-based optimizer (CBO) to take advantage of Stored Outlines or the **DBMS_STATS** package.

New SQL Keywords for Computing Subtotals

Oracle has added two new aggregate operators that help you create reports with multiple subtotals and grand totals—commonly known as cross-tabular (or cross-tab) reports. These reports include subtotals for each column in a row, as well as for each row in a column. (Confused? See Listing 9.3 for a sample cross-tabular report.) The new **ROLLUP** and **CUBE** operations are used with the **GROUP BY** clause, and they can be used with all the other valid **GROUP BY** functions (MIN, MAX, and so on).

The **ROLLUP** and **CUBE** operators execute very efficiently and reduce the complexity of the SQL required to produce a cross-tab report. To get similar results without these aggregate operators, you would have to create a complex query that utilizes multiple occurrences of the **UNION ALL** clause. These new operations are more efficient than client-side tools because, instead of sorting and processing locally to get the desired subtotal format, the aggregate operations occur at the server. Queries with **CUBE** or **ROLLUP** can also be optimized by adding hints and using the cost-based optimizer. **CUBE** and **ROLLUP** are efficient for data warehouse applications. The **GROUPING** function has also been introduced to help clarify the meaning of **NULL** values in **CUBE** and **ROLLUP** reports.

Listing 9.3 Sample cross-tab report.

```
                                  1998
Division                       Department
                Research        Marketing              Total
East            100,000           150,000            250,000
West             45,000           103,000            148,000
Total           145,000           203,000            398,000
```

ROLLUP

The **ROLLUP** operator is useful for creating simple cross-tab reports with multiple levels of subtotals and a grand total. See Listing 9.4 for **ROLLUP** syntax and Listing 9.5 for a sample **ROLLUP** report. **ROLLUP** will create a row for the **GROUP BY** aggregate and then progressively subtotal the **ROLLUP** dimensions from right to left. In our example, we sum the **Expenses** and then

ROLLUP by **Department** within **Division** for each **Year**. Along the way, we get a subtotal for each **Division** for each **Year**, a subtotal for each **Year**, and finally a grand total for all **Years**.

Listing 9.4 ROLLUP syntax.

```
SELECT ... GROUP BY
   ROLLUP(grouping_column_reference_list)
```

Listing 9.5 ROLLUP usage.

```
SELECT Year, Division, Dept, sum(expenses) AS Expenses
FROM SCOTT.EXPENSE_ACCT
GROUP BY ROLLUP(Year, Division, Dept);

YEAR DIVISION                  DEPT              EXPENSES
---- --------                  ----              --------
1998 East                      Marketing           150000
1998 East                      Research            100000
1998 East                                          250000
1998 West                      Marketing           103000
1998 West                      Research             45000
1998 West                                          148000
1998                                               398000
1999 East                      Marketing           153000
1999 East                      Research            110000
1999 East                                          263000
1999 West                      Marketing           125000
1999 West                      Research             42000
1999 West                                          167000
1999                                               430000
                                                   828000
15 rows selected.
```

The blanks in the report above are **NULL** values and represent a subtotal. Many text examples will show **[NULL]** in **ROLLUP** and **CUBE** reports. These **NULLs** appear as blanks in a real SQL query report. The **GROUPING** function can be used to indicate when **NULLs** are part of a subtotal or when they are actual database values.

CUBE

The CUBE operator is similar to ROLLUP but returns subtotals for all groupings in the result set. See Listing 9.6 for CUBE syntax and Listing 9.7 for a CUBE example. As with ROLLUP, using CUBE is much more efficient than issuing multiple **SELECT** statements strung together with **UNION ALL** clauses. Not only is the SQL easier to read, but it also requires far fewer table reads and sorts, resulting in faster queries.

Listing 9.6 **CUBE** syntax.

```
SELECT ... GROUP BY
   CUBE(grouping_column_reference_list)
```

Listing 9.7 **CUBE** usage and sample output.

```
SELECT Year, Division, Dept, sum(expenses) AS Expenses
FROM SCOTT.EXPENSE_ACCT
GROUP BY CUBE(Year, Division, Dept);

YEAR DIVISION                  DEPT               EXPENSES
---- --------                  -----              --------
1998 East                      Marketing            150000
1998 East                      Research             100000
1998 East                                           250000
1998 West                      Marketing            103000
1998 West                      Research              45000
1998 West                                           148000
1998                           Marketing            253000
1998                           Research             145000
1998                                                398000
1999 East                      Marketing            153000
1999 East                      Research             110000
1999 East                                           263000
1999 West                      Marketing            125000
1999 West                      Research              42000
1999 West                                           167000
1999                           Marketing            278000
1999                           Research             152000
1999                                                430000
     East                      Marketing            303000
     East                      Research             210000
     East                                           513000
     West                      Marketing            228000
     West                      Research              87000
     West                                           315000
                               Marketing            531000
                               Research             297000
                                                    828000
27 rows selected.
```

The GROUPING Function

As we mentioned earlier, a subtotal in the report is indicated by a blank cell value. This is a problem when the value returned from the database by the query is actually **NULL**: how are we to tell the difference? The **GROUPING** function allows the query developer to modify output based on the **NULL** value of a cell. See Listing 9.8 for the syntax of the **GROUPING** function, and see Listing 9.9 for an example.

The **GROUPING** function creates a nice bitmap that indicates the level of subtotal grouping. With this tool, you can easily see if there is a **NULL** where you would expect something else. In Listing 9.10, we've inserted into the **EXPENSE_ACCT** table a row that has a **NULL** value for the **Dept** column. This row is rolled up into the **Year** 1999 and the East **Division**, but the **Dept** column is blank. The only way to distinguish the **ROLLUP** subtotal from a legitimate **GROUP BY** aggregate value is with the bitmap. You could always add up the values manually to determine which rows truly have **NULL** values and which are subtotals, but that's tedious. The **GROUPING** function can be used with **DECODE** to create a more meaningful bitmap. The **HAVING** clause can also be used with the results of the **GROUPING** function to generate a filtered and sorted report.

Listing 9.8 GROUPING function syntax.

```
SELECT ...  [GROUPING(dimension_column)...]  ...
  GROUP BY ...    {CUBE | ROLLUP}
```

Listing 9.9 GROUPING function usage and sample output.

```
SELECT Year, Division, Dept, sum(expenses) AS Expenses,
GROUPING (Year) as Y,
GROUPING (Division) as D,
GROUPING (Dept) as T
FROM SCOTT.EXPENSE_ACCT
GROUP BY ROLLUP(Year, Division, Dept);

YEAR DIVISION     DEPT            EXPENSES        Y       D       T
---- --------     ----            --------        -       -s
1998 East         Marketing         150000        0       0       0
1998 East         Research          100000        0       0       0
1998 East                           250000        0       0       1
1998 West         Marketing         103000        0       0       0
1998 West         Research           45000        0       0       0
1998 West                           148000        0       0       1
```

```
1998                               398000          0        1        1
1999 East        Marketing         153000          0        0        0
1999 East        Research          110000          0        0        0
1999 East                          263000          0        0        1
1999 West        Marketing         125000          0        0        0
1999 West        Research           42000          0        0        0
1999 West                          167000          0        0        1
1999                               430000          0        1        1
                                   828000          1        1        1
15 rows selected.
```

Listing 9.10 The GROUPING function with suspicious output.

```
YEAR DIVISION        DEPT         EXPENSES          Y        D        T
---- --------        ----         -------           -        -        -
1998 East            Marketing      150000          0        0        0
1998 East            Research       100000          0        0        0
1998 East                           250000          0        0        1
1998 West            Marketing      103000          0        0        0
1998 West            Research        45000          0        0        0
1998 West                           148000          0        0        1
1998                                398000          0        1        1
1999 East            Marketing      153000          0        0        0
1999 East            Research       110000          0        0        0
1999 East                           150000          0        0        0 <—
*****Investigate the previous row!!
1999 East                           413000          0        0        1
1999 West            Marketing      125000          0        0        0
1999 West            Research        42000          0        0        0
1999 West                           167000          0        0        1
1999                                580000          0        1        1
                                    978000          1        1        1
16 rows selected.
```

Top-N SQL Queries

Top-N queries are optimized for selecting a discrete number of ordered rows from a table. The Top-N query is great for answering questions like "Who earned the top-five salaries in SCOTT's corporation?" (See Listing 9.12 for the answer.)

The Top-N query is constructed by creating a special subquery within a query. The *inner query (subquery)* determines the columns that will be returned to the outer query and determines the sort order of the rows. The *outer query* determines which columns from the inner query will be displayed and how many rows to display. The outer-query cutoff uses the **ROWNUM** pseudo-column along with one of the following operators: <, >, <=, or >=. See Listing 9.11 for the Top-N SQL syntax and format.

The main difference between a regular subquery and one in a Top-N query is the use of the **ORDER BY** clause. Use the **DESC** keyword in the **ORDER BY** clause to return the *n* highest-value rows based on the **ORDER BY** columns; use the **ASC** keyword in the **ORDER BY** clause to return the *n* lowest-value rows.

A Top-N query can contain nested subqueries, complex **WHERE** conditions, and compound **ORDER BY** clauses. The **SELECT** clause in the outer query cannot refer to a column that isn't selected in the inner query. See Listing 9.13 for an example Top-N query that doesn't work. (The query doesn't work because the Empno column isn't one of the columns returned from the subquery.) Top-N queries are faster than regular queries because of the in-line view and enhanced sorting mechanisms.

The main difference between a regular subquery and one in a Top-N query is the use of the **ORDER BY** clause.

Listing 9.11 Framework for a Top-N SQL query.

```
SELECT displayed_column_list FROM
  (SELECT inner_column_list FROM table
   WHERE condition_list
   ORDER BY Top-N_column ASC|DESC)
WHERE  ROWNUM <=  N;
```

Listing 9.12 A sample Top-N SQL query.

```
SELECT * FROM
   (SELECT *
    FROM scott.emp
    ORDER BY sal desc)
WHERE rownum < 6;

EMPNO ENAME   JOB         MGR HIREDATE    SAL  COMM  DEPTNO
----- -----   ---         --- --------    ---  ----  ------
 7839 KING    PRESIDENT       17-NOV-81  5000            10
 7788 SCOTT   ANALYST    7566 19-APR-87  3000            20
 7902 FORD    ANALYST    7566 03-DEC-81  3000            20
 7566 JONES   MANAGER    7839 02-APR-81  2975            20
 7698 BLAKE   MANAGER    7839 01-MAY-81  2850            30
5 rows selected.
```

Listing 9.13 Incorrect usage of a Top-N SQL query.

```
SELECT empno FROM
  (SELECT ename, sal FROM scott.emp
     ORDER BY sal desc)
WHERE rownum < 4;
SELECT empno FROM
       *
ERROR at line 1:
ORA-00904: invalid column name
```

The TRIM Function

New in Oracle8i is the implementation of the ANSI-standard **TRIM** function. This new Oracle function enables you to trim a recurring leading or trailing digit from a number, or trim a leading and/or trailing recurring character from a character string. As always, characters must be enclosed in single quotes.

The **LEADING** keyword causes Oracle to remove all leading symbols equal to **TRIM_CHARACTER**. The **TRAILING** keyword causes the same action for trailing symbols. The **BOTH** keyword (default) trims leading and trailing symbols that match the **TRIM_CHARACTER**. The default value for **TRIM_CHARACTER** is a blank space. See Listing 9.14 for the syntax of the **TRIM** function. The return data type for **TRIM** is **VARCHAR2**, but the **TRIM** function can be embedded in a math function; see Listing 9.15 for sample uses of the function. If you specify a **NULL** value for the **TRIM_CHARACTER** (''), **TRIM** returns a **NULL** value for all rows. If **TRIM_SOURCE** is a **NULL** value, then the **TRIM** function returns a **NULL** value for that row.

Listing 9.14 Syntax of the TRIM function.

```
TRIM (LEADING/TRAILING/BOTH(default) trim_character
FROM trim_source)
```

Listing 9.15 Sample queries that use the TRIM function.

```
SELECT TRIM ('  this is a test.  ') "TrimTest" from dual;
TrimTest
--------
this is a test.

SELECT TRIM('x' FROM 'xxxxthis is a test.xxxx') "BothEndsTrim"
from dual;
BothEndsTrim
--------
this is a test.
```

```
SELECT TRIM (LEADING 'x' FROM 'xxxxthis is a test.xxxx')
"LeadTrim" from dual;
LeadTrim
--------
this is a test.xxxx

SELECT sqrt(trim('9' FROM '9259')) "SqrtTrim" from dual;
SqrtTrim
--------
       5

SELECT TRIM('xxx' FROM 'xxx_test_xxx_this_xxx') from dual;
       *
ERROR at line 1:
ORA-30001: trim set should have only one character

SELECT sqrt(trim('9' FROM 'bob99')) "SqrtTrim" from dual;
           *
ERROR at line 1:
ORA-01722: invalid number
```

New Sort Processing Options

The following init.ora parameters are no longer supported in Oracle8i: SORT_DIRECT_WRITES, SORT_WRITE_BUFFERS, SORT_WRITE_BUFFER_SIZE, SORT_READ_FAC, and SORT_SPACEMAP_SIZE.

The new parameter SORT_MULTIBLOCK_READ_COUNT specifies how many database blocks to read from a temporary segment when a read request occurs during a sort operation. The read from a temporary segment on disk occurs only if the sort isn't accomplished in memory. The SORT_MULTIBLOCK_READ_COUNT parameter is similar to the DB_FILE_MULTIBLOCK_READ_COUNT parameter in that increasing the value causes more blocks to be read with each read request, thereby performing larger and fewer I/Os. If you notice a high ratio of I/O per second to CPU usage during sort operations, you might consider increasing the value of the SORT_MULTIBLOCK_READ_COUNT parameter. The default value for SORT_MULTIBLOCK_READ_COUNT is 2.

Automatic Parallel Execution

Parallel execution improves performance for the following types of operations:

- Large table scans and joins
- The creation of large indexes

- Partitioned index scans
- Large amounts of inserts, updates, and/or deletions

Parallel executions are worthwhile only on multiprocessor systems (symmetric or massively parallel) that have sufficient memory and I/O capabilities.

The first step you must take is to determine whether to use manual or automatic parallel tuning. Oracle recommends that you use automatic tuning, and that will suffice for most systems. You enable automatic tuning by setting the initialization parameter **PARALLEL_AUTOMATIC_ TUNING=TRUE**. When this parameter is set, automatic parallel execution will determine the values for related parameters, unless you explicitly set them in the init.ora file. See Table 9.1 for parameters and their default settings when parallel automatic tuning is enabled. Beware that you might need to adjust the parameter values to optimize your system performance. For example, automatic tuning can set the **LARGE_POOL_SIZE** parameter value larger than real memory, causing poor performance.

Note: Parallel execution isn't the same as Oracle Parallel Server, a separately licensed product.

Table 9.1 Parameter values when parallel_automatic_ tuning=true.

Parameter	Value
LARGE_POOL_SIZE	600kb +
	Parallel execution pool +
	backup buffer requests +
	MTS heap requirements
PARALLEL_ADAPTIVE_MULTI_USER	true
PARALLEL_EXECUTION_MESSAGE_SIZE	2kb
PARALLEL_MAX_SERVERS	CPU x 10
PROCESSES	**PARALLEL_MAX_SERVERS** x 1.2, or
	PARALLEL_MAX_SERVERS + 6 + 5+ (CPUs x 4), whichever is larger.
SESSIONS	5 + PROCESSES x 1.1

Practice Questions

Question 1

Increasing the value of the following init.ora parameter might improve the performance of larger sort operations.

❍ a. **SORT_MULTI_BLOCK_READ_COUNT**

❍ b. **SORT_MULTI_BLOCKDISK_READS**

❍ c. **SORT_MULTIBLOCK_READ_COUNT**

❍ d. **SORT_READ_MULTIBLOCK_COUNT**

Answer c is correct. Increasing the value of the **SORT_MULTIBLOCK_READ_COUNT** init.ora parameter can improve the performance of larger sorts by increasing the number of temporary segment blocks that are read in each read request. This reduces the total number of read I/O requests, but might not decrease the number of write requests needed to complete the sort. As always, test any change to this value in a test environment before making the change to a production instance. Oracle recommends the default value. Answers a, b, and d are incorrect because they aren't valid init.ora parameters.

Question 2

Specify the **LEADING** option of the _____ function to remove leading zeroes from a number.

The ANSI-standard **TRIM** function can be used to trim one or many occurrences of a single character or digit from a character string or number. The **LEADING** option removes from the left, and the **TRAILING** option removes from the right. The default behavior is to remove from **BOTH** ends of the source.

Question 3

The following init.ora parameter must be set to enable multiblock reads from disk during sort operations.

- ❍ a. **SORT_MULTIBLOCK_READ_COUNT**
- ❍ b. **SORT_MULTIBLOCK_READS**
- ❍ c. **SORT_BLOCKS_FROM_DISK**
- ❍ d. **SORT_DIRECT_WRITES**

Answer a is correct. This question is intentionally ambiguous. The value of **SORT_MULTIBLOCK_READ_COUNT** is 2 by default, so there is really no need to set it in the init.ora file. However, the other answers are incorrect. Answers b and c are incorrect because they are fictitious parameters. Answer d is incorrect because it's no longer supported in Oracle8i. By increasing the value of **SORT_MULTIBLOCK_READ_COUNT**, you can potentially improve the I/O efficiency of sort operations requiring reads from disk.

Question 4

In the following Top-N SQL query, what information will be displayed?

```
SELECT * FROM
   (SELECT *
    FROM scott.emp
    ORDER BY hire_date desc)
WHERE rownum < 6;
```

- ❍ a. The rows with the five highest row numbers
- ❍ b. The last six employees hired, sorted by hire date
- ❍ c. The first five employees hired, sorted by hire date
- ❍ d. The last five employees hired, sorted by hire date

Answer d is correct. Remember, by using the **DESC** keyword, we sort from highest value to lowest value; therefore, our query will sort the employees with the highest value (most recent) **hire_date** to the top. Because the **rownum** condition is less than six, we'll see the five employees with the most recent hire date.

Question 5

The **ROLLUP** and **CUBE** operators are used along with the following clause to create cross-tabular reports.

❍ a. **HAVING**

❍ b. **ORDER BY**

❍ c. **GROUP BY**

❍ d. **SELECT**

❍ e. **WHERE**

Answer c is correct. The ROLLUP and CUBE aggregate operators are used with the GROUP BY clause to create cross-tabular reports. Although you might argue that answer d is essential, it isn't the most correct answer. Answers a and b are incorrect because the HAVING and ORDER BY clauses are optional. Answer e is incorrect because the WHERE clause isn't required to create a cross-tabular report.

Question 6

By dynamically setting the following parameter, you cause the creation of stored outlines.

❍ a. **CREATE_USER_STORED_OUTLINES**

❍ b. **USE_STORED_OUTLINES**

❍ c. **USE_USER_STORED_OUTLINES**

❍ d. **CREATE_SYSTEM_STORED_OUTLINES**

❍ e. **CREATE_STORED_OUTLINES**

Answer e is correct. When you dynamically set the parameter CREATE_STORED_OUTLINES =TRUE or **named_category**, Oracle begins recording stored outlines for executing queries. You stop the creation of stored outlines by setting the parameter value to FALSE. Answer b is incorrect because setting USE_STORED_OUTLINES=TRUE or **named outline** will cause Oracle to use existing stored outlines. Answers a, c, and d are incorrect because they don't exist.

Question 7

The ______ package is preferred over the **ANALYZE** command for creating statistics on a table, index, schema, or database. [Fill in the blank]

The **DBMS_STATS** package allows you to customize statistics gathering for the database, a schema, a table, or an index. Some of the really neat features of **DBMS_STATS** are that it allows parallel statistics gathering, block or row sampling, and statistics mobility.

Question 8

You manage a large hybrid database that is in OLTP mode during the daytime and DSS mode at night. As the DBA, you can optimize query performance for all users by issuing what command after OLTP startup? [Choose two]

- ❑ a. **ALTER SESSION SET USE_STORED_OUTLINES=TRUE;**
- ❑ b. **ALTER SYSTEM SET USE_STORED_OUTLINES=TRUE;**
- ❑ c. **ALTER SESSION SET USE_STORED_OUTLINES=OLTP;**
- ❑ d. **ALTER SYSTEM SET USE_STORED_OUTLINES=OLTP;**
- ❑ e. **ALTER SESSION SET CREATE_STORED_OUTLINES=OLTP;**

Answers b and d are correct because we assume that you've named your default category **OLTP**. If you named it something else, that would only serve to confuse your successor. If you made DSS your default category, and your scheduled job that changes the value of **USE_STORED_OUTLINES** fails, you'll probably hear from angry customers because query performance isn't what they expect. Answers a and c are incorrect because the question specifically asks you to optimize query performance for *all* users, not just for the current session. Answer e is incorrect because it will start the collection of stored outlines in the OLTP category.

Question 9

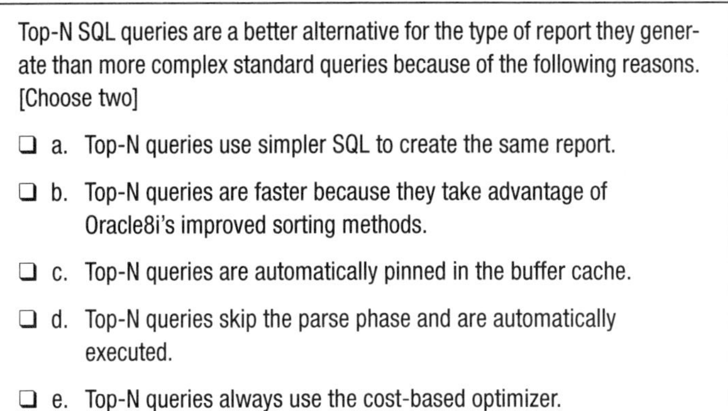

Top-N SQL queries are a better alternative for the type of report they generate than more complex standard queries because of the following reasons. [Choose two]

- ❑ a. Top-N queries use simpler SQL to create the same report.
- ❑ b. Top-N queries are faster because they take advantage of Oracle8i's improved sorting methods.
- ❑ c. Top-N queries are automatically pinned in the buffer cache.
- ❑ d. Top-N queries skip the parse phase and are automatically executed.
- ❑ e. Top-N queries always use the cost-based optimizer.

Answers a and b are correct. Top-N queries are far simpler to develop and read than an alternative query that accomplishes the same results. Also, improved performance of Top-N queries makes them even more preferable. Answer c is incorrect; Top-N queries aren't automatically pinned in either the library cache or the buffer cache. Answer d is incorrect because all queries must be parsed at least once. Answer e is incorrect because the query doesn't force the use of the CBO if RULE is specified in a hint, if **OPTIMIZER_GOAL=RULE** (precedence) for the session, or if **OPTIMIZER_MODE =RULE** for the instance. Using cost-based optimizer hints with Top-N queries is another way to improve their performance. You might think some of these answers are crazy, but remember, some of the OCP exam answers should be eliminated immediately.

Question 10

Which of the following functions will help the report developer differentiate between **NULL** values in the database and **NULL** subtotal values in a **ROLLUP** or **CUBE** report? [Choose one]

- ❍ a. **GROUP_BY**
- ❍ b. **GROUPING_BY**
- ❍ c. **GROUPING**
- ❍ d. **GROUP_NULLS**
- ❍ e. **GROUTING**

Answer c is correct. The **GROUPING** function can be used by the report developer to create a bitmap column for each dimension in a **ROLLUP** or **CUBE** report. If the value of the bit is **0**, then the database value for the dimension is actually **NULL**. If the value is **1**, then the **NULL** indicates a subtotal row for the dimension. The remaining answers are incorrect because they aren't valid Oracle-supplied functions.

Need to Know More?

Austin, David, Meghraj Thakkar, and Kurt Lysy. *Migrating to Oracle8i.* Sams Publishing, 2000. ISBN 0-672-31577-7. See Chapter 30, "Application Development," for a Top-N query example and Chapter 31, "Data Warehousing Enhancements," for detailed information on the **DBMS_STATS** package and the **ROLLUP** and **CUBE** operations.

Scherer, Douglas, et al. *Oracle8i Tips & Techniques.* Oracle Press, 1999. ISBN 0-07-212103-3. See the discussions in Chapter 5, "Performance," on the **DBMS_STATS** package and Plan Stability.

The following documents are available on the Oracle server installation CD, or you can download them from **http://technet.oracle.com**.

Lorentz, Diana and Denise Oertel. *SQL Reference, Release 8.1.5.* Oracle Corporation, 1999 (Part No. A67779-01). This is the syntax reference for Oracle8i SQL statements.

Mark Bauer, *Oracle8i Tuning, Release 8.1.5.* Oracle Corporation, 1999 (Part No. A67775-01). See Chapter 26 for details about automatic parallel execution.

Tablespace Management

Terms you'll need to understand:

- ✓ Dictionary-managed tablespace
- ✓ Locally-managed tablespace
- ✓ Transportable tablespace
- ✓ **DBMS_TTS** package
- ✓ Read-only tablespace

Techniques you'll need to master:

- ✓ Creating a locally-managed tablespace
- ✓ Verifying that all of the objects in a transportable tablespace set are self-contained
- ✓ Transporting a tablespace set from one Oracle8i database to another by using the Export and Import utilities
- ✓ Putting a tablespace in read-only mode

This chapter focuses on the enhancements to tablespace management in Oracle8i. Locally-managed tablespaces reduce the data-dictionary overhead associated with extent management. Transportable tablespaces make mobile computing and data distribution easier to manage. Enhancements in read-only tablespaces make it easier for you to manage the process of placing a tablespace in read-only mode.

Space Management in Tablespaces

In Oracle7 and 8, tablespace extent management was handled by the data dictionary. In Oracle8i, tablespace extent management can be either *dictionary managed* or *locally managed*. When you create a tablespace, you can choose which format to use. A database can contain a mix of locally-managed and dictionary-managed tablespaces. (The latest versions of Oracle still don't support system tablespaces in locally-managed format, however.) After a tablespace is created as either dictionary-managed or locally managed, it can't be changed to the other format. To change the extent management, you must drop and recreate the tablespace.

Dictionary-Managed Tablespaces

Dictionary-managed tablespaces are the default, but you can use the clause **EXTENT MANAGEMENT DICTIONARY** when creating the tablespace. When an extent is allocated or freed, appropriate tables in the data dictionary are updated; therefore, very active databases can suffer from contention in the data dictionary when dictionary-managed tablespaces are used. Also, Oracle stores rollback information about each update of the dictionary tables, thus creating even more opportunity for contention. Extents are allocated based on the storage parameters **INITIAL**, **NEXT**, and **PCTINCREASE**. Free space is coalesced manually by using the **ALTER TABLESPACE <tablespace_name> COALESCE** statement.

Locally-Managed Tablespaces

Locally-managed tablespaces are built by using the new clause **EXTENT MANAGEMENT LOCAL** when you create the tablespace. Oracle uses a bitmap in each data file to keep track of the used or free status of each extent in the data file. This bitmap approach reduces the contention that is caused by data-dictionary extent allocation and de-allocation. With locally managed tablespaces, data-dictionary updates and rollback generation due to data dictionary updates occur only in special cases.

A bitmap in each data file in a locally-managed tablespace keeps track of extent allocation. You'll need to know this for the exam!

Extent management is either *uniform* or *system managed*. Use the **UNIFORM** keyword for a uniform extent size; the default size is 1MB. Use the **AUTOALLOCATE** keyword for system-managed space allocation; extents default to 64K, and Oracle determines the optimal size for additional extents. Temporary tablespaces must use uniform extent management. Permanent tablespaces can use uniform or system extent management, with system as the default.

Only the **INITIAL** storage parameter is allowed when you're creating a locally managed tablespace because **NEXT** extents are based on free blocks in the bitmap. The storage parameters **NEXT**, **PCTINCREASE**, **MINEXTENTS**, **MAXEXTENTS**, and **DEFAULT STORAGE** aren't valid for extents that are managed locally. Locally-managed tablespaces don't require coalescing. See Listing 10.1 for the correct syntax to create a locally-managed tablespace.

Listing 10.1 Creating a locally-managed tablespace.

```
CREATE TABLESPACE mylocalauto
DATAFILE 'mylocalauto_01.dbf' SIZE 100M
EXTENT MANAGEMENT LOCAL AUTOALLOCATE;

CREATE TEMPORARY TABLESPACE mytemp
TEMPFILE 'mytemp_01.dbf' SIZE 50M
EXTENT MANAGEMENT LOCAL UNIFORM SIZE 2M;
```

Locally-managed temporary tablespaces must use the **UNIFORM** allocation. Locally-managed permanent tablespaces—also referred to as *system-managed* tablespaces—default to **AUTOALLOCATE**.

Transportable Tablespaces

New to Oracle8i is the ability to move an entire tablespace or set of tablespaces from one 8i database to another 8i database. This feature can be used to quickly rebuild a test database from a production system, distribute tablespaces to a mobile client, or update a data warehouse. The process to move a *transportable tablespace* from one database to another is much faster than Export/Import, SQL*Plus table copying, or backup and recovery. A *transportable tablespace set* is defined as all of the datafiles that make up the tablespaces that will be moved, and an export that contains the data dictionary information about those tablespaces.

Note: Make sure that the **COMPATIBLE** *parameter in the init.ora file in both the source database and the target database is set to 8.1.*

The general steps are very simple:

1. Verify that the set of source tablespaces is self-contained.
2. Generate a transportable tablespace set.
3. Transport the tablespace set.
4. Import the tablespace set into the target database.

Figure 10.1 illustrates the basic steps in transporting a tablespace set from one Oracle8i database to another Oracle8i database.

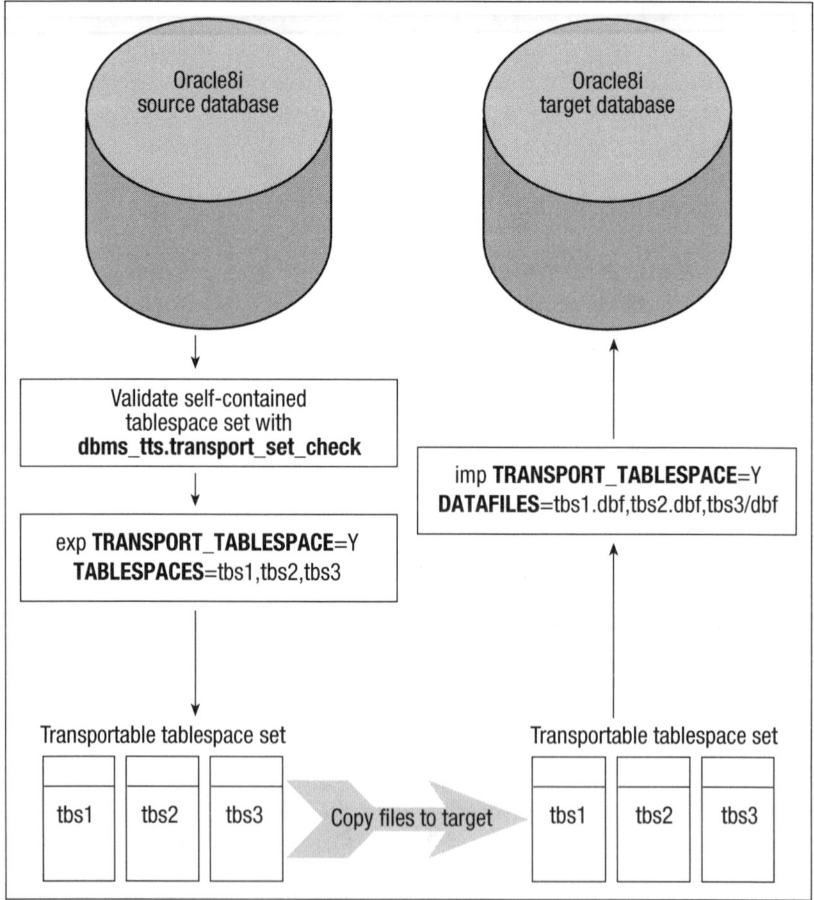

Figure 10.1 Oracle8i transportable tablespaces.

Verify Self-Contained Status with the DBMS_TTS Package

Self-contained, as it sounds, means that there are no references to objects outside the tablespace set. All indexes for a table in the tablespace must also reside in the tablespace set. For partitioned tables, all partitions must reside in the tablespace set. If a table contains LOB columns, they must also exist in the tablespace set. Referential integrity constraint checking is optional.

You use the DBMS_TTS package to confirm that a transportable set is self-contained. The TRANSPORT_SET_CHECK procedure tests whether a set of tablespaces is self-contained. The procedure takes as input a comma-separated list of tablespace names, plus either TRUE or FALSE to indicate whether or not to include referential integrity constraints in the test. After calling this procedure, you can select from the TRANSPORT_SET_VIOLATIONS view to see a list of violations. No violations means that the set of tablespaces is self-contained. REFs aren't checked by the procedure, so object references outside the set can result in "dangling REFs" in the target database. See Listing 10.2 for a sample DBMS_TTS.TRANSPORT_SET_CHECK session.

Listing 10.2 Using the DBMS_TTS.TRANSPORT_SET_CHECK procedure.

```
EXECUTE TRANSPORT_SET_CHECK('mydata,myindx', TRUE);
SELECT * FROM TRANSPORT_SET_VIOLATIONS;
VIOLATIONS
--------------------
Constraint STAMPS_FK between table MY.STAMPS
in tablespace MYDATA
and table MY.ENVELOPES in tablespace MYDATA_2

Partitioned table MY.TV_DINNER is partially
contained in the transportable set
```

Execute the **DBMS_TTS.TRANSPORT_SET_CHECK** procedure before you attempt to transport a tablespace set. It may save you from having to repeat steps later in the process.

Generate a Transportable Tablespace Set

Now that your tablespace set has passed the self-containment test, you can begin the transport process. Again, the steps are straightforward:

1. Place each tablespace in the set in read-only mode with the command **ALTER TABLESPACE <tablespace_name> READ ONLY**. Before you do this, make a note of which tablespaces in the set were already in read-only mode.

2. Use the Oracle Export utility program to export the tablespace data-dictionary information. Use the **TRANSPORT_TABLESPACE=Y** parameter to indicate that you want to transport tablespaces. Specify the tablespace set with the parameter **TABLESPACES=** followed by a comma-delimited list of the tablespaces to be transported. Specify the dump file name with the **FILE=** parameter. The parameters **TRIGGERS=Y/N**, **CONSTRAINTS=Y/N**, and **GRANTS=Y/N** determine what additional information from the data dictionary will go into the export dump file. The default for each parameter is Y. Triggers aren't checked for validity during the export. The export will fail if the tablespace set isn't self-contained. See Listing 10.3 for a sample **EXPORT** command.

3. Using an operating-system copy program, copy the data files and the export dump file from the source to the target location or to a staging area.

4. In the source database, place each tablespace in the set back to read-write mode, unless it was in read-only mode before you started this process.

Listing 10.3 Sample transportable tablespace settings for the Oracle Export utility.

```
EXP TRANSPORT_TABLESPACE=y TABLESPACES=mydata,myindx TRIGGERS=y
CONSTRAINTS=y GRANTS=y FILE=mystuff.dmp
```

Transport the Tablespace Set

If you copied the data files to a temporary staging area, now is the time to copy them to their final destination on the target system. Also make sure that the export dump file is in a staging area that can be accessed by the Oracle Import utility program on the target system.

Import the Tablespace Set

We're almost there, and the most difficult and time-consuming steps are behind us. If you haven't already moved the data files to their final destination, do it now. Use the Oracle Import utility program to bring the tablespace set's data-dictionary information into the target database. See Listing 10.4 for a sample **IMPORT** command. There are two required parameters: **TRANSPORT _TABLESPACE=Y**, and the **DATAFILES=** parameter followed by the comma-delimited list of data files that make up the tablespace set. Other, optional parameters are:

- **TABLESPACES=** followed by the comma-delimited list of tablespace names in your set. If the list doesn't match what is in the export dump file, then you'll get an error.
- **TTS_OWNERS=** followed by a list of all users who own data in the tablespace set. Again, mismatches cause an error.
- The **FROMUSER** and **TOUSER** parameters allow you to change ownership of the objects moving into the target database. If these parameters aren't included, the source data owners must exist in the target database.

TRANSPORT_TABLESPACE and **DATAFILES** are the two required parameters when you're importing transportable tablespaces into an Oracle8i database. You'll need to know this for the exam.

Listing 10.4 Sample transportable tablespace settings for the Oracle Import utility.

```
IMP TRANSPORT_TABLESPACE=y
DATAFILES='/ora075/oracle/data/ORCL/mydat_01.dbf,
/ora078/oracle/data/ORCL/myindx_01.dbf'
TABLESPACES=mydata,myindx TTS_OWNERS=my FROMUSER=my
TOUSER=yours FILE=mydat.dmp
```

Final Cleanup

When the tablespace import is successfully completed, the new tablespaces are in read-only mode in the target database. If you intend to use the tablespaces for read-write, now is the time to alter them.

Known Limitations of Transportable Tablespaces

Of course, there are some limitations, and these are pretty straightforward:

- The source and target databases must be on the same type of hardware and operating-system platform.
- The source and target databases must have the same database block size.
- The source and target databases must have the same character set.
- A tablespace with the same name must not already exist in the target database.

- Materialized views, function-based indexes, scoped REFs, 8.0-compatible advanced queues with multiple recipients, and domain indexes can't be transported in this manner.

Enhancements in Read-Only Tablespaces

The major difference between read-only tablespace management in Oracle8.0 and Oracle8i is the way pending transactions affect the request to place a tablespace in read-only mode. When you issue the **ALTER TABLESPACE <tablespace name> READ ONLY** command in Oracle8, any active transaction in the database will cause the command to fail. When the **COMPATIBLE** parameter is set to **8.1** in an 8i database, pending transactions don't cause the **ALTER** command to fail. Instead, the tablespace is put into *transitional read-only mode,* which allows existing transactions to be completed but doesn't allow new transactions to start in the tablespace. After the **ALTER** command is issued, new transactions see the tablespace as read-only, while pending transactions can be completed with either a commit or a rollback. This means that you don't have to repeatedly submit the command until all transactions are complete. You can submit the command once, and the instance will take care of the rest.

If you need to make the tablespace read-only immediately, you might want to verify that no transactions are currently modifying objects in the tablespace. The query in Listing 10.5 will show active transactions, the sessions that have created the transactions, the objects they have locked, and the rollback segments they are using. You can use **SID** and **SERIAL#** to kill the offending sessions. Be aware that when you kill an active session, Oracle will roll back the block changes in the transaction; this could cause the tablespace to be in transitional read-only mode for a longer time period than it would have taken to complete the transaction. Knowing the application and its processes will help you decide whether to kill the session or let the transaction continue. Also, you should always contact the person who owns the session (or the application owner) before you kill the active session.

Listing 10.5 Sample query to display active transactions and associated tablespaces.

```
SELECT a.os_user_name "Os User ",
       a.oracle_username "db user ",
       e.sid,
       e.serial#,
       b.owner "schema",
       b.object_name "name",
       b.object_type "type",
```

```
       f.tablespace_name "tbs",
       c.segment_name "rbs",
       d.used_urec "#"
FROM   v$locked_object a,
       dba_objects b,
       dba_rollback_segs c,
       v$transaction d,
       v$session e,
       dba_segments f
WHERE  a.object_id      = b.object_id   and
       a.xidusn         = c.segment_id  and
       a.xidusn         = d.xidusn      and
       a.xidslot        = d.xidslot     and
       d.addr           = e.taddr       and
       f.segment_name = b.object_name and
       f.segment_type = b.object_type
/
Os User  db user   SID serial# schema  name  type  Tbs     rbs  #
-- ----  -- ----   --- ------- ------  ----  ----  ---     ---  -
bob      bobbijoe   25 134     USERDA  TAB1  TABLE MYDATA  RB3  13
joe      joebob     26 313     USERDA  TAB1  TABLE MYDATA  RB1  89
```

Read-Only Tablespace Requirements

Just for a refresher, let's go over the requirements to place a tablespace in read-only mode:

- The tablespace and data files in the tablespace must be online.
- If there are any rollback segments in the tablespace, they must not have any active transactions. To be safe, take the rollback segments offline and drop them before you make the tablespace read-only.
- If you're running in **ARCHIVELOG** mode, check that the tablespace isn't in backup mode.
- The **COMPATIBLE** parameter in the init.ora file must be set to **7.1.0** or higher.
- To enable transitional read-only mode, set the **COMPATIBLE** parameter to **8.1**.
- You can't place the **SYSTEM** tablespace in read-only mode.
- You can't add data files to a read-only tablespace.
- You can drop objects from a read-only tablespace, but you can't create or modify objects in the tablespace.

Practice Questions

Question 1

Which of the following statements will build a locally-managed temporary tablespace?

- ❍ a. **CREATE TEMPORARY TABLESPACE MYTEMP......EXTENT MANAGEMENT LOCAL AUTOALLOCATE;**
- ❍ b. **CREATE TEMPORARY TABLESPACE MYTEMP......EXTENT MANAGEMENT LOCAL UNIFORM SIZE 2M;**
- ❍ c. **CREATE TABLESPACE MYTEMP......EXTENT MANAGEMENT LOCAL;**
- ❍ d. **CREATE TEMPORARY TABLESPACE MYTEMP......LOCAL EXTENT MANAGEMENT;**
- ❍ e. **CREATE TEMPORARY TABLESPACE MYTEMP......EXTENT MANAGEMENT DICTIONARY UNIFORM SIZE 2M;**

Answer b is correct. Locally managed temporary tablespaces must use uniform extent sizes. If you want to use extents of some other size than the default 1MB, use the UNIFORM SIZE clause when you create the tablespace. Answer a is incorrect because AUTOALLOCATE isn't an option for temporary tablespaces. Answer e is incorrect because the DICTIONARY keyword indicates that extent management will be in the data dictionary. Answer c is incorrect because the TEMPORARY keyword is used when creating a temporary tablespace for session sort segments.Answer d is incorrect because LOCAL EXTENT MANAGEMENT isn't a valid clause; it should be EXTENT MANAGEMENT LOCAL.

Question 2

A _____ in each data file of a locally managed tablespace keeps track of free and used extents.

A bitmap, stored in each data file, is responsible for keeping track of extent allocation and de-allocation.

Question 3

Which of the following are valid types of extent allocation for locally-managed tablespaces? [Choose two]

- ❑ a. Uniform
- ❑ b. System
- ❑ c. Dictionary
- ❑ d. Hash
- ❑ e. Composite

Answers a and b are correct. Locally-managed temporary tablespaces must use uniform extent management. Locally-managed permanent tablespaces may use system or uniform. Remember, to enable system-allocated extents in a locally-managed permanent tablespace, use the keyword **AUTOALLOCATE** when you create the table. Answers c, d, and e are incorrect because they aren't valid means of extent management.

Question 4

Which one of the following **IMPORT** parameters is required when you transport tablespaces?

- ❍ a. **TABLESPACES**
- ❍ b. **TTS_OWNERS**
- ❍ c. **DATAFILES**
- ❍ d. **FROMUSER**
- ❍ e. **TOUSER**

Answer c is correct. The **DATAFILES** parameter must be followed by a comma-delimited list of the data files to import into the database. The other parameter required for transporting tablespaces (not listed) is **TRANSPORT_TABLESPACE=Y**. Answer a is incorrect because the **TABLESPACES** parameter isn't required, but it can be used to verify that the tablespaces listed match the tablespace set in the export dump file. Answer b is incorrect because the **TTS_OWNERS** parameter isn't required, but it can be used to verify that the data owners listed match those in the export dump file. Answers d and e are incorrect because the **FROMUSER** and **TOUSER** parameters aren't required, but they can be used to change the ownership of objects when they are imported into the target database.

Question 5

Which of these methods is the preferred way to move big chunks of self-contained data from one database to another?

❍ a. Export/Import

❍ b. Backup/Restore

❍ c. Stand-by database

❍ d. SQL*Plus copy through database links

❍ e. Transportable tablespaces

Answer e is correct. Transportable tablespaces provides the quickest way to move large amounts of self-contained data from one system to another. Of course, certain limitations apply. Answer e is the best option given the context that both databases are on the same OS and hardware platforms, both have the same database block size, and both are Oracle8i databases with **COMPATIBLE** set to **8.1**. Each of the other answers could be correct given a different context. Also, keep in mind that this exam is about Oracle8i new features, so it's a good idea to assume that, all other things being equal, the new feature is preferred.

Question 6

Which of the following **EXPORT** parameters is required when you transport tablespaces? [Choose two]

❑ a. **TRANSPORT_TABLESPACES**

❑ b. **DATAFILES**

❑ c. **TABLESPACES**

❑ d. **FROM_USER**

❑ e. **GRANTS**

❑ f. **TRIGGERS**

Answers a and c are correct. Set **TRANSPORT_TABLESPACES=Y**, and follow the **TABLESPACES** parameter with the list of tablespaces in the tablespace set. Answer b is incorrect because the **DATAFILES** parameter is used with the Import utility when you're importing tablespace data files into the target database. Answer d is incorrect because **FROM_USER** isn't a valid **EXPORT** parameter. Answers e and f aren't mandatory parameters.

Question 7

The DBMS_TTS.________ procedure is used to verify that a transportable tablespace set is self-contained.

The **TRANSPORT_SET_CHECK** procedure is used to verify that a tablespace set is self-contained. Self-contained means that all related objects, such as tables and indexes, and all the partitions in a partitioned table are in the tablespace set. Any failures to the validity check show up in the view **TRANSPORT_SET_VIOLATIONS**.

Question 8

Why are locally-managed tablespaces preferable to dictionary-managed tablespaces? [Choose two]

- ❑ a. Data files in locally-managed tablespaces are smaller.
- ❑ b. Data-dictionary contention for extent allocation is reduced.
- ❑ c. Locally-managed tablespaces use a bitmapped-index to speed up access to each extent.
- ❑ d. The bitmap in each data file tracks adjacent free space so coalescing isn't required.
- ❑ e. Dictionary-managed tablespaces aren't transportable.

Answers b and d are correct. Locally managed tablespaces reduce data-dictionary contention due to extent allocation and de-allocation. In dictionary-managed tablespaces, the data dictionary is updated every time an extent is allocated or de-allocated. In locally-managed tablespaces, the bitmap in each data file is updated when extents are allocated or de-allocated. Also, the locally-managed tablespace doesn't require coalescing, which further reduces DBA intervention. Although it's possible to make all of your locally-managed tablespaces smaller than dictionary-managed tablespaces, it's not a requirement; therefore, answer a is incorrect. Answer c is incorrect because a bitmap is used to track extents in each data file, but no bitmapped-index is used to improve access to each extent. Watch out for questions that use ambiguous or incorrect terms. Answer e is incorrect because dictionary-managed tablespaces are transportable.

Question 9

Your database has a large number of active transactions, as noted by querying the **V$TRANSACTION** view. You attempt to place the **USER_DATA** tablespace in read-only mode, but your command appears to hang. What has happened ? [Choose two]

- ❑ a. New transactions are modifying objects in the tablespace.
- ❑ b. Existing transactions are waiting to commit or roll back.
- ❑ c. The tnsnames.ora file has been corrupted.
- ❑ d. The tablespace is in transitional read-only mode.
- ❑ e. The tablespace was already in read-only mode.

Answers b and d are correct. The tablespace is in transitional read-only mode and is waiting for existing transactions to be completed. Answer a is incorrect because new transactions are blocked from modifying objects in the tablespace after the **ALTER TABLESPACE <tablespace_name> READ ONLY** command has been entered. Answer c is interesting, but it's out of context. Answer e is incorrect because Oracle will return an error message if the tablespace is already in read-only mode.

Question 10

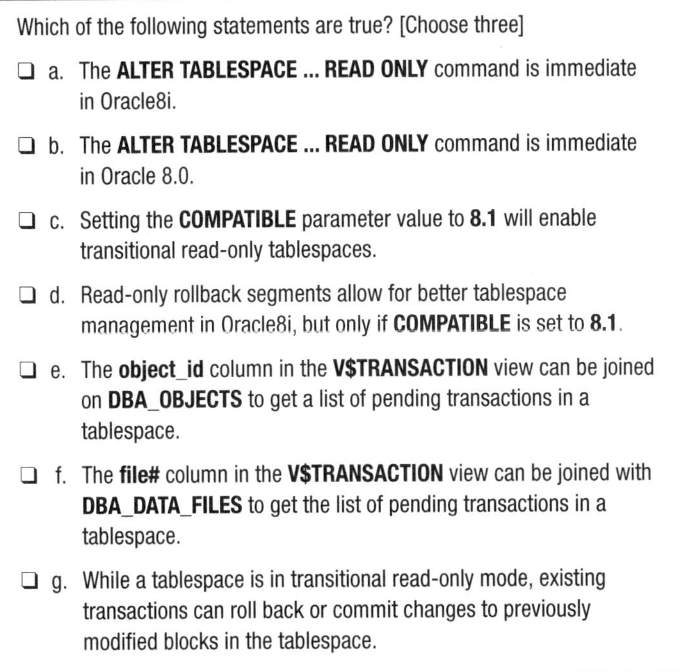

Which of the following statements are true? [Choose three]

- ❑ a. The **ALTER TABLESPACE ... READ ONLY** command is immediate in Oracle8i.
- ❑ b. The **ALTER TABLESPACE ... READ ONLY** command is immediate in Oracle 8.0.
- ❑ c. Setting the **COMPATIBLE** parameter value to **8.1** will enable transitional read-only tablespaces.
- ❑ d. Read-only rollback segments allow for better tablespace management in Oracle8i, but only if **COMPATIBLE** is set to **8.1**.
- ❑ e. The **object_id** column in the **V$TRANSACTION** view can be joined on **DBA_OBJECTS** to get a list of pending transactions in a tablespace.
- ❑ f. The **file#** column in the **V$TRANSACTION** view can be joined with **DBA_DATA_FILES** to get the list of pending transactions in a tablespace.
- ❑ g. While a tablespace is in transitional read-only mode, existing transactions can roll back or commit changes to previously modified blocks in the tablespace.

Answers b, c, and g are correct. Answer a is incorrect because the command will wait while pending transactions either roll back or commit if the **COMPATIBLE** parameter is set to **8.1**. Answer d is incorrect because read-only rollback segments don't exist. Answers e and f are incorrect because the **V$TRANSACTION** view doesn't contain the **object_id** or **file#** columns.

Need to Know More?

Loney, Kevin and Marlene Theriault. *Oracle8i DBA Handbook.* Oracle Press (Osborne/McGraw-Hill), 2000. ISBN 0-07-212188-2. See Chapter 12 for a description of transportable tablespaces and locally-managed tablespaces.

Ault, Mike. *Oracle8i Administration and Management.* Wiley Computer Publishing, 2000. ISBN 0-471-35453-8. See Chapter 3 for Mike's discussion on using transportable tablespaces.

Austin, David, Meghraj Thakkar, and Kurt Lysy. *Migrating to Oracle8i.* Sams Publishing, 2000. ISBN 0-672-31577-7. Good information on downgrading an 8i database that contains transported tablespaces to an 8.0 database, in addition to good sections on transportable and locally-managed tablespaces.

The following documents are available on the Oracle server installation CD, or you can download them from **http://technet.oracle.com**.

Fee, Joyce. *Oracle8i Administrator's Guide* (Part No. A67772-01). Oracle Corporation, 1999.

Leverenz, Lefty and Diana Rehfield. *Oracle8i Concepts* guide (Part No. A67781-01). Oracle Corporation, 1999.

Indexes and Index-Organized Tables

Terms you'll need to understand:

- ✓ Index-organized table (IOT)
- ✓ Row overflow
- ✓ Logical **ROWID**
- ✓ Reverse-key index
- ✓ Function-based index
- ✓ **QUERY_REWRITE_ENABLED** parameter
- ✓ **QUERY_REWRITE_INTEGRITY** parameter
- ✓ Descending index
- ✓ Online index create/rebuild
- ✓ **ANALYZE INDEX**

Techniques you'll need to master:

- ✓ Creating an index-organized table
- ✓ Describing row overflow in IOTs
- ✓ Listing IOT restrictions and data dictionary information
- ✓ Creating multiple indexes on IOTs
- ✓ Creating a reverse-key index
- ✓ Creating a function-based index
- ✓ Creating a descending index
- ✓ Creating and rebuilding indexes online
- ✓ Computing index statistics

This chapter focuses on enhancements to index-organized tables (IOTs), new and improved index types, and improved index maintenance features. For index-organized tables, the important new enhancements include the ability to rebuild the IOT with the **MOVE** clause and the **ONLINE** option, the **CREATE AS SELECT** option, and the ability to create secondary indexes. The important new and improved index types are reverse-key indexes, function-based indexes, and descending indexes. The important maintenance features are rebuilding indexes online and collecting statistics while creating or altering an index.

Index-Organized Tables

As an Oracle DBA, you should already know about index-organized tables (IOTs) from Oracle8. In this section, we'll focus on enhancements to IOTs in Oracle8i. However, we'll review IOT basics before we jump into the enhancements.

What Is an Index-Organized Table?

An index-organized table is an object that combines a primary key with its associated table data. The primary key is required because it is the unique identifier for each row in the IOT. Storage is reduced because the primary key data is not duplicated in a separate index. See Figure 11.1 for an illustration comparing a key search on an ordinary table to a key search on an index-organized table.

Creating an Index-Organized Table

To create an index-organized table, you use the same syntax as when you create a regular table, except that you need to include a primary key constraint and include the **ORGANIZATION INDEX** clause. If you intend to make the IOT a partitioned table, you also include the partitioning definition when you create the IOT.

New in 8i is the ability to create an IOT from data in an existing table with the **CREATE TABLE ... AS SELECT** clause. See Listing 11.1 for the correct syntax to use when you're building a nonpartitioned index-organized table from the data in an existing regular table.

Listing 11.1 Creating an index-organized table.

```
CREATE TABLE my_iot_tab
(empno,ename,job,mgr,hiredate,sal,comm,deptno,
CONSTRAINT my_iot_tab_pk PRIMARY KEY (empno))
ORGANIZATION INDEX
OVERFLOW TABLESPACE USERS
AS
SELECT * FROM SCOTT.EMP;
```

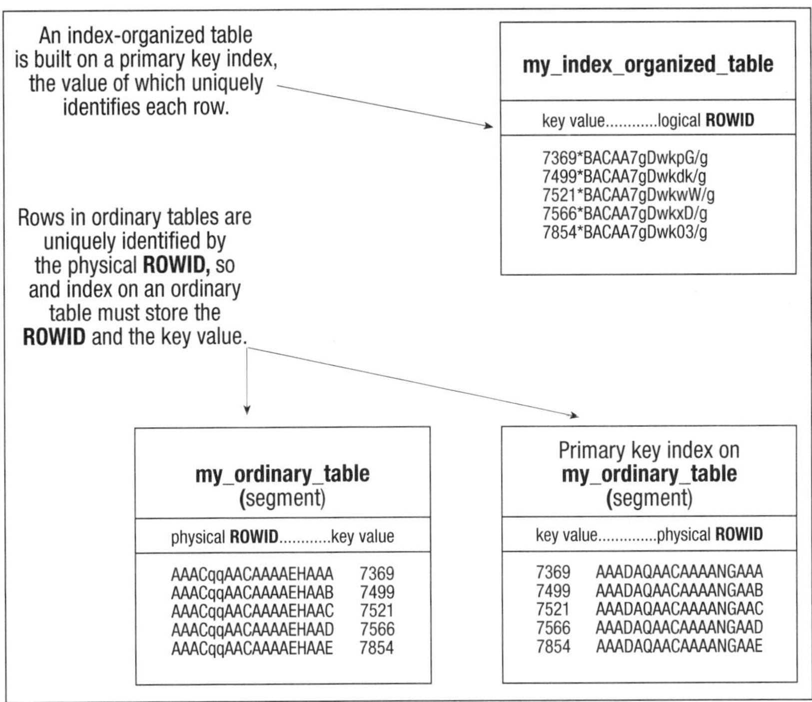

Figure 11.1 Key searches on an ordinary table and an index-organized table.

Logical ROWIDs

Because the physical ROWID isn't used in an IOT, secondary indexes must use a logical ROWID to find a row. A logical ROWID is based on the primary key value and a "guess" as to the location of the row in a data block. Logical ROWIDs do not have a permanent physical address. In a query WHERE clause, logical ROWIDs are used just as physical ROWIDs are, and they provide the fastest possible access to a row.

Applications can use the **Universal ROWID** data type in Oracle8i to access physical or logical **ROWIDs** with PL/SQL statements.

Creating Secondary Indexes on IOTs

One of the new features of Oracle8i is the ability to create additional indexes on IOT columns to improve performance on queries that do not use the primary key. Secondary indexes use the logical ROWID instead of the physical ROWID used by regular tables. Because the logical ROWID is not a physical location, moving an IOT does not invalidate its secondary indexes. No special syntax is required to create a secondary index on an IOT.

The locical **ROWID** and guess are important for secondary index performance. Without a guess, a secondary index scan and a primary key index scan are required to fetch the data block. The guess can become stale when rows are moved to new blocks, leading to inaccurate guesses. When a guess is inaccurate, Orace scans the secondary index, gets the wrong data block, and then scans the primary key index to get the correct data block.

Note: You can create unique, nonunique, and function-based secondary indexes. You cannot create bitmapped secondary indexes on IOTs.

Partitioning IOTs

Range partitioning on IOTs is supported in Oracle8i. The partition key must be a subset of the primary key. The **ORGANIZATION INDEX, OVERFLOW, PCTTHRESHOLD,** and **INCLUDING** clauses are considered table-level attributes. Overflow segments are equipartitioned with the partition key, so each partition has an index segment and an overflow segment. You can specify tablespaces for each overflow partition. Moving or splitting partitions in an IOT does not invalidate its partitioned or nonpartitioned indexes because they rely on logical **ROWIDs**. The **MERGE** partitioning maintenance option is not allowed with IOTs.

IOTs and LOBs

IOTs work with both internal and external **LOB** columns. **LOB** data and index segments are created in the same tablespace as the IOT primary key segment. **LOBs** in IOTs are stored out-of-line if no overflow segment is created. **LOBs** are not supported in partitioned IOTs.

IOTs and Overflow Storage

When you create an IOT, you can specify a tablespace to hold an overflow storage segment. Overflow columns are matched to the parent row columns by using **ROWIDs**. The **PCTTHRESHOLD** parameter determines the cutoff column—for those columns that stay in the IOT and those that are in the overflow. Overflow storage is useful for keeping the primary key data densely packed while maintaining a connection to additional row information. If you did not create an overflow data segment when you created the IOT, you can add one with the command **ALTER TABLE <table_name> ADD OVERFLOW**.

Moving IOTs

You can reorganize an IOT online with the **ALTER TABLE MOVE** command. Because secondary indexes rely on the logical **ROWID**, you can reorganize an index-organized table or an index-organized table partition without rebuilding its indexes. So IOTs are a good choice in a 24x7 system. The **ONLINE** keyword can be used to move the table and allow user DML at the same time. The **ONLINE** move is not supported for IOTs that have an overflow segment. The init.ora parameter **COMPATIBLE** must be set to **8.1.3** or higher to allow **ONLINE** moves.

IOT Data Dictionary Views

Index-organized tables are tables, but they show up in different data dictionary views. Look in **DBA_TABLES** for your IOT, and look for the columns **IOT_NAME** and **IOT_TYPE**. If you query **DBA_OBJECTS**, you will find a reference to your IOT and a reference to the primary key index. If you query **DBA_SEGMENTS**, you will find no reference to your IOT, but you will find a reference to the primary key index segment.

The **IOT** has an entry in **DBA_TABLES**; note the columns **IOT_NAME** and **IOT_TYPE**. The IOT primary key appears in **DBA_SEGMENTS**, and the primary key index appears in **DBA_INDEXES**.

IOT Restrictions

Just about anything that can be done to a regular table can also be done to an IOT. There are, of course, some exceptions:

- Bitmapped secondary indexes are not allowed.
- **LONG** data types are not allowed.
- Parallel execution of secondary-index-only scan queries is not supported.
- Object tables (**TABLE OF <object type>**) cannot be created as IOTs.
- The primary key constraint cannot be dropped.
- Unique constraints are not allowed.
- Distribution and replication are not supported.

Why Use an IOT?

IOTs are good for very large databases (VLDBs) because of the decreased storage and improved online-maintenance features. IOTs are good for 24x7 operations because you can reorganize the table without invalidating the indexes, and you can rebuild an IOT **ONLINE**. Object types, **VARRAY**s, nested tables, **REF** columns, and **LOB**s are supported. Function-based, reverse-key, and descending indexes are supported. Gathering statistics on an IOT with the **ANALYZE** command will analyze the primary key segment and the overflow segment. The **ALTER TABLE** options **ADD, MODIFY,** and **DROP COLUMN** (as well as others) that are available to regular tables are available to IOTs.

Index Enhancements

The major enhancements to indexes in Oracle8i can be split into two basic groups. New or improved index features designed to *improve application performance* include reverse-key indexes, function-based indexes, and descending-key indexes. New or improved *administration features* include rebuilding indexes online, coalescing indexes, and computing statistics when creating or altering an index.

Reverse-Key Indexes

In a reverse-key index, the bytes are the reverse of the bytes in the associated column in the table. For one sample row, if the table column value is 123, then the value stored in the index is 321 because the bytes are reversed. This is a simplistic example, but one that might appear as a question on the exam. A reverse-key index is a good way to index data that is very skewed when in its original order. Reverse-key indexes are useful when applications insert ascending values into a table and delete lower values, as with time-series data. Reverse-key indexes also reduce pinging in an OPS environment. See Listing 11.2 for the correct syntax to use when you build a reverse-key index.

Listing 11.2 Creating a reverse-key index.

```
CREATE INDEX myindx_desc on mytab (emplid) REVERSE;
```

Function-Based Indexes

Simply put, a function-based index is an index that is based on an expression. A function-based index contains a PL/SQL function, a C callout, a SQL function, or a package function. A function-based index can be an arithmetic expression. You can use function-based indexes to support NLS (National Language Support) collating sequences (linguistics sorts). Function-based indexes can be used with complex mathematical expressions to calculate and store the results and reduce query execution time.

See Listing 11.3 for the correct syntax used to create a function-based index. To use a function-based index, you must set **QUERY_REWRITE_ENABLED=TRUE** and **QUERY_REWRITE_INTEGRITY=TRUSTED.** You can set these in the init.ora file, use **ALTER SYSTEM** to enable function-based indexes for the instance, or use **ALTER SESSION** to enable function-based indexes for the session.

The parameters **QUERY_REWRITE_ENABLED=TRUE** and **QUERY_REWRITE_INTEGRITY=TRUSTED** must be set in order for function-based indexes to work.

Advantages of function-based indexes include the following:

- Function-based indexes increase the likelihood of an index-range scan instead of a full table scan, thus improving query performance.
- A function-based index stores the results of complex mathematical expressions in the index, thus reducing query execution time.
- You can create indexes on object and **REF** columns.
- You can implement case-insensitive or NLS sorts, using built-in functions.

Restrictions on function-based indexes include the following:

- The rule-based optimizer doesn't understand function-based indexes and ignores them. You must use the cost-based optimizer if you want to use function-based indexes.
- Function-based indexes cannot be built on **LOB** columns.
- PL/SQL procedures must be deterministic.
- Aggregate functions are not allowed.
- PL/SQL functions that return **RAW** or **VARCHAR2** data types are not allowed because of size.

Also, it is important to remember that the index expression in the query *must match* the expression in the index. For example, if the index is built on **UPPER(ENAME))**, then for a query to use the index, it must use a comparison, such as: **WHERE UPPER(ENAME)) = 'SMITH'**. The comparison **WHERE TRIM(UPPER(ENAME)) = 'SMITH'** will not use the index based on the function **UPPER(ENAME))**.

Listing 11.3 Creating a function-based index.

```
CREATE INDEX myfunc_indx ON mydata (upper(ename));
```

Descending Indexes

You define a descending-key index by using the keyword **DESC** when you create the index. When DESC is specified, the columns in the index are sorted in descending order according to the database character set. In prior versions of Oracle, the **DESC** keyword was ignored. Oracle8i treats descending-key indexes as function-based indexes. However, you do not need the **QUERY REWRITE** privileges to create a **DESC** index. Oracle needs statistics on the **DESC** index and its base table, so they must be analyzed at least once or else the **DESC** index will not be used. Reverse or bitmapped indexes cannot use the **DESC** option. See Listing 11.4 for the correct syntax used to create a descending index.

Listing 11.4 Creating a descending index.

```
CREATE INDEX myindx_desc ON mytab (emplid DESC);
```

Creating or Rebuilding an Index Online

In previous versions of Oracle, it was not possible to perform DML (Data Manipulation Language) operations on a table during an associated index build or rebuild because of read-shared (DML S-lock) locking on the table. Index maintenance usually occurred with no users in the database—something that is difficult to schedule on a 24x7 database. In Oracle8i, the **ONLINE** index build keyword gives you the option to rebuild the index while the base table is in use. By using the **ONLINE** option, you tell Oracle to allow DML operations on the base table during the index build or rebuild process. The **ONLINE** option means that you don't have to kick users out of the database to build or rebuild an index. However, be aware that active DML on the base table can slow down the performance of the online build. For example, when users attempt to retrieve and modify columns at the same time that Oracle is trying to build indexes based on the column values, index build time suffers because the index structure changes. Index maintenance will also slow down the build process if a large number of rows are deleted or inserted.

Users cannot perform DDL (Data Definition Language) operations during an **ONLINE** index build because DML SS-locks are placed on the base table. Parallel DML is not supported during **ONLINE** index building. The **ONLINE** option is supported with **B*-tree** indexes on index-organized, partitioned, and nonpartitioned tables. Cluster, bitmap, and secondary indexes on index-organized tables are not supported. See Listing 11.5 for examples of online index building operations.

Rebuilding an index requires free space equivalent to the size of the existing index unless you modify the storage parameters. Because the index is actually rebuilt in different data blocks from the original index, always check free space in the target tablespace to make sure that there is enough space.

Listing 11.5 Sample online index building operations.

```
ALTER INDEX myindx_01 REBUILD ONLINE;
CREATE INDEX myindx_01 ON mytab (name, emplid) ONLINE;
```

Oracle places a brief initial lock on the table before it actually builds the index, so pending transactions against the table must commit or roll back before the online index build or rebuild can continue. You will need to know this for the exam.

Coalescing an Index

If you want to defragment an index, use the **COALESCE** option with the **ALTER INDEX** statement. Coalescing can be done while users have shared DML locks on the base table but not if the table is locked in exclusive mode. You might want to coalesce an index if rebuilding the index, or dropping and re-creating the index, is not an option. Listing 11.6 shows the syntax for coalescing an index.

Listing 11.6 Coalescing an index.

```
ALTER INDEX myindx_01 COALESCE;
```

Computing Index Statistics

You can now gather statistics when creating or altering an index. This action is relatively inexpensive and saves the extra step of analyzing the index after you've created or altered it. See Listing 11.7 for the syntax. The key term to remember is **COMPUTE STATISTICS**. The **ESTIMATE STATISTICS** clause is not supported. You can rebuild and compute statistics at the same time, but the **REBUILD** keyword must immediately follow the index name. The **REBUILD ONLINE** option is not supported with **COMPUTE STATISTICS**.

When Oracle analyzes the index, the statistics are gathered according to the following general rules and stored in the data dictionary:

- When Oracle is analyzing an index on a nonpartitioned table, statistics are gathered for the index and the table.
- When Oracle is analyzing a concatenated index, statistics are gathered for the index and the leftmost column.
- When Oracle is analyzing an index on a partitioned table, only the index statistics are gathered.

Listing 11.7 Computing statistics when an index is created or altered.

```
CREATE INDEX myindx_01 ON mytab (name, emplid) COMPUTE STATISTICS;
ALTER INDEX myindx_01 COMPUTE STATISTICS;
```

Practice Questions

Question 1

You have a badly fragmented index on a heavily used table in a 24x7 production DSS system. Performance is suffering, so you need to rebuild the index. What do you do?

❍ a. Shut down the database by using **SHUTDOWN NORMAL**; then open the database in restricted mode and rebuild the index.

❍ b. Rebuild the index online.

❍ c. Place the index tablespace in read-only mode so that no one can modify it; then rebuild the index, and place the tablespace in read-write mode.

❍ d. Drop the index and create it from saved DDL.

❍ e. Export the index, drop it in the source database, and then import the index into the target database.

Answer b is correct. Rebuild the index online. Although the online index rebuilding process briefly places locks on the table, end users will probably not be affected. Answer a will definitely cause the users some pain and suffering and is probably your least likely option. Answer c is unfeasible because you cannot build an index in a read-only tablespace. Answers d and e are incorrect and essentially the same—you're in a 24x7 environment and you don't want to severely impact your users. You would use the technique loosely described in answer e to export the DDL for the index, then use the DDL to create the index. Neither d nor e is optimal, but they might be your only hope if you cannot rebuild the index online—that is, if your init.ora **COMPATIBILITY** parameter is set to **8.0** or less.

Question 2

A _____ index would be used if you had multiple NLS collating sequences.

A function-based index is used to implement multiple NLS collating sequences. Any time you see references to NLS and indexes in the same sentence, think function-based indexes.

Question 3

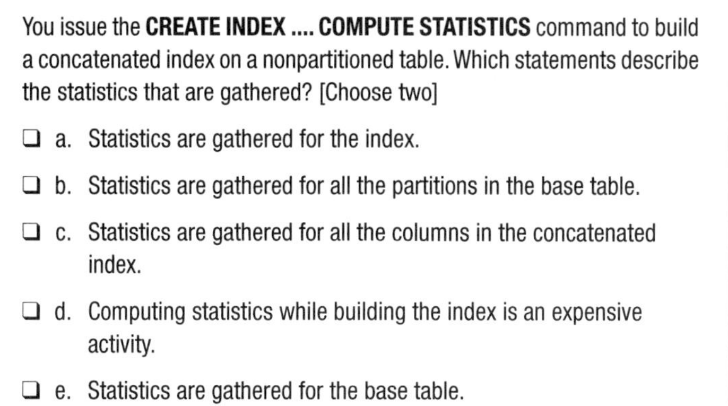

You issue the **CREATE INDEX .... COMPUTE STATISTICS** command to build a concatenated index on a nonpartitioned table. Which statements describe the statistics that are gathered? [Choose two]

- ❑ a. Statistics are gathered for the index.
- ❑ b. Statistics are gathered for all the partitions in the base table.
- ❑ c. Statistics are gathered for all the columns in the concatenated index.
- ❑ d. Computing statistics while building the index is an expensive activity.
- ❑ e. Statistics are gathered for the base table.

Answers a and e are correct. Because this is a concatenated index on a nonpartitioned table, statistics are gathered for the table, the index, and the leftmost column in the concatenated index. Answer b is incorrect because the question specifically states that this is a nonpartitioned table. Answer c is incorrect because statistics are gathered for only the leftmost column (not all columns) in the concatenated index. Answer d is incorrect because computing statistics during the index building process is relatively inexpensive.

Question 4

In the following code, which type of index are we creating?

```
CREATE INDEX emp_name_nls_indx
ON emptab (NLSSORT(name, 'NLS_SORT = Italian'));
```

- ❍ a. Reverse-key
- ❍ b. Descending
- ❍ c. Bitmapped
- ❍ d. Function-based
- ❍ e. Procedure-based

Answer d is correct. A function-based index includes a user-defined, third-party, or Oracle-supplied function on one or more columns in the table. Function-based indexes are very useful with NLS collating sequences. Answers a, b, and c are actual index types, but we're not creating them in this question. Reverse-key indexes actually reverse the table column data in the index, and they are created by adding the keyword **REVERSE** to the **CREATE INDEX** statement. Descending indexes are sorted in a descending order, and we use the **DESC** keyword when creating the index. Bitmap indexes are useful for low-cardinality data, and we use the **BITMAP** keyword when creating the index. Answer e is incorrect because there is no such thing as a procedure-based index.

Question 5

Which of these statements about building indexes online are true? [Choose two]

- ❑ a. No locks are placed on the base table when an index is built online.
- ❑ b. An online index rebuild will be delayed if users have row-level locks on the base table.
- ❑ c. DDL is allowed during online index rebuilds.
- ❑ d. DML is allowed, but large transactions affecting more than half the data should be avoided.
- ❑ e. Bitmap indexes can be rebuilt online, but you must also use the **COMPUTE STATISTICS** option.

Answers b and d are correct. If there are active transactions on the base table, or someone has an exclusive lock on the table, the online index build will simply wait for the lock or locks to be released. DML is allowed, but large-scale changes will slow down the process. Answer a is incorrect because locks are briefly placed on the base table. Answer c is incorrect because DDL is not allowed during the building process. Answer e is incorrect because you cannot rebuild bitmap indexes online, and you cannot use the **COMPUTE STATISTICS** option with the **ONLINE** option.

Question 6

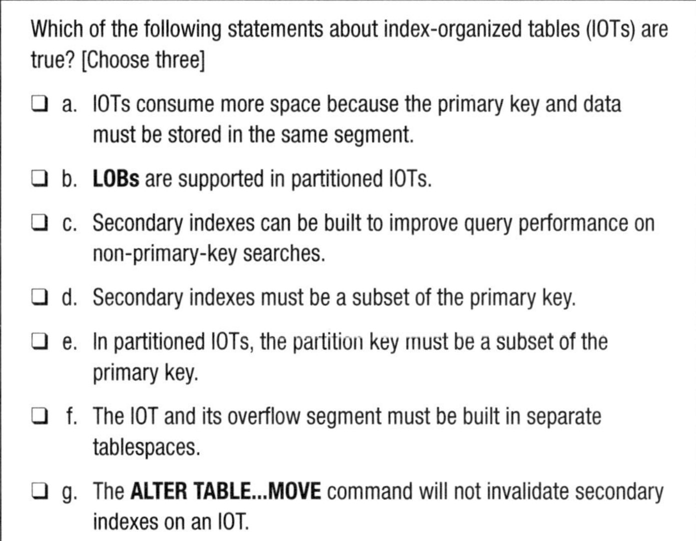

Which of the following statements about index-organized tables (IOTs) are true? [Choose three]

- ❑ a. IOTs consume more space because the primary key and data must be stored in the same segment.
- ❑ b. **LOBs** are supported in partitioned IOTs.
- ❑ c. Secondary indexes can be built to improve query performance on non-primary-key searches.
- ❑ d. Secondary indexes must be a subset of the primary key.
- ❑ e. In partitioned IOTs, the partition key must be a subset of the primary key.
- ❑ f. The IOT and its overflow segment must be built in separate tablespaces.
- ❑ g. The **ALTER TABLE...MOVE** command will not invalidate secondary indexes on an IOT.

Answers c, e, and g are correct. In Oracle8i, you can build secondary indexes on IOTs. The partition key must be a subset of the primary key, which means that only one partition needs to be searched to verify uniqueness. Because secondary indexes rely on a logical **ROWID**, reorganizing a table will not invalidate the **ROWID** reference, as it would in an ordinary table. Answer a is incorrect because IOTs consume less space than storing the primary key and base table separately. Answer b is incorrect because **LOBs** are not supported in partitioned IOTs, but they are supported in nonpartitioned IOTs. Answer d is incorrect because secondary indexes need not be a part of the primary key. Answer f is incorrect because the overflow segment is by default built in the same tablespace as the IOT primary key.

Question 7

Secondary _______ can be built on an IOT to improve query performance.

Secondary indexes can be built on an IOT to improve non-primary-key searches. Remember that bitmap secondary indexes on IOTs are not supported.

Question 8

Which of the following columns in the **DBA_TABLES** view would you query to view IOT information? [Choose two]

- ❑ a. **IOT_PK**
- ❑ b. **IOT_TYPE**
- ❑ c. **IOT_NAME**
- ❑ d. **IOT_OBJECT**
- ❑ e. **IOT_PART**

Answers b and c are correct. The columns **IOT_TYPE** and **IOT_NAME** are not new to Oracle8i, and they indicate that a table is an IOT. Answers a, d, and e are not valid columns in the **DBA_TABLES** view.

Question 9

IOTs are a good choice for 24x7 operations because of which of the following reasons? [Choose three]

- ❑ a. IOTs can be partitioned, allowing partition maintenance while the other partitions are online.
- ❑ b. IOTs can be **MOVED ONLINE**, which allows user DML while the table is reorganized.
- ❑ c. You can rebuild the primary key index in an IOT without rebuilding the base table, making maintenance easier.
- ❑ d. You can create multiple primary keys on an IOT, making the table more reliable.
- ❑ e. Partitioned IOTs support **LOBs** and bitmapped indexes, so you can reorganize the IOT offline while the users still have access to the **LOBs**.
- ❑ f. IOTs and their overflow segments can be taken offline separately for maintenance.
- ❑ g. Secondary indexes on IOTs can be rebuilt online.

Answers a, b, and g are correct. Partitioning and its associated maintenance features are definitely beneficial in a 24x7 environment. You can move one partition without locking the entire table. Moving the index online complements the partitioning feature, allowing DML during the table moving operation. Secondary indexes can be rebuilt using the **ONLINE** clause, as with ordinary tables. Answer c is incorrect because the primary key and the base table are integrated, meaning that rebuilding or moving the IOT affects the primary key and the base table data. Answer d is incorrect because there can be only one primary key on an IOT, just as there can be only one primary key on an ordinary table. Answer e is incorrect because bitmapped indexes are not supported in partitioned IOTs. Answer f is incorrect because overflow segments are not taken offline for maintenance.

Question 10

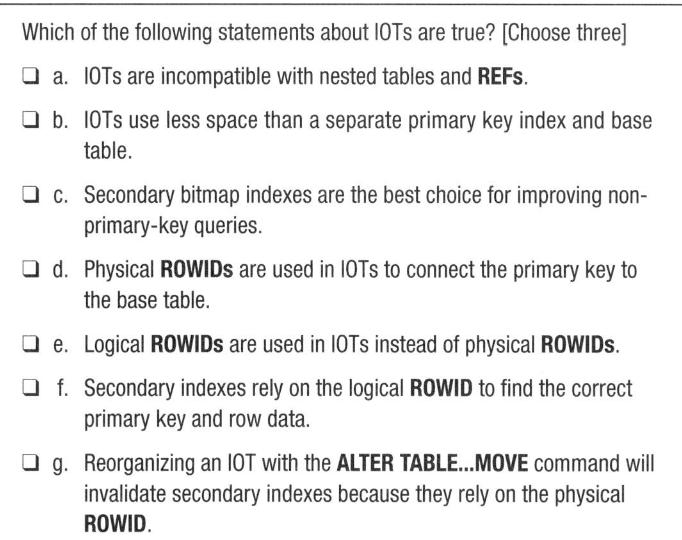

Which of the following statements about IOTs are true? [Choose three]

- ❑ a. IOTs are incompatible with nested tables and **REFs**.
- ❑ b. IOTs use less space than a separate primary key index and base table.
- ❑ c. Secondary bitmap indexes are the best choice for improving non-primary-key queries.
- ❑ d. Physical **ROWIDs** are used in IOTs to connect the primary key to the base table.
- ❑ e. Logical **ROWIDs** are used in IOTs instead of physical **ROWIDs**.
- ❑ f. Secondary indexes rely on the logical **ROWID** to find the correct primary key and row data.
- ❑ g. Reorganizing an IOT with the **ALTER TABLE...MOVE** command will invalidate secondary indexes because they rely on the physical **ROWID**.

Answers b, e, and f are correct. One of the major selling points of the IOT is that it uses less space because primary key data is not duplicated. Logical **ROWIDs** are used to locate the actual data when you're using a secondary index. The primary key, not the physical **ROWID**, is the IOT unique identifier. Answer a is incorrect because IOTs are compatible with nested tables and **REFs**. Answer c is incorrect because bitmapped indexes are not allowed as secondary indexes. Answer d is incorrect because physical **ROWIDs** are not used; the base table information is stored in the leaf blocks of the index. Answer g is incorrect because secondary indexes rely on a logical **ROWID**, which is not invalidated when an IOT is moved.

Need to Know More?

Austin, David, Meghraj Thakkar, and Kurt Lysy. *Migrating to Oracle8i.* Sams Publishing, 2000. ISBN 0-672-31577-7. A good discussion on migration and upgrade issues related to index-organized tables.

Scherer, Douglas, et al. *Oracle8i Tips & Techniques.* Oracle Press, 1999. ISBN 0-07-212103-3. Some practical examples of function-based indexes.

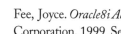

The following documents are available on the Oracle server installation CD, or you can download them from **http://technet.oracle.com.**

Fee, Joyce. *Oracle8i Administrator's Guide* (Part No. A67772-01). Oracle Corporation, 1999. See Chapter 14 for a description of managing index-organized tables.

Raphaely, Denis. *Oracle8i Application Developer's Guide—Fundamentals* (Part No. A68003-01). Oracle Corporation, 1999. See chapters 6 and 7 for a thorough discussion of indexing strategies and index-organized tables.

Leverenz, Lefty and Diana Rehfield. *Oracle8i Concepts* (Part No. A67781-01). Oracle Corporation, 1999. See Chapter 10 for a description of indexes and index-organized tables.

Visit the Oracle Technet Website: **http://technet.oracle.com/**.

Recovery Manager (RMAN) Enhancements

Terms you'll need to understand:

✓ RMAN recovery catalog

✓ Media Management API

✓ Crosscheck

✓ **LIST** and **REPORT** commands

✓ **CREATE CATALOG** command

✓ **UPGRADE CATALOG** command

✓ **DROP CATALOG** command

✓ **DUPLICATE** command

✓ Node affinity detection

✓ Tablespace point-in-time recovery (TSPITR)

✓ **V$BACKUP_SYNC_IO** view

✓ **V$BACKUP_ASYNC_IO** view

Techniques you'll need to master:

✓ Using RMAN without a recovery catalog

✓ Crosschecking backup sets

✓ Issuing new **LIST**, **REPORT**, and database maintenance commands

✓ Creating, upgrading, and dropping a recovery catalog

✓ Using new RMAN performance views

The Oracle Recovery Manager (RMAN) utility was introduced in Oracle8 and has been enhanced for Oracle8i. New commands have been added to crosscheck backups, make catalog maintenance easier, and make recovery less cumbersome. In this chapter, we'll explain the enhancements in detail.

Optional Recovery Catalog

The recovery catalog is not essential, but more backup and recovery options are available when the recovery catalog is used; also, Oracle recommends that you use the recovery catalog. Given that a recovery catalog gives you more options, why wouldn't you use one? Here are a few reasons why you might not want to use a recovery catalog:

- The recovery catalog requires storage space in a schema in an Oracle database.
- You will need to back up the database that contains the recovery catalog.
- The recovery catalog must exist in a database other than the target database.

If you choose not to use a recovery catalog, RMAN will look in the control file of the target database for needed information. In this case, Oracle recommends that you use multiple multiplexed or mirrored control files on separate disks, and back them up regularly. Also, many RMAN commands are not available unless you use a recovery catalog. Here is a list of RMAN commands that require the use of a recovery catalog:

- CHANGE...AVAILABLE
- DROP CATALOG
- LIST INCARNATION
- CHANGE...UNAVAILABLE
- CREATE SCRIPT
- REGISTER DATABASE
- CHANGE...UNCATALOG
- DELETE SCRIPT
- REPORT SCHEMA AT TIME
- CHANGE BACKUPSET...CROSSCHECK
- REPLACE SCRIPT
- RESET DATABASE

- CHANGE BACKUPPIECE...CROSSCHECK
- PRINT SCRIPT
- RESTORE (without a control file)
- CREATE CATALOG
- CROSSCHECK BACKUP
- RESYNC CATALOG
- UPGRADE CATALOG
- DELETE EXPIRED BACKUP
- SET AUXNAME

Even without the recovery catalog, you can verify that a backup is good by issuing the command **VALIDATE BACKUPSET**. You can use the **RESTORE...VALIDATE** command without a recovery catalog to confirm that the backup is good. Also, you can clean up the control file and remove unwanted backups on disk by using the **CHANGE...DELETE** command.

If you lose all of your control files, you weren't using a recovery catalog, and you need to recover a database, then you'll need to call Oracle Support for assistance.

The Media Management API

RMAN now supports the Oracle Media Management API v2.0, and support for v1.1 is maintained. The API is used to interface between RMAN and third-party tape-backup software so that different types of storage devices can be used for backup and recovery.

The Oracle Media Management API is also known as the System Backup to Tape (SBT) API, the media management layer, or the Media Management Library (MML).

Enhancements in media management include the following:

- *Proxy copy*—A new enhancement called *proxy copy* enables media-management software to handle the data transfer involved in a backup or restore operation. When the **PROXY** keyword is used with the **BACKUP** command, RMAN provides a list of files that need backup or recovery, and the media-management software takes over the transfer of data between disk and storage device. (Not all third-party media-management software supports this option.)
- *Media pool selection*—The new **POOL** keyword is used with the **BACKUP** command to assign a backup set to a storage pool, as defined in the media-management software.
- *Vendor identification*—The RMAN log indicates the media-management product used for backup when a channel is allocated.
- *Improved error messages*—The RMAN log indicates errors encountered by the media-management software.
- *SEND command*—You can send commands directly from an RMAN session to the media-management software by using the **SEND** command. Use this to control runtime options of the media management software that can not be controlled using other RMAN commands.

Crosschecking Backup Sets

If you're backing up to tape and you want to synchronize the recovery catalog information with the information stored in your tape media manager's catalog, or if you're backing up to disk and you want to verify that a backup exists, you can use the new crosschecking commands. To use these new commands, you must have a recovery catalog. The new commands are:

- CROSSCHECK BACKUP—Allows you to check whether an **AVAILABLE** or an **EXPIRED** backup set or proxy copy exists on disk or tape. You must allocate a channel before you issue this command at the RMAN prompt.
- DELETE EXPIRED BACKUP—Updates a backup set's recovery catalog status from **EXPIRED** to **DELETED**. You must issue this command at the RMAN prompt, and do so only after allocating a channel for maintenance or deletion.
- CHANGE...CROSSCHECK—Changes the status of a backup set or copy. Use this command to crosscheck backup sets or image copies and to change the status if the backup set or copy is not found.

With both the CHANGE...CROSSCHECK and CROSSCHECK BACKUP commands, if a backup piece or copy is not found, it will be marked EXPIRED in the catalog. The status of the backup in the RMAN recovery catalog can then match the information in the media-management software for tape backups, and match the information on disk for disk backups.

New and Enhanced Maintenance Commands

Oracle8i has improved and added various commands for getting information about backups and for managing recovery catalogs and databases.

LIST and REPORT Commands

In Oracle8i, the output from the LIST BACKUP command has been improved, and a new report for data-file redundancy has been added:

- LIST BACKUP—The output is easier to read, showing backups in a backup set in their own section.
- REPORT NEED BACKUP REDUNDANCY—This new command indicates when you have fewer than a user-specified number of backups of a data file.

Recovery-Catalog Maintenance Commands

In Oracle8, you had to execute the catrman.sql script to create an RMAN recovery catalog. Upgrading the catalog also required running a script. Oracle8i has simplified the process to create, upgrade, and drop a catalog by using the following commands:

- CREATE CATALOG—Replaces the catrman.sql script.
- UPGRADE CATALOG—Upgrades any previous version of the catalog to the current version. No data in the recovery catalog is lost.
- DROP CATALOG—Drops the catalog. Recovery is still possible as long as a control file or duplicate catalog is available.

To create the RMAN recovery catalog in Oracle8i, issue the **CREATE CATALOG** command at the RMAN prompt. This replaces the **catrman.sql** script used in Oracle8.

Database Maintenance Commands

It is now possible to run some database maintenance commands from within RMAN, simplifying the recovery process. The following commands are supported:

- STARTUP—Starts up the database, as you would with SQL*Plus or Server Manager.
- SHUTDOWN—Shuts down the database, as you would with SQL*Plus or Server Manager.
- ALTER DATABASE MOUNT—Mounts an unmounted database, following an instance startup with STARTUP NOMOUNT.
- ALTER DATABASE OPEN—Opens a mounted database, following STARTUP MOUNT, or following STARTUP NOMOUNT and then ALTER DATABASE MOUNT.

Other Commands

The duplicate command doesn't fall into any of the above categories of new commands:

- DUPLICATE—Allows you to use the backup from one database to create another database. This is handy if you want to create a test or development database that is a copy of a production database.

The **DUPLICATE** command can be used to create a database from a backup copy.

Node Affinity Detection

In a parallel server environment on some cluster platforms (AIX and Pyramid Mesh clusters), some nodes in the cluster have faster access to specific data files. The term *affinity* is used to describe this relationship. RMAN automatically detects affinity, and RMAN tries to improve backup performance by using an allocated channel between a node and a data file that have this relationship.

Note: Not all parallel server platforms support node affinity detection.

Backups

New features have been added to safeguard backups. You can now create multiple copies of a backup piece, RMAN now names backup pieces automatically, and RMAN now includes overwrite protection on backup pieces with duplicate names:

- *Duplexed backup sets*—RMAN can now create up to four concurrent copies of each backup piece.
- *Backup piece naming*—In Oracle8 RMAN, you used the **FORMAT** parameter to name backup pieces. This is no longer the case in Oracle8i because RMAN (by default) assigns a unique name to each backup piece.
- *Overwrite protection*—In Oracle8i, RMAN issues an error if you attempt to create a backup piece with the same name as an existing backup piece. In previous versions, the existing backup piece was overwritten if you attempted to create a backup piece with the same name.

TSPITR Without a Recovery Catalog

Tablespace point-in-time recovery (TSPITR) allows you to recover a tablespace to a point in time different from the other tablespaces in the database. In Oracle8i, you can use RMAN to perform TSPITR without a recovery catalog. However, some restrictions apply:

- RMAN assumes that the current rollback segments were the same ones present at the recovery point in time.
- When you're recovering to a remote time (really far back), it might not be possible to perform TSPITR because Oracle might have reused the records of the copies and backups.

TSPITR is a complex exercise, so please review the Oracle backup and recovery documentation before you attempt it. Experiment in a test environment before you attempt it in a production environment.

V$ Performance Views for RMAN Backups

Oracle8i includes two new views to monitor RMAN backup progress and performance. Use these views to identify backup performance issues and to monitor backup and restoration progress on a file-by-file basis.

V$BACKUP_SYNC_IO

When the backup operation I/O is synchronous, the **V$BACKUP_SYNC_IO** view will contain rows. With synchronous I/O, you evaluate potential performance issues by comparing the bytes-per-second rate to the maximum throughput of the backup device. Compare the expected throughput of the device to the actual I/O rate value, which is in the DISCRETE_BYTES_PER_SECOND column.

V$BACKUP_ASYNC_IO

When the backup operation I/O is asynchronous, the V$BACKUP_ASYNC_IO view will contain rows. To determine if a file is a bottleneck to the operation, add the values of the LONG_WAITS and SHORT_WAITS columns, and compare the sum to the value of the IO_COUNT column. If you compare these values across all files in the operation, you'll see which files are potential bottlenecks.

For detailed information on tuning RMAN performance by using the **V$BACKUP_ASYNC_IO** and **V$BACKUP_SYNC_IO** views, see *Oracle8i Performance Tuning,* Chapter 20, "Tuning I/O."

Additional New Features in Release 2

New features in release 8.1.6 include the following:

- The **autolocate** option of the SET command causes RMAN to automatically discover which nodes of an OPS cluster contain the backups that you want to restore.
- The CONFIGURE COMPATIBLE command controls the compatibility of the recovery catalog packages with the RMAN executable.
- The **resetlogs** option of the ALTER DATABASE command allows you to open the datbase with the RESET LOGS option.
- The CHANGE...DELETE, DELETE EXPIRED, and BACKUP ...DELETE INPUT commands can now remove catalog records rather than update them to status DELETED.

Practice Questions

Question 1

Which of the following views are used for RMAN performance monitoring? [Choose two]

- ❑ a. **V$RMAN_THROUGHPUT**
- ❑ b. **V$BACKUP_SYNC_IO**
- ❑ c. **V$BACKUP_PERFORMANCE**
- ❑ d. **V$BACKUP_ASYNC_IO**
- ❑ e. **V$RMAN_BACKUP_IO**

Answers b and d are correct. The **V$BACKUP_SYNC_IO** view is used to monitor synchronous I/O throughput, and the **V$BACKUP_ASYNC_IO** view is used to monitor asynchronous I/O throughput. During RMAN backup operations, each view will be populated if the corresponding I/O type is used. Answers a, c, and e are incorrect because they are not valid V$ performance views.

Question 2

You can recover a tablespace to a point in time other than that of the rest of the database by using ________.

The answer is TSPITR (tablespace point-in-time recovery). TSPITR is used to recover a tablespace that contains objects that might have been inadvertently dropped or modified. You can use TSPITR to recover the objects in a tablespace without affecting the rest of the database.

Question 3

Which of the following statements about the recovery catalog is true?

- ❍ a. Issue the command **CREATE CATALOG** to build a recovery catalog.
- ❍ b. Issue the command **DELETE CATALOG** to remove a recovery catalog.
- ❍ c. The command **MIGRATE CATALOG** migrates Oracle7 RMAN catalogs to the current version.
- ❍ d. The command **UPGRADE CATALOG** upgrades the catalog structure but removes the contents of the catalog.

Answer a is correct. The RMAN command **CREATE CATALOG** has been added in Oracle8i to make recovery catalogs easier to create. In previous versions, the DBA ran the catrman.sql script to create the recovery catalog. Answer b is incorrect because the **DROP CATALOG** command is used to remove a recovery catalog. Answer c is incorrect because the **UPGRADE CATALOG** command is used to upgrade a recovery catalog to the current version, and RMAN wasn't available with Oracle7. Answer d is incorrect because the **UPGRADE CATALOG** command upgrades the catalog structure and keeps the contents intact.

Question 4

Which of the following statements about node affinity detection in RMAN are true? [Choose two]

- ❑ a. It is available on all parallel server platforms.
- ❑ b. It improves backup performance on non-parallel server systems.
- ❑ c. It is available on some, but not all, parallel server platforms.
- ❑ d. It improves backup performance on selected parallel server systems.
- ❑ e. It improves performance by selecting the least-busy communication channel between disks and tape in a parallel backup environment.

Answers c and d are correct. This feature is available on some, but not all, parallel server platforms. Node affinity detection speeds up backup operations by using nodes that have faster access to the disks. Answer a is incorrect because not all parallel server platforms are supported. Answer b is incorrect because node affinity detection is specific to parallel server systems. Answer e is incorrect because communication channel usage between disk and tape is not a factor in determining node-to-disk affinity.

Question 5

What is the maximum number of concurrent copies of a backup piece that you can make in RMAN?

- ❍ a. 1
- ❍ b. 2
- ❍ c. 4
- ❍ d. 8
- ❍ e. 16

Answer c is correct. RMAN can now create up to four concurrent copies of each backup piece. This is called *duplexing*.

Question 6

Which of the following commands are used to verify that a backup set is valid? [Choose two]

- ❑ a. **CROSSCHECK BACKUP**
- ❑ b. **CHANGE...CROSSCHECK**
- ❑ c. **VALIDATE BACKUP CROSSCHECK**
- ❑ d. **DELETE...CROSSCHECK**
- ❑ e. **CROSSCHECK RESTORE**

Answers a and b are correct. Use the **CROSSCHECK BACKUP** command or the **CHANGE...CROSSCHECK** command to validate that a backup set is available. Answers c, d, and e are not valid RMAN commands.

Question 7

Which of the following RMAN commands is used to create a new database by using a backup from another database?

- ❍ a. **REPLICATE**
- ❍ b. **DUPLICATE**
- ❍ c. **RESTORE NEW**
- ❍ d. **CREATE NEW DATABASE FROM BACKUP**
- ❍ e. **REPLICATE...STANDBY**

Answer b is correct. With the **DUPLICATE** command, you can use the backup from one database to create another database. Answer a is incorrect because the **REPLICATE** command is used to replicate control files. Answers c, d, and e are incorrect because they are not valid RMAN commands.

Question 8

Which of the following database commands are valid in RMAN? [Choose two]

- ❑ a. **ALTER DATABASE OPEN**
- ❑ b. **ALTER SYSTEM**
- ❑ c. **ALTER TABLESPACE**
- ❑ d. **ALTER DATAFILE**
- ❑ e. **SHUTDOWN**

Answers a and e are correct. **STARTUP**, **SHUTDOWN** (answer e), **ALTER DATABASE MOUNT**, and **ALTER DATABASE OPEN** (answer a) are valid database commands that you can issue from within RMAN. Answers b, c, and d are incorrect because they are not valid RMAN commands.

Question 9

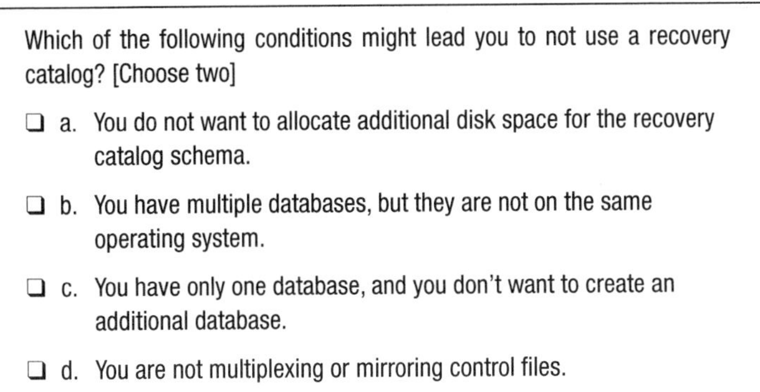

Which of the following conditions might lead you to not use a recovery catalog? [Choose two]

- ❑ a. You do not want to allocate additional disk space for the recovery catalog schema.
- ❑ b. You have multiple databases, but they are not on the same operating system.
- ❑ c. You have only one database, and you don't want to create an additional database.
- ❑ d. You are not multiplexing or mirroring control files.

Answers a and c are correct. The RMAN recovery catalog requires storage space in a database schema. If you do not want to allocate space to create the recovery catalog, you can still use RMAN to recover your database. If you have only one database and you don't want to create a second, RMAN can still use the control file to obtain information needed for recovery. Answer b is incorrect because you can create your recovery catalog in a database that resides on a different hardware platform or operating system. Answer d is incorrect because if you are not multiplexing or mirroring control files, you should use a recovery catalog. If you lose your control files and you are not using a recovery catalog, you should call Oracle Support for assistance.

Question 10

Which of the following RMAN commands require a recovery catalog? [Choose two]

- ❑ a. **SHUTDOWN**
- ❑ b. **CROSSCHECK BACKUP**
- ❑ c. **ALTER DATABASE OPEN**
- ❑ d. **RESTORE** (without a control file)
- ❑ e. **DUPLICATE**

Answers b and d are correct. To crosscheck a backup, you must have a recovery catalog. If you don't have a control file and you attempt to recover a database, you'll need a recovery catalog. Answers a, c, and e are valid RMAN commands even if you don't have a recovery catalog.

Need to Know More?

Ault, Michael. *Oracle8i Administration and Management.* Wiley Computer Publishing, 2000. Chapter 15 provides fundamental information on RMAN and then walks readers through RMAN installation and an incomplete-recovery scenario.

Austin, David, Meghraj Thakkar, and Kurt Lysy. *Migrating to Oracle8i.* Sams Publishing, 2000. ISBN 0-672-31577-7. See Chapter 21 for a thorough explanation of RMAN, backup and recovery strategies, and recovery scenarios.

Freeman, Robert. *Oracle DBA 7.3 to 8 Upgrade Exam Cram.* The Coriolis Group, 2000. Chapter 10 covers the RMAN essentials for Oracle8, most of which apply in Oracle8i.

The following resources are available on the Oracle server installation CD, or you can download them from **http://technet.oracle.com**.

Bauer, Mark. *Oracle8i Parallel Server Concepts and Administration* (Part No. A67778-01). Oracle Corporation, 1999. See the chapter that contains a description of node affinity detection and information on using RMAN in a parallel server environment.

Bauer, Mark. *Oracle8i Tuning, Release 8.1.5* (Part No. A67775-01). Oracle Corporation, 1999. The "Tuning I/O" chapter covers the V$ views that you'll want to monitor while performing backup and recovery operations with RMAN.

Baylis, Ruth and Paul Lane. *Getting to Know Oracle8i* (Part No. A68020-01). Oracle Corporation, 1999. See the chapter that lists the Oracle8i RMAN enhancements, with links to detailed descriptions.

Dialeris, Connie, Joyce Fee, and Lance Ashdown. *Oracle8i Backup and Recovery Guide* (Part No. A67773-01 for version 8.1.5, A76993 for version 8.1.6). Oracle Corporation, 1999. The 8.1.5 version of this document includes backup & recovery using RMAN; the 8.1.6 version includes some information on RMAN, but the 8.1.6 RMAN guide has the complete details.

Beusee, Don, Greg Pongracz, Francisco Sanchez, and Steve Wertheimer. *Oracle8i Recovery Manager User's Guide and Reference Release* (Part No. A76990-01). Oracle Corporation, 1999. RMAN has its own document for 8.1.6.

Visit the Oracle Technet Web site: **http://technet.oracle.com**.

Partitioning Tables and Indexes in Oracle8i

Terms you'll need to understand:

- ✓ Partition
- ✓ Subpartition
- ✓ Range partitioning
- ✓ Hash partitioning
- ✓ Composite partitioning
- ✓ Equipartitioned
- ✓ Nonequipartitioned
- ✓ Partition pruning
- ✓ Partition-wise joins
- ✓ Global indexes
- ✓ Local indexes
- ✓ DML locks

Techniques you'll need to master:

- ✓ Describing the new methods of partitioning tables in Oracle8i
- ✓ Partitioning a table in Oracle8i with the new partitioning methods introduced in Oracle8i
- ✓ Describing the new methods of partitioning indexes in Oracle8i
- ✓ Partitioning an index in Oracle8i with the new partitioning methods introduced in Oracle8i
- ✓ Describing the restrictions that pertain to the new partitioning methods introduced in Oracle8i

Oracle8 introduced table and index partitioning, and Oracle8i improves on these features. In this chapter, we'll cover all the partitioning information you need to know for the Oracle8i OCP upgrade exam. This will include basic partition concepts, such as partitioned tables and indexes, and new Oracle8i partition features, such as hash partitioning, composite partitioning, and partitioning of large objects. Likewise, you'll need to understand how to maintain partitions and how to use the various data dictionary views that are required to manage them.

Overview of Partitioned Tables

In this section, we'll look at the reasons for partitioning, the types of systems that might benefit from partitioning, and Oracle8i partition options, including range partitioning, hash partitioning, and composite partitioning. We'll then look at the difference between equipartitioning and nonequipartitioning of Oracle objects. Finally, we'll review the concepts of partition pruning and partition-wise joins.

Basics of Partitioning Tables

Partitioning is a method of splitting an object (a table or index) into separate parts (*partitions*) based on some criterion that is assigned to the partition. The criterion might be a date range, a number range, or any other possible value. Imagine, for example, that you have a huge table that is driving you crazy because queries on it are really slow. You get so mad at this table that you take a logical hatchet and begin to slice the table up into many smaller tables, based on the date of the record in each row. Each of these smaller tables is a partition. Each table has the same columns, and each stores a certain amount of data. Oracle collectively deals with these physical partitions as a single logical object—called the partitioned table or index—that you can access.

In Oracle8i, you can partition the following items: tables, indexes on tables, index-organized tables, materialized views, and indexes on materialized views. Currently Oracle doesn't support partitioning of clusters or indexes on clusters.

Why partition tables and indexes? As time goes on, certain objects tend to grow quickly, some becoming very large indeed. This can lead to several problems. As a nonpartitioned table grows larger:

- Queries take longer and longer to run.
- More time is needed to back up the tablespace in which the table resides.
- More time is needed to recover the tablespace, because the tablespace grows larger.

- The table becomes harder to manage. Object management issues, such as storage parameters and defragmentation, become more complicated as an object gets bigger.
- You cannot assign different parts of the nonpartitioned table to other tablespaces. This ability might make for better performance and faster backup and recovery.

Partitioning is one method of dealing effectively with these problems. It's a particularly effective strategy with certain types of very large databases (VLDBs). Partitioning can be used with Decision Support System (DSS) databases, which typically store and process large amounts of data using complex queries. Partitioning might also assist with VLDBs that handle Online Transaction Processing (OLTP). These databases may store large amounts of data, have high rates of concurrent activity, and have relatively simple queries processing a small amount of data.

In version 8i, Oracle has improved on the partitioning benefits introduced in Oracle8. In Oracle8, you could only partition based on data values in a column using a partitioning method called *range partitioning*. Now, in Oracle8i, you can use range partitioning or you can partition a table based on a hash algorithm created in a column using a partitioning method called *hash partitioning*. In Oracle8i you also can use a combination of both methods, called *composite partitioning*.

The general benefits of partitioning include the following:

- *Performance*—Partitioning allows you to segment your data in different tablespaces. For example, if you had two sets of disks to choose from—slow ones and very fast ones—you might choose to partition your general-ledger data differently. You might partition the most current (and most commonly accessed) dates in your general-ledger table into one or more tablespaces residing on the faster disks because the performance on these often-accessed partitions will be better. You might also partition the older (and less frequently accessed) dates into different tablespaces created on the slower disks.

  There are significant potential performance gains from queries executed against partitioned tables. In an action known as *partition pruning*, the optimizer in Oracle8 removes partitions that don't need to be accessed during a query. If the rows in the partition aren't needed, based on the partition range with which the partition was created, then Oracle will prune (remove) that partition from the query, and Oracle won't scan that partition, although it will scan the needed partitions of the same table. This pruning reduces the total I/O required, and thus the time required, to execute a query.

By using partitioned tables, you can further expand on Oracle8's parallel DML and DDL capabilities. These offer even greater potential performance gains.

- *Recoverability and availability*—You can create multiple partitions on separate tablespaces (and thus on different physical devices), and this potentially reduces the scope of an outage if a disk device fails. Individual partitions can be recovered by the DBA, and while the partition is being recovered, other partitions in the table can still be used. Also, you can back up specific partitions rather than the entire table. In addition, spreading the object across several disks reduces the impact of the failure of a single disk. Should a disk fail, the user would only encounter an error if an attempt were made to access the partition on that disk.
- *Maintenance*—Partitions are easy to control. Each partition can have its own storage parameters, and you can control where each partition is created. You can maintain a particular partition's data (e.g., perform a data load that locks the partition) while the other partitions remain available to the user population, although in some cases indexes might be unavailable for the duration of the load. Also, you can load data into multiple partitions at the same time.
- *Reduction of backup windows*—Tablespaces for a partition can be read-only if that partition isn't going to be modified. This relieves backup requirements completely for that partition. Because you can define tablespaces as read-only, you can force parts of a partitioned object to be read-only and other parts to be read-write. This can reduce backup requirements and reduce the time needed for backups because read-only tablespaces don't need to be constantly backed up.

Table Partitioning Methods in Oracle8i

Oracle8i provides three methods of partitioning tables: range partitioning, hash partitioning, and composite partitioning. In the examples throughout this section, we'll use a table called **sales_detail_data**. Listing 13.1 provides an example of this table.

Listing 13.1 Description of the **sales_detail_data** table.

```
SQL> DESC sales_detail_data
 Name                           Null?    Type
 ------------------------------ -------- ----
 date_of_sale                   NOT NULL DATE
 invoice_number                 NOT NULL NUMBER
 item_line_no                   NOT NULL NUMBER
 item_sku                       NOT NULL CHAR(20)
 qty_sold                       NOT NULL NUMBER
```

Range-Partitioned Tables

Using the sample **sales_detail_data table** shown earlier, you might decide to partition by the **date_of_sale** column. This is a logical choice because the date of a record falls into a logical range of values, and records stored by date should be evenly distributed over the date range that you'll partition on. In this case, you might choose to include one quarter's worth of data in each partition. Partitioning the table in this manner is known as *range partitioning*. Range partitioning was the only kind of partitioning available in Oracle8, but it's one of three partitioning options in Oracle8i.

With range partitioning, you are partitioning the table based on a range of values defined in the partition key. In this example, because we're partitioning on the **date_of_sale** column, we have made it the partition key. The *partition key* is a column or a series of up to 16 columns that contains a range of values by which you partition an object. You choose the partition key of a table based on a number of factors, including the nature of the data, its volume, and its volatility. The partition key *cannot* consist of the following:

- A LEVEL or **ROWID** pseudo-column
- A column of the **ROWID** data type
- A nested table, **VARRAY**, object type, or **REF** column (discussed in Chapter 12)
- Any LOB column (**BFILE, CLOB, BLOB, NCLOB**)

See the Creating Partitioned Tables section later in this chapter for more details on partitioning tables using the range partition method. Figure 13.1 provides an example of a range partitioned table.

Hash-Partitioned Tables and Their Benefits

You might discover that your sales are a bit unbalanced in the range you have partitioned it over (for example, Christmas sales might be significantly higher than March sales). In this case, you might decide that you want to use hash partitioning on the **sales_detail_data** table.

When you use hash partitioning, Oracle will create a hash value based on a list of columns that you provide as the partition key. That hash value is then used to determine which partition to store the data in. This has the effect of balancing the data across the partitions of the table. Hash partitioning should be considered for the following reasons:

- Hash partitioning might provide a better opportunity than range partitioning to take full advantage of partition pruning, partition-wise joins, and parallel DML.
- The sizes of range partitions will differ dramatically.
- You aren't sure how data is distributed for a given range.

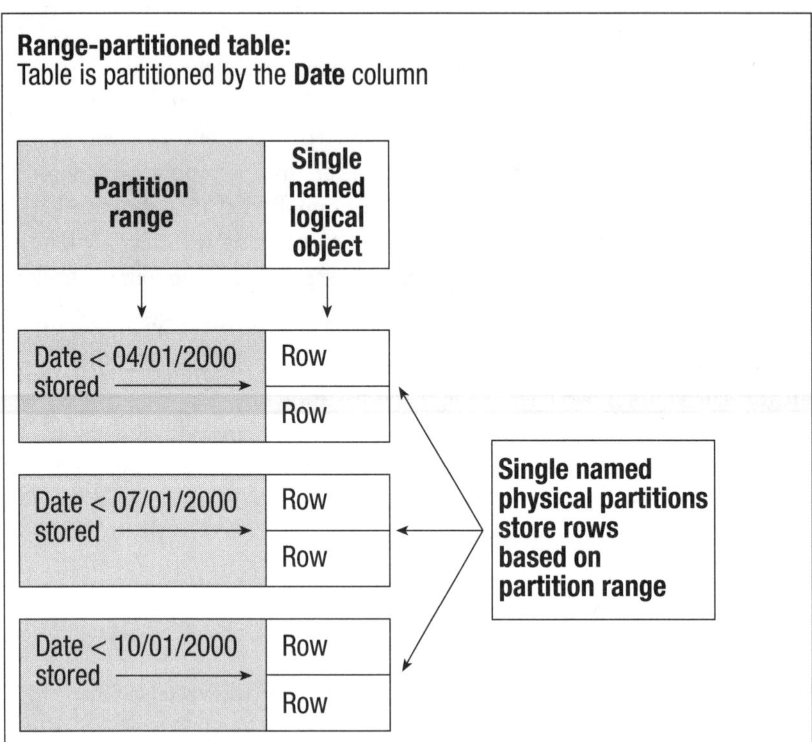

Figure 13.1 Example of a range-partitioned table.

When you create a hash-partitioned table, Oracle suggests that you make the number of partitions a power of two (two, four, eight, and so on) to obtain the most even data distribution. Also, when creating a hash partitioned table, you can specify partition names for associated local partitioned indexes that are created on a hash-partitioned table. See the Creating Partitioned Tables section later in this chapter for more details on partitioning tables using the range partition method. An example of a hash partitioned table is shown in Figure 13.2.

Composite-Partitioned Tables and Their Benefits

Composite partitioning combines range partitioning and hash partitioning into one powerful partitioning option. With composite partitioning, Oracle first partitions the data based on a range partition key that you define (for example, by date of sale). The data in the each partition range is then subpartitioned based on a hash-partition column (for example, invoice number). Thus, you have the benefit of range partitioning (i.e. partition maintenance operations, such as being able to truncate all of January's data) while also benefiting from a more even distribution of the data via the hash subpartitions.

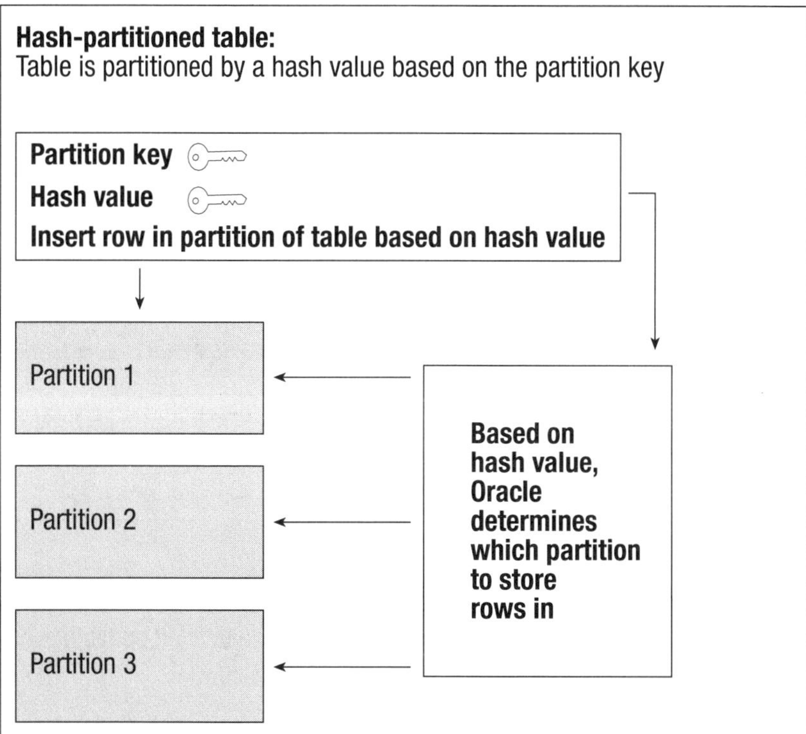

Figure 13.2 Example of a hash-partitioned table.

Note that the composite table's range partitions are never actually created. Rather, they define where a row can be stored in the underlying hash subpartitions of that partitioned table, so the range partitions are really more logical in nature.

A composite partitioned table's hash partitions are grouped based on the range partition key(s). Therefore, when you truncate a given range partition, it will result in the truncation of the underlying, associated hash partitions. Also, there is a one–to-many relationship between a partition range and its underlying hash subpartitions. Thus, one defined range partition can have one or more hash subpartitions. The reverse is not true, however, as any given hash subpartition can belong to only one defined range partition.

Composite partitioning provides several benefits over both range partitioning and hash partitioning. These benefits include:

- The ease of management of range partitioning
- The data placement and parallelism advantages that hash partitioning might provide over range partitioning on a specific table

- The ability to build both local indexes and global range-partitioned indexes on composite-partitioned tables
- The ability to name index subpartitions and their tablespaces
- The ability to name both the partition and the subpartitions

Figure 13.3 provides an example of a composite partitioned table.

Equipartitioned and Nonequipartitioned Objects

You can create *equipartitioned* objects or *nonequipartitioned* objects. Two tables or indexes are said to be equipartitioned if they have *identical logical partitioning attributes*. However, objects don't have to be of the same type to be equipartitioned; a table and an index can be equipartitioned if they have identical logical partitioning attributes.

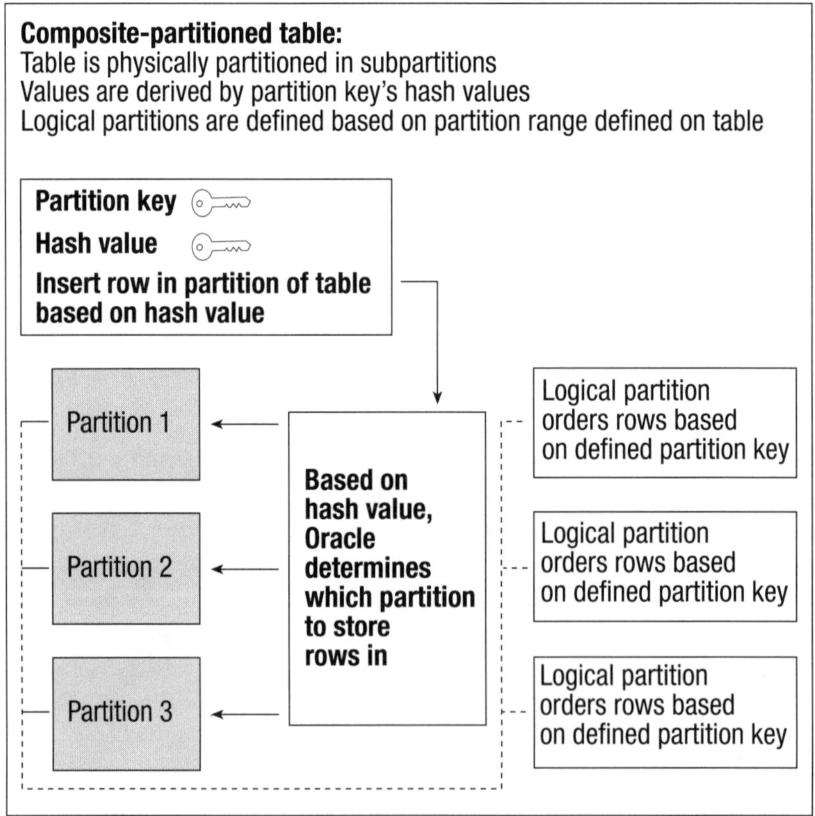

Figure 13.3 Example of a composite-partitioned table.

The benefits of equipartitioning include the following:

- Equipartitioning offers possible performance increases in SQL operations. Equipartitioning table partitions and index partitions can reduce the number of sorts and joins required by the statement.
- Equipartitioning makes tablespace recovery much easier. For example, you can equijoin a parent table and a child table, placing them in the same tablespace. Thus, you could recover corresponding table and index partitions to a specific point in time by using the tablespace point-in-time recovery feature (in the form of the new transportable tablespace feature) available in Oracle8 (see Chapter 10).

  Equipartitioning might also make development platforms easier to use if you often have to recover certain large tables because of data-destructive testing. If you can partition the data being changed into its own partition and its own tablespace, you might get faster recovery back to the point in time before the destructive testing occurred. For an example of the difference between equipartitioning and nonequipartitioning of objects, see Figure 13.4.

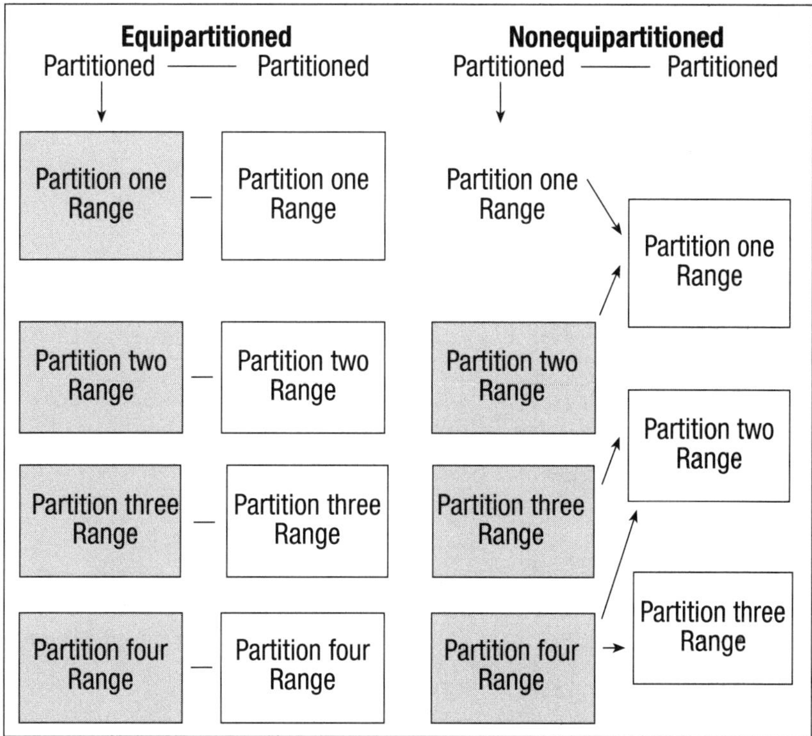

Figure 13.4 Equipartitioned versus nonequipartitioned objects.

- Creating and maintaining equipartitioned indexes on a partitioned table is generally easier than creating and maintaining nonequipartitioned indexes.

Creating Partitioned Tables

This section examines how to create a partitioned table. Using our sample **sales_detail_data** table, we'll partition it first as a range-partitioned table, then as a hash partitioned table, and then as a composite-partitioned table. Along the way, we'll provide more information on partitioned tables, such as how Oracle assigns rows to partitions.

Creating a Range-Partitioned sales_detail_data Table

In this section, we'll create a range-partitioned **sales_detail_data** table with four partitions (each partition will store one quarter's worth of data). We'll store each of these partitions in separate tablespaces (named **quarter_one**, **quarter_two**, **quarter_three**, and **quarter_four**).

Creating the Range-Partitioned Table

To create any partitioned table, you use the Oracle CREATE TABLE command. So, without further ado, let's create the **sales_detail_data** range-partitioned table. Listing 13.2 shows the DDL (Data Definition Language) code for this creation. Note that we've included several comments inside the code.

Listing 13.2 Creating the sales_detail_data table.

```
CREATE TABLE sales_detail_data
(date_of_sale      DATE      NOT NULL,
invoice_number     NUMBER    NOT NULL,
item_line_no       NUMBER    NOT NULL,
item_sku           NUMBER    NOT NULL,
qty_sold           NUMBER    NOT NULL
)
/* Below are the default partition storage
   attributes. Partitions without any defined attributes take
   on the attributes defined on these lines. */
PCTFREE 10
PCTUSED 60
STORAGE (INITIAL 10K NEXT 10K)
/* The table partition clause and the rest of the
   syntax make up the partition specification.
   date_of_sale is the partition key. */
PARTITION BY RANGE (date_of_sale)
(
```

```
   /* Now the partition description clauses:
      The name of the first partition is sales_q1_99.
      It contains values for all
      dates inserted that are earlier than  Feb 02 1999.
      This partition is assigned to the quarter_one(q1)
      tablespace.
      Note that we have now added storage clauses to
      the partitions, so they are created as we defined.  */
  PARTITION sales_q1_99 VALUES LESS THAN
  (TO_DATE('1999-04-01','YYYY-MM-DD') )
  PCTFREE 10
  PCTUSED 60
  TABLESPACE quarter_one
  STORAGE (INITIAL 10K NEXT 10K),
  PARTITION sales_q2_99 VALUES LESS THAN
  (TO_DATE('1999-07-01','YYYY-MM-DD') )
  PCTFREE 10
  PCTUSED 60
  TABLESPACE quarter_two
  STORAGE (INITIAL 10K NEXT 10K ),
  PARTITION sales_q3_99 VALUES LESS THAN
  (TO_DATE('1999-10-01','YYYY-MM-DD') )
  PCTFREE 10
  PCTUSED 60
  TABLESPACE quarter_three
  STORAGE (INITIAL 20K NEXT 20K ),
  PARTITION sales_q4_99 VALUES LESS THAN
  (TO_DATE('2000-01-01','YYYY-MM-DD') )
  PCTFREE 10
  PCTUSED 60
  TABLESPACE quarter_four
  STORAGE (INITIAL 40K NEXT 40K ) );
CREATE TABLE sales_detail_data
*
ERROR at line 1:
ORA-00439: feature not enabled: Partitioning
```

Now we've run into some sort of problem. Note the unfortunate error that occurred when we tried to create the partitioned table. The reason we got this error is that we chose not to install partitioning when we first installed the database software on our system. That's because partitioning was not licensed at the time on that box. In this case, although partitioning is installed by default, I had chosen not to install it. Because partitioning is a separately purchased option from

Oracle (even though it does come on the same media as the database software and does install by default), you must consider licensing issues when installing the database. Partitioning is available with Oracle8i Enterprise Edition and Personal Edition but not with Oracle8i Standard Edition. After we installed the Partitioning option (having, of course, paid the licensing fee), the partitioned table was created successfully. (See Chapter 14 for information on maintaining hash-partitioned tables.)

Some Details on Creating Range-Partitioned Tables

Let's look at the **CREATE TABLE** statement in Listing 13.2 and the comments included in it. The first several lines look like the old **CREATE TABLE** syntax we are familiar with. Next, looking like the normal storage specifications you would find in the **CREATE TABLE** statement, we find the default physical attributes of the partitions to be associated with the partitioned table.. Any partition that is created in that table but is not given specific physical storage attributes derives its attributes from the default attributes defined.

The next section of code involves syntax known as the *partition specification* (this section is commented in the code). The partition specification consists of the following:

- *A PARTITION BY RANGE clause*—This clause specifies that the table is partitioned based on the set of one or more columns enclosed in parentheses after the **PARTITION BY RANGE** clause. The partition column (**date_of_sale**, in the example) defines the *partition key* on which the table will be partitioned. This part of the SQL statement is known as the *table partition clause*. The table partition clause is used to define the type of partitioning that will occur: range partitioning, hash partitioning, or (with the **SUBPARTITION_ CLAUSE**) composite partitioning.
- *A list of partition descriptions* (**PARTITION SPECIFICATION CLAUSE**)— This clause defines the partitions, the data they hold, the storage characteristics, and so on. Each partition is assigned a unique name, and this name must remain unique within the partitioned table.

The **date_of_sale** column listed in the **PARTITION BY RANGE** clause is known as the *partition column*. The values in the partition column(s) are the *partition keys*. A partition column can consist of up to 16 columns and is an ordered list of the values for the partitioned columns. Returning to the example of the **sales_detail_data** table, assume that you want to partition not only on the **date_of_sale** column but perhaps also on what was sold (the **item_sku**). In the environment in which we created our demonstration tables, perhaps further partitioning of the table would allow partitioning of sales by the date and the items being sold (jeans, shoes, and other items). Listing 13.3, later in this section, provides an example of a partitioned table with multiple partition columns.

Along with other column restrictions on partitioned tables, a partition key cannot contain the **LEVEL**, **ROWID**, or **MLSLABEL** pseudo-columns or any column that is of the type **ROWID**. The partition key is sorted by its binary value.

In Listing 13.2, note that the partitions are created with different storage size values. Partitioning allows you to size each partition as you want to. Controlling the size of each partition is handy when the data is cyclical: large volumes come in during well-defined times, and smaller volumes come in during others. You can manage your disk space more effectively, allocating a smaller amount of space to one partition and allocating a larger amount to another.

It's always a good idea to carefully analyze the data that you intend to partition. Carefully look at the data, and size the partitions relative to the partition key and to the volume and nature of data related to that key. Look at historical volumes and how they might fluctuate over time, and determine how to split the partitions based on the key you select.

Let's look at different elements of the **PARTITION BY RANGE** clause. It starts with the keyword **PARTITION** followed by the name of the partition. Each partition has a name, and this name must conform to Oracle naming rules for objects. In addition, each partition name that belongs to the same table must be unique.

The next section is the *partition bounds*. Every partition has a noninclusive upper bound that is represented by the **VALUES LESS THAN** clause. All partitions but the first have an inclusive lower bound. This bound is specified by the **VALUES LESS THAN** clause of the partition before it. These partition bounds define the order of the partitions in the table (and the partition that rows will be stored in). The first partition has the lowest **VALUES LESS THAN** value. Each subsequent partition is ordered based on the relationship of its partition bounds to those of the others. The partition with the highest partition-bound value becomes the highest partition in the table.

In the **sales_detail_data** table, the order of the partitions is **sales_q1_99**, **sales_q2_99**, **sales_q3_99**, and then **sales_q4_99**. The ordering is defined by the **VALUES LESS THAN** clauses associated with these partitions. The date range in **sales_q1_99** is less than that of **sales_q2_99**, so **sales_q1_99** is ordered first, then **sales_q2_99**.

Note the use of the **TO_DATE** function format mask used in the example in Listing 13.3. The use of the format mask is required. If you don't use the **TO_DATE** function format mask, an error will occur when you're trying to create the table if the **nls_date_format** date format doesn't specify the century with the year. Also, partition pruning won't be possible if the **nls_date_format** doesn't specify the century with the year.

Remember that the values stored in each partition are less than the partition bounds defined for a specific partition. Thus, if you create a partition with a partition key of the letters A through Z and then make "Z" the last partition's **VALUES LESS THAN**, you cannot store any value with a Z in that partition. In this case, a Z is an ASCII value of 90. In order to store the value Z, you need to define the partition's **VALUES LESS THAN** clause as ASCII character 91, which is a "[".

Note: Partition boundary limits have implications with lowercase values as well because these limits start at ASCII values of 97 and up. When partitioning a table, take care that you don't inadvertently prevent yourself from inserting the data that you want to store, such as lowercase letters.

Partition Boundaries and MAXVALUE

When you're dealing with a range-partitioned table, you can attempt to insert into a partitioned table a value that doesn't conform to the partition bounds defined for that table. In this case, the insertion will fail. For example, in **sales_detail_data** (referring to Listing 13.2), if we tried to insert sales data for March 1, 2001, the insertion would fail because no partition is defined that would include the date being inserted within its partition bounds. If you'll need to insert into a partitioned table partition-key values greater than the maximum partitioned boundary, then you'll need to include the **MAXVALUE** clause when you create the partitioned table. The **MAXVALUE** clause represents all values possible that are higher than the greatest partition boundary in a partitioned table. Thus, in our sample **sales_detail_data** table, if we want to enter any dates greater than December 31, 1999, we have to add a new partition by using the **MAXVALUE** clause instead of a specific date.

Note that Oracle sorts **NULL** values higher than all other values except **MAXVALUE**. **NULL**s sort less than **MAXVALUE**. This means that if a table's partition bounds are defined on a column that is nullable, you must include a **MAXVALUE** clause in the table's creation statement. If you don't, any **NULL**s inserted will map above the highest partitioned value, and the insertion will fail.

Listing 13.3 shows an example of this changed code. The listing includes multiple partitions and partitioning on two separate columns, and it uses the MAXVALUE clause.

Make sure you understand what **MAXVALUE** is, how to use it when you're creating partitioned tables, and why you need to use it.

Listing 13.3 Another example of a range-partitioned table.

```
CREATE TABLE sales_detail_data
(date_of_sale     DATE      NOT NULL,
invoice_number    NUMBER    NOT NULL,
item_line_no      NUMBER    NOT NULL,
item_sku          NUMBER    NOT NULL,
qty_sold          NUMBER    NOT NULL
)
/* Below are the default partition storage attributes. Partitions
   without any defined attributes take on the attributes defined
   on these lines. */
PCTFREE 10
PCTUSED 60
STORAGE (INITIAL 10K NEXT 10K)
/* Now the table partition clause and the whole rest of the syntax
   make up the partition specification. */
PARTITION BY RANGE (date_of_sale,item_sku)
(
   /* Now the partition description clauses: */
   /* The name of the first partition is sales_q1_99. It
      contains values for all */
   /* dates inserted less than Feb 02 1999. */
   /* This partition is assigned to the quarter_one
      tablespace. */
   /* Note that we have added storage clauses to the
      partitions, so they are created as we defined. */
PARTITION sales_q1_99_jeans VALUES LESS THAN
(TO_DATE('1999-04-01','YYYY-MM-DD'),100000 )
  PCTFREE 10
  PCTUSED 60
  TABLESPACE quarter_one
  STORAGE (INITIAL 10K NEXT 10K ),
PARTITION sales_q1_99_shirts VALUES LESS THAN
(TO_DATE('1999-04-01','YYYY-MM-DD'),200000 )
  PCTFREE 10
  PCTUSED 60
```

```
  TABLESPACE quarter_one
  STORAGE (INITIAL 10k NEXT 10k ),
PARTITION sales_q1_99_allelse VALUES LESS THAN
(TO_DATE('1999-04-01','YYYY-MM-DD'),MAXVALUE )
  PCTFREE 10
  PCTUSED 60
  TABLESPACE quarter_one
  STORAGE (INITIAL 10k NEXT 10k ),
PARTITION sales_q2_99_jeans VALUES LESS THAN
(TO_DATE('1999-07-01','YYYY-MM-DD'),100000 )
  PCTFREE 10
  PCTUSED 60
  TABLESPACE quarter_two
  STORAGE (INITIAL 10k NEXT 10k ),
PARTITION sales_q2_99_shirts VALUES LESS THAN
(TO_DATE('1999-07-01','YYYY-MM-DD'),200000 )
  PCTFREE 10
  PCTUSED 60
  TABLESPACE quarter_two
  STORAGE (INITIAL 10k NEXT 10k ),
PARTITION sales_q2_99_allelse VALUES LESS THAN
(TO_DATE('1999-07-01','YYYY-MM-DD'),MAXVALUE )
  PCTFREE 10
  PCTUSED 60
  TABLESPACE quarter_two
  STORAGE (INITIAL 10k NEXT 10k ),
PARTITION sales_q3_99_jeans VALUES LESS THAN
(TO_DATE('1999-10-01','YYYY-MM-DD'),100000 )
  PCTFREE 10
  PCTUSED 60
  TABLESPACE quarter_three
  STORAGE (INITIAL 10k NEXT 10k ),
PARTITION sales_q3_99_shirts VALUES LESS THAN
(TO_DATE('1999-10-01','YYYY-MM-DD'),200000 )
  PCTFREE 10
  PCTUSED 60
  TABLESPACE quarter_three
  STORAGE (INITIAL 10k NEXT 10k ),
PARTITION sales_q3_99_allelse VALUES LESS THAN
(TO_DATE('1999-10-01','YYYY-MM-DD'),MAXVALUE )
  PCTFREE 10
  PCTUSED 60
  TABLESPACE quarter_three
  STORAGE (INITIAL 10k NEXT 10k ),
PARTITION sales_q4_99_jeans VALUES LESS THAN
(TO_DATE('2000-01-01','YYYY-MM-DD'),100000 )
```

```
  PCTFREE 10
  PCTUSED 60
  TABLESPACE quarter_four
  STORAGE (INITIAL 30k NEXT 30k ),
PARTITION sales_q4_99_shirts VALUES LESS THAN
(TO_DATE('2000-01-01','YYYY-MM-DD'),200000 )
  PCTFREE 10
  PCTUSED 60
  TABLESPACE quarter_four
  STORAGE (INITIAL 20k NEXT 20k ),
PARTITION sales_q4_99_allelse VALUES LESS THAN
(TO_DATE('2000-01-01','YYYY-MM-DD'),MAXVALUE )
  PCTFREE 10
  PCTUSED 60
  TABLESPACE quarter_four
  STORAGE (INITIAL 10k NEXT 10k ) );
```

Row Partition Assignments

In a partitioned table with a single partition key, the order of the partitions starts with the lowest sorted partition based on the partition key. A new row is inserted into the partition based on that row's relationship to the partition key. If the value of the partition-key column being inserted is less than the value of the partition bound for that partition, then the row is in that partition. For example, if the partition bounds are 5, 10, and 15, and the value being inserted into the partitioned table is 7, the insertion would occur in the partition bounded by 10. Rows with partition-key insertions equal to the range boundary end up in the next-higher partition. Therefore, an attempt to insert a value of 10 causes the row to be inserted into the partition bounded by 15. An attempt to insert a value outside valid partition boundaries results in an error.

Placement of a row in a multicolumn partition-keyed table is a bit more complex than single-column partition-keyed tables are. Here are the rules:

- Oracle looks at the range values from left to right to determine in which partition the row belongs.
- Oracle looks at the value in the leftmost partition-key column in the row to be inserted. If that value is less than the first partition-key range boundary of the partitioned table, Oracle will move to the next partition-key column. Oracle will continue to move left to right, through the partition-key columns of the row, comparing them to the partition-range values of the table's key columns, until it finds the correct partition to insert the row into.
- If all the columns are equal to the range boundaries, then the row is assigned to the next-higher partition.

How Rows are Assigned to a Partition in a Range-Partitioned Table

This section offers some examples that might make it easier for you to understand how a row is assigned to a partition. In addition, Figure 13.5 shows a graphical depiction of what is happening. For these examples, review the table created in Listing 13.3.

- *Example One*—The user inserts a row with a partition-key value for **date_of_sale** of **1999-01-01** with an **item_sku** of **'99000'**. Which partition will this be assigned to? Remember, the rules say that you must start from left to right. Look for the first value that is less than the range value, and that is the partition to which the row is assigned. So, look at the first partition, **sales_q1_99_jeans** (remember that partitions are ordered based on the ordering of the partition keys). The **date_of_sale** column is the first in the partition key, so start comparing its value in the inserted row with the partition-bound value of the first partition. The first partition's partition-bound range starts with a **date_of_sale** earlier than **01-apr-1999**. Next, compare the **item_sku** value. The **item_sku** value is less than the partition range of the partition for **item_sku**, so the row is inserted into the first partition, **sales_q1_99_jeans.**

- *Example Two*—Assume the next row to be inserted has a value of **1999-04-01** for the **date_of_sale** column and a value of **'954333'** for the **item_sku** column. Starting with the first partition, **sales_q1_99_jeans**, compare the **date_of_sale** to the range value allowed by the first partition for this column. The two values should be equal, so you must move to the next range defined in the partition key. You skip the next two partitions (**sales_q1_99_shirts** and **sales_q1_99_allelse**) for the same reason. Then you compare the **item_sku** to the range allowed in the fourth partition (**sales_q2_99_jeans**). Comparing the **date_of_sale**, you find that it's now less than the range of the **date_of_sale** for the partition.

  Next, start comparing the next key, **item_sku**. The **item_sku** range in the fourth partition is **'100000'**. The **item_sku** value that you want to insert is higher than that range, so you must go to the next (fifth) partition, **sales_q2_99_shirts**. This partition has the **date_of_sale** range that's greater than your date, again, so look at the **item_sku** value, which is now **'200000'**. Again, your inserted value is higher than this. Your next move is to the next (sixth) partition, **sales_q2_99_allelse**. Here you find the two **date_of_sale** values to be equal; therefore, you have to move to the next **item_sku** range defined in the partition key. You find the next **item_sku** range to be **MAXVALUE**, which allows you an unlimited ceiling for row values. The insertion of the **item_sku** is—and will always be—less than **MAXVALUE**, so insert the row in the sixth partition, **sales_q2_99_allelse**.

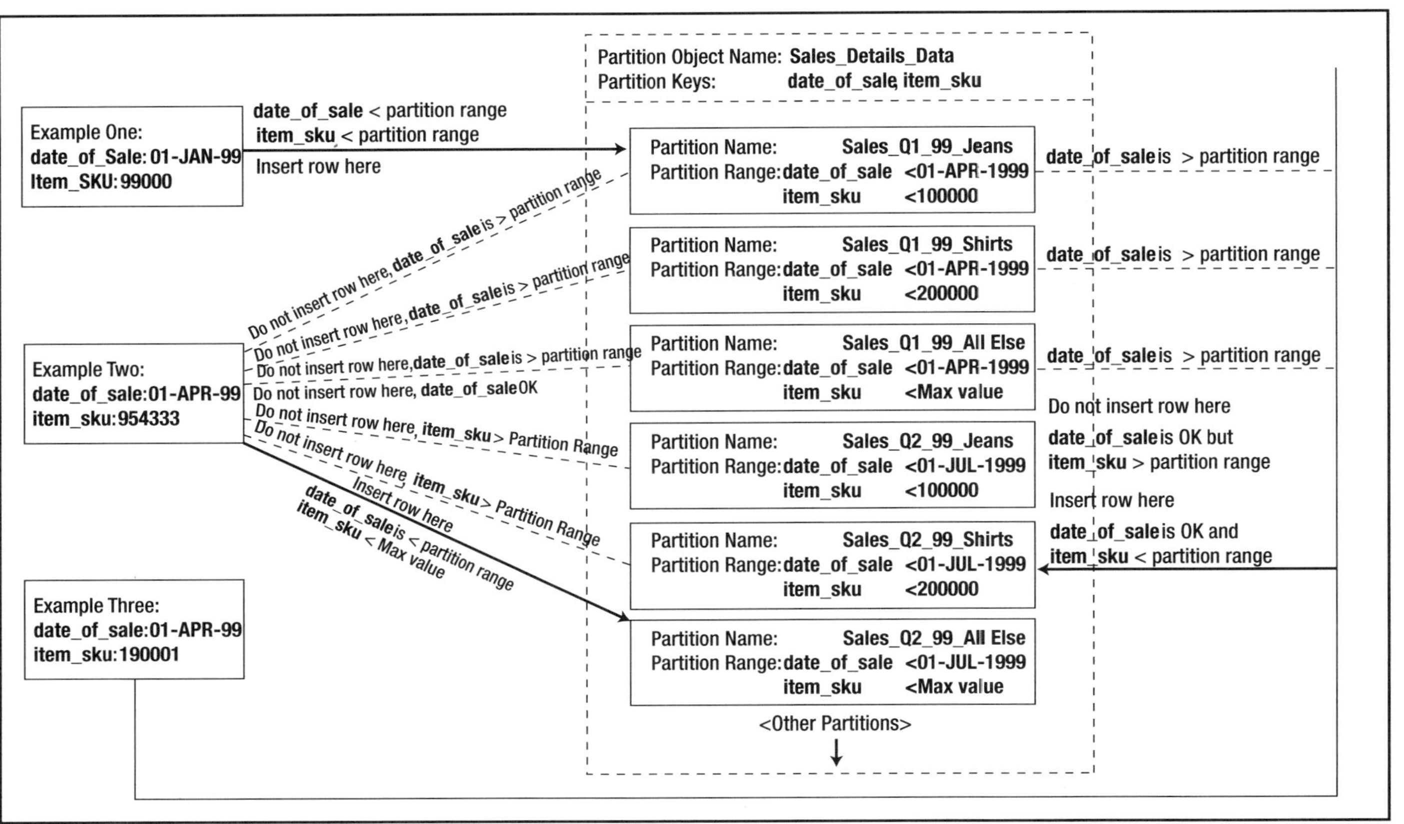

Figure 13.5 Examples of assigning rows to range-partitioned tables.

- *Example Three*—Assume that a **date_of_sale** of **1999-04-04** and an **item_sku** of **'190001'** are being inserted. In this example, you again skip the first three partitions because the first partition boundary of each is less than the **date_of_sale** value of **04-apr-1999**. You then arrive at the fourth partition, **sales_q2_99_jeans**, where the **date_of_sale** is less than the partition boundary of **01-jul-1999**. Comparing the **item_sku**, you find that your row's **item_sku** is greater than the partition range of that partition's **item_sku** column. Proceed to the next partition. There again, the partition boundary remains **01-jul-1999**, greater than your **date_of_sale**. Your **item_sku** in this case is less than the **'200000'** boundary for the partition. Therefore, this insertion goes into the **sales_q2_99_shirts** partition.

Creating a Hash-Partitioned sales_detail_data Table

We introduced hash-partitioned tables earlier in this chapter. Now let's look at how we create one. In Listing 13.4, we create the hash-partitioned table **sales_detail_data**. The example has several comments in it so you can better understand what is happening in the code.

When a hash-partitioned table is created and a row is inserted, the hash value of the row's partition key is determined. Based on that hash value, the row is stored in the correct partition. The partition hash ranges are totally controlled by Oracle. The partition sizes cannot be set individually, but they each take the default settings defined for the partitioned table. As with range partitioning, partitions can reside in different tablespaces.

Listing 13.4 Creating the sales_detail_data hash-partitioned table.

```
CREATE TABLE sales_detail_data
(date_of_sale       DATE      NOT NULL,
invoice_number      NUMBER    NOT NULL,
item_line_no        NUMBER    NOT NULL,
item_sku            NUMBER    NOT NULL,
qty_sold            NUMBER    NOT NULL
)
PCTFREE 10
PCTUSED 60
/* This is where we define the sizes of all
   the partitions. Partitions cannot be sized by
   themselves with hash partitioning. */
STORAGE (INITIAL 10K NEXT 10K)
/* Define this as a hash-partitioned table
   we are partitioning on date_of_sale */
PARTITION BY HASH(date_of_sale)
(
```

```
/* Creating four partitions, in different tablespaces */
PARTITION sales_p1  TABLESPACE quarter_one,
PARTITION sales_p2  TABLESPACE quarter_two,
PARTITION sales_p3  TABLESPACE quarter_three,
PARTITION sales_p4  TABLESPACE quarter_four );
```

As with the range-partitioned table, here we use the table partition clause, substituting the **HASH** keyword instead of **RANGE**. We then define the hash key by defining—in parentheses at the end of the table partition clause—the column or columns that the hash value should be calculated on. (See Chapter 14 for information on maintenance operations and on where to find data dictionary information on hash-partitioned tables.)

Creating a Composite-Partitioned sales_de tail_data Table

We introduced the composite-partitioned table earlier, so let's create one now. In Listing 13.5, we create the composite-partitioned table **sales_detail_data**. The example has several comments in it so you can better understand what is happening in the code.

When a composite-partitioned table is created and a row is inserted, the partition in which the row belongs is determined based on the column defined in the **PARTITION BY RANGE** clause. Next, based on this, the hash value of the column defined in the **SUBPARTITION BY HASH** is defined, and the correct sub-partition in which to actually store the row is identified. Remember that the range part of the partition is really only a logical structure; it's the hash value that determines the physical placement of the data. The partition hash ranges are totally controlled by Oracle, as with hash partitioning.

Note that the storage clauses specified apply to the subpartitions, because the data is stored at the sub-partition level. The subpartition sizes cannot be set individually, as with range partitioning, but each subpartition can reside in a different tablespace. You can name both the partition and the subpartitions, or you can allow Oracle to name them for you. The names of the partitions and subpartitions must be distinct because Oracle stores these in the same namespace.

Listing 13.5 Creating the sales_detail_data composite-partitioned table.

```
CREATE TABLE sales_detail_data
(date_of_sale      DATE      NOT NULL,
invoice_number     NUMBER    NOT NULL,
item_line_no       NUMBER    NOT NULL,
item_sku           NUMBER    NOT NULL,
qty_sold           NUMBER    NOT NULL
```

```
)
PCTFREE 10
PCTUSED 60
/* This is where we define the default sizes and
   storage allocation of the partitions. In this example,
   though, we'll specify sizes at the partition level. */
STORAGE (INITIAL 10K NEXT 10K)
/* Define the composite partitioning details.
   We'll cover these items below in more detail. */
PARTITION BY RANGE(date_of_sale)
SUBPARTITION BY HASH(invoice_number) subpartitions 4
STORE IN (quarter_one, quarter_two, quarter three, quarter_four)
(
      PARTITION sales_q1_99 VALUES LESS THAN
         (TO_DATE('2000-04-01','YYYY-MM-DD') )
          /* We have defined our first partition. Remember,
             though, partitions are logical structures and
             not physical. What we are really doing by defining
             the STORAGE clause here is defining the storage of
             the subpartitions because they don't have specific
             storage clauses. */
         PCTFREE 10
         PCTUSED 60
         TABLESPACE quarter_one
         STORAGE (INITIAL 10K NEXT 10K)
         ( subpartition q1s1 tablespace quarter_one,
           subpartition q1s2 tablespace quarter_one,
           subpartition q1s3 tablespace quarter_one,
           subpartition q1s4 tablespace quarter_one
         ),
       PARTITION sales_q2_99 VALUES LESS THAN
         (TO_DATE('2000-07-01','YYYY-MM-DD') )
         PCTFREE 10
         PCTUSED 60
         TABLESPACE quarter_two
         STORAGE (INITIAL 10K NEXT 10K)
         ( subpartition q2s1 tablespace quarter_two,
           subpartition q2s2 tablespace quarter_two,
           subpartition q2s3 tablespace quarter_two,
           subpartition q2s4 tablespace quarter_two
         ),
      PARTITION sales_q3_99 VALUES LESS THAN
         (TO_DATE('2000-10-01','YYYY-MM-DD') )
         PCTFREE 10
         PCTUSED 60
         TABLESPACE quarter_three
```

```
    STORAGE (INITIAL 10K NEXT 10K)
    ( subpartition q3s1 tablespace quarter_three,
      subpartition q3s2 tablespace quarter_three,
      subpartition q3s3 tablespace quarter_three,
      subpartition q3s4 tablespace quarter_three
    ),
  PARTITION sales_q4_99 VALUES LESS THAN
    (TO_DATE('2001-01-01','YYYY-MM-DD') )
    PCTFREE 10
    PCTUSED 60
    TABLESPACE quarter_four
    STORAGE (INITIAL 10K NEXT 10K)
    ( subpartition q4s1 tablespace quarter_four,
      subpartition q4s2 tablespace quarter_four,
      subpartition q4s3 tablespace quarter_four ) );
```

Let's review some of the details of the creation of this partitioned table. Here are the two lines that define this as a composite-partitioned table:

```
PARTITION BY RANGE(date_of_sale)
SUBPARTITION BY HASH(invoice_number) subpartitions 4
```

These lines look much like the lines used to define a range-partitioned table and a hash-partitioned table, and in fact they are. The first line defines the partition column on which the range partitions will be keyed. The second line defines the partition column on which the hash value should be calculated, and this line defines how many subpartitions should be created by default. You can—as we did in the partition **sales_q4_99** in our example—define a different number of subpartitions from the default as data volumes warrant.

Next, look at the **STORE IN** clause. Again, this is a default value defining the tablespaces to store the subpartitions in. Again, this can be overridden (as we did) when you're defining the subpartitions. You don't need to specify the same number of partition tablespaces in the **STORE IN**clause as you define for the table. If there are fewer tablespaces defined, Oracle will simply cycle through them as it assigns tablespaces to the subpartitions.

See Chapter 14 for information on maintenance operations and on where to find data dictionary information on composite-partitioned tables.

Partitioning Index-Organized Tables

Oracle8i now allows you to partition index-organized tables (IOTs) but only by using the range partitioning method. You must partition an IOT on the primary key or on a subset of the primary-key columns of the table that you want to partition. You can also partition an IOT without row overflow by using the **ORGANIZATION INDEX** clause at the table level rather than at the partition level.

If you create an IOT with an overflow segment, the IOT's **OVERFLOW** segments are always equipartitioned with the Index Organized Tables (IOTs). Each IOT partition has associated overflow and index segments associated with it. The **OVERFLOW** segments are equipartitioned with the primary-key-index segments of the partitioned IOT table. The storage specifications for partitioned IOTs can be defined at the table or partition level for both the table data and the **OVERFLOW** segments.

Assuming that we wanted to create our **sales_detail_data** table as an IOT and partition it, we might do something like the example shown in Listing 13.6. To save some space, we've reduced this table to only two partitions. We've also removed the **PCTUSED** statement because it isn't valid with an IOT.

Listing 13.6 Creating the sales_detail_data table as an IOT.

```
CREATE TABLE sales_detail_data
(date_of_sale      DATE      NOT NULL,
invoice_number     NUMBER    NOT NULL,
item_line_no       NUMBER    NOT NULL,
item_sku           NUMBER    NOT NULL,
qty_sold           NUMBER    NOT NULL,
/* Define the PK. This MUST be defined or you cannot create
 this as a partitioned IOT. */
Constraint pk_sales_detail_data
PRIMARY KEY(date_of_sale,invoice_number)
)
/* Here we'll define the table as an IOT. */
ORGANIZATION INDEX
PCTTHRESHOLD 20
OVERFLOW TABLESPACE users
-- Note no PCTUSED; not available for an IOT.
PCTFREE 10
STORAGE (INITIAL 10K NEXT 10K)
/* The table partition clause and the rest of the
   syntax make up the partition specification.
   date_of_sale is the partition key. */
PARTITION BY RANGE (date_of_sale)
(
/* A partitioned IOT can ONLY be range-partitioned in 8i. */
PARTITION sales_q1_99 VALUES LESS THAN
  (TO_DATE('1999-02-01','YYYY-MM-DD') )
```

```
PCTFREE 10
TABLESPACE quarter_one
STORAGE (INITIAL 10K NEXT 10K),
PARTITION sales_q2_99 VALUES LESS THAN
(TO_DATE('1999-07-01','YYYY-MM-DD') )
PCTFREE 10
TABLESPACE quarter_two
STORAGE (INITIAL 10K NEXT 10K ));
```

Partitioning Tables with LOBs

Oracle8i allows you to partition tables that contain large objects (LOBs), a feature not available in Oracle8. (Chapter 15 addresses LOBs in more detail.) Some special consideration should be given when you're going to partition a table that contains LOB columns.

First, you should know that a table's partition key can't contain a LOB column. For each partition of an object containing a LOB, two additional equipartitioned segments are created: a LOB data segment and a LOB index segment. Thus, for every partition of a partitioned table that contains a LOB column, there's a LOB data segment and a LOB index segment. Likewise, when you're using composite-partitioned tables, for every subpartition that contains a LOB column, there's a separate equipartitioned LOB data segment and a LOB index segment.

Various rules also exist regarding tablespace assignment of LOB segments. If a tablespace for the LOB segment is defined, then that tablespace will be used (as opposed to the default tablespace). You can also define the default tablespaces for LOB segments within the **CREATE TABLE** command, just as you would do with hash or composite partitioning. Otherwise, Oracle defaults by creating the LOB segments in the same tablespace as the partition they are associated with. Note that the LOB index segments and the LOB data segments are always stored together in the same tablespace.

Special rules also exist regarding storage considerations for LOB segments. You can use the **lob_storage_clause** to specify storage for LOB segments. You can define default storage specifications for LOB storage, or you can define specific partition or subpartition LOB storage clauses. For a hash partition or subpartition, you can only define a tablespace in the **lob_storage_clause**.

A Few More Words on Table Partitioning

Oracle doesn't support partitioning tables that contain **LONG** or **LONG RAW** data types. You cannot specify **NULL** as a value for a partition boundary. Nor can blank strings be defined as values because they are treated as **NULLs** within the server.

A new Oracle8i feature allows you to enable updates of the partition-key column's values for a row in a partitioned table. Before Oracle8i, the only way to update these column values was to drop the row and re-create it with the new values. In Oracle8i, you can update the column in a row that belongs to a table's partition key. To do so, you must first **CREATE** or **ALTER** the table specifications to allow for such an action by using the **ENABLE ROW MOVEMENT** clause in the **CREATE TABLE** or **ALTER TABLE** commands.

Other restrictions include the inability to define a synonym that points to a partition of a table and the inability to use the new SQL syntax to access partitions directly in PL/SQL code. This latter problem can be overcome by using views or by using dynamic SQL.

Restrictions on Partitioned Tables

Having covered the creation of various partitioned tables, we should review the numerous rules on the creation of various types of partitioned tables. Following is a summary of creation rules for partitioned tables:

- A partitioned table cannot be part of a cluster.
- A partitioned table cannot be a temporary table.
- A partitioned table cannot contain **LONG** or **LONG RAW** data types.
- A partitioned table can have partitioned or nonpartitioned indexes associated with it. (See Chapter 14 for more on partitioned indexes.)
- A nonpartitioned table can have only global partitioned indexes or nonpartitioned indexes associated with it.
- A partitioned index-organized table cannot contain **LOB** columns or **VARRAY** column types.
- A partitioned table cannot be set to **UNRECOVERABLE**.
- A partitioned table can have up to 64,000 partitions.

Partitioning Indexes

From partitioned tables we move into partitioned indexes. In this section, we'll discuss the different index partitioning options and how you create partitioned indexes. Finally, this section reviews the restrictions on partitioning indexes.

Basics of Partitioning Indexes

In Oracle, there are four general types of indexes:

- Nonpartitioned indexes
- Global prefixed indexes
- Local prefixed indexes
- Local nonprefixed indexes

As with tables, partitioned indexes have to have a partition key that is used to separate the values into different partitions based on the range defined for the key. An index is *prefixed* if the leftmost column (leading edge) of the index is the same as the leftmost column on which the table is partitioned. If this isn't the case, the index is *nonprefixed*. For example, if we were to create a multicolumn index on the partitioned table created in Listing 13.3, and we created the index on the **date_of_sale** column, then that index would be considered prefixed. This is because the index has the partition key as its leading or only key. If, however, we created an index on **item_sku**, it would be a nonprefixed because **item_sku** isn't the leading edge of the partition key. In a multicolumn index, as long as **date_of_sale** were the leftmost value that the index was created on, it would be a prefixed index.

Unique prefixed indexes can have performance advantages over nonprefixed indexes by allowing the database to access only one index partition to find the data it requires. As with any index, the contents of the WHERE clause in a SELECT statement can control the efficiency of the index lookup. Take care to index properly. Finally, note that you cannot create a partitioned index on an index cluster.

The benefits (and a gotya thrown in for good measure) of using partitioned indexes include the following:

- Only one partition of an index is searched if the index is a unique, prefixed, partitioned index and the WHERE clause specifies the value(s) of the column(s) in the index.
- Only one partition of an index is searched if the index is a prefixed, nonunique index and if the WHERE clause specifies a value for all the columns in the index. If this isn't the case, all the index's partitions are scanned.
- If the index is a unique, nonprefixed index, you might still be able to scan only one partition. If the WHERE clause of the SELECT statement contains the partition key, Oracle uses only the partition that contains the data requested.

➤ One "gotcha" is in the case where the index is nonunique and nonprefixed, Oracle must search all the partitions of that index to get the data queried.

Global Indexes

Global indexes allow you to define the partitions of the index differently than the partition of the table. This means that the partitioned index can contain partition-key range values different from those of the associated table. By using a global index, you can create a nonequipartitioned index with a partitioned table.

If you create a global index, Oracle doesn't maintain the relationship between the table and the index as it does with a local index, so global indexes are harder to manage. Oracle allows the creation of only range-partitioned global indexes. A global index can only be range-partitioned, but it can be defined on any kind of partitioned table (range, hash, or composite). Execution of DDL on the table associated with the global index can cause the index to become invalid (for example, splitting a partition in an underlying table). A bitmap index cannot be partitioned as a global index.

To rebuild a global index, you can use the **ALTER INDEX REBUILD PARTITION** statement. We'll discuss partitioned index maintenance operations in greater detail in Chapter 14.

Note: All global indexes must be prefixed.

Listing 13.7 shows an example of creating a global index on the **sales_detail_data** table. Note that the index is partitioned differently than is the **sales_detail_data** table. Note that previous to Oracle8i, if you did not use the **MAXVALUE** clause and you attempted to insert a value out of the range of the index partition defined in Listing 13.2, the statement would fail. Oracle8i forces you to include the **MAXVALUE** clause, or you will get an ORA-14021 error. In addition, you explicitly name the partitions when creating the index. Naming the partitions isn't required, though it's good practice; Oracle assigns default partition names if they aren't explicitly defined. Finally, note that the partition definition syntax for a global index is essentially the same as that for partitioning a table.

Generally, local prefixed indexes are preferable to global indexes. Local prefixed indexes are less of a maintenance burden and generally provide better performance than global indexes do.

Listing 13.7 Creating a global index.

```
CREATE INDEX ix_sales_dos_01 ON sales_detail_data(date_of_sale)
-- the GLOBAL keyword makes this a global index.
GLOBAL
PARTITION BY RANGE(date_of_sale)
(PARTITION par1 VALUES LESS THAN
(TO_DATE('01-APR-1999','DD-MON-YYYY') )
 TABLESPACE quarter_one
 STORAGE (INITIAL 10k NEXT 10k),
 PARTITION par2 VALUES LESS THAN
(TO_DATE('01-JUL-1999','DD-MON-YYYY') )
 TABLESPACE quarter_three
STORAGE (INITIAL 20k NEXT 10k),
 PARTITION par3 VALUES LESS THAN (MAXVALUE)
 TABLESPACE quarter_four
STORAGE (INITIAL 10k NEXT 10k) );
```

Always name your partitions explicitly. Doing so makes administration much easier down the road.

Local Indexes

Local indexes, when created, automatically inherit both the same number of partitions as the partitioned table referred to and the names of those partitions. Oracle can even provide the storage specifications for the partitions. When created, the partitions are automatically equipartitioned with the associated table. If you don't specify a tablespace for the local index, the index will use the same tablespace of the corresponding partition of the underlying table being indexed. To specify an alternate location for an index, use the **LOCAL STORE IN** clause of the **CREATE INDEX** statement. With composite-partitioned tables, the first **STORE IN** statement defines a default tablespace, which you can override as you define each partition of the index. You can also specify the name of the index in the **ON_RANGE_PARTITIONED_TABLE_CLAUSE**, **ON_HASH_PARTITIONED_TABLE_CLAUSE**, or the **ON_CLUSTER _PARTITIONED_TABLE** clause of the **CREATE INDEX** statement, or Oracle will supply a system-generated index name.

Local prefixed indexes generally offer more performance and maintenance advantages than global indexes do. Oracle maintains local indexes so that changes in the associated table structure (e.g., adding a new partition) don't require significant DBA involvement to revalidate the indexes. In addition, you can create a local nonprefixed index for columns that aren't members of the partition key. Partitioned, local, nonprefixed indexes can offer performance advantages in that they allow range scans on the index key to be executed in parallel; therefore, finding data that isn't part of the partition key is much faster than for a nonpartitioned, nonprefixed index.

Some operations may require you to rebuild a local index. These operations include moving a partition and truncating a partition. Use the **ALTER TABLE MODIFY PARTITION REBUILD UNUSABLE LOCAL INDEXES** statement to rebuild the invalidated index. See Chapter 14 for more information on partitioned index maintenance operations.

Listing 13.8 shows an example of creating a prefixed local index on the **sales_detail_data** table. Note how much less work is required to create the local index as opposed to creating global indexes. You can still include storage requirements, if you want to, but you don't need to define the partition key or the partition range values.

Listing 13.8 Creating a prefixed index and a nonprefixed local index.

```
/* A very simple local index creation. Oracle provides all the
PARTITION sales_q1_99 VALUES LESS THAN

   partition information and storage. */
CREATE INDEX test_id ON sales_detail_data
(date_of_sale, item_sku) LOCAL;
/* Prefixed index creation. */
CREATE INDEX ix_sales_dos_01 ON sales_detail_data(date_of_sale)
LOCAL
(PARTITION sales_q1_99 TABLESPACE quarter_one,
PARTITION sales_q2_99 TABLESPACE quarter_two,
PARTITION sales_q3_99 TABLESPACE quarter_three,
PARTITION sales_q4_99 TABLESPACE quarter_four);

/* Nonprefixed index creation. */
CREATE INDEX ix_sales_sku_01 ON sales_detail_data(item_sku)
LOCAL
(PARTITION sales_q1_99 TABLESPACE quarter_one,
PARTITION sales_q2_99 TABLESPACE quarter_two,
PARTITION sales_q3_99 TABLESPACE quarter_three,
PARTITION sales_q4_99 TABLESPACE quarter_four);
```

Secondary Indexes on IOTs

You can create secondary, partitioned indexes on IOTs in Oracle8i. You can create nonpartitioned indexes, partitioned local prefixed indexes, partitioned local nonprefixed indexes, and global prefixed indexes on IOTs. Oracle constructs secondary indexes on index-organized tables by using logical row identifiers (*logical ROWIDs*) that are based on the IOT's primary key. (See Chapter 11 for more on IOTs and logical **ROWIDs**.) A logical **ROWID** can also include additional guess information that identifies the block location of the row. Oracle can use these guesses to probe directly into the leaf block of the index-organized table, bypassing the primary key search. But because rows in index-organized tables don't have permanent physical addresses, the guesses can become stale when rows are moved to new blocks.

For an ordinary table, an index scan involves a scan of the index and an additional I/O to fetch the data block containing the row. For index-organized tables, access by a secondary index varies depending on the use and accuracy of physical guesses. Three types of access scenarios are possible:

- *Access of the secondary IOT index without guesses*—Access involves two index scans: a secondary index scan followed by a scan of the primary key index.
- *Access of the secondary IOT with accurate guesses*—Access involves a secondary index scan and an additional I/O to fetch the data block containing the row.
- *Access of the secondary IOT with inaccurate guesses*—Access involves a secondary index scan and an I/O to fetch the wrong data block (as indicated by the guess), followed by scanning the primary key index.

From looking at the different scenarios, you can see that guess information is important to have and important to keep current. (See Chapter 11 for more information on Index Organized Tables and analyzing the guess information.) If you find that the guess information is stale, consider rebuilding the IOT secondary index.

Restrictions on Partitioned Indexes

Having covered the creation of various indexes, we should review the restrictions on creating the various types of partitioned indexes. Following is a summary of rules for creating partitioned indexes:

- A partitioned index cannot be a clustered index.
- A partitioned index cannot be defined on a clustered table.

- If you create a partitioned bitmap index on a partitioned table, the index must be a local index. Also, you cannot create a partitioned bitmap index on a nonpartitioned table.
- To create a local index, you must partition the underlying table.
- You cannot create a partitioned index on a temporary table. (See Chapter 15 for more on temporary tables.)
- Partitioned indexes in Oracle8i cannot contain **LONG**, **LONG RAW**, **LOB**, or **REF** columns, except those **REF** columns or attributes defined with the **SCOPE** clause.
- If you're using a function-based index as a globally partitioned index, the columns that the index is being built on cannot be the partitioning key.
- A partitioned index can have a maximum of 64,000 partitions.
- If you are partitioning an object table, you cannot use the OID as the partition key. If the object identifier is user-defined, then you can use some or all of the columns constituting the user-defined OID in the partition key.

Locks, Pruning, and Joins: Miscellaneous Partitioning Information

This section will discuss partition and subpartition locks as they relate to table partitioning. Then we'll look at partition pruning and partition-wise joins.

Oracle DML Locks

Just as Oracle uses locking mechanisms to protect rows in a table that have been changed, it also uses locking mechanisms to synchronize actions that occur on partitioned tables. For example, Oracle provides *DML table locks,* which are used when a table's structure is being modified by a DDL statement (for example, when a partition is being added) to prevent DML statements (**INSERT**, **UPDATE** or **DELETE**) from trying to access the table. These locks likewise prevent a DDL operation from occurring while outstanding DML operations are in progress or while other DDL operations are ongoing.

Two other DML locks specific to partitioning that Oracle uses are the DML partition lock and the DML subpartition lock. These locking mechanisms allow you to perform DDL operations on specific partitions while other partitions in the same object remain available for other DDL or DML operations. The priority and ordering of partition and subpartition DML locks is as shown here:

1. Table locks
2. Partition/subpartition locks
3. Row locks

As you can see, these locks are one level higher than row level locking and one level lower than table level locks. This implies that a partition/subpartition lock will prevent you from changing a row in a given partition, but that it will not lock out the entire partitioned table.

Thus, even though you're doing maintenance on one partition of a partitioned table, other partitions are not affected. This has positive implications for performance, as users won't experience blocking situations as they access the other partitions of the partitioned table.

Partition locks and subpartition locks, much like other locking mechanisms in Oracle, can be acquired in one of several modes. The available modes are: Share (S), Exclusive (X), Row Share (SS), Row Exclusive (SX), and Share Row Exclusive (SSX).

So, when are DML partition locks used and when are DML subpartition locks used? DML partition locks are used during operations on range-partitioned or hash-partitioned tables. DML subpartition locks then are used during operations on composite partitioned tables.

Partition Pruning and Partition-Wise Joins

To further improve the performance of partition operations, Oracle supports two operations on partitions: partition pruning and partition-wise joins.

Partition pruning is the process of keeping partitions from being accessed during a SQL query if those partitions don't contain data relevant to the query. For each SQL statement, one or more partitions can be pruned based on the criteria in the **WHERE** clause of the statement. Take, for example, the **sales_detail_data** table. Assume that it was partitioned on the **date_of_sale** column, with a partition for every month's sales. If the **WHERE** clause of a query wanted sales for January, then all the partitions that do not contain sales dates in January can be removed from consideration by the optimizer.

Partition pruning has some restrictions. Specifically, if the SQL statement applies a function to the partition column, then partition pruning will be unavailable. The only exception to this rule is the use of the **TO_DATE** function. A function can be applied to a column on an index partition lookup when that index is a function-based index.

Partition pruning can also eliminate partitions in indexes, even when the underlying table partitions cannot be eliminated. Thus, if the table was partitioned on one value and the index on another, it's possible that partition pruning will still be available on the index.

The use of partition pruning can significantly reduce the number of accesses—logical or physical—that may be required to return the result of the SQL query. Partition pruning also affects availability, system-level performance, reorganization, and index building.

Partition-wise joins involve the breaking down of a large join operation between two equijoined objects into smaller units of work. These smaller joins can then be performed in serial or in parallel. The optimizer will determine whether a partition-wise join can be used and whether it's likely to be effective. In addition, Oracle can combine partition pruning and partition join operations, thus further improving performance of a query on a partitioned table.

Practice Questions

Question 1

What are the three methods of partitioning a table in Oracle8i?

- ❑ a. Range
- ❑ b. Subpartition
- ❑ c. Hash
- ❑ d. Consolidated
- ❑ e. Composite

Trick! question!

Answers a, c, and e are correct. Answer b is incorrect because *subpartition* is a term used in relation to composite partitioning. You might have opted to select this incorrect choice, and thus this is a trick question. Answer d is incorrect because it isn't a partitioning method.

Question 2

What type of partitioning method is supported for non-prefixed global partitioned indexes?

- ❍ a. Range
- ❍ b. Subpartition
- ❍ c. Hash
- ❍ d. Consolidated
- ❍ e. Composite

Answer a is correct. Range partitioning is the only partitioning method supported for indexes. Answers b, c, d, and e are incorrect for this reason.

Question 3

Which statement is true in relation to composite partitioning?

- ❍ a. Data in a composite partition is stored in partitions determined by the partition range.
- ❍ b. Composite partitioned tables cannot contain LOBs.
- ❍ c. The partitions store the actual partitioned data determined by hash value, and the subpartitions are logical structures that provide access to the partitioned data as determined by range.
- ❍ d. When created, the composite-partitioned table creates two storage segments: the partition and the subpartition. The partition stores rows as determined by the range value of the partition key. The subpartition stores the rows as determined by the hash value of the partition-key columns.
- ❍ e. Data in a composite partition is stored in subpartitions determined by hash value.

Answer e is correct. In a composite-partitioned table, the data is physically stored in the subpartitions as determined by the hash value of the partition key. The partitions, which represent the range partitions of the table, are logical structures, which don't actually store data. Answer a is incorrect because data is never stored in the partition of a composite-partitioned table; data is stored only in the subpartitions. Answer b is incorrect because composite-partitioned tables can store LOBs. Answer c is incorrect because the partition component of a composite-partitioned table never stores data. Answer d is incorrect because data is stored only in a subpartition segment determined by the hash value.

Question 4

If you are partitioning a table that contains a LOB column, which of the following statements is true?

❍ a. The LOB column can be part of the partition key as long as it's the leading edge of the key.

❍ b. The LOB column can be part of the partition key as long as it's the trailing edge of the key.

❍ c. The LOB column cannot be part of the partition key.

❍ d. The LOB column can be part of a partition key if you are creating a hash-partitioned table.

❍ e. The LOB column must be part of the primary key.

Answer c is correct. When you're creating a partitioned table with a LOB column, the LOB column cannot be part of the partition key. Therefore, answers a, b, d, and e are incorrect because they assume that the LOB column can be part of the partition key.

Question 5

Range and __________ partitioning are the two basic partitioning methods available in Oracle8i.

Hash is the correct answer.

Question 6

You have created a partitioned table called **acct_payable_data**, the DDL of which is shown in the following code. Which invoice numbers cannot be stored in a partition of this table?

```
CREATE TABLE acct_payable_data
(invoice_number    NUMBER   NOT NULL,
date_of_invoice    DATE     NOT NULL,
amount            NUMBER   NOT NULL,
vendor_code       NUMBER   NOT NULL
)
-- TABLESPACE part_table_store
STORAGE (INITIAL 10K NEXT 10K)
PARTITION BY RANGE (invoice_number)
(
PARTITION invoices_0_1999 VALUES LESS THAN
  (2000),
PARTITION invoices_2000_2999 VALUES LESS THAN
  (3000),
PARTITION invoices_3000_3999 VALUES LESS THAN
  (4000) );
```

❍ a. 0

❍ b. 1,000

❍ c. 2,000

❍ d. 4,000

❍ e. 500

Answer d is correct. The value 4,000 cannot be stored because the last partition of the table will hold invoice numbers only up to 3,999. Attempting to insert a row with a value of 4,000 will result in an error. Answers a, b, c, and e are all valid invoice numbers.

Question 7

When you're creating a local index on a composite-partitioned table, which statement will be true?

- ❍ a. The local index won't be equipartitioned with the composite-partitioned table.
- ❍ b. By default, the partitions of the local index will be stored in the same tablespace as the subpartition of the composite-partitioned table with which they're associated.
- ❍ c. You cannot create a local index on a composite-partitioned table.
- ❍ d. You cannot define the location of the local index partitions of a local index built in a composite-partitioned table.
- ❍ e. You cannot create any indexes on partitioned tables.

Answer b is correct. You can create only local indexes on composite-partitioned tables, and by default the partitions are always stored in the same tablespace as the associated subpartition. Answer a is incorrect because local partitioned indexes are always equipartitioned. Answer c is incorrect because you can create a local index on a composite-partitioned table. Answer d is incorrect because you can define the location of a local index partition by using the **LOCAL STORE IN** clause of the **CREATE INDEX** statement. Answer e is incorrect because you can indeed create indexes on partitioned tables.

Question 8

Which of the following isn't a restriction involving the partitioning of a table?

- ❍ a. A partitioned table cannot be a clustered table.
- ❍ b. A partitioned table cannot contain a **LONG** data type.
- ❍ c. A partitioned table cannot contain a **BFILE** data type.
- ❍ d. A partitioned table cannot contain a **LONG RAW** data type.
- ❍ e. A nonpartitioned table can have only global partitioned indexes or nonpartitioned indexes associated with it.

Answer c is correct. A partitioned table can contain a **LOB** data type. Because **BFILE** is a **LOB** data type, it can be included in a partitioned table except for the restriction that it can't be a part of the partition key. Answer a is incorrect because a partitioned table can't be a clustered table. Answers b and d are incorrect because a **LONG** or **LONG RAW** data types can't be contained in a partitioned table. Answer e is incorrect because it does properly describe a restriction involving a table partition.

Question 9

When is an index considered prefixed?

- ❍ a. An index is considered prefixed when the leftmost columns of the index are based on the partition key of the index.
- ❍ b. A prefixed index is an index that contains the second or later columns of the partition key of the index and one or more columns that aren't part of the partition key of the same table.
- ❍ c. A prefixed index is an index that is equijoined with the table it's related to.
- ❍ d. A prefixed index is an index that contains one or more nonpartition-key columns of the related partitioned table and no partition-key columns.
- ❍ e. A prefixed index is a **LOB** index that is contained in the same tablespace as the **LOB** data segment.

Answer a is correct. An index is prefixed when the leftmost columns of the index are based on the partition key of the index. Answer b is incorrect because a prefixed index should contain the leftmost column of the partitioned table. Answer c is incorrect because a prefixed index has no relationship to equipartitioning of a table and an index. Answer d is incorrect because a prefixed index must contain at least the leftmost column of the partition key. Answer e is incorrect because a prefixed index isn't the same as a **LOB** index.

Question 10

Which statement is true in relation to **MAXVALUE**?

- ❍ a. The **MAXVALUE** hint in a SQL statement will cause the optimizer to use only the last partition of the table when processing a query, thus speeding up execution of the query.
- ❍ b. The **MAXVALUE** clause of a partition on a range-partitioned or composite-partitioned table will allow all values beyond the range of the other partitions of the table to be stored without error.
- ❍ c. The **MAXVALUE** clause indicates that no value should be allowed to enter a partition beyond the **MAXVALUE** specified in the statement.
- ❍ d. The **MAXVALUE** clause defines an alternate LOB storage tablespace for partitioned tables that contain LOB columns, if the LOB column stored exceeds the length defined in the **MAXVALUE** clause.
- ❍ e. The **MAXVALUE** setting is no longer valid in Oracle8i.

Answer b is correct. You define the last partition of a partitioned table with MAXVALUE to allow that partition to become a "catch-all" partition, holding values that are beyond the normal ranges defined in the partition boundaries of the partitioned table. Answer a is incorrect because MAXVALUE isn't a hint. Answers c and d are incorrect because they don't correctly define the purpose of the MAXVALUE clause. Answer e is incorrect because MAXVALUE is still valid in Oracle8i.

Question 11

Fill in the blank in the following code.

```
CREATE INDEX ix_sales_dos_01 ON
sales_detail_data(date_of_sale)
________________
PARTITION BY RANGE(date_of_sale)
(PARTITION par1 VALUES LESS THAN
(TO_DATE('01-APR-1999','DD-MON-YYYY') )
 TABLESPACE quarter_one
 STORAGE (INITIAL 10k NEXT 10k),
 PARTITION par2 VALUES LESS THAN
(TO_DATE('01-JUL-1999','DD-MON-YYYY') )
 TABLESPACE quarter_three
STORAGE (INITIAL 20k NEXT 10k),
 PARTITION par3 VALUES LESS THAN (MAXVALUE)
 TABLESPACE quarter_four
STORAGE (INITIAL 10k NEXT 10k) );
```

GLOBAL is the correct answer. Because this index creation statement includes a **PARTITION BY RANGE** statement, the index must be global.

Need to Know More?

Ault, Mike. *Oracle8i Administration and Management.* Wiley Computer Publishing, 2000. ISBN 0-471-35453-8. Contains good information on partitioning tables and indexes.

Oracle's documentation is good reference material. Oracle has numerous guides available on CD or in hardcover. The *Oracle8i Concepts* guide and the *Oracle8i SQL Reference* guide have very good sections on partitioning.

Scherer, Douglas. *Oracle8i Tips & Techniques.* Osborne/McGraw-Hill (Oracle Press), 2000. ISBN 0-07-2121903-3. With a good chapter on partitioning of indexes and tables, this book is a worthy read.

www.revealnet.com is a wonderful site with Oracle tips for DBAs and PL/SQL developers.

support.oracle.com is Oracle's Metalink Web site, a wonderful resource if you have Oracle metals support.

14

Administration of Partitioned Tables and Indexes in Oracle8i

Terms you'll need to understand:

- ✓ Merged partitions
- ✓ Splitting partitions
- ✓ **NOLOGGING**
- ✓ **UNUSABLE** status

Techniques you'll need to master:

- ✓ Following Oracle8i table and index partitioning rules
- ✓ Recognizing Oracle8i table and index types
- ✓ Managing new Oracle8i partitioned tables
- ✓ Managing new Oracle8i partitioned indexes
- ✓ Rebuilding indexes that have a status of **UNUSABLE**
- ✓ Generating statistics for partitioned and subpartitioned objects
- ✓ Accessing specific partitions and subpartitions with SQL
- ✓ Using the Oracle Import/Export utility on partitioned and subpartitioned tables
- ✓ Using SQL*Loader on partitioned tables

In this chapter, we'll cover what you need to know about managing partitioned objects for the Oracle8i OCP upgrade exam. We'll discuss the various DDL statements used to maintain partitions, plus the various data dictionary views that are required to manage them. We'll also discuss the special SQL syntax that Oracle provides for accessing partitions, analyzing partitioned objects, and analyzing explain plans for queries that access partitioned objects. We'll then discuss importing data into and exporting data from partitioned objects, and finally, we'll look at using SQL*Loader to load outside data into partitioned objects.

Managing Partitioned Objects

In Chapter 13, we talked about creating partitioned objects. After you've created them, you'll sometimes need to change an individual partition or an entire object. You might need to rebuild an index or add a partition to a table. In this section, we'll cover the management of partitioned objects.

General Information on Managing Partitioned Tables

After a partitioned table is created, several management issues arise from time to time. You might sometimes need to modify the partition table's storage parameters, or add, drop, or split partitions. The three partitioning methods in Oracle8i generally use the same command set for partition-maintenance operations, but if a certain operation does not apply to a particular partitioning method, we'll point that out. Most commands you use on nonpartitioned tables (for example, **DROP TABLE** and **ANALYZE**) can also be used on partitioned tables. Other commands work pretty much the same, although they might contain syntax specific to partitioning.

The **ALTER TABLE** Command

Generally, you use the **ALTER TABLE** statement to perform maintenance functions on partitioned tables. With the **ALTER TABLE** command, you can perform several functions that should already seem like second nature. These functions include:

- Altering the physical characteristics and default settings of a partition or subpartition.
- Adding a partition or subpartition to a table (this can be done only at the end of a partitioned table's partition range).
- Coalescing partitions (in hash-partitioned tables) or subpartitions (in composite-partitioned tables). This redistributes the contents of a partition or subpartition into remaining partitions or subpartitions.

- Dropping a partition (for range or composite partitioning only).
- Exchanging a partition or subpartition—swapping the data (and possibly local index segments) of a table partition or subpartition with the data (and index segments) of a nonpartitioned table.
- Loading, importing, and exporting data to or from a partition or subpartition.
- Marking as **UNUSABLE** all local index partitions or subpartitions associated with a table partition or subpartition.
- Merging partitions (for range- or composite-partitioned tables only).
- Modifying a partition's or subpartition's physical attributes, including a composite-partitioned table's default attributes.
- Moving a table partition or subpartition—moving it to another tablespace, or reclustering it, or changing any of its parameters.
- Moving a partition (this allows you to move a table partition to another tablespace).
- Renaming a partition or subpartition.
- Rebuilding an index partition or subpartition.
- Splitting a single partition into two partitions (for range and composite partitioning only).
- Truncating a partition (with an option to reuse or not reuse storage).

Maintaining Partitions in Partitioned Tables with LOBs

Certain specific operations occur when you perform maintenance operations on partitioned tables with **LOB** columns. A summary of these operations follows:

- When you're adding a partition with the **ADD PARTITION** command, for every **LOB** column in a table, a new **LOB** data partition and a **LOB** index partition are created. You can specify the physical attributes of the new **LOB** data partitions.
- When you're dropping a partition with the **DROP PARTITION** command, for every **LOB** column in a table, the **LOB** data partition and the **LOB** index partition corresponding to the table partition being dropped are also dropped.
- When you're creating a new partitioned table with the **EXCHANGE PARTITION** command, an algorithm is used to determine whether a given nonpartitioned table can be exchanged with a partition of a partitioned table. This algorithm has been updated so that it can also handle **LOB** columns.

- When you're importing or exporting data into a partition of a table, you can import or export partitions of tables containing **LOB** columns.
- When you're loading data into partitions, if the data contains **LOB** columns, then the data will also be loaded into **LOB** data partitions (while making appropriate changes to **LOB** index partitions) corresponding to the partition of the partitioned table into which you're loading the data.
- When you're modifying partitions with the **MODIFY PARTITION** command, you can modify attributes of **LOB** data partitions associated with a given table partition. Although you cannot specify attributes for a **LOB** index partition, changes to an attribute of a **LOB** data partition might result in changes to the corresponding attribute of a **LOB** index partition associated with it.
- When you're moving partitions with the **MOVE PARTITION** command, for every **LOB** column in a table, a **LOB** data partition and a **LOB** index partition corresponding to the table partition being moved can also be moved. These partitions do not have to be moved; for example, a **LOB** data partition may reside on a read-only device. You can specify new physical attributes of **LOB** data partitions.
- When you're splitting a partition with the **SPLIT PARTITION** command, for every **LOB** column in a table, two new **LOB** data partitions and **LOB** index partitions are created. **LOB** instances (or values) are divided between the new partitions based on the values of the partitioning column(s) in the row of which they are a part. You can specify physical attributes for the new **LOB** data partitions.
- When you're truncating a partition with the **TRUNCATE PARTITION** command, for every **LOB** column in a table, the **LOB** data partition and **LOB** index partition corresponding to the table partition being truncated are also truncated.

Managing Partitioned Tables

In this section, we'll discuss the **ALTER TABLE** command, **NOLOGGING** mode, and the **ALTER TABLE EXCHANGE** command.

Using the ALTER TABLE Command to Modify Partitioned Tables

When you're altering range-partitioned tables, you can perform a variety of operations, such as changing the default storage of a table, changing storage for particular partitions, or dropping, adding, or splitting a partition. You alter a partitioned table by using the **ALTER TABLE** command. Listing 14.1 shows several examples of partitioned-table maintenance operations along with comments describing their functions.

Make sure you make yourself familiar with the various operations you can perform on partitioned tables. In particular, you should know how to split, drop, truncate, move, and perform exchange operations on partitioned tables. You should also be clear on the effects of these operations on indexes associated with these tables.

Listing 14.1 Using the **ALTER TABLE** command on a range-partitioned table.

```
/* Change the default storage for a partitioned table. */
ALTER TABLE sales_detail_data MODIFY
DEFAULT ATTRIBUTES STORAGE (INITIAL 10M NEXT 10M);

/* Change the storage parameters for a specific partition. */
ALTER TABLE sales_detail_data modify
PARTITION sales_q1_99 STORAGE (NEXT 10m);

/* Drop a partition in a partitioned table. */
ALTER TABLE sales_detail_data
DROP PARTITION sales_q1_99;

/* Move a partition in a partitioned table to another
   tablespace. */
ALTER TABLE sales_detail_data
MOVE PARTITION sales_q1_99 TABLESPACE quarter_one;

ALTER TABLE sales_detail_data
RENAME PARTITION sales_q1_99 TO sales_q1_1999;

ALTER TABLE sales_detail_data
TRUNCATE PARTITION sales_q1_1999 DROP STORAGE;

ALTER TABLE sales_detail_data ADD PARTITION sales_q1_00
VALUES LESS THAN(TO_DATE('2000-04-01','YYYY-MM-DD') )
PCTFREE 10
PCTUSED 60
TABLESPACE quarter_one
STORAGE (INITIAL 10K NEXT 10K);

-- This next operation would cause ALL partitions of a global
-- index to take on an UNUSABLE status and require rebuilding.
ALTER TABLE sales_detail_data SPLIT PARTITION sales_q1_99_jeans
AT (TO_DATE('1999-04-01','YYYY-MM-DD')) INTO
( PARTITION sales_q1_99_bluejean STORAGE (INITIAL 10k NEXT 10k),
PARTITION sales_q1_99_blackjean STORAGE (INITIAL 10k NEXT 10k) );
```

Some **ALTER TABLE** operations are not supported for hash-partitioned tables. Operations not supported are:

- ALTER TABLE...SPLIT PARTITION
- ALTER TABLE...DROP PARTITION
- ALTER TABLE...MERGE PARTITIONS

Two maintenance operations exist for hash-partitioned tables. They are:

- **ALTER TABLE ADD PARTITION**—Adds a partition to a hash-partitioned table.
- **ALTER TABLE COALESCE PARTITION**—Causes a hash partition to be removed, and Oracle redistributes the data among the remaining partitions.

All **ALTER TABLE** options that can be used with range-partitioned tables can be used with composite-partitioned tables. Also, there are specific subpartition-maintenance operations available. These actions generally are the same as the corresponding actions on partitioned tables, but they specifically refer to subpartitions of a composite-partitioned table. These actions include:

- ALTER TABLE EXCHANGE SUBPARTITION
- ALTER TABLE MODIFY PARTITION ADD SUBPARTITION
- ALTER TABLE MODIFY PARTITION COALESCE SUBPARTITION
- ALTER TABLE MODIFY SUBPARTITION
- ALTER TABLE MOVE SUBPARTITION
- ALTER TABLE RENAME SUBPARTITION
- ALTER TABLE REBUILD SUBPARTITION
- ALTER TABLE TRUNCATE SUBPARTITION

Using NOLOGGING Mode

Some partition operations can be performed in **NOLOGGING** mode if the object has been set to **NOLOGGING** mode. These operations include:

- Parallel **CREATE TABLE...AS SELECT** operations
- **CREATE INDEX** operations
- **SPLIT, MOVE,** or **REBUILD PARTITION** operations

- Direct-path SQL*Loader operations
- Direct-load **INSERT** operations

The default for all operations in **ARCHIVELOG** mode is **LOGGING**. The default for all operations that support **NOLOGGING** mode when the database is in **NOARCHIVELOG** mode is **NOLOGGING**.

Using the **ALTER TABLE EXCHANGE** Command

The **ALTER TABLE EXCHANGE** command is used to move partitioned data into a separate table or to move data from a separate table into a partitioned object. Certain restrictions apply to moving a table into a partitioned table:

- The columns and constraints must be identical.
- The table coming into the partitioned table must not be clustered.
- The table or partition to be exchanged must, obviously, already exist.

An option of the **ALTER TABLE EXCHANGE** command is the **EXCLUDING INDEXES** clause, which leaves indexes intact or excludes them when you're creating tables out of partitions. Listing 14.2 shows an example of moving tables into and out of a partition.

Listing 14.2 Using the ALTER TABLE EXCHANGE command.

```
ALTER TABLE sales_detail_data EXCHANGE PARTITION sales_q1_99
WITH TABLE sales_quarter_99 EXCLUDING INDEXES;
```

General Information on Managing Partitioned Indexes

Managing partitioned indexes is similar in some respects to managing partitions of tables. There are several rules that you should be aware of, however, and these rules are often specific to the type of partitioned index you are dealing with (local or global). Oracle manages many operations on local indexes for you automatically when you affect the associated tables. Some of these operations include:

- When you add a partition to the underlying table, Oracle automatically creates a new index partition with the same partition bound as the new table partition.
- When you drop a partition in the underlying table, Oracle automatically drops the associated index partition.
- When you split a partition in an underlying table, Oracle automatically splits the corresponding index partition. The two new index partitions have the same partition bounds as the new table partitions. Global index partitions

whose partition boundaries are affected by this split are marked **UNUSABLE** if the table partition being split is nonempty.

You can perform the following operations on indexes, with exceptions being noted:

- Alter the default and partition storage clauses.
- Drop a partition. (This cannot be done to a local index.)
- Rebuild a partition. (This allows you to move an index partition to another tablespace, rebuild the partition to recover space, repair an index partition due to media failure or other corruption, or rebuild the index partition if it is made **UNUSABLE** by some operation.)
- Rename a partition.
- Split a partition. (This allows you to take one partition of a global index and split it into two partitions.)

A rule about index partitions: You cannot add a partition to a partitioned index. As we stated earlier, if you add a partition to a table that has local indexes associated with it, Oracle adds a partition to those indexes for you. With a global index, you might want to split an existing partition, drop or rebuild the index, or do nothing. Listing 14.3 shows examples of each of these operations.

Managing Partitioned Indexes

To manage partitioned indexes, you use the **ALTER INDEX** statement. This statement allows you to change default storage for an index, change storage for an index partition, and drop, split, or rebuild an index partition. Listing 14.3 provides several examples of operations performed with the **ALTER INDEX** command.

Listing 14.3 Variations on the **ALTER INDEX** command.

```
/* Change the default storage for a partitioned index. */
ALTER INDEX ix_sales_isku_01
MODIFY DEFAULT ATTRIBUTES STORAGE (NEXT 10M);

/* Drop a partition in a global index. */
ALTER INDEX ix_sales_isku_01
DROP PARTITION parta-1;

/* Change the storage parameters for a specific partition. */
ALTER INDEX ix_sales_dos_01
MODIFY PARTITION PAR1 STORAGE (NEXT 10M);
```

```
/* Drop a partition in an index. This operation cannot be done
   in a local index. */
ALTER INDEX ix_sales_dos_01 DROP PARTITION par1;

/* Rebuild the index partition in another tablespace. */
ALTER INDEX ix_sales_dos_01
REBUILD PARTITION par2 TABLESPACE quarter_two;

/* Rename a partition */
ALTER INDEX ix_sales_dos_01
RENAME PARTITION par2 TO ix_sales_q1_1999;

/* Split a partition of a global index. Will NOT make the
   resulting partitions UNUSABLE! */
ALTER INDEX sales_detail_data
SPLIT PARTITION sales_q1_99_jeans
AT (TO_DATE('1999-04-01','YYYY-MM-DD'),5000) INTO
( PARTITION sales_q1_99_bluejean STORAGE (INITIAL 10k NEXT 10k),
PARTITION sales_q1_99_blackjean STORAGE (INITIAL 10k NEXT 10k) );
```

Partitioned Indexes in an UNUSABLE State

Several operations might put an index into an **UNUSABLE** state. This state might affect a nonpartitioned index or one or more partitions of a partitioned index. If you try to perform DML or **SELECT** operations against a table, and the optimizer decides to access index partitions in an **UNUSABLE** state, Oracle will raise an error (usually an ORA-1502).

Operations that can cause an index to be in an **UNUSABLE** state include the following:

- In certain cases, the Import utility can cause this if it is set to bypass updates on the partitioned index (e.g., the **SKIP_UNUSABLE_INDEXES** parameter in the Import utility).
- If you move, split, truncate, or drop a table partition that contains data in it, these operations will mark nonpartitioned and global indexes as **UNUSABLE**.
- If you drop a partition in a global index, the next highest partition will be marked as **UNUSABLE**.
- You use SQL*Loader to do a direct-path load. Also, in Oracle8i, a SQL*Loader option called **SKIP_INDEX_MAINTENANCE** will cause indexes to become **UNUSABLE**.

- **DROP, EXCHANGE, MOVE, SPLIT**, and **TRUNCATE** operations on tables will cause all partitions of a global index to become **UNUSABLE**. After these operations, you must rebuild each partition of the partitioned indexes.
- A **DROP** operation on a partition of a global index will cause all partitions of the index to acquire a status of **UNUSABLE**.

Note that you can split or rename a partition in an **UNUSABLE** state, and you can also drop a partition of a global index that is in an **UNUSABLE** state.

If an index on a partitioned table shows a status of **UNUSABLE** in the **DBA_INDEXES** view, or if you know that an operation to be performed will set the status of the indexes to such a state, then you must plan to rebuild the indexes accordingly. The command to rebuild partitioned indexes depends on the type of index that needs to be rebuilt. To rebuild the indexes, use the **ALTER INDEX REBUILD PARTITION** statement. Note that you must execute this command for *each partition* that you want to rebuild because there is no statement available to rebuild all partitions of a partitioned index.

Views for Administering Partitioned Tables and Indexes

Several views are used to administer partitioned indexes and tables. Following is a summary list of these views and their purposes:

- DBA_IND_PARTITIONS—Provides information on all index partitions in the database.
- DBA_IND_SUBPARTITIONS—Provides information on all index subpartitions in the database.
- DBA_INDEXES—Shows the name, tablespace, associated table, and other statistics for all indexes in the database.
- DBA_OBJECTS—Provides information on all objects within the database.
- DBA_PART_COL_STATISTICS—Provides the ability to review the statistics collected by the cost-based optimizer for partitioned tables.
- DBA_PART_HISTOGRAMS—Displays the distribution of data in partitions, for all analyzed partitions in the database.
- DBA_PART_INDEXES—Provides information on indexes and how they are partitioned for the tables in the database.
- DBA_PART_KEY_COLUMNS—Identifies partition keys used for all tables and indexes.

- DBA_PART_TABLES—Provides information on partitioned tables in the database, including partition keys.
- DBA_SEGMENTS—Shows segment-level information. Each partition is a segment, so each partition appears in the DBA_SEGMENTS view along with the partitioned table.
- DBA_SUBPART_COL_STATISTICS—Provides a way to review the statistics collected by the cost-based optimizer for subpartitions.
- DBA_TAB_COL_STATISTICS— Provides a way to review the statistics collected by the cost-based optimizer for partitioned indexes.
- DBA_TAB_PARTITIONS—Provides information on all table partitions in the database.
- DBA_TAB_SUBPARTITIONS—Provides information on all table subpartitions in the database.
- DBA_TABLES—Shows the name, tablespace, and statistics on all tables in the database.

The following sections examine these views in more detail and show you what information they can provide.

Note: The DBA_TAB_COLUMNS, DBA_TAB_COL_STATISTICS, DBA_TAB_HISTOGRAMS, and DBA_IND_COLUMNS views have not changed significantly for partitioning in Oracle8i, so they are not addressed in this chapter.

The **DBA_IND_PARTITIONS** View

The DBA_IND_PARTITIONS view provides granular partition-level information for all partitions of an object. Many of the columns are similar to those in the DBA_TAB_PARTITIONS table. In this view, you can find a variety of information on specific partitions, including the tablespace the partitions are assigned to, partition storage parameters, and various statistics gathered for each partition by the ANALYZE command. Many of the columns are similar to the columns you already use in DBA_INDEXES.

Note: If you are looking for an index partition with an UNUSABLE status, this is the table you query.

The **DBA_IND_SUBPARTITIONS** View

The DBA_IND_SUBPARTITIONS view provides granular partition-level information for all subpartitions of an object. Many of the columns are similar to those in the DBA_TAB_SUBPARTITIONS table. In this view, you can find a variety of information on specific partitions, including the tablespace the partitions are assigned to, partition storage parameters, and various statistics gathered for each partition by the **ANALYZE** command. Many of the columns are similar to the columns you already use in **DBA_INDEXES**.

Note: If you are looking for an index subpartition with an **UNUSABLE** *status, this is the table you query.*

Listing 14.4 shows a sample query against the view.

Listing 14.4 Sample query of the DBA_IND_SUBPARTITIONS view.

```
SQL> SELECT index_owner,index_name,partition_name,tablespace_name,
  2  FROM dba_ind_subpartitions;
INDEX_OW INDEX_NAME                 PARTITION_N TABLESPACE_NAME
-------- -------------------------- ----------- ---------------
SYSTEM   IX_L_SALES_DETAIL_DATA_01  SALES_Q1_99 QUARTER_ONE
SYSTEM   IX_L_SALES_DETAIL_DATA_01  SALES_Q1_99 QUARTER_ONE
SYSTEM   IX_L_SALES_DETAIL_DATA_01  SALES_Q1_99 QUARTER_ONE
SYSTEM   IX_L_SALES_DETAIL_DATA_01  SALES_Q1_99 QUARTER_ONE
SYSTEM   IX_L_SALES_DETAIL_DATA_01  SALES_Q2_99 QUARTER_TWO
SYSTEM   IX_L_SALES_DETAIL_DATA_01  SALES_Q2_99 QUARTER_TWO
SYSTEM   IX_L_SALES_DETAIL_DATA_01  SALES_Q2_99 QUARTER_TWO
SYSTEM   IX_L_SALES_DETAIL_DATA_01  SALES_Q2_99 QUARTER_TWO
SYSTEM   IX_L_SALES_DETAIL_DATA_01  SALES_Q3_99 QUARTER_THREE
SYSTEM   IX_L_SALES_DETAIL_DATA_01  SALES_Q3_99 QUARTER_THREE
SYSTEM   IX_L_SALES_DETAIL_DATA_01  SALES_Q3_99 QUARTER_THREE
SYSTEM   IX_L_SALES_DETAIL_DATA_01  SALES_Q3_99 QUARTER_THREE
SYSTEM   IX_L_SALES_DETAIL_DATA_01  SALES_Q4_99 QUARTER_FOUR
SYSTEM   IX_L_SALES_DETAIL_DATA_01  SALES_Q4_99 QUARTER_FOUR
SYSTEM   IX_L_SALES_DETAIL_DATA_01  SALES_Q4_99 QUARTER_FOUR
15 rows selected.
```

The DBA_INDEXES View

In Oracle8i, the **DBA_INDEXES** view was changed to allow the management of partitioned indexes. The tablespace names for the partitions of indexes are in the **DBA_PART_INDEXES** view. Listing 14.5 shows a sample query of the **DBA_INDEXES** view.

Listing 14.5 Query of the DBA_INDEXES view, showing partitioned indexes on a partitioned table.

```
SQL> SELECT owner, index_name, index_type,
  2  status, partitioned
  3  FROM dba_indexes where TABLE_NAME
  4  = 'SALES_DETAIL_DATA';
```

```
OWNER  INDEX_NAME        INDEX_TYPE   STATUS  PARTITIONED
------ ----------------  ----------   ------  -----------
OBJOWN IX_SALES_DOS_01   NORMAL       N/A     YES
OBJOWN IX_SALES_ISKU_01  NORMAL       N/A     YES
```

The DBA_OBJECTS View

The DBA_OBJECTS view is used to support partitioning of objects in Oracle8i. For a single partitioned object, this view lists each partition as a separate object. For a partitioned object, the **OBJECT_NAME** column contains the name of the partitioned object, and the **SUBOBJECT_NAME** column contains an entry for each partition of the object. The **OBJECT_TYPE** column lists object types of both partitions and subpartitions. Listing 14.6 shows an example of the pertinent output from this view.

Listing 14.6 Sample query of the DBA_OBJECTS view for a partitioned table.

```
SQL> SELECT owner, subobject_name, object_id, data_object_id,
  2  object_type, status
  3  FROM dba_objects
  4  WHERE object_name = 'SALES_DETAIL_DATA';

OWNER  SUBOBJECT_N OBJECT_ID DATA_OBJECT_ID OBJECT_TYPE     STATUS
------ ----------  --------  -------------- -------------   ------
OBJOWN SALES_Q1_99 2578      2578           TABLE PARTITION VALID
OBJOWN SALES_Q2_99 2579      2579           TABLE PARTITION VALID
OBJOWN SALES_Q3_99 2580      2580           TABLE PARTITION VALID
OBJOWN SALES_Q4_99 2581      2581           TABLE PARTITION VALID
OBJOWN             2577                     TABLE           VALID
```

The DBA_PART_COL_STATISTICS View

The DBA_PART_COL_STATISTICS view provides granular partition-level column information for all columns of an object. This includes statistical and histogram information that is populated after an ANALYZE command is executed on the table. Listing 14.7 shows a sample query against the table.

Listing 14.7 Description and sample query of the DBA_PART_COL_STATISTICS view.

```
SQL> SELECT owner, partition_name, column_name, num_distinct
  2  FROM dba_part_col_statistics
  3  WHERE table_name = 'SALES_DETAIL_DATA';

OWNER  PARTITION_NAME  COLUMN_NAME     NUM_DISTINCT
------ --------------  --------------  ------------
SYSTEM SALES_Q1_99     DATE_OF_SALE               1
SYSTEM SALES_Q1_99     INVOICE_NUMBER             2
SYSTEM SALES_Q1_99     ITEM_LINE_NO               2
```

```
SYSTEM SALES_Q1_99      item_sku                     1
SYSTEM SALES_Q1_99      QTY_SOLD                     1
SYSTEM SALES_Q2_99      date_of_sale                 2
SYSTEM SALES_Q2_99      INVOICE_NUMBER               2
SYSTEM SALES_Q2_99      ITEM_LINE_NO                 2
SYSTEM SALES_Q2_99      item_sku                     3
SYSTEM SALES_Q2_99      QTY_SOLD                     2
SYSTEM SALES_Q3_99      date_of_sale                 2
SYSTEM SALES_Q3_99      INVOICE_NUMBER               2
SYSTEM SALES_Q3_99      ITEM_LINE_NO                 1
SYSTEM SALES_Q3_99      item_sku                     2
SYSTEM SALES_Q3_99      QTY_SOLD                     1
SYSTEM SALES_Q4_99      date_of_sale                 1
SYSTEM SALES_Q4_99      INVOICE_NUMBER               1
SYSTEM SALES_Q4_99      ITEM_LINE_NO                 1
SYSTEM SALES_Q4_99      item_sku                     1
SYSTEM SALES_Q4_99      QTY_SOLD                     1
```

The DBA_PART_HISTOGRAM View

The DBA_PART_HISTOGRAM view provides histogram data for all partitions of a table. Listing 14.8 shows a sample query against the table, looking at columnar distinct values.

Listing 14.8 Description and sample query of the DBA_PART_HISTOGRAM view.

```
SQL> SELECT owner, partition_name, column_name,
  2  bucket_number, endpoint_value from dba_part_histograms
  2  WHERE table_name LIKE 'SALES_DETAIL_DATA' AND
  3  partition_name LIKE 'SALES_Q3_99';

                                                BUCKET
OWNER   PARTITION_NAME     COLUMN_NAME          NUMBER ENDPOINT_VALUE
------  ------------------ --------------       ------ --------------
SYSTEM  SALES_Q3_99        date_of_sale              0        2451361
SYSTEM  SALES_Q3_99        date_of_sale              1        2451423
SYSTEM  SALES_Q3_99        INVOICE_NUMBER            0              4
SYSTEM  SALES_Q3_99        INVOICE_NUMBER            1              5
SYSTEM  SALES_Q3_99        ITEM_LINE_NO              0              1
SYSTEM  SALES_Q3_99        ITEM_LINE_NO              1              1
SYSTEM  SALES_Q3_99        item_sku                  0        2000000
SYSTEM  SALES_Q3_99        item_sku                  1        4000000
SYSTEM  SALES_Q3_99        QTY_SOLD                  0              1
SYSTEM  SALES_Q3_99        QTY_SOLD                  1              1
```

The DBA_PART_INDEXES View

The DBA_PART_INDEXES view provides partitioning information for all partitioned indexes. Listing 14.9 shows a sample query against the view. In the query, you see the owner and name of the index. No table information is provided in the view, so you have to join this view with **DBA_INDEXES** to get the associated table information. The **PARTITIONING_TYPE** column can be **RANGE** or **HASH**, and a new column called **SUBPARTITION_TYPE** can be **NULL**, **HASH**, or **NONE**. The **PARTITIONING_COUNT** column returns the number of partitions (four), and the **PARTITIONING _KEY_COUNT** column returns the number of columns that make up the partition key (**1** equals **sales_date**). The **LOCALITY** column tells you whether the index is **LOCAL** or **GLOBAL**, and the **ALIGNMENT** column tells you whether the index is **PREFIXED** or **NON_PREFIXED**. This view also contains the default settings used if you add new partitions.

Listing 14.9 Description and sample query of the DBA_PART_INDEXES view.

```
SQL> SELECT owner, partitioning_type, partition_count,
  2  partitioning_key_count,locality, alignment
  3  FROM dba_part_indexes
  4  WHERE index_name LIKE 'IX_SALES_ISKU_01';

OWNER  PART    PARTITION PARTITIONING LOCALITY ALIGNMENT
       TYPE    COUNT     KEY_COUNT
------ ------  -------- ------------ -------- --------
OBJOWN RANGE          4            1 LOCAL    NON_PREFIXED

SQL> SELECT owner, partitioning_range, partition_count,
  2  partitioning_key_count, locality, alignment FROM
     dba_part_indexes
  3  WHERE index_name LIKE 'IX_SALES_DOS_01';

OWNER  PART    PARTITION PARTITIONING LOCALITY ALIGNMENT
       RANGE   COUNT     KEY_COUNT
------ ------  -------- ------------ -------- --------
OBJOWN RANGE          3            1   GLOBAL  PREFIXED
```

The DBA_PART_KEY_COLUMNS View

The DBA_PART_KEY_COLUMNS view provides partitioning information for all partitioned indexes. Listing 14.10 shows a sample query against the view. The view provides information about the columns on which a partitioned object is keyed. The **OWNER** and **NAME** columns are the owner and name of the object. The

OBJECT_TYPE column is either **TABLE** or **INDEX**. The **COLUMN_NAME** column displays the name of the column(s) on which the object is keyed. The **COLUMN_POSITION** column shows the order of that column in the composite key.

Listing 14.10 Description and sample query of the DBA_PART_KEY_COLUMNS view.

```
SQL> SELECT * FROM dba_part_key_columns;

OWNER  NAME                OBJECT_TYPE COLUMN_NAME   COLUMN_POS
------ ------------------  ----------  ------------  ----------
OBJOWN IX_SALES_DOS_01     INDEX       date_of_sale           1
OBJOWN IX_SALES_ISKU_01    INDEX       date_of_sale           1
OBJOWN SALES_DETAIL_DATA   TABLE       date_of_sale           1
```

The DBA_PART_TABLES View

The **DBA_PART_TABLES** view provides partitioning information for all partitioned tables. Listing 14.11 shows a sample query against the view. In the query, you see:

- The name of the table returned in the **TABLE_NAME** column
- The type of partitioning being used in the **PARTITIONING_TYPE** column (**RANGE** or **HASH** is the only valid method)
- The number of partitions (four) in the **PARTITION_COUNT** column
- The number of columns that make up the partition key in the **PARTITION _KEY_COUNT** column

In addition, this view shows the partition's default settings used (if you are adding a new partition).

Listing 14.11 Description and sample query of the DBA_PART_TABLES view.

```
SQL> SELECT owner,partitioning_type, partition_count,
  2  partitioning_key_count
  3  FROM dba_part_tables
  4  WHERE table_name LIKE 'SALES_DETAIL_DATA';

OWNER  PART    PARTITION_COUNT PARTITIONING_KEY_COUNT
       RANGE
-----------------------------------------------------
OBJOWN RANGE                 4                      1
```

The DBA_SEGMENTS View

The DBA_SEGMENTS view provides a row for each partition (or subpartition) of a partitioned object and the partitioned object itself. For a partitioned object, the **SEGMENT_NAME** column contains the name of the partitioned table and the name of each partition. The **PARTITION_NAME** column defines the partitioned table that each partition belongs to. The **SEGMENT_TYPE** column indicates the type of segment that you're dealing with, such as an index subpartition, a **LOB** segment, a table subpartition, and so on. Listing 14.12 shows an example of the pertinent output from this view.

Listing 14.12 Sample query of the DBA_SEGMENTS view for a partitioned table.

```
SQL> SELECT owner, segment_name,
  2  partition_name, segment_type,
  3  tablespace_name
  4  FROM dba_segments
  5  WHERE segment_type = 'TABLE PARTITION';

OWNER  SEGMENT_NAME       PARTITION  SEGMENT_TYPE    TABLESPACE
                          _NAME                      _NAME
------ -------------      ---------  -------------   ------------
SYSTEM  SALES_DETAIL_DATA  SALES_Q1_  TABLE PARTITION QUARTER_ONE
                          _99_SHIRTS
SYSTEM  SALES_DETAIL_DATA  SALES_Q1_  TABLE PARTITION QUARTER_ONE
                          _99_ALLELSE
SYSTEM  SALES_DETAIL_DATA  SALES_Q2_  TABLE PARTITION QUARTER_TWO
                          _99_JEANS
SYSTEM  SALES_DETAIL_DATA  SALES_Q2_  TABLE PARTITION QUARTER_TWO
                          _99_SHIRTS
SYSTEM  SALES_DETAIL_DATA  SALES_Q2_  TABLE PARTITION QUARTER_TWO
                          _99_ALLELSE
SYSTEM  SALES_DETAIL_DATA  SALES_Q3_  TABLE PARTITION QUARTER_THREE
                          _99_JEANS
SYSTEM  SALES_DETAIL_DATA  SALES_Q3_  TABLE PARTITION QUARTER_THREE
                          _99_SHIRTS
SYSTEM  SALES_DETAIL_DATA  SALES_Q3_  TABLE PARTITION QUARTER_THREE
                          _99_ALLELSE
SYSTEM  SALES_DETAIL_DATA  SALES_Q4_  TABLE PARTITION QUARTER_FOUR
                          _99_JEANS
SYSTEM  SALES_DETAIL_DATA  SALES_Q4_  TABLE PARTITION QUARTER_FOUR
                          _99_SHIRTS
SYSTEM  SALES_DETAIL_DATA  SALES_Q4_  TABLE PARTITION QUARTER_FOUR
                          _99_ALLELSE
SYSTEM  SALES_DETAIL_DATA  SALES_Q1_  TABLE PARTITION QUARTER_ONE
                          _99_BLUEJEAN
SYSTEM  SALES_DETAIL_DATA  SALES_Q1_  TABLE PARTITION QUARTER_ONE
                          _99_BLACKJEAN
```

The **DBA_SUBPART_COL_STATISTICS** View

The DBA_SUBPART_COL_STATISTICS view, new to Oracle8i, provides a method of reviewing the current statistics on columns in subpartitions of a partitioned table. These statistics include the last time the subpartition was analyzed. This view also provides the various settings for each subpartition, which advanced DBAs might want to explore for tuning purposes. Listing 14.13 provides a sample query of this table and its output.

Listing 14.13 Sample query of the DBA_SUBPART_COL_STATISTICS view for a partitioned table.

```
SQL> select owner,table_name,subpartition_name,last_analyzed
  2   from dba_subpart_col_statistics

OWNER      TABLE_NAME                     SUBPART    LAST_ANAL
                                          NAME
---------- ------------------------------ ---------- ---------
SYSTEM     SALES_DETAIL_DATA              Q1S1       29-MAY-00
SYSTEM     SALES_DETAIL_DATA              Q1S2       29-MAY-00
SYSTEM     SALES_DETAIL_DATA              Q1S3       29-MAY-00
SYSTEM     SALES_DETAIL_DATA              Q1S4       29-MAY-00
SYSTEM     SALES_DETAIL_DATA              Q1S1       29-MAY-00
SYSTEM     SALES_DETAIL_DATA              Q1S2       29-MAY-00
SYSTEM     SALES_DETAIL_DATA              Q1S3       29-MAY-00
SYSTEM     SALES_DETAIL_DATA              Q1S4       29-MAY-00
SYSTEM     SALES_DETAIL_DATA              Q1S1       29-MAY-00
SYSTEM     SALES_DETAIL_DATA              Q1S2       29-MAY-00
SYSTEM     SALES_DETAIL_DATA              Q1S3       29-MAY-00
SYSTEM     SALES_DETAIL_DATA              Q1S4       29-MAY-00
```

The **DBA_TAB_PARTITIONS** View

The DBA_TAB_PARTITIONS view provides granular partition-level information for all partitions of a table. Here, you can find a variety of information on specific partitions, including the tablespace that the partitions are assigned to, partition storage parameters, and various statistics gathered for each partition by the ANALYZE command. Many of the columns are similar to the columns you already use in the DBA_TABLES view. Listing 14.14 shows a sample query against the table.

Listing 14.14 A sample query of the DBA_TAB_PARTITIONS view.

```
SQL> SELECT table_owner "OWNER",table_name,partition_name,
     partition_position,tablespace_name
  2  FROM dba_tab_partitions;
```

```
                                             PARTITION
OWNER   TABLE_NAME         PARTITION_NAME POSITION  TABLESPACE_NAME
------  ----------------   -------------- --------  ---------------
OBJOWN  SALES_DETAIL_DATA SALES_Q1_99           1  QUARTER_ONE
OBJOWN  SALES_DETAIL_DATA SALES_Q2_99           2  QUARTER_TWO
OBJOWN  SALES_DETAIL_DATA SALES_Q3_99           3  QUARTER_THREE
OBJOWN  SALES_DETAIL_DATA SALES_Q4_99           4  QUARTER_FOUR
```

The DBA_TAB_SUBPARTITIONS View

The DBA_TAB_SUBPARTITIONS view, much like the DBA_TAB_PARTITIONS view, provides granular subpartition-level information for all subpartitions of a table. Here, you can find a variety of information on specific subpartitions, including the tablespace that the subpartitions are assigned to, subpartition storage parameters, and various statistics gathered for each subpartition by the ANALYZE command. Many of the columns are similar to the columns you already use in the DBA_TABLES view. Listing 14.15 shows a sample query against the table.

Listing 14.15 A sample query of the DBA_TAB_SUBPARTITIONS view.

```
SQL> SELECT table_owner, table_name, subpartition_name,
     tablespace_name FROM dba_tab_subpartitions;

TABLE_OWNER  TABLE_NAME           SUBPARTITI TABLESPACE_NAME
-----------  -------------------- ---------- ---------------
SYSTEM       SALES_DETAIL_DATA    Q1S1       QUARTER_ONE
SYSTEM       SALES_DETAIL_DATA    Q1S2       QUARTER_ONE
SYSTEM       SALES_DETAIL_DATA    Q1S3       QUARTER_ONE
SYSTEM       SALES_DETAIL_DATA    Q1S4       QUARTER_ONE
SYSTEM       SALES_DETAIL_DATA    Q2S1       QUARTER_TWO
SYSTEM       SALES_DETAIL_DATA    Q2S2       QUARTER_TWO
SYSTEM       SALES_DETAIL_DATA    Q2S3       QUARTER_TWO
SYSTEM       SALES_DETAIL_DATA    Q2S4       QUARTER_TWO
SYSTEM       SALES_DETAIL_DATA    Q3S1       QUARTER_THREE
SYSTEM       SALES_DETAIL_DATA    Q3S2       QUARTER_THREE
SYSTEM       SALES_DETAIL_DATA    Q3S3       QUARTER_THREE
SYSTEM       SALES_DETAIL_DATA    Q3S4       QUARTER_THREE
SYSTEM       SALES_DETAIL_DATA    Q4S1       QUARTER_FOUR
SYSTEM       SALES_DETAIL_DATA    Q4S2       QUARTER_FOUR
SYSTEM       SALES_DETAIL_DATA    Q4S3       QUARTER_FOUR
```

The DBA_TABLES View

The DBA_TABLES view provides various information on partitioned tables. In the query in Listing 14.16, you will see the owner of the table and the name of the table. Note that the TABLESPACE_NAME column is blank because the table is partitioned. The tablespace names for each partition appear in the **DBA_PART_TABLES** view, which is described shortly. Nothing substantial has changed in this view, and most partition-specific information is contained in the **DBA_PART%** views.

The PARTITIONED column indicates whether or not the table is partitioned.

Listing 14.16 A sample query of the DBA_TABLES view.

```
SQL> SELECT owner,table_name, tablespace_name, table_lock,
     partitioned
  2  FROM dba_tables WHERE table_name LIKE 'SALES_DETAIL_DATA';

OWNER  TABLE_NAME           TABLESPACE_NAME    TABLE    PARTITION
                                               LOCK
------ -------------------- ------------------ ------
SYSTEM SALES_DETAIL_DATA                       DISABLED
```

Using Partitions

In this section, we'll discuss various utilities and the support they provide for partitioning in Oracle8i. We'll examine how to address a partition explicitly through SQL statements. In addition, we'll review the process required to analyze partitioned and subpartitioned objects, and we'll discuss how using partitioned objects can change the output of the **EXPLAIN PLAN** command and its associated **PLAN_TABLE** table. We'll then discuss Import and Export issues related to partitioned objects, and finally we'll discuss SQL*Loader issues.

Accessing Partitions Directly in SQL

Oracle has added new syntax to SQL to allow you to manipulate partitions and subpartitions directly. In the **FROM** clause of a **SELECT** statement, you can now directly refer to a partition that you want to query. To do so, you append the keyword **PARTITION** or **SUBPARTITION** after the **FROM** clause, and then, in parentheses, you list the partition or subpartition that you want to restrict the search to. The advantage of this capability is that you can direct Oracle where to look for the data if you know where it is. The disadvantage is that if you instruct Oracle to look at only one specific partition, and that partition is incorrect (the data actually resides in another partition), the results returned will be incorrect.

It bears noting again that the SQL syntax, allowing direct access to partitions, is not yet supported in PL/SQL. Some parallel operations—including parallel updates and deletes—can be used only on partitioned tables. Certain hints have been added to Oracle to accommodate the new partitioning features in combination with the new parallel processing features of Oracle8. (See Chapter 6 for more information on this topic.) Listing 14.17 shows an example of selecting a row from a specific partition.

Listing 14.17 Selecting a row from a specific partition of the sales_detail_data table.

```
--First look at all of the data.
SQL> SELECT * FROM sales_detail_data;

date_of_s INVOICE_NUMBER ITEM_LINE_NO  item_sku  QTY_SOLD
--------  -------------- ------------  --------  --------
01-JAN-99              1            1   1000000         1
01-JAN-99              2            1   1000000         1
01-JAN-99              2            2   1000000         1
01-APR-99              2            1   2000000         1
01-APR-99              2            2   9000000         5
30-JUN-99              3            1   1000000         1
01-JUL-99              4            1   2000000         1
01-SEP-99              5            1   4000000         1
31-DEC-99              6            1   1000000         2

--Now just the data in the SALES_Q1_99 partition.
SQL> SELECT * FROM sales_detail_data partition (sales_q1_99);

DATE_OF_S INVOICE_NUMBER ITEM_LINE_NO  item_sku  QTY_SOLD
--------  -------------- ------------  --------  --------
01-JAN-99              1            1   1000000         1
01-JAN-99              2            1   1000000         1
01-JAN-99              2            2   1000000         1
--Note the problem if we are looking for specific data in the
--wrong partition.
--This query works fine.
SQL> SELECT * FROM sales_detail_data PARTITION (sales_q1_99)
  2  WHERE TO_CHAR(date_of_sale,'DD-MON-YY')=
  3  TO_DATE('01-JAN-99','DD-MON-YY');

DATE_OF_S INVOICE_NUMBER ITEM_LINE_NO  item_sku  QTY_SOLD
--------  -------------- ------------  --------  --------
01-JAN-99              1            1   1000000         1
01-JAN-99              2            1   1000000         1
01-JAN-99              2            2   1000000         1
--This query does not return any rows
-- because the wrong partition is selected.
SQL> SELECT * FROM sales_detail_data PARTITION (sales_q2_99)
  2   WHERE TO_CHAR(date_of_sale,'DD-MON-YY')=
  3   TO_DATE('01-JAN-99','DD-MON-YY');
no rows selected
```

Analyzing the Partitioned or Subpartitioned Object

To get the benefit of using partitioned objects, you must be using cost-based optimization. Therefore, it is important to create statistics on the partitioned objects. You use the **ANALYZE** command to facilitate statistics collection on both partitioned and nonpartitioned objects. Again, much like accessing partitions or subpartitions directly in SQL code, you can use the **PARTITION** or **SUBPARTITION** keyword to analyze a specific partition or subpartition.

Listing 14.18 shows examples of analyzing a partitioned table, a partitioned index, and specific partitions of both.

Listing 14.18 Analysis of a partitioned table and a partitioned index.

```
SQL> ANALYZE TABLE sales_detail_data COMPUTE STATISTICS;
Table analyzed.
SQL> ANALYZE TABLE sales_detail_data PARTITION (sales_q1_99)
     COMPUTE STATISTICS;
Table analyzed.
SQL> ANALYZE index IX_SALES_ISKU_01 COMPUTE STATISTICS;
Index analyzed.
SQL> ANALYZE TABLE sales_detail_data ESTIMATE STATISTICS
     SAMPLE 30 PERCENT;
Table analyzed.
SQL> ANALYZE TABLE sales_detail_data PARTITION (sales_q1_99)
     ESTIMATE STATISTICS SAMPLE 20 PERCENT;
Table analyzed.
SQL> ANALYZE TABLE sales_detail_data SUBPARTITION (q4s3)
     ESTIMATE STATISTICS SAMPLE 20 PERCENT;
Table analyzed.
```

Oracle also makes the **DBMS_UTILITY.ANALYZE_PART_OBJECT** package available to DBAs. This package allows DBAs to analyze a partition in a partitioned object. This procedure can only be used to analyze partitioned objects. The call to the **DBMS_UTILITY.ANALYZE_PART_OBJECT** takes this format:

```
PROCEDURE DBMS_UTILITY.ANALYZE_PART_OBJECT
(schema IN VARCHAR2 DEFAULT NULL,
 object_name IN VARCHAR2 DEFAULT NULL,
 object_type IN CHAR DEFAULT 'T',
 command_type IN CHAR DEFAULT 'E',
 command_opt  IN  VARCHAR2 DEFAULT NULL,
 sample_clause IN VARCHAR2 DEFAULT 'SAMPLE 5 PERCENT');
```

Note: Oracle documentation is not clear on the question of whether the DBMS_UTILITY.ANALYZE_PART_OBJECT package will provide statistics for all the new partitioning methods in Oracle8i. Our personal testing seems to indicate that it will work for all methods of partitioning.

The **DBMS_UTILITY.ANALYZE_PART_OBJECT** package has the following parameters:

- **SCHEMA**—The schema that owns the object to be analyzed.
- **OBJECT_NAME**—The name of the object to be analyzed.
- **OBJECT_TYPE**—The type of object being analyzed (T = Table and I = Index).
- **COMMAND_TYPE**—Indicates the type of analysis to be performed. Valid codes are **C** (Compute Statistics), **E** (Estimate Statistics), **D** (Delete Statistics), and **V** (Validate Structure).
- **COMMAND_OPT**—Indicates options for different command types. If the **COMMAND_TYPE** code is **C** or **E**, then valid **COMMAND_OPT** values are: **FOR TABLE**, **FOR ALL LOCAL INDEXES**, and **FOR ALL COLUMNS**. Also valid are combinations of the **FOR** options for the **ANALYZE STATISTICS** command. If the **COMMAND_TYPE** code is **V** and the **OBJECT_TYPE** is **T** (Table), then **CASCADE** is a valid **COMMAND _OPT** entry.
- **SAMPLE_CLAUSE**—Contains the sample clause for estimating statistics.

See Listing 14.19 for an example of using this package.

Listing 14.19 Using the DBMS_UTILITY.ANALYZE_PART_OBJECT package.

```
EXEC DBMS_UTILITY.ANALYZE_PART_OBJECT('ACCT_OWN',
'GENERAL_LEDGER_DETAIL','T','E',NULL,'SAMPLE 20 PERCENT');
```

Using the EXPLAIN PLAN Command

If you have used **EXPLAIN PLAN** before, you'll notice that the **PLAN_TABLE** table has some columns just for partition operations. The **PARTITION_START**, **PARTITION_STOP**, and **PARTITION_ID** columns have been added. They indicate, respectively, the starting partition in the range of accessed partitions, the ending partition in the range of accessed partitions, and the step that determines the values for these partitions.

In Oracle8i, explain plans now indicate which form of partitioned table the data is coming from: range, hash, or composite. You also might see special partition operations, such as the partition concatenation operation, as shown in the explain plan in Listing 14.20. Also, in the last query in Listing 14.20, you'll find an access plan for a query against a composite-partitioned table. Using **AUTOTRACE**, if you access a partition directly, nothing is displayed in the plan to indicate that a specific partition is being used. You can tell by the difference in the block gets and consistent gets, or you can run a manual **EXPLAIN PLAN** and look at the **PLAN_TABLE** table results for more information.

Listing 14.20 Sample EXPLAIN PLANs for queries on partitioned tables.

```
SQL> SELECT * FROM sales_detail_data;

DATE_OF_S INVOICE_NUMBER ITEM_LINE_NO  ITEM_SKU QTY_SOLD
--------  -------------- ------------  -------- --------
01-JAN-99              1            1   1000000        1
01-JAN-99              2            1   1000000        1
01-JAN-99              2            2   1000000        1
01-APR-99              2            1   2000000        1
01-APR-99              2            2   9000000        5
30-JUN-99              3            1   1000000        1
01-JUL-99              4            1   2000000        1
01-SEP-99              5            1   4000000        1
31-DEC-99              6            1   1000000        2

Execution Plan
----------------------------------------------------------
0       SELECT STATEMENT Optimizer=CHOOSE (Cost=1 Card=9 Bytes=207)
1    0  PARTITION (CONCATENATED)
2    1   TABLE ACCESS (FULL) OF 'SALES_DETAIL_DATA' (Cost=1 Card=
         9 Bytes=207)

SQL> select * from sales_detail_data
  2  where date_of_sale < TO_DATE('01-APR-1999','DD-MON-YYYY');

DATE_OF_SALE INVOICE_NUMBER ITEM_LINE_NO  item_sku  QTY_SOLD
--------     -------------- ------------  --------  --------
01-JAN-99                 1            1   1000000         1
01-JAN-99                 2            1   1000000         1
01-JAN-99                 2            2   1000000         1
Execution Plan
----------------------------------------------------------
   0  SELECT STATEMENT Optimizer=CHOOSE (Cost=1 Card=3 Bytes=69)
   1  0  PARTITION (CONCATENATED)
   2  1   TABLE ACCESS (FULL) OF 'SALES_DETAIL_DATA' (Cost=1 Card=
        3 Bytes=69)
```

```
SQL> select * from sales_detail_data;

DATE_OF_S INVOICE_NUMBER ITEM_LINE_NO  ITEM_SKU  QTY_SOLD
--------- -------------- ------------ --------- ---------
28-MAY-00              1            1         1         1

Execution Plan
----------------------------------------------------------
   0      SELECT STATEMENT Optimizer=CHOOSE (Cost=46 Card=6075
             Bytes=370575)
   1    0  PARTITION RANGE (ALL)
   2    1  PARTITION HASH (ALL)
   3    2  TABLE ACCESS (FULL) OF 'SALES_DETAIL_DATA' (Cost=46
             Card=6075 Bytes=370575)
```

Importing and Exporting Partitions

You can use the Oracle Import/Export utility to export data from an entire partitioned table or from specific partitions or subpartitions. You can export a partitioned table in table, user, and full modes. One restriction is that if you want to export individual partitions, these can be exported in table mode only.

Oracle8i has added some new functionality to the Import/Export process. This functionality includes the ability to specify a query for the SELECT statement that the export user uses when unloading tables and the ability to create multiple dump files.

To export just a partition of a partitioned table, use the TABLES = syntax, and format the table and partition in the manner of [TABLE_NAME:PARTITION NAME or SUBPARTITION NAME]. Listing 14.21 shows an example of exporting a complete partitioned table and a single partition of a partitioned table.

Listing 14.21 Sample export of a partitioned table and a partition in partitioned table.

```
oracle@sun002>$ exp system file=test.dmp tables=sales_detail_data
Export: Release 8.1.6.0.0 - Production on Tue Aug 10 13:18:53 1999
(c) Copyright 1998 Oracle Corporation.  All rights reserved.
Password:
Connected to: Oracle8 Enterprise Edition Release
8.1.6.0.0 - Production
With the Partitioning and Objects options
PL/SQL Release 8.1.6.0.0 - Production
Export done in US7ASCII character set and US7ASCII NCHAR character
set About to export specified tables via Conventional Path ...
```

```
. . exporting table                  SALES_DETAIL_DATA
. . exporting partition                SALES_Q1_99    3 rows exported
. . exporting partition                SALES_Q2_99    3 rows exported
. . exporting partition                SALES_Q3_99    2 rows exported
. . exporting partition                SALES_Q4_99    1 rows exported
Export terminated successfully without warnings.
oracle@sun002>$ exp system file=test_part.dmp
tables=sales_detail_data:sales_q1_99
Export: Release 8.1.6.0.0 - Production on Tue Aug 10 13:19:37 1999
(c) Copyright 1998 Oracle Corporation.  All rights reserved.
Password:
Connected to: Oracle8 Fnterprise Edition Release
8.1.6.0.0 - Production
With the Partitioning and Objects options
PL/SQL Release 8.1.6.0.0 - Production
Export done in US7ASCII character set and US7ASCII NCHAR character
set
About to export specified tables via Conventional Path ...
. . exporting table                  SALES_DETAIL_DATA
. . exporting partition              SALES_Q1_99   3 rows exported
Export terminated successfully without warnings.
```

Oracle8i also supports the importing of partitions. When you import an entire partitioned table, or even specific partitions exported from a partitioned table, Oracle creates a partitioned table, the partitions you import, and the associated indexes. You can also use the **SKIP_UNUSABLE_INDEXES** clause to have the Import utility not create indexes that were in an **UNUSABLE** status when you did the export.

Using SQL*Loader with Partitions

You can use SQL*Loader with partitioned tables using both the conventional-path load and the direct-path load. Note that SQL*Loader can now handle **LOB** types, objects, and collections within partitioned and nonpartitioned tables. Also, versions before Oracle8i had a 64K size limit for records; this limit has been removed in Oracle8i.

Following are some of the SQL*Loader features related to using the conventional path to load a partitioned table:

- DBAs can run multiple loads into different partitions of the same table at the same time.
- DBAs can load data into specific partitions. They do so by changing the control file to indicate into which partition to load the data.

- When any user is using SQL*Loader to load data, row data that does not meet the partition criterion is dumped into the bad file for DBAs to review. Be mindful of the data that you're trying to load into a partition. The data's key values might lie outside the partition-key range boundaries for the partition into which you're trying to load the data.

Changes in the direct-path load include the following:

- DBAs can run multiple loads into different partitions of the same table at the same time, in parallel (parallel direct path).
- Only one direct-path load to a partitioned table (as opposed to a specific partition) can occur at one time.
- The direct load method can be used to load data into a single partition.
- The direct load method can be used to load partitioned index-organized tables, even those with secondary indexes.

Practice Questions

Question 1

If you split a partition of a partitioned table that contains data, what will be the impact on the related partitions of a local index?

- ❍ a. The associated local index partitions will become **UNUSABLE**, and you will need to execute the command **ALTER INDEX REBUILD PARTITION** to rebuild the local index partitions that are in an **UNUSABLE** status.
- ❍ b. The associated local index will be maintained by Oracle and no DBA action will be required.
- ❍ c. The associated local index partitions will become **UNUSABLE**, and you will need to execute the **ANALYZE** command to rebuild the local index partition that is **UNUSABLE**.
- ❍ d. You cannot split a partition of a table with a local index.
- ❍ e. You cannot split a partition of a partitioned table that contains data. You must first truncate the table and then split it.

Answer b is correct. If you split a partition of a table that contains a local index, Oracle will maintain that index for you. No action on the part of the DBA is required. Answer a is incorrect because the index is not marked UNUSABLE. If the index happened to be a global index, then the associated partitions of that index would be marked UNUSABLE. Answer c is incorrect because, again, the index is not marked UNUSABLE. Also, you do not use the ANALYZE command to rebuild an index if it's marked UNUSABLE. Answers d and e are incorrect because you can indeed split a partition of a partitioned table that contains data.

Question 2

Which of the following operations will not result in a global index becoming **UNUSABLE**?

- ❍ a. Truncating a partition in a table
- ❍ b. Splitting partitions in a table
- ❍ c. Dropping a partition in a table
- ❍ d. Splitting a partition in a global index
- ❍ e. Performing an exchange operation on a partitioned table

Answer d is correct. If you split a partition in a global index, the resulting partitions are not marked **UNUSABLE**. Answers a, b, c, and e are all incorrect because all of these operations do result in the marking of global index partitions as **UNUSABLE**.

Question 3

Which Oracle partitioning method uses both partitions and subpartitions?

- ❍ a. Range
- ❍ b. Hash
- ❍ c. Composite
- ❍ d. Combination
- ❍ e. Oracle does not allow you to use partitions and subpartitions together.

Answer c is correct. Composite partitioning is a combination of the range and hash partitioning methods. The data is physically stored in hash subpartitions, and the range partition is a logical structure created over those subpartitions. Answers a and b are both incorrect because the range and hash partitioning methods have to be combined for you to use partitions and subpartitions. Answer d is incorrect because this is not a valid partitioning method. Answer e is incorrect because Oracle does allow a combination of the two partitioning methods.

Question 4

Which action will result in the addition of a partition to a local partitioned index?

- ❍ a. **ALTER INDEX ADD PARTITION**
- ❍ b. **ALTER TABLE TRUNCATE**
- ❍ c. **ALTER INDEX SPLIT PARTITION**
- ❍ d. **ALTER TABLE ADD PARTITION**
- ❍ e. **ALTER INDEX COALESCE PARTITION**

Answer d is correct. The **ALTER TABLE ADD PARTITION** statement will add a partition to a partitioned table and will also automatically add a partition to all local partitioned indexes. This occurs because local indexes are always equipartitioned. Answer a is incorrect because there is not an **ADD PARTITION** command for indexes. Answer b is incorrect because the **ALTER TABLE TRUNCATE** operation will not add a partition to the index. Answer c is incorrect because you cannot issue an **ALTER INDEX SPLIT PARTITION** command on a local partitioned index. Answer e is incorrect because the **ALTER INDEX COALESCE PARTITION** operation cannot be executed on a local partitioned index (and would have the reverse effect of what you wanted to accomplish on a global index, anyway).

Question 5

Fill in the blank for the missing keyword in the SQL statement below. Assume that you want to determine which partitions of a global partitioned index are **UNUSABLE** due to a recent operation.

```
SELECT table_name, partition_name, status
FROM DBA________________________
Where status='UNUSABLE';
```

The correct answer is **_IND_PARTITIONS**. The **DBA_IND_PARTITIONS** view will show you each partition and its status.

Question 6

Which view provides you with the statistics generated by an **ANALYZE** command, collected for a specific column of a specific subpartition?

- ❍ a. **DBA_IND_SUBPARTITIONS**
- ❍ b. **DBA_IND_PARTITIONS**
- ❍ c. **DBA_COL_PARTITIONS**
- ❍ d. **DBA_COL_SUBPARTITIONS**
- ❍ e. **DBA_TAB_SUBPARTITIONS**

Answer d is correct. The **DBA_COL_SUBPARTITIONS** view provides you with information—including generated statistics—about columns in a subpartition of a partitioned table. Answer a is incorrect because **DBA_IND _SUBPARTITIONS** does not provide column-level information. Answer b is incorrect because this view does not provide any information at the subpartition level, nor does it provide column-level information. Answer c is incorrect because the **DBA_COL_PARTITIONS** view provides no subpartition information. Answer e is incorrect because this view doesn't provide column-level information. Note this is a trick question because it requires careful reading. If you don't read it closely, you might choose answer c, thinking that you're being asked about partitions instead of subpartitions. Also, you might be tempted to choose answer e if you don't catch that the question is asking about column-level information.

Question 7

You want to use SQL*Loader to load data into a partitioned index-organized table with a secondary index. What is required to perform this action?

- ❍ a. Load the data as you normally would.
- ❍ b. Drop the secondary index before loading the data.
- ❍ c. Rebuild the secondary index after loading the data.
- ❍ d. You cannot use SQL*Loader to load data into an IOT.
- ❍ e. SQL*Loader will not load data into a partitioned IOT, but it will load data into a nonpartitioned IOT.

Answer a is correct. In Oracle8i, SQL*Loader can load data directly into a partition of an index-organized table, and can do so as a direct load for even better performance. Answer b is incorrect because you do not need to drop any secondary index. Answer c is incorrect because you do not need to rebuild the secondary index after a successful load. Answer d is incorrect because you can use SQL*Loader to load data into an IOT. Finally, answer e is incorrect because you can use SQL*Loader to load data into an IOT whether or not it's partitioned.

Question 8

You have a partitioned table with several global indexes. At the end of the year, you need to truncate the data for the previous year's four quarters. What is the best way to perform this maintenance action and avoid having the table's global indexes being set to **UNUSABLE** and/or having to rebuild the indexes?

❍ a. **TRUNCATE** each partition of the table that you want to have the data removed from. **DROP** the table partitions that you no longer need, and then **DROP** the associated global index partitions.

❍ b. **DELETE** the data you need to remove, and then **TRUNCATE** the partitions that are empty.

❍ c. **DROP** the table partitions containing the data you no longer need.

❍ d. Using the **CREATE TABLE AS SELECT** command, copy the data that you want to keep in the table to a copy of that table; then rename that table. Re-create the indexes as required.

❍ e. **DELETE** the data that you no longer want. Oracle will automatically drop both the table and the index partitions when they are no longer in use.

Answer b is correct. In some cases, it is imperative that you do not allow your indexes to become UNUSABLE because they might affect queries on the system. Answer b is the only method you can use to make sure you do not cause your indexes to become UNUSABLE. Answer a is incorrect because if you TRUNCATE a partition with data, index partitions will become UNUSABLE on global indexes. Answer c is incorrect because, again, global index partitions will become UNUSABLE and will need to be rebuilt. Answer d is not only a slow solution, but it will certainly take much longer to implement than any of the other solutions. In addition, it will require a rebuild of the indexes. Answer e is incorrect because Oracle will not drop unused partitions.

Question 9

Which of the following views does not provide partitioning information?

- ❍ a. **DBA_TAB_COLUMNS**
- ❍ b. **DBA_INDEXES**
- ❍ c. **DBA_PART_INDEXES**
- ❍ d. **DBA_PART_TABLES**
- ❍ e. **DBA_TAB_PARTITIONS**

Answer a is correct. The **DBA_TAB_COLUMNS** table does not provide any information about partitioned objects. Answers b, c, d, and e each provide some level of information about a partitioned object.

Question 10

Which action would be invalid when applied to a hash-partitioned table?

- ❍ a. **ALTER TABLE...DROP PARTITION**
- ❍ b. **ALTER TABLE...SPLIT PARTITION**
- ❍ c. **ALTER TABLE...ADD PARTITION**
- ❍ d. **ALTER TABLE...COALESCE PARTITION**
- ❍ e. **ALTER TABLE...MOVE SUBPARTITION**

Answer b is correct. The **ALTER TABLE...SPLIT PARTITION** operation is not supported for a hash-partitioned table. Answers a, c, d, and e are all supported operations.

Need to Know More?

Ault, Mike. *Oracle8i Administration and Management*. Wiley Computer Publishing, 2000. ISBN 0-471-35453-8. Includes a whole chapter on Oracle8i objects, including all the new features.

Austin, David, Meghraj Thakkar, and Kurt Lysy. *Migrating to Oracle8i*. Sams Publishing, 2000. ISBN 0-672-31577-7. This book provides an introduction to partitioning and partition maintenance operations.

www.revealnet.com is a wonderful site with Oracle tips for DBAs and PL/SQL developers.

support.oracle.com is Oracle's Metalink Web site, a wonderful resource if you have Oracle metals support.

Manageability Enhancements

Terms you'll need to understand:

- ✓ **ALTER TABLE MOVE** command
- ✓ **ALTER TABLE DROP COLUMN** command
- ✓ **ALTER TABLE SET UNUSED COLUMN** command
- ✓ **ALTER TABLE DROP UNUSED COLUMNS** command
- ✓ **ALL_UNUSED_COL_TABS** view
- ✓ Temporary table
- ✓ **DEFAULTIF/NULLIF**
- ✓ **V$SESSION_LONGOPS** view
- ✓ **DBMS_APPLICATION_INFO.SET_SESSION_LONGOPS** procedure
- ✓ **RELY/NORELY**
- ✓ **DISABLE VALIDATE** constraint

Techniques you'll need to master:

- ✓ Identifying database limits
- ✓ Moving a table
- ✓ Removing unused columns from a table
- ✓ Building temporary tables
- ✓ Identifying SQL*Loader enhancements
- ✓ Identifying new Import/Export features
- ✓ Monitoring long-running operations
- ✓ Defining new constraint features

Database Limits

Oracle8i has certain limitations that are part of the server application or that are necessary because of the operating system or hardware. See Table 15.1 for Oracle8i database limits.

Table 15.1 Oracle8i database limits.

Type	Minimum	Maximum
Database block size	2	32K; operating system dependent
Database blocks per data file	2	2^{22} –1; platform dependent
Control files	1	Not applicable
Control file size	N/A	20,000 database blocks
Database files per tablespace	1	1022; operating system dependent
Data files per database	Mn=1	65,533; dependent on operating system, **DB_BLOCK_SIZE**, **MAXDATAFILES**, and **DB_FILES**
Database file size	Not applicable	Operating system dependent; usually 4 million blocks
Maxextents	1	Unlimited
Redo log files	Mn=2	Dependent on operating system, **MAXLOGFILES**, and **LOG_FILES**
Redo log file size	50K	Operating system dependent—usually 2GB
Tablespaces	1	Unlimited
SGA size	N/A	2 to 4GB for 32-bit systems; more than 4GB for 64-bit systems
Nested queries	0	255
Columns per table	1	1000
Columns per index	1	32; 30 for bitmap indexes
Indexes per table	0	Unlimited
VARCHAR2 data type	1	4000 bytes
NUMBER data type	-999...(38 9's) x10^{125}	999...(38 9's) x10^{125}
LONG	N/A	2GB
BFILE, **BLOB**, **CLOB**	N/A	4GB

Moving Tables

Oracle8i allows you to move a nonpartitioned ordinary table, a nonpartitioned index-organized table (IOT), or a LOB data segment to a new segment, effectively reorganizing the table. You can modify the storage parameters and even move the table to a different tablespace. See Listing 15.1 for **MOVE** syntax, and Listing 15.2 for a sample command that moves a table to another tablespace. Indexes, grants, and constraints are retained when you move a table. You can't move an entire partitioned table--you have to move the partitions individually. DML is not allowed on ordinary tables during the **MOVE**. The **MOVE** on an ordinary table is offline.

For an IOT, you can specify the **ONLINE** clause, which allows DML on the table while you're rebuilding its primary key index B*-tree. Parallel DML is not allowed during the **ONLINE** move. Also with an IOT, the **COMPRESS** keyword enables key compression, which eliminates repeated occurrences of primary-key-column values.

Listing 15.1 Syntax for moving a table.

```
ALTER TABLE (ONLINE)
(index_organized_table_clause|segment_attribute_clause)
(LOB_storage_clause)
table_name
MOVE TABLESPACE (tablespace_name)
```

Listing 15.2 Moving a table.

```
ALTER TABLE my_tab MOVE TABLESPACE users;
```

Removing Unused Columns from a Table

In previous versions of Oracle, removing a column wasn't easy. You had to create a new table excluding the columns you wanted to drop, populate the new table with data from the old table, drop the old table, and then rename the new table. Indexes and constraints were also part of the headache. Oracle8i makes it easy. You can drop columns from a table, or set columns unused and drop them later. You can't drop all of the columns from a table, however; you would need to use the **DROP TABLE** command to accomplish that.

So that you don't create performance bottlenecks for current sessions, defer column drops for tables with a large amount of data until a time when the system is not as busy.

Dropping a Column or Columns

If you want to drop a column or columns immediately, simply issue the **ALTER TABLE** command to drop the columns. See Listing 15.3 for an example. When you issue the **DROP COLUMN** command, the column is completely removed from the table. The data is removed from that column; the column doesn't appear in the **DESCRIBE table_name** output; you can't query on the column; and any index on the table that included the dropped column will also be dropped.

Listing 15.3 Dropping a column.

```
ALTER TABLE my_tab DROP COLUMN col_x;
```

Setting a Column Unused

If you want to defer the column drop to a later time, then simply alter the table to set the column unused. When you tell Oracle8i to set a column unused, the column is no longer visible in queries or in a **DESCRIBE** statement, but the data still exists in the table. Any index that includes the marked column is dropped. The view **ALL_UNUSED_COL_TABS** indicates any tables with partially dropped columns. See Listing 15.4 for a sample command.

Listing 15.4 Setting unused columns.

```
ALTER TABLE my_tab SET UNUSED COLUMN col_y;
```

Dropping Unused Columns

Now that you've set columns unused, you'll want to actually drop the data. See Listing 15.5 for an example of how to drop unused columns. Dropping the column frees the disk space previously used by the dropped column.

Listing 15.5 Dropping unused columns.

```
ALTER TABLE my_tab DROP UNUSED COLUMNS;
```

Restrictions

Of course, there are restrictions to dropping columns. You can't drop a column in the following circumstances:

- The column is from tables owned by **SYS**.
- The column is a parent key column.

- The column is from an object type table or a nested table.
- The column is the only column in a table (you can't drop all columns in a table).
- The column is a key column for partitioning.

Also, if you export a table that has an unused column, the unused column will not be imported into the target. When you drop a column or set a column unused, you can immediately create a new column with the same name.

Temporary Tables

In Oracle8i, you can create *temporary tables*—tables that you can use just like any other table, except that the rows in the temporary tables go away when your session ends. You can build indexes, views, triggers, and constraints on a temporary table. You can export and import a temporary table. See Listing 15.6 for an example of how to build a temporary table.

Listing 15.6 Creating a temporary table.

```
CREATE GLOBAL TEMPORARY TABLE my_temp_tab
AS SELECT * FROM my_tab;
```

Restrictions

Other sessions can see the definition of your temporary table, but they can't see the rows in it. You can't specify storage parameters or a TABLESPACE parameter for a temporary table. Temporary tables are created in the user's session sort space, or in the user's temporary tablespace if the sort space isn't large enough. Transaction save points are supported, so you can roll back to a save point if needed. Otherwise, a COMMIT or a ROLLBACK removes all rows from your temporary tables.

The value **Y** in the **TEMPORARY** column of the **DBA_TABLES/ALL_TABLES** view indicates that a table is temporary.

SQL*Loader Enhancements

In Oracle8i, SQL*Loader has been enhanced in the following ways:

- The 64K limit for physical record size has been removed.
- The FILLER keyword indicates a column that exists in the data file but doesn't exist in the target table. Use this keyword in the position of the datafile column that you don't want loaded into the target table.

- SQL*Loader now supports the loading of objects, collections, and **LOBs**.
- There are new length-value pair data types similar to **VARCHAR**: **VARCHARC**, **VARRAW**, **VARRAWC**, and **LONG VARRAW**.
- There is now support for a user-specified record separator.
- A field delimiter can now be more than one character in length.
- **DEFAULTIF** and **NULLIF** can be chained by using the **AND** operator.

Export/Import Enhancements

The following are enhancements specific to the Export and Import utility programs:

- You can specify a query for the **SELECT** statements that Export uses to get data from the tables.
- You can circumvent the previous 2GB limit for Export dump files by specifying multiple dump files.
- You can export to larger dump files and dump tapes.
- You can export tables containing **LOBs** and objects; direct mode is supported.
- You can export and import optimizer statistics on certain exports and tables.
- In the Import utility, you can inhibit type-object-identifier validation.

For details on how to use SQL*Loader or Export/Import, see the *Oracle8i Utilities* document referred to at the end of the chapter.

Monitoring Long-Running Operations

The **V$SESSION_LONGOPS** view lets you monitor the progress of long-running operations and estimate their completion times. Backup, recovery, hash-cluster creation, and complex queries are examples of operations that can be monitored. This view existed in Oracle8, and it has been enhanced in Oracle8i. Oracle8i monitors long-running operations, collects statistics, and updates the **V$SESSION_LONGOPS** view. Compare the columns **SOFAR** and **TOTALWORK** to estimate the time until completion.

If you want to gather statistics from an application, use the procedure **DBMS_APPLICATION_INFO.SET_SESSION_LONGOPS**.

New Constraints Options

In Oracle8i, you can use ALTER TABLE ... MODIFY CONSTRAINT to change the attributes of a constraint. The RELY/NORELY option specifies whether an enabled constraint is to be enforced. RELY enables an existing constraint without enforcing the constraint. The default NORELY enables and enforces an existing constraint. You cannot set a NOT NULL constraint to RELY. Unenforced constraints (RELY) are useful for the query rewrite function of materialized views.

The DISABLE VALIDATE Constraint

All four combinations of DISABLE/ENABLE and VALIDATE/NOVALIDATE are now allowed. The DISABLE VALIDATE constraint guarantees constraint validity but doesn't require a unique or primary key index. Index lookups and DML are not allowed on a table with DISABLE VALIDATE constraints.

Practice Questions

Question 1

Which view can you use to monitor long-running operations?

❍ a. **V$OPERATION_LONGSESS**

❍ b. **V$LONG_SESSIONS**

❍ c. **V$LONG_OPERATIONS**

❍ d. **V$SESSION_LONGOPS**

❍ e. **V$SESSION_LONGOPERATION**

Answer d is correct. V$SESSION_LONGOPS is used to view the statistics gathered for a long-running session. From the statistics—specifically, the columns SOFAR and TOTALWORK—you can estimate the time of completion. The rest of the answers are incorrect because they are not valid views.

Question 2

The ________ constraint tells Oracle to enable and enforce an existing constraint.

Answer: NORELY. NORELY is the default, and it tells Oracle to enforce the constraint. Using the RELY option enables the constraint but doesn't enforce it.

Question 3

What is the maximum number of columns in a table?

❍ a. 255

❍ b. 1024

❍ c. Unlimited

❍ d. 1000

Answer d is correct. The maximum number of columns in a table is 1000. Each of the other answers is simply wrong.

Question 4

You want to drop a column from a table but do not want to cause system overhead at this time. Which of the following scenarios describes the best action to take?

❍ a. Issue the **ALTER TABLE DROP COLUMN** command.

❍ b. Issue the **ALTER TABLE SET UNUSED COLUMN** command; then issue the **ALTER TABLE DROP COLUMN** command.

❍ c. Issue the **ALTER TABLE MARK UNUSED COLUMN** command; then issue the **ALTER TABLE DROP COLUMN** command.

❍ d. Issue the **ALTER TABLE SET UNUSED COLUMN** command; then issue the **ALTER TABLE DROP UNUSED COLUMN** command.

❍ e. Create a new table without the column; copy the data from the old table to the new table; drop the old table; then rename the new table.

Answer d is correct. So that you don't negatively affect system performance, set the column unused, and then drop the unused column later. Answer a is incorrect because you're trying to avoid the overhead at this time. Answer b is incorrect for the same reason; and it will return an error if you try to drop the column that was just set unused. Answer c is incorrect because MARK is not a valid option. Answer e is how it was done in versions before Oracle8i.

Question 5

Use the **ALTER TABLE** __________ command to reorganize a table without using Export/Import.

Answer: MOVE. Use the ALTER TABLE MOVE command to move the table to a new segment, thus reorganizing the table. You can modify the storage parameters as part of the ALTER TABLE command.

Question 6

Which of the following accurately describes what users can do while you are moving a table? [Choose two]

- ❑ a. DML is not allowed on ordinary tables.
- ❑ b. Inserts are allowed, but deletes are not allowed on ordinary tables.
- ❑ c. DML is allowed on index-organized tables.
- ❑ d. Deletes are allowed, but inserts are not allowed on ordinary tables.
- ❑ e. Updates are always allowed during a move.

Answers a and c are correct. DML is not allowed during a **MOVE** on ordinary tables, but DML is allowed during a move on IOTs. Answers b, d, and e are not correct because they involve DML on ordinary tables.

Question 7

Which of the following views shows columns that have been set unused but not yet dropped?

- ❍ a. **V$UNUSED_COLUMNS**
- ❍ b. **ALL_UNUSED_COLUMNS**
- ❍ c. **ALL_UNUSED_COL _TABS**
- ❍ d. **ALL_DROPPED_COLS**

Answer c is correct. The view **ALL_UNUSED_COL_TABS** indicates an owner and tables with unused columns. Each of the other views is not a valid view.

Question 8

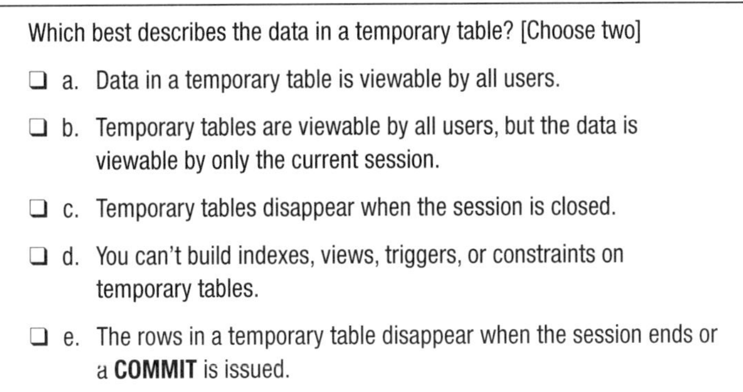

Which best describes the data in a temporary table? [Choose two]

- ❑ a. Data in a temporary table is viewable by all users.
- ❑ b. Temporary tables are viewable by all users, but the data is viewable by only the current session.
- ❑ c. Temporary tables disappear when the session is closed.
- ❑ d. You can't build indexes, views, triggers, or constraints on temporary tables.
- ❑ e. The rows in a temporary table disappear when the session ends or a **COMMIT** is issued.

Answers b and e are correct. Temporary table data is viewable by only the current session, and the rows disappear when the session ends or a COMMIT is issued. Save points are supported, as are rollbacks to a save point. Answer c is incorrect because the table remains; just the data disappears. Answer d is incorrect because you can build views, indexes, constraints, and triggers on temporary tables.

Need to Know More?

The followinrg documents are available on the Oracle server installation CD, or you can download them from **http://technet.oracle.com**.

Baylis, Ruth and Paul Lane. *Getting to Know Oracle8i* (Part No. A68020-01). Oracle Corporation, 1999. Introduction to each of the topics presented in this chapter.

Durbin, Jason. *Oracle8i Reference* (Part No. A67790-01). Oracle Corporation, 1999. See Chapter 3 for a detailed description of **V$SESSION_LONGOPS**. See Chapter 4 for the list of Oracle8i database limits.

Durbin, Jason. *Oracle8i Utilities* (Part No. A67792-01). Oracle Corporation, 1999. See the chapters on export information, import information, and SQL*Loader details.

16

The Database Resource Manager

Terms you'll need to understand:

- ✓ Resource plan
- ✓ Resource consumer group
- ✓ Resource plan directive
- ✓ Resource allocation method
- ✓ **DBMS_RESOURCE_MANAGER** package
- ✓ **DBMS_RESOURCE_MANAGER_PRIVS** package
- ✓ **RESOURCE_MANAGER_PLAN** initialization parameter
- ✓ Pending area

Techniques you'll need to master:

- ✓ Creating a resource plan
- ✓ Creating resource consumer groups
- ✓ Managing shared resources
- ✓ Switching between consumer groups
- ✓ Setting the resource plan for an instance

This chapter covers the Database Resource Manager, a new feature in Oracle8i that you can use to manage system and database resources. We'll discuss the items that you'll create with this feature—resource plans, resource consumer groups, and resource plan directives—and the packages you'll use to create them.

Using the Database Resource Manager

The Database Resource Manager (DRM)—which is new in Oracle 8i—allows you to manage system and database resources. The DRM is used to assign different levels of database resources to different groups of users. Currently, CPU utilization and parallelism are the only two resources manageable with the DRM. The DBA can use the DRM to do the following:

- Designate a minimum amount of resources to consumer groups.
- Allocate percentages of CPU resources to consumer groups.
- Limit the degree of parallelism that a consumer group can use.
- Dynamically change resource parameter values for consumer groups.

These are the basic steps to creating and using resource plans:

1. Create resource plans with the **DBMS_RESOURCE_MANAGER** package.
2. Create resource consumer groups with the **DBMS_RESOURCE_MANAGER** package.
3. Create resource plan directives with the **DBMS_RESOURCE_MANAGER** package.
4. Assign users to consumer groups with the **DBMS_RESOURCE_MANAGER** package.
5. Specify a plan for an instance by setting the init.ora parameter **RESOURCE_MANAGER_PLAN** to the name of a valid resource plan.

Resource Plans

As the name suggests, a *resource plan* is a plan for how system resources will be allocated to users. Currently, *percentage of CPU resources* and *maximum degrees of parallelism* are the only two configurable resources. You can define multiple resource plans in a database, but only one plan can be active in an instance. You can also create *subplans,* or plans within a plan. A resource plan can have up to 32 levels, and 32 groups per level.

The init.ora parameter **RESOURCE_MANAGER_PLAN** specifies the top-level plan for an instance. If the **RESOURCE_MANAGER_PLAN** is not specified, the DRM is disabled. The DRM loads the plan as well as its descendants: subplans, directives, and consumer groups. You can change the active plan dynamically by using the command **ALTER SYSTEM SET RESOURCE_MANAGER_PLAN=<plan name>**. If the plan doesn't exist in the data dictionary, an error will be displayed. The data dictionary view **DBA_RSRC_PLANS** lists the resource plans in the instance's data dictionary.

Resource Consumer Groups

A *resource consumer group* is a logical grouping of users who have similar resource needs. A resource consumer group should be built around user sessions that have similar priority and resource usage requirements. As of Oracle 8.1.5, percentage of CPU usage is the only configurable resource at the resource-consumer-group level. Each user has a default resource consumer group, and all sessions owned by a user belong to that user's default resource consumer group.

Remember that parallelism is managed by the *resource plan*, and CPU usage is managed by both the *resource consumer group* and the *resource plan*.

A few special consumer groups are already set up for you:

- DEFAULT_CONSUMER_GROUP—Used for all sessions that don't belong to a consumer group. You can't modify or delete this group.
- OTHER_GROUPS—Used for all sessions that belong to a consumer group that is not part of the active plan. You can't modify or delete this group.
- SYS_GROUP—Used for the users **SYS** and **SYSTEM**.
- LOW_GROUP—Used for low-priority sessions.

Query the **DBA_RSRC_CONSUMER_GROUPS** view to see resource consumer groups and their attributes. You can see a session's resource consumer group by querying the **RESOURCE_CONSUMER_GROUP** column of the **V$SESSION** view.

Resource Plan Directives

You use *resource plan directives* to assign consumer groups or subplans to resource plans. You create a resource plan directive, specifying CPU and parallelism parameters, for each subplan or consumer group that you wish to manage in the resource plan. Query the **DBA_RSRC_PLAN_DIRECTIVES** view to see the resource plan directives for the database.

Resource Allocation Methods

Consumer groups and resource plans use *resource allocation methods* to determine how a resource such as a CPU will be allocated. Valid methods for CPU are *emphasis* and ***round-robin***. The CPU method *emphasis* indicates that CPU will be allocated to sessions in a group based on the percentage of CPU assigned for that group. You assign CPU *levels* 1-8, and percentages within each level.

The default value for **cpu_method** when creating a plan is 'EMPHASIS'. The default value for **cpu_method** when creating a group is 'ROUND-ROBIN'. The default value for **parallel_degree_limit**, which you set when creating resource plans, is "PARALLEL DEGREE_LIMIT_ABSOLUTE". When you create a resource plan directive, you have the opportunity to set the parallel degree limit; this limit applies only to groups, not to subplans.

Resource Plan Directive parallel degree limit applies only to groups, not to the subplans.

Database Resource Manager PL/SQL Packages

Oracle provides us with two packages to configure DRM objects: DBMS_RESOURCE_MANAGER and DBMS_RESOURCE_MANAGER _PRIVS. Procedures in the DBMS_RESOURCE_MANAGER package are used to create, modify, and delete plans, consumer groups, and plan directives. This package is also used to create, validate changes in, and submit changes to the pending area. The *pending area* is a work area for changes to plans, consumer groups, and plan directives.

Procedures in the DBMS_RESOURCE_MANAGER_PRIVS package are used to grant system privileges to and revoke system privileges from users or roles, and to allow or deny users the privilege to switch consumer groups.

Oracle also provides us with a DBMS_SESSION procedure that allows us to switch consumer groups for our current session.

The DBMS_RESOURCE_MANAGER Package

The DBMS_RESOURCE_MANAGER package maintains resource plans, resource plan directives, and resource consumer groups. To execute any of the procedures in the package, the invoker must have the ADMINISTER _RESOURCE_MANAGER system privilege. See Table 16.1 for the complete list of package procedures and their purposes. Here are a few very important ones:

- CREATE_PENDING_AREA must be run first when you're creating a plan.
- VALIDATE_PENDING_AREA is used to validate a newly created or modified consumer group, resource plan, or resource plan directive (DRM objects).
- SUBMIT_PENDING_AREA must be run to activate a modified DRM object. This procedure also validates, so you can save a step in the process by just executing SUBMIT_PENDING_AREA.
- CREATE_PLAN is used to create a resource plan.
- CREATE_CONSUMER_GROUP is used to create a resource consumer group.
- CREATE_PLAN_DIRECTIVE is used to create a resource plan directive.

Later in this chapter we'll give examples of how to use the procedures in the DBMS_RESOURCE_MANAGER package, and we'll indicate the exact steps you need to take to make it all work.

Table 16.1 Procedures in the DBMS_RESOURCE_MANAGER package.

Procedure	Purpose
CREATE_PENDING_AREA	Create a work area for changes to plans, consumer groups, and plan directives.
VALIDATE_PENDING_AREA	Validate changes in the work area.
CLEAR_PENDING_AREA	Clear the work area.
SUBMIT_PENDING_AREA	Submit changes in the work area.
CREATE_PLAN	Create resource-plan entries.
UPDATE_PLAN	Update resource-plan entries.
DELETE_PLAN	Delete the plan and its plan directives.
DELETE_PLAN_CASCADE	Delete the plan and its descendants.
CREATE_CONSUMER_GROUP	Create resource-consumer-group entries.
UPDATE_CONSUMER_GROUP	Update resource-consumer-group entries.
DELETE_CONSUMER_GROUP	Delete entries that define resource consumer groups.
SET_INITIAL_CONSUMER_GROUP	Set a user's default resource consumer group.
SWITCH_CONSUMER_GROUP _FOR_SESS	Switch the resource consumer group for a session.
SWITCH_CONSUMER_GROUP _FOR_USER	Switch the resource consumer group for all of a user's sessions.
CREATE_PLAN_DIRECTIVE	Create resource plan directives.
UPDATE_PLAN_DIRECTIVE	Update resource plan directives.
DELETE_PLAN_DIRECTIVE	Delete resource plan directives.

The **DBMS_RESOURCE_MANAGER_PRIVS** Package

The DBMS_RESOURCE_MANAGER_PRIVS package is used by the DBA to grant system privileges to and revoke system privileges from users. This package is also used by the users to switch the resource consumer group for a session. As with the DBMS_RESOURCE_MANAGER package, the invoker must have been granted the ADMINISTER_RESOURCE_MANAGER system privilege to execute any of the procedures. See Table 16.2 for a list of the procedures in the DBMS_RESOURCE_MANAGER_PRIVS package.

Query the view DBA_RSRC_CONSUMER_GROUP_PRIVS to see the switch privileges for consumer groups. Query the view DBA_RSRC _MANAGER_SYSTEM_PRIVS to see the system privileges for the resource manager.

The **DBMS_SESSION.SWITCH_CURRENT_CONSUMER _GROUP** Procedure

The procedure SWITCH_CURRENT_CONSUMER_GROUP allows a user to change the consumer group for the current session. Listing 16.1 shows the correct syntax for the procedure. The user passes to the procedure the name of the consumer group that the user wants to switch to. The current consumer group name is returned. The INITIAL_GROUP_ON_ERROR parameter, when set to TRUE, will revert to the initial consumer group if there is an error.

Listing 16.1 Syntax for the **DBMS_SESSION.SWITCH_CURRENT _CONSUMER_GROUP** procedure.

```
EXEC DBMS_SESSION.SWITCH_CURRENT_CONSUMER_GROUP
(new_consumer_group in VARCHAR2,
old_consumer_group out VARCHAR2,
initial_group_on_error in BOOLEAN)
```

Table 16.2 Procedures in the **DBMS_RESOURCE_MANAGER_PRIVS** package.

Procedure	Purpose
GRANT_SYSTEM_PRIVILEGE	Grant **ADMINISTER_RESOURCE_MANAGER** privilege to a user or role.
REVOKE_SYSTEM_PRIVILEGE	Revoke **ADMINISTER_RESOURCE_MANAGER** privilege to a user or role.
GRANT_SWITCH_CONSUMER_GROUP	Grant the privilege to switch to another resource consumer group.
REVOKE_SWITCH_CONSUMER_GROUP	Revoke the privilege to switch to another resource consumer group.

Example of Using the Database Resource Manager

Earlier in the chapter, we listed the steps to using the DRM. Now we'll walk through a simple DRM session, creating one resource plan, one resource consumer group, and two resource plan directives. We'll create two resource plan directives because the group **OTHER_GROUPS** must always be considered. We'll validate and submit the changes, and then make the resource plan active for the instance. We'll grant a user the privilege to switch to a group, then use **DBMS_SESSION** to switch the user's consumer group. See Listing 16.2 for a sample DRM session. Note that, in this example, we dynamically set the plan for the instance; we could have edited the init.ora file and restarted the instance, but we just wanted to make this plan active temporarily. To start, here are the steps to create and implement resource plans:

1. Grant resource manager privileges to the plan administrator.
2. Create a pending area.
3. Create a resource plan, which consists of a top-level plan and optional subplans.
4. Create resource groups and optional subgroups.
5. Create resource plan directives.
6. Validate the pending area.
7. Submit the pending area.
8. Grant groups to users, grant switch privileges, etc.
9. Set the resource plan for the instance.

Listing 16.2 Using the DBMS_RESOURCE_MANAGER package.

```
--create the pending area
EXEC DBMS_RESOURCE_MANAGER.CREATE_PENDING_AREA();

--create a resource plan
exec dbms_resource_manager.create_plan
(plan => 'MY_PLAN',
comment => 'this is a sample resource plan');

--create a resource group
exec dbms_resource_manager.create_consumer_group
(consumer_group =>'MY_GROUP',
comment => 'my sample resource consumer group');
```

```
--create a resource plan directive
exec dbms_resource_manager.create_plan_directive
(plan => 'MY_PLAN',
group_or_subplan=> 'MY_GROUP',
comment => 'My level 0 plan directive',
cpu_p1 => 75, cpu_p2 => 50,
parallel_degree_limit_p1 => 16);

--create another resource plan directive
exec dbms_resource_manager.create_plan_directive
(plan => 'MY_PLAN', group_or_subplan=> 'OTHER_GROUPS',
comment => 'My level 0 plan directive', cpu_p1 => 25,
cpu_p2 => 25, parallel_degree_limit_p1 => 4);

--validate and submit the pending area
exec dbms_resource_manager.validate_pending_area();
exec dbms_resource_manager.submit_pending_area();

--set the active resource plan for the instance
ALTER SYSTEM SET RESOURCE_MANAGER_PLAN='MY_PLAN';

--grant the user SCOTT the privilege to switch to a group
exec dbms_resource_manager_privs.grant_system_privilege
('SCOTT' ,'MY_GROUP',TRUE);

--use DBMS_SESSION in a code block to switch
the consumer group for a user's current session

CREATE OR REPLACE PROCEDURE my_drm is
old_group varchar2(30);
BEGIN
dbms_session.switch_current_consumer_group
('MY_GROUP', old_group, TRUE);
END my_drm;
/
```

Restrictions on Using the Database Resource Manager

Following is a list of general usage restrictions:

- Loops aren't allowed—no plan can contain loops.
- A plan directive can't reference a plan or consumer group that doesn't exist.

- Each plan must contain plan directives that reference groups or other plans.
- The plan directive parameter **PARALLEL_DEGREE_LIMIT_P1** is used with resource consumer groups. It can't appear in plan directives that refer to other resource plans (subplans).
- The init.ora parameter **COMPATIBLE** must be set to 8.1 or higher for the Database Resource Manager to function.
- The Database Resource Manager is available only in Oracle8i Enterprise Edition.
- You cannot delete the plan that is currently the top-level plan in an active instance.
- Plans and consumer groups cannot have the same name.
- The **OTHER_GROUPS** consumer group must have a resource plan.
- No plan can have more than 32 plan directives.
- An active plan cannot have more than 32 consumer groups.
- Percentages for a resource allocation method at a plan level cannot add up to more than 100 percent.

The dynamic performance views **V$SESSION, V$RSRC_CONSUMER_GROUP, V$RSRC_PLAN, V$MYSESSION, V$RSRC_CONSUMER_GROUP_CPU_MTH, V$RSRC_PLAN_CPU_MTH,** and **V$PARALLEL_DEGREE_LIMIT_MTH** contain DRM-related information. The static data dictionary views **DBA_RSRC_PLANS, DBA_RSRC_CONSUMER_GROUP_PRIVS, DBA_USERS, USERS_USERS, DBA_RSRC_MANAGER_SYSTEM_PRIVS, DBA_RSRC_CONSUMER_GROUPS, DBA_RSRC_PLAN_DIRECTIVES, USER_RSRC_CONSUMER_GROUP_PRIVS,** and **USER_RSRC_MANAGER_SYSTEM_PRIVS** contain DRM-related information.

Practice Questions

Question 1

Which Oracle-supplied PL/SQL package will you use to create a resource plan?

- ❍ a. **DBMS_RESOURCE_PLAN**
- ❍ b. **DBMS_RESOURCE_CREATE_PLAN**
- ❍ c. **DBMS_RESOURCE_MANAGER_PRIVS**
- ❍ d. **DBMS_RESOURCE_MANAGER**
- ❍ e. **DBMS_RESOURCE_PRIVS**

Answer d is correct. The **CREATE_PLAN** procedure in the **DBMS_RESOURCE_MANAGER** package is used to create resource plans. Answer c is incorrect because **DBMS_RESOURCE_MANAGER_PRIVS** is used to assign users to consumer groups. Answers a, b, and e are incorrect because they are not Oracle-supplied packages.

Question 2

Creating a _____ is the first step when you use the Database Resource Manager.

The correct answer is **pending area**. Remember that you must create a pending area before you create a plan. Creating a resource plan is the next step to using the Database Resource Manager. You create a pending area by using the procedure **DBMS_RESOURCE_MANAGER.CREATE_PENDING_AREA**. After you create the pending area, plan, consumer groups, and plan directives, you can validate and submit the pending area.

Question 3

Before you specify your own resource plan for an instance, which of the following steps must you perform? [Choose two]

- ❑ a. Create a resource plan.
- ❑ b. Create a consumer plan allocation method.
- ❑ c. Create a CPU resource function for each user in the consumer group.
- ❑ d. Create a resource consumer group.
- ❑ e. Set the init.ora parameter **CPU_RESOURCE_PERCENT**.

Answers a and d are correct. The correct steps are to create a resource plan, create consumer groups, create plan directives, assign users to consumer groups, and then specify a default plan for the instance. Answer b is incorrect because we made it up. Answer c is incorrect because you don't have to create a function to manage CPU resources. Answer e is incorrect because it is not a valid Oracle8i init.ora parameter.

Question 4

Which of the following statements about the Database Resource Manager are true? [Choose three]

- ❑ a. CPU resources are allocated by percentage.
- ❑ b. CPU resources are allocated by number of CPUs.
- ❑ c. DB Buffer Cache maximum buffer allocation is configured for each consumer group.
- ❑ d. A database can have an unlimited number of resource plans but only one active plan per instance.
- ❑ e. Degree of parallelism is controlled at the resource-plan level.
- ❑ f. Degree of parallelism is controlled at the resource-consumer-group level.
- ❑ g. Currently, CPU usage, shared pool open cursors, degree of parallelism, and transactions per second are controllable by resource plans.

Answers a, d, and e are correct. CPU utilization is specified by percentage, not by number of CPUs. There's no limit on the number of resource plans, but only one can be active at any given time. You can **ALTER** the parameter **RESOURCE_MANAGER_PLAN**, changing the active resource plan dynamically. Degree of parallelism and CPU usage are controlled at the resource-plan level, and the consumer group can also specify the CPU resource. Answer b is incorrect because it directly conflicts with answer a. Answer c is incorrect because DB buffer cache allocation isn't configurable with the DRM. Answer f is incorrect because it conflicts with answer e. Answer g is incorrect because currently only CPU percentage and degree of parallelism are controllable by resource plans.

Question 5

Users can change to a different consumer group by using which of the following procedures?

- ❍ a. **DBMS_SESSION.SWITCH_CONSUMER_GROUP**
- ❍ b. **DBMS_APPLICATION.SWITCH_CONSUMER_GROUP**
- ❍ c. **DBMS_SESSION.SWITCH_CURRENT_CONSUMER_GROUP**
- ❍ d. **DBMS_SESSION.SET_CURRENT_CONSUMER_GROUP**
- ❍ e. **DBMS_RESOURCE_MANAGER_PRIVS.GRANT_SWITCH_CONSUMER_GROUP**

Answer c is correct. Use the procedure **DBMS_SESSION.SWITCH_CURRENT_CONSUMER_GROUP** to switch the current session to a different consumer group. The user must have been granted permission to switch to the target group before the command is executed. Answer e is incorrect, but the DBA or a user with the **ADMINISTER_RESOURCE_MANAGER** system privilege must have granted the user the privilege to switch to the target consumer group. Answers a, b, and d are not valid Oracle-supplied procedures.

Question 6

You need to determine a session's current consumer group. Which view and column will you query?

❍ a. **V$SESSION.CONSUMER_GROUP**

❍ b. **V$SESSION.CURRENT_CONSUMER_GROUP**

❍ c. **V$SESSION.RESOURCE_CONSUMER_GROUP**

❍ d. **V$SESSION.CONSUMER_RESOURCE_GROUP**

❍ e. **DBA_RESOURCE_CONSUMER_GROUP.CURRENT_SESSIONS**

Answer c is correct. The RESOURCE_CONSUMER_GROUP column displays each session's current resource consumer group. If a user switches to a different consumer group, the column will be updated. The other columns are not valid columns.

Question 7

A user can dynamically switch to a different resource ______ .

The correct answer is **consumer group**. The user can dynamically switch to another consumer group by using the procedure DBMS_SESSION.SWITCH_CURRENT_CONSUMER_GROUP. Users can switch to only a consumer group that they have been granted the privilege to use. Privilege to use a consumer group is granted with the DBMS_RESOURCE_MANAGER_PRIVS.GRANT_SWITCH_CONSUMER_GROUP procedure.

Question 8

Which of the following statements accurately describes Database Resource Manager packages?

❍ a. **DBMS_RESOURCE_MANAGER** is used to create plans, create consumer groups, and assign privileges to consumer groups.

❍ b. **DBMS_RESOURCE_MANAGER** is used to assign privileges to consumer groups, and **DBMS_RESOURCE_MANAGER_PRIVS** is used to create consumer groups.

❍ c. **DBMS_RESOURCE_MANAGER** is used to create plans and consumer groups, and **DBMS_RESOURCE_MANAGER_PRIVS** is used to assign privileges to users or roles.

❍ d. Either **DBMS_SESSION** or **DBMS_RESOURCE_MANAGER_PRIVS** can be used to assign or switch privileges to consumer groups.

❍ e. **DBMS_RESOURCE_MANAGER_PRIVS** is used to assign privileges to resource plan directives and allocation methods.

Answer c is correct. The package DBMS_RESOURCE_MANAGER contains the procedures to manage resource plans, resource consumer groups, and resource plan directives. The package DBMS_RESOURCE_MANAGER_PRIVS contains the procedures to grant and revoke valid switch groups and system privileges to users.

Question 9

If you are creating a new resource plan, which of the following are necessary steps before you set the active plan for the instance? [Choose two]

❑ a. Create a pending area with the procedure **DBMS_RESOURCE_MANAGER.CREATE_PENDING_AREA**.

❑ b. Create a pending area with the procedure **DBMS_RESOURCE_MANAGER_PRIVS.CREATE_PENDING_AREA**.

❑ c. Clear the pending area with the procedure **DBMS_RESOURCE_MANAGER.CLEAR_PENDING_AREA**.

❑ d. Edit the init.ora parameter **RESOURCE_MANAGER_PLAN**; set it to the name of the new plan; then restart the instance.

❑ e. Submit the pending area with the procedure **DBMS_RESOURCE_MANAGER.SUBMIT_PENDING_AREA**.

❑ f. Update the pending area with the procedure **DBMS_RESOURCE_MANAGER.UPDATE_PENDING_AREA**.

Answers a and e are correct. Before you create a resource plan or modify a DRM object, you must create a pending area. When you've completed your work and you're ready to implement the changes, execute the **SUBMIT_PENDING_AREA** procedure. You might want to execute **VALIDATE_PENDING_AREA** before you submit, just to check your work. However, the submit procedure implicitly calls the validate procedure before updating the data dictionary.

Question 10

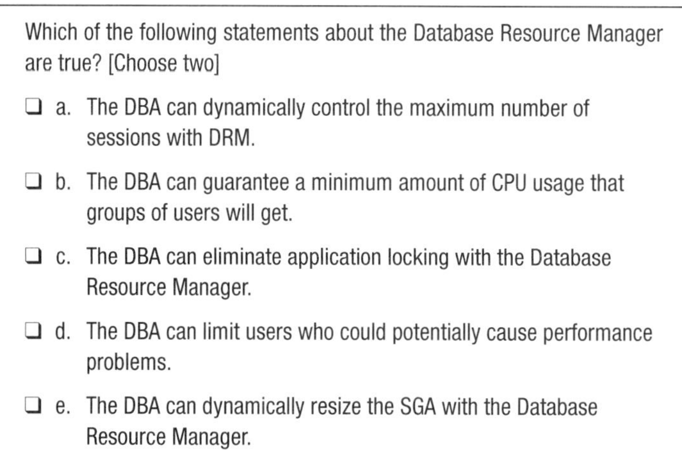

Which of the following statements about the Database Resource Manager are true? [Choose two]

- ❑ a. The DBA can dynamically control the maximum number of sessions with DRM.
- ❑ b. The DBA can guarantee a minimum amount of CPU usage that groups of users will get.
- ❑ c. The DBA can eliminate application locking with the Database Resource Manager.
- ❑ d. The DBA can limit users who could potentially cause performance problems.
- ❑ e. The DBA can dynamically resize the SGA with the Database Resource Manager.

Answers b and d are correct. The DBA can guarantee a minimum CPU percentage to a resource consumer group. The DBA can also limit the degree of parallelism for users who might cause potential bottlenecks, as in Denial of Service attacks from Internet users. Answers a, c, and e are all dreams that we have as DBAs, but the Database Resource Manager cannot dynamically control the maximum number of sessions, eliminate application locking, or dynamically resize the SGA. Maybe in Oracle 9?

Need to Know More?

Austin, David, Megh Thakkar, and Kurt Lysy. *Migrating to Oracle8i*. Sams Publishing, 2000. ISBN 0-672-31577-7. Chapter 27 includes a discussion on the Database Resource Manager and Internet security.

Ault, Mike. *Oracle8i Administration and Management*. Wiley Computer Publishing, 2000. ISBN 0-471-35453-8. Chapter 9, User and Security Administration, contains a good section on DB Resource Manager.

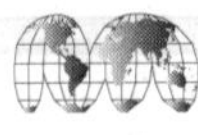

The following documents are available on the Oracle server intallation CD, or you can download them from **http://technet.oracle.com**.

Joyce Fee. *Oracle8i Administrator's Guide* (Part No. A67772-01). Oracle Corporation, 1999. Chapter 11 explains DB Resource Manager.

Leverenz, Lefty, and Diana Rehfield. *Oracle8i Concepts* (Part No. A67781-01). Oracle Corporation, 1999.

Cyran, Michele. *Oracle8i Supplied Packages Reference* (Part No. A68001-01). Oracle Corporation, 1999. See Chapter 39 for details on the **DBMS_RESOURCE_MANAGER** package, Chapter 40 for the same with **DBMS_RESOURCE_MANAGER_PRIVS**, and Chapter 43 for correct usage of DBMS_SESSION.

Visit the Oracle Technet Web site: **http://technet.oracle.com/**.

Sample Test

In this chapter, we provide pointers to help you develop a successful test-taking strategy. We discuss how to choose proper answers, how to decode ambiguity, how to work within the Oracle testing framework, how to decide what you need to memorize beforehand, and how to prepare in general for the test. At the end of this chapter, we include a set of 60 questions on subject matter that is pertinent to Exam 1Z0-020, "Oracle8i: New Features for Administrators." In Chapter 18, you'll find the answer key to this test. Good luck!

Questions, Questions, Questions

There should be no doubt in your mind that you are facing a test full of specific and pointed questions. The "Oracle8i: New Features for Administrators" test consists of 60 questions that you must complete in 90 minutes.

Questions belong to one of three basic types: multiple-choice with a single answer, multiple-choice with more than one answer, and fill-in-the-blank questions. You must answer the fill-in-the-blank questions with the exact answer, including spelling, or you will miss the question.

Always take the time to read a question at least twice before selecting an answer, and always look for an Exhibit button as you examine each question. Exhibits include graphics information that pertains to the question. (An exhibit is usually a screen capture of program output, a specific SQL statement, or GUI information that you must examine to analyze the question's scenario and formulate an answer.)

Not every question has only one answer; many questions require multiple answers. Therefore, it's important to read each question carefully—not only to determine how many answers are necessary or possible, but also to look for additional hints or instructions when you're selecting answers. Such instructions often occur in brackets immediately following the question itself (as they do for all multiple-choice questions in which one or more answers are possible).

Picking Proper Answers

Obviously, the only way to pass any exam is to select enough of the right answers to obtain a passing score. However, Oracle's exams are not standardized like the SAT and GRE exams required for entrance to college or graduate school in the U.S.; they are far more diabolical and convoluted. In some cases, questions are strangely worded, and deciphering them can be a real challenge. In those cases, you might need to rely on answer-elimination skills. Almost always, at least one answer out of a question's possible choices can be eliminated immediately because it matches one of these conditions:

- It doesn't apply to the situation.
- It describes a nonexistent issue, an invalid option, or an imaginary state.

After you eliminate all answers that are obviously wrong, you can apply your retained knowledge to eliminate further answers. Look for items that sound correct but that refer to actions, commands, or features that are not present or available in the situation that the question describes. Also look in other test questions for possible answers to the question you're struggling with.

If you're still faced with a blind guess among two or more potentially correct answers, reread the question. Try to picture how each of the possible remaining answers would alter the situation. Be especially sensitive to terminology because sometimes the choice of words ("remove" instead of "disable") can make the difference between a right answer and a wrong one.

Only when you've exhausted your ability to eliminate answers should you guess at an answer. An unanswered question offers you no points, but guessing gives you at least some chance of getting a question right. Just don't be too hasty when making a blind guess.

You can wait until the last round of reviewing marked questions (just as you're about to run out of time, or out of unanswered questions) before you start making guesses.

Decoding Ambiguity

Exams are meant to test knowledge on a given topic, and the scores from a properly designed test will have the classic bell-shaped distribution for the target audience, meaning that a certain number will fail. A problem with this exam is that it has been tailored to Oracle's training materials, and some of the questions in the exam are just plain ambiguous. In the practice questions in the previous chapters, we have tried to represent the types of questions you will see in the OCP exam. We have done the same with the questions in this chapter.

The only sure way to overcome some of the exam's limitations is to be prepared. You will discover that many of the questions test your knowledge of something that is not directly related to the issues that the questions raise. This means that the answers offered to you, even the incorrect ones, are as much a part of the skill assessment as are the questions themselves. If you do not have a thorough grasp of all the aspects of an exam topic (in this case, Oracle8i), you will not be able to eliminate answers that are obviously wrong because they relate to a different aspect of the topic than the one the question addresses.

Questions can reveal answers, especially when dealing with commands. So read a question and then evaluate the answers in light of common terms, names, and structure.

Another problem is that Oracle uses some terminology in its training materials that isn't found anywhere else in its documentation sets. Whether this is a deliberate attempt to force you to take its classes to pass the exam or simply a case of documentation oversight is unknown.

Working within the Framework

The test questions appear in random order, and many elements or issues that receive mention in one question also crop up in other questions. It's not uncommon to find that an incorrect answer to one question is the correct answer to another question, or vice versa. Take the time to read every answer to each question, even if you recognize the correct answer to a question immediately. This extra reading may spark a memory or remind you about a feature or function that helps you on another question elsewhere in the exam.

You can revisit any question as many times as you like. If you're uncertain of the answer to a question, check the box that's provided to mark it for easy return later on. You should also mark questions that you think might offer information that you can use to answer other questions. We usually mark somewhere between 25 and 50 percent of the questions. The testing software is designed to let you mark every question if you choose, so use this feature to your advantage. Everything you will want to see again should be marked; the testing software can then help you return to marked questions quickly and easily.

Deciding What to Memorize

The amount you must memorize for an exam depends on how well you remember what you've read and how well you intuitively know the software. If you are a visual thinker and you can see the drop-down menus and dialog boxes in your head, you won't need to memorize as much as someone who's less visually oriented. Because the tests will stretch your recollection of new commands, tools, utilities, and functions in Oracle8i, you'll want to memorize—at a minimum—the following kinds of information:

- The various new utilities introduced in Oracle8i
- The various new features and related SQL commands introduced in Oracle8i
- Which existing features have been enhanced (such as partitioning) and how those enhancements work
- Which existing features have been changed (such as the creation of the recovery catalog in RMAN) and how those changes affect the database and its operation

If you work your way through this book while sitting at a machine with Oracle8i, try to manipulate the features and functions of the various commands, tools, and utilities as they're discussed. In doing so, you should have little or no difficulty mastering this material. Also, don't forget that the Cram Sheet at the front of the book captures the material that is most important to memorize, so use it to guide your studies as well.

Preparing for the Test

The best way to prepare for the test—after you've studied—is to take at least one practice exam. We've included one in this chapter for that reason; the test questions are located in the pages that follow. (Unlike the preceding chapters in this book, the answers don't follow the questions immediately; you'll have to flip to Chapter 18 to review the answers.)

Give yourself 90 minutes to take the exam. Keep yourself on the honor system, and don't look at earlier text in the book or jump ahead to the answer key. When your time is up or you've finished the questions, you can check your work in Chapter 18. Pay special attention to the explanations for the incorrect answers; these can also help to reinforce your knowledge of the material. Knowing how to recognize correct answers is good, but understanding why incorrect answers are wrong can be equally valuable.

Taking the Test

Relax. Once you're sitting in front of the testing computer, there's nothing more you can do to increase your knowledge or preparation. Take a deep breath, stretch, and start reading that first question.

There's no need to rush; you have plenty of time to complete each question and to return to those questions that you skip or mark for return. If you read a question twice and remain clueless, you can mark it. Both easy and difficult questions are intermixed in random order throughout the test. Don't cheat yourself by spending too much time on a hard question early in the test, which deprives you of the time you need to answer the questions at the end of the test.

You can read through the entire test and, before returning to marked questions for a second visit, figure out how much time you've got per question. As you answer each question, remove its mark. Continue to review the remaining marked questions until you run out of time or you complete the test.

That's it for pointers. Here are some questions for you to practice on.

Sample Test

Question 1

What are the two installation modes supported by the Oracle Universal Installer? [Choose two]

- ❑ a. Interactive
- ❑ b. Silent
- ❑ c. Quiet
- ❑ d. Batch
- ❑ e. Net-based

Question 2

To install the Java Virtual Machine in an Oracle8i database, you will need to run which of the following scripts?

- ❍ a. catproc.sql
- ❍ b. loadjava.sql
- ❍ c. initjvm.sql
- ❍ d. loadjvm.sql
- ❍ e. catalog.sql

Question 3

Which of the following is a new feature that was introduced in Net8 with Oracle8i and that requires no application changes to utilize?

- ❍ a. Load balancing
- ❍ b. Automated instance registration
- ❍ c. Client runtime failover
- ❍ d. ODBC connectivity
- ❍ e. None of the above

Question 4

Which is not a benefit of fine-grained access control (FGAC)?

❍ a. Data access is controlled at the database level, rather than at the application level.

❍ b. FGAC is easy to set up.

❍ c. FGAC is very flexible.

❍ d. FGAC allows for much more sophisticated security policies with regard to data availability.

❍ e. FGAC allows you to change security policies without requiring that changes be made to the application.

Question 5

Which of the following commands is not a valid new SQL*Plus command in Oracle8i?

❍ a. **STARTUP**

❍ b. **SHUTDOWN**

❍ c. **SHOW SGA**

❍ d. **SHOW PGA**

❍ e. **ARCHIVE LOG LIST**

Question 6

In Oracle8i, what type of object can be partitioned that could not be partitioned in Oracle8?

❍ a. Table

❍ b. Local index

❍ c. Global index

❍ d. Bitmap index

❍ e. All of these could be partitioned in Oracle8

Question 7

Complete the following SQL statement:

```
________________________.SET_CONTEXT  -
('cont_tab_hr','f_hr_stuff',hr_variable);
```

Question 8

What will happen if the **ARCH** process cannot copy an archived redo log to a mandatory archive-log destination?

- ❍ a. Nothing; the **ARCH** process will continue to attempt the copy until it's successful.
- ❍ b. An Oracle error message will be sent to all connected users, and the database will crash.
- ❍ c. The Oracle database will suspend operations when it attempts to reuse the online redo log that is waiting to be archived to the mandatory destination.
- ❍ d. The mandatory destination will be marked **INVALID**, and **ARCH** will no longer attempt to copy archived redo logs to it.
- ❍ e. The **ARCH** process will fail, and the database will revert to **NOARCHIVELOG** mode.

Question 9

What are the two refresh modes of a materialized view?

- ❑ a. **ON COMMIT**
- ❑ b. **AFTER COMMIT**
- ❑ c. **AFTER UPDATE**
- ❑ d. **ON DEMAND**
- ❑ e. **FULL**

Question 10

In the following Top-N SQL query, what information will be displayed?

```
SELECT * FROM
(SELECT * FROM scott.emp
 ORDER BY hire_date asc)
WHERE ROWNUM < 11;
```

❍ a. The rows with the 10 lowest row numbers will be displayed.

❍ b. The first 10 employees hired will be displayed, sorted by **hire_date**.

❍ c. The rows with the 10 highest row numbers will be displayed.

❍ d. The last 10 employees hired will be displayed, sorted by **hire_date**.

❍ e. The first 11 employees hired will be displayed, sorted by **hire_date**.

Question 11

Which of the following two **IMPORT** parameters are required when you transport tablespaces?

❑ a. **DATAFILES**

❑ b. **TRANSPORT_TABLESPACE**

❑ c. **IMPORT_METADATA**

❑ d. **TRIGGERS**

❑ e. **FROMUSER**

Question 12

Which of the following RMAN commands are new in Oracle8i? [Choose two]

- ❑ a. **CREATE CATALOG**
- ❑ b. **MIGRATE CATALOG**
- ❑ c. **UPGRADE CATALOG**
- ❑ d. **DUPLICATE CATALOG**
- ❑ e. **DROP DATABASE**

Question 13

When you create a partitioned table that contains a **LOB** column, what other objects are created? [Choose two]

- ❑ a. **LOB** index partition
- ❑ b. **LOB** locator partition
- ❑ c. **LOB** data partition
- ❑ d. **LOB** rowid index
- ❑ e. No additional objects are created. With partitioned tables, all **LOB** storage is maintained within the partitioned table itself.

Question 14

Which of the following is not a valid **ALTER TABLE** command when you're modifying a hash-partitioned table?

- ❍ a. **ALTER TABLE...ADD PARTITION**
- ❍ b. **ALTER TABLE...COALESCE PARTITION**
- ❍ c. **ALTER TABLE...SPLIT PARTITION**
- ❍ d. **ALTER TABLE...RENAME PARTITION**
- ❍ e. None of the above operations is supported for a hash-partitioned table.

Question 15

What types of DML statements are allowed during a table move?

❍ a. No DML is allowed on any types of tables.

❍ b. DML is allowed on an IOT while you're rebuilding its primary key index.

❍ c. **INSERT** and **UPDATE** activity is allowed, but **DELETE** activity is restricted.

❍ d. All DML activities are supported during a table move on all table types.

❍ e. DML is allowed only if the move operation is moving the table to a new tablespace.

Question 16

Based on the following SQL, what kind of index will be built?

```
CREATE INDEX ix_test_me
ON emp (UPPER(name) )
TABLESPACE data
STORAGE (INITIAL 100k NEXT 100k);
```

❍ a. Reverse key

❍ b. Bitmap

❍ c. Primary key

❍ d. Descending

❍ e. Function-based

Question 17

After you complete the migration of an Oracle7 database to Oracle8i, you should run which script to ensure that all PL/SQL modules are valid?

❍ a. utlval.sql

❍ b. utlrp.sql

❍ c. u0703040.sql

❍ d. catproc.sql

❍ e. catalog.sql

Question 18

Which SQL statement would you use to cause the database to use stored outlines?

❍ a. **ALTER DATABASE USE OUTLINE**

❍ b. **ALTER SYSTEM SET STORED_OUTLINES=TRUE**

❍ c. **ALTER SYSTEM SET USE_STORED_OUTLINES=TRUE**

❍ d. **ALTER DATABASE SET USE_STORED_OUTLINES=TRUE**

❍ e. **ALTER STORED OUTLINES ENABLE**

Question 19

In Oracle8i, when you're issuing the command **ALTER TABLESPACE tablespace_name READ ONLY**, what happens? [Choose two]

❑ a. The tablespace is immediately made read-only even if transactions are actively updating objects in the tablespace.

❑ b. The tablespace is placed in transitional read-only mode.

❑ c. The command fails if there are any active transactions in the database.

❑ d. The command might appear to hang because it is waiting for transactions to complete.

❑ e. This is not a valid SQL command.

Question 20

Which of the following statements will take an existing table and register it as a materialized view?

❍ a. **CREATE VIEW my_view MATERIALIZED AS SELECT * FROM emp;**

❍ b. **CREATE MATERIALIZED VIEW mat_my_view FROM EXISTING_VIEW my_view;**

❍ c. **CREATE MATERIALIZED VIEW mat_my_view ON PREBUILT TABLE my_view ENABLE QUERY REWRITE AS SELECT * FROM emp;**

❍ d. **ALTER VIEW my_view AS mat_my_view (OPTION MATERIALIZED)**

❍ e. No direct method is provided by Oracle to convert an existing view to a materialized view.

Question 21

Which of the following RMAN commands require the presence of a recovery catalog? [Choose two]

- ❑ a. **RECOVER**
- ❑ b. **RESTORE**
- ❑ c. **STARTUP**
- ❑ d. **CREATE SCRIPT**
- ❑ e. **RESTORE** without a control file
- ❑ f. **DUPLICATE**

Question 22

Which of the following utilities should you use to load a **Java** class into the database?

- ❍ a. compilejava
- ❍ b. loadjava
- ❍ c. installjava
- ❍ d. classloader
- ❍ e. orajava

Question 23

Which Oracle8i commands are used to temporarily halt all IO on the database and then continue normal database operations? [Choose two]

- ❑ a. **ALTER SYSTEM SUSPEND**
- ❑ b. **ALTER SYSTEM RESTART**
- ❑ c. **ALTER DATABASE RESUME**
- ❑ d. **ALTER SYSTEM RESUME**
- ❑ e. **STARTUP**
- ❑ f. **SHUTDOWN**

Question 24

Which of the following are new standby-database features introduced in Oracle8i? [Choose two]

- ❑ a. Automated application of archived redo logs
- ❑ b. Read-only database
- ❑ c. Automated failover
- ❑ d. The ability to issue DML commands against objects in the standby database while it's in managed recovery mode
- ❑ e. The ability to have the standby database on a different version of Oracle than the primary database

Question 25

A locally managed temporary tablespace must use the ________________ extent allocation parameter for extent management.

Question 26

You drop a partition from a partitioned global index. How will this operation affect the other partitions in that index?

- ❍ a. There will be no impact.
- ❍ b. Oracle will mark all partitions unusable in that index, and you will need to rebuild the entire index.
- ❍ c. The next highest partition will be marked unusable and will need to be rebuilt.
- ❍ d. Oracle will automatically rebuild all partitions that would be marked unusable.
- ❍ e. You cannot drop a partition from a global index.

Question 27

What will be the result of the following SQL statements?

```
CREATE TABLE test_table
(id   NUMBER,
 test VARCHAR2(10) )
PARTITION BY RANGE (id)
(
     PARTITION ONE VALUES LESS THAN (100),
     PARTITION TWO VALUES LESS THAN (200),
     PARTITION THREE VALUES LESS THAN (300)
)
/

CREATE INDEX ix_test_table ON test_table(id)
GLOBAL
PARTITION BY RANGE(id)
(
     PARTITION ONE VALUES LESS THAN (100),
     PARTITION TWO VALUES LESS THAN (200),
     PARTITION THREE VALUES LESS THAN (300)
)
/
```

❍ a. The statements will successfully create a partitioned table called **test_table** and a global partitioned index called **ix_test_table**. The table and the index both will have three partitions.

❍ b. The table creation statement will fail because no **MAXVALUE** is defined for the upper limit of the **test_table** table. This will also cause the index creation to fail because no table will be present.

❍ c. The table creation will succeed, but the index creation will fail because no **MAXVALUE** is defined for the upper limit of the last partition of the global index.

❍ d. The SQL syntax of both statements is incorrect, so they will fail.

❍ e. The creation of the global index will fail because you cannot create a global index on a partitioned table in which the last defined partition of the table does not have a partition boundary set to **MAXVALUE**.

Question 28

Select the three partitioning methods supported in Oracle8i:

- ❑ a. Hash
- ❑ b. Cluster
- ❑ c. Range
- ❑ d. Composite
- ❑ e. Index

Question 29

What tool is provided in Oracle8i to help you create an Oracle database?

- ❍ a. Database Creation Wizard
- ❍ b. Database Creation Assistant
- ❍ c. Database Configuration Wizard
- ❍ d. Database Configuration Assistant
- ❍ e. Server Manager

Question 30

You need to create a dictionary file in preparation for using LogMiner to analyze some archived redo logs. How do you create the dictionary file?

- ❍ a. Use the SQL command **CREATE LOGMNR DICTIONARY**.
- ❍ b. Make sure the **UTL_FILE_DIR** init.ora parameter is set, and then use the Oracle procedure **DBMS_SYSTEM.LOGMNR_DICTIONARY_BUILD** to build the dictionary file.
- ❍ c. Make sure the **UTL_FILE_DIR** init.ora parameter is set, and then use the Oracle procedure **DBMS_LOGMNR_D.BUILD** to build the dictionary file.
- ❍ d. Run the creldict.sql script.
- ❍ e. Use RMAN to create the dictionary file with the **CREATE LOG MINER DICTIONARY** command.

Question 31

Which of the following system resources can be controlled with the Database Resource Manager? [Choose two]

- ❑ a. Percentage of CPU resources used
- ❑ b. Degree of parallelism
- ❑ c. Disk utilization
- ❑ d. Memory utilization
- ❑ e. Number of CPUs utilized

Question 32

Which of the following is not a step in creating and using a resource plan?

- ❍ a. Create a resource consumer group.
- ❍ b. Create resource plan directives.
- ❍ c. Assign users to consumer groups.
- ❍ d. Specify a plan for an instance by setting the init.ora parameter **RESOURCE_MANAGER_PLAN**.
- ❍ e. Configure the resconf.ora operating-system-level file to interface with the Database Resource Manager.

Question 33

What will be the result of the following SQL statement?

```
ALTER TABLE emp
SET UNUSED COLUMN old_empl_id;
```

❍ a. This SQL statement will succeed. It will mark the **old_empl_id** column as unused, staging it for later deletion.

❍ b. This SQL statement will drop the **old_empl_id** column, including its data, from the table.

❍ c. This SQL statement will cause user queries to return **NULL** values on any query of the column.

❍ d. This SQL statement will cause a column previously marked **UNUSED** to be usable again.

❍ e. This SQL statement will fail.

Question 34

Which of the following statements describe rows in a temporary table? [Choose two]

❑ a. All sessions with the same **USERID** can see the shared data in a temporary table.

❑ b. Only the current session can see data in a temporary table created by that session.

❑ c. Temporary tables do not support save points and rollback operations.

❑ d. Data in temporary tables is truncated when the session ends.

❑ e. You can create views, but not indexes, on a temporary table.

Question 35

Which refresh mode would you use when creating a materialized view, if you wished to use only the warehouse refresh facility to update the contents of the view? [Choose two]

- ❑ a. On demand
- ❑ b. Refresh
- ❑ c. Never
- ❑ d. On commit
- ❑ e. Complete

Question 36

If you have a large partitioned table that you want to load data into, and you want to guarantee unique constraint validity without the use of a unique key index, which combination of constraint options in the **ALTER TABLE** command would you use?

- ❍ a. **DISABLE VALIDATE**
- ❍ b. **DISABLE NOVALIDATE**
- ❍ c. **ENABLE VALIDATE**
- ❍ d. **ENABLE NOVALIDATE**

Question 37

The ______________________ aggregate operator should be used to create a report that generates subtotals and totals for all possible groupings.

Question 38

Parallel execution improves performance for which of the following types of operations? [Choose two]

- ❑ a. OLTP transactions
- ❑ b. Large-table scans and joins
- ❑ c. Partitioned index scans
- ❑ d. Truncate operations
- ❑ e. Dropping of large indexes

Question 39

Stored plans are kept in which of the following tables? [Choose one]

- ❍ a. **OUTLN.OL$**
- ❍ b. **SYS.OL$**
- ❍ c. **OUTLN.OL$HINTS**
- ❍ d. **OUTLN.OUTLINE$**
- ❍ e. **SYS.V$OUTLINE**

Question 40

If you create a PL/SQL procedure, and you want the privileges to be resolved with the rights of the user that is calling the procedure, which authorization clause will you use in your code?

- ❍ a. **AUTHID CURRENT_ID**
- ❍ b. **AUTHID CURRENT_USER**
- ❍ c. **AUTHID DEFINER**
- ❍ d. **AUTHID OWNER**

Question 41

If you don't set the **NATIONAL_CHARACTER_SET** value when you create a database, it will default to which value?

❍ a. The same as the database character set

❍ b. The USASCII7 character set

❍ c. **NULL**

❍ d. There will be no NLS value set, so NLS functions will not be allowed on the database

Question 42

It is now possible to execute dynamic SQL in PL/SQL code by using which one of the following commands?

❍ a. **EXECUTE DYNAMIC**

❍ b. **DYNAMIC EXECUTE**

❍ c. **EXECUTE IMMEDIATE**

❍ d. **EXECUTE DYNAMIC SQL**

Question 43

Which of the following procedures can you call from your PL/SQL code to gather statistics for a long-running operation?

❍ a. **DBMS_APPLICATION_INFO.SET_PROCEDURE_LONGOPS**

❍ b. **DBMS_APPLICATION_INFO.SET_SESSION_LONGOPS**

❍ c. **DBMS_SESSION.SET_SESSION_LONGOPS**

❍ d. **DBMS_SESSION.SET_PROCEDURE_LONGOPS**

Question 44

To create a dictionary-managed tablespace, which of the following **EXTENT MANAGEMENT** clauses of the **CREATE TABLESPACE** command will you use? [Choose two]

- ❑ a. **CREATE TABLESPACE...DICTIONARY MANAGED**
- ❑ b. **CREATE TABLESPACE...EXTENT MANAGEMENT DICTIONARY**
- ❑ c. **CREATE TABLESPACE...EXTENT MANAGEMENT SYSTEM**
- ❑ d. **DICTIONARY MANAGED** is the default, so no clause is required if you want to create a dictionary-managed tablespace.
- ❑ e. **CREATE TABLESPACE...EXTENT MANAGEMENT UNIFORM**

Question 45

You create a transportable tablespace set, but one of a table's partitions is in a tablespace that is not in the tablespace set. What will happen to the transport process?

- ❍ a. The export/import will work, but the missing partition will not be in the target database.
- ❍ b. The export will work, but the import will fail because a tablespace is missing.
- ❍ c. The export will work, but Oracle will log a non-fatal error message on the import.
- ❍ d. When you run the **TRANSPORT_SET_CHECK** procedure, the view **TRANSPORT_SET_VIOLATIONS** will have an entry indicating that the partitioned table is not fully contained in the tablespace set.
- ❍ e. No errors will be logged; this is a good way to transport only the partitions that you want to move.

Question 46

Which of the following is true about index-organized tables?

❍ a. When you rebuild an index-organized table with the **ALTER TABLE...MOVE** command, you must also rebuild any secondary performance indexes.

❍ b. When you rebuild an index-organized table with the **ALTER TABLE...MOVE** command, you do not need to rebuild any secondary performance indexes.

❍ c. You can't build secondary performance indexes on an index-organized table because there is no physical rowid in an IOT.

❍ d. To build a secondary performance index on an IOT, you must use the special syntax **CREATE IOT SECONDARY INDEX**.

Question 47

Which of the following statements accurately describe descending-key indexes? [Choose two]

❑ a. In previous versions of Oracle, the **DESC** keyword was used to create accurate descending-key indexes.

❑ b. Descending-key indexes are really function-based indexes, so the **QUERY_REWRITE** privileges must be granted to the user before the index is created.

❑ c. Descending-key indexes are really function-based indexes, but the **QUERY_REWRITE** privileges do not have to be granted.

❑ d. Statistics must be run at least once on a descending-key index, or it will not be used.

❑ e. Descending-key indexes are not implemented in Oracle8i.

❑ f. Bitmap indexes usually perform better if they are also descending key.

Question 48

You can gather statistics for an index when you create or rebuild it by using which of the following commands?

❍ a. **ALTER INDEX...ESTIMATE STATISTICS**

❍ b. **ALTER INDEX...ESTIMATE STATISTICS SAMPLE 10%**

❍ c. **ALTER INDEX...COMPUTE STATISTICS**

❍ d. **CREATE INDEX...ESTIMATE STATISTICS**

❍ e. **CREATE INDEX...ESTIMATE STATISTICS VALIDATE STRUCTURE CASCADE**

Question 49

When you create a locally-managed tablespace, which of the following **EXTENT** clauses is allowed?

❍ a. **NEXT**

❍ b. **INITIAL**

❍ c. **PCTINCREASE**

❍ d. **MAXEXTENTS**

❍ e. **MINEXTENTS**

Question 50

A subpartition is defined in what kinds of partitioned tables?

❍ a. Range

❍ b. Hash

❍ c. Nonpartitioned

❍ d. Composite

❍ e. None of the above

Question 51

You have just executed a direct-path SQL*Loader load using the parameter **SKIP_INDEX_MAINTENANCE=Y**. How will this operation affect the tables indexes?

❍ a. The partitioned global and partitioned local indexes of the table will be marked **UNUSABLE**.

❍ b. The partitioned global indexes of the table will be marked **UNUSABLE**.

❍ c. All indexes on the table will be marked **UNUSABLE** or will be in **DIRECT LOAD** state.

❍ d. Oracle will wait until the load is complete to rebuild all indexes.

❍ e. No indexes will be affected by the load.

Question 52

After you've created a dimension, what Oracle-supplied procedure can you use to validate the dimension created?

❍ a. **DBMS_OLAP.VALIDATE_DIMENSION**

❍ b. **DBMS_OLAP.CHECK_DIMENSION**

❍ c. **DBMS_OLAP.CONFIRM_DIMENSION**

❍ d. **DBMS_SYSTEM.VALIDATE_DIMENSION**

❍ e. **DBMS_MVIEW.VALIDATE_DIMENSION**

Question 53

What procedure is used to manage materialized views?

❍ a. **DBMS_SYSTEM.MVIEW_BUILD**

❍ b. **DBMS_DDL.BUILD_MVIEW**

❍ c. **DBMS_SCHEDULE.RUN_MVIEW**

❍ d. **DBMS_MVIEW.REFRESH_ALL_MVIEWS**

❍ e. **DBMS_MVIEW.FULL_REFRESH**

Question 54

What mode would you use the Universal Installer in if you needed to install database software over the network with no user interaction?

❍ a. Update mode

❍ b. Quiet mode

❍ c. Automated mode

❍ d. Perky mode

❍ c. Silent mode

Question 55

Which functionality is supported by the Data Migration Assistant?

❍ a. New database creation

❍ b. Database removal

❍ c. Modification of Net8 network files

❍ d. Upgrade of an Oracle database

❍ e. None of the above

Question 56

Fill in the blank to complete this SQL statement.

```
CREATE TABLE audit_table
( timestamp               DATE,
   user_id        VARCHAR2(30),
   message       VARCHAR2(100)
)
STORAGE (INITIAL 1M NEXT 1M)
PARTITION BY _______________(timestamp)
(
     PARTITION   part_001
     TABLESPACE  part_tbs_001,
     PARTITION   part_002
     TABLESPACE  part_tbs_002,
     PARTITION   part_003
     TABLESPACE  part_tbs_003,
     PARTITION   part_004
     TABLESPACE  part_tbs_004,
     PARTITION   part_005
     TABLESPACE  part_tbs_005 );
```

Question 57

Which of the following operations, if performed on partitions with data, will never cause one or more partitions of a global index to be marked **UNUSABLE**?

❍ a. **ALTER INDEX...SPLIT PARTITION**

❍ b. **ALTER INDEX...DROP PARTITION**

❍ c. **ALTER TABLE...MOVE PARTITION**

❍ d. **ALTER TABLE...EXCHANGE PARTITION**

❍ e. **ALTER TABLE...ADD PARTITION**

❍ f. None of the above

Question 58

Which of the following operations can't be performed in **NOLOGGING** mode?

- ❍ a. Parallel **CREATE TABLE...AS SELECT**
- ❍ b. **CREATE INDEX**
- ❍ c. **REBUILD PARTITION** operation
- ❍ d. Direct-load inserts
- ❍ e. Conventional-path SQL*Loader operations

Question 59

You want to add a partition to a global index. Which command would you use to perform this operation?

- ❍ a. **ALTER INDEX...ADD PARTITION**
- ❍ b. **ALTER INDEX...DIVIDE PARTITION**
- ❍ c. **ALTER INDEX...SPLIT PARTITION**
- ❍ d. **ALTER INDEX...MODIFY PARTITION**
- ❍ e. **ALTER INDEX...USE PARTITION**

Question 60

What new Oracle8i feature is useful when you need to establish user-session context settings upon sign-on to the database?

- ❍ a. Setting a logon event trigger
- ❍ b. Setting the init.ora parameter **RECORD_LOGON=TRUE**
- ❍ c. Issuing the command **ALTER SYSTEM CONFIGURE LOGGING=TRUE;**
- ❍ d. Issuing the command **CREATE LOGON PROCEDURE**
- ❍ e. Using the **DBMS_RLS** package

Answer Key

1. a,b
2. c
3. b
4. b
5. d
6. d
7. **DBMS_SESSION**
8. c
9. a, d
10. b
11. a, b
12. a, c
13. a, cc
14. c
15. b
16. e
17. b
18. c
19. b, d
20. c
21. d, e
22. b
23. a, d
24. a, b
25. **UNIFORM**
26. c
27. c
28. a, c, d
29. d
30. c
31. a, b
32. e
33. a
34. b, d
35. a
36. a
37. **CUBE**
38. b, c
39. a
40. b
41. a
42. c
43. b
44. b, d
45. b
46. d
47. c, d
48. c
49. b
50. d
51. c
52. a
53. d
54. e
55. d
56. **HASH**
57. f
58. e
59. c
60. a

This is the answer key to the sample test presented in Chapter 17.

Question 1

Answers a and b are correct. You use the interactive mode installation to install the Oracle software interactively, and you use the silent mode to install the Oracle software (and even a database) without requiring user interaction. This allows you to automate the installation process. Answers c, d, and e are all incorrect because they are not valid installation modes.

Question 2

Answer c is correct. You run initjvm.sql as **SYS** to install the Java Virtual Machine. Answer a is incorrect because catproc.sql is used to install PL/SQL in the database. Answer b is incorrect because there is no loadjava.sql script. Rather, loadjava (an executable) loads javal class, java, and jar files into the database. Answer d is incorrect because there is no loadjvm.sql script in Oracle8i. Answer e is incorrect because catalog.sql doesn't load the JVM into the database, but rather installs the Oracle data dictionary views.

Question 3

Answer b is correct. Automated instance registration is a new feature in Oracle8i. This feature allows the database to register itself with the Oracle listener process automatically. Answer a is incorrect because load balancing was not introduced in Oracle8i but has existed since Oracle 7.3. It has been improved on, however. Answer c is incorrect. Client runtime failover is not a new feature, and it does require application changes to implement. Answer d is incorrect because ODBC connectivity was previously available through NET8 (and before). Answer e is incorrect because there is a correct answer to this question.

Question 4

Answer b is correct. FGAC-based security can be quite complex to set up and establish. Therefore, answer b is not a benefit of FGAC. Answers a, c, d, and e are all incorrect because they are all features of FGAC. Controlling data access at the database level rather than at the application level makes the data and the database much more secure, so this is a benefit. Answers c and d are benefits because FGAC is very flexible; it allows you to write customized security packages that can enforce specific and sophisticated database-security requirements that might be outside the scope of Oracle's normal security features. Answer e is a feature because you can change security requirements at the database level without requiring changes to the application.

Question 5

Answer d is correct. There is no **SHOW PGA** command, even though you might want to be watching Tiger Woods while you are defragmenting your database. Answers a, b, c, and e are all new valid SQL*Plus commands in Oracle8i.

Question 6

Answer d is correct. In Oracle8i, you can partition bitmap indexes for the first time. Answers a, b, and c are all incorrect because these objects could be partitioned in Oracle8. Answer e is incorrect because there is a correct answer to this question.

Question 7

DBMS_SESSION is correct. The **SET_CONTEXT** procedure is part of the **DBMS_SESSION** package.

Question 8

Answer c is correct. Oracle will continue to cycle through the other online redo log groups until it returns to the group that the **ARCH** process is trying to copy to the mandatory archive-log destination. If the mandatory archive-log destination copy has not occurred, then database operations will suspend until the copy is successful or the DBA has intervened. Answer a is incorrect because all database activity will eventually be halted until the **ARCH** process has copied the online redo log(s) to the mandatory destination(s). Answer b is incorrect because this situation should not cause a database crash. Answer d is incorrect because the archive-log destination is not marked **INVALID** and **ARCH** will continue to attempt the copy operation. Answer e is incorrect because the **ARCH** process won't fail and the database won't revert to **NOARCHIVELOG** mode.

Question 9

Answers a and d are correct. The **ON COMMIT** and **ON DEMAND** modes allow you to define when a materialized view is refreshed. When the **ON COMMIT** mode is used, the view will be updated when a commit occurs on the table that the view is built on. The use of the **ON COMMIT** option when creating a materialized view is also subject to several restrictions. The **ON DEMAND** mode allows you to use the Oracle warehouse refresh feature to determine when you want to update the materialized view. Answers b and c are incorrect and are not valid refresh modes. Answer e is incorrect because it is a refresh option, not a refresh mode.

Question 10

Answer b is correct. The first 10 employees whom the company hired will be displayed, and this display will be sorted by **hire_date**. Answer a is incorrect because the subquery doesn't order by **ROWNUM**; rather, it orders by **hire_date**. Answer c is incorrect for the same reason. Answer d is incorrect because the first 10 employees will be displayed. Answer e is incorrect because 10 rows will be displayed, rather than 11.

Question 11

Answers a and b are correct. You use the **DATAFILES** parameter to determine which data files will be imported into the database. Use the **TRANSPORT _TABLESPACE** parameter to indicate that tablespaces will be imported; this is a Y/N flag. Answers c and d are incorrect because these are not valid **IMPORT** parameters. Answer e is incorrect because **FROMUSER** is not required when you transport tablespaces.

Question 12

Answers a and c are correct. You use the **CREATE CATALOG** command to create the recovery catalog, and you use the **UPGRADE CATALOG** command to upgrade your recovery catalog to the more recent version of the Oracle database. Answers b, d, and e are all incorrect because they are not valid RMAN commands.

Question 13

Answers a and c are correct. Two additional segments are created that are equipartitioned with the original partitioned table. These segments are the **LOB** index partition and the **LOB** data partition for out-of-line **LOB** storage. Answers b and d are incorrect because these partitions don't exist. Answer e is incorrect because additional objects are created.

Question 14

Answer c is correct. The **ALTER TABLE...SPLIT PARTITION** command is not a valid command. With a hash-partitioned table, this command is not supported because the table is partitioned on a hash value rather than on a range value. Answer a is incorrect because you can add a partition to a hash-partitioned table. This causes the data in the partitioned table to be redistributed among the existing and new partitions. Answer b is incorrect because you can coalesce a hash-partitioned table's partition. Again, this causes the contents of the partition being coalesced to be redistributed to the other partitions. Answer d is incorrect because you can rename a partition in a hash-partitioned table. Because answer c is the correct answer, answer e is incorrect.

Question 15

Answer b is correct. DML operations are supported on an index-organized table only when it is being moved with the **ALTER TABLE...MOVE** command. Answers a, c, d, and e are all incorrect because you can issue DML statements against an index-organized table while it is being moved with the **ALTER TABLE...MOVE** command.

Question 16

Answer e is correct. This SQL statement will create a function-based index called **IX_TEST_ME**. Answers a, b, c, and d are incorrect. Though these are valid index types, the given SQL statement won't create any of these.

Question 17

Answer b is correct. The utlrp.sql script is used to recompile any invalid PL/SQL objects in the migrated database. Answer a is incorrect because this is not a valid script. Answer c is incorrect because this is one of the scripts used to actually do the migration process. Answers d and e are both incorrect because these scripts are used when you're creating a database for the first time.

Question 18

Answer c is correct. Use the **ALTER SYSTEM SET USE_STORED_OUTLINES=TRUE** statement to force the database to use stored outlines. You can also designate a name category instead of **TRUE** if you have stored your outlines using a specific identifier. Answers a, b, d, and e are all invalid SQL statements and will cause an Oracle error message to appear.

Question 19

Answers b and d are correct. When you issue the command to put the tablespace in **READ ONLY** mode, the tablespace will be placed in transitional read-only mode until all transactions updating objects in that tablespace are completed. After those transactions are complete, the tablespace will be placed in **READ ONLY** mode. This might cause the command to appear to hang for a short period of time, until the transactions are completed. Answer a is incorrect because Oracle must wait for all transactions in that tablespace to be completed before putting the tablespace in read-only mode. Answer c is incorrect because this is a changed behavior in Oracle8i, as opposed to Oracle8. Answer e is obviously incorrect because there are correct answers provided for this question.

Question 20

Answer c is correct. Use the **ON PREBUILT TABLE** clause of the **CREATE MATERIALIZED VIEW** command to create a materialized view using an existing table. You can choose to enable query rewrite, as we did in answer c. Answers a, b, and d are all incorrect SQL statements and will generate errors. Answer e is incorrect because you can convert an existing view to a materialized view.

Question 21

Answers d and e are correct. These operations require that the recovery catalog be present. Answers a, b, c, and f all can be executed without the presence of the recovery catalog.

Question 22

Answer b is correct. The loadjava utility loads the **Java** class into the database. Answers a, c, d, and e are all incorrect as they are not used to load javal classes into the database.

Question 23

Answers a and d are correct. Use the **ALTER SYSTEM SUSPEND** and **ALTER SYSTEM RESUME** commands to start and stop IO operations on the database. Answers b and c are invalid SQL statements. Answers e and f, while effectively starting or stopping IO on the database, are not the most correct answers.

Question 24

Answers a and b are correct. Oracle8i and Net8 work together to permit the automated application of archived redo logs from the primary database to the standby database. Also, the standby database can be opened in read-only mode to allow user reporting against the database. Answers c, d, and e are all incorrect because these are not features supported by Oracle8i.

Question 25

UNIFORM is the correct parameter. You must use uniform extent allocation because each extent in a temporary tablespace must be the same size.

Question 26

Answer c is correct. The partition with the next highest partition range will be marked unusable, and it will need to be rebuilt. Answer a is incorrect because the next highest partition will need to be rebuilt. Answer b is incorrect because not all partitions of the index are marked unusable. Answer d is incorrect because Oracle won't automatically rebuild all the partitions marked unusable. Answer e is incorrect. Though you can't drop the last partition of a global index, you can drop other partitions of a global index.

Question 27

Answer c is correct. The table creation will be successful because the use of **MAXVALUE** is not required when you're defining a partitioned table. However, you must define **MAXVALUE** as the upper limit in the last partition of a global index in Oracle. Because this wasn't done in this example, the index creation will fail with an ORA-14021 error. Answer a is incorrect because the index creation will fail. Answer b is incorrect because the table will be created successfully. Answer d is incorrect because the syntax of the **CREATE TABLE** statement is correct. Answer e is incorrect because you can create a global index on a partitioned table, even if that table's last partition boundary is not set to **MAXVALUE**.

Question 28

Answers a, c, and d are correct. Answers b and e are incorrect because these are not partitioning methods in Oracle8i.

Question 29

Answer d is correct. The Database Configuration Assistant is provided in Oracle8i to help you with database creation. Answers a, b, and c are all incorrect representations of the actual name of the product. Answer e is incorrect. Though you can create a database with Server Manager, the question is asking about a tool that you can use to create the Oracle database.

Question 30

Answer c is correct. After you make sure the **UTL_FILE_DIR** parameter in the init.ora file is set correctly, use the **DBMS_LOGMNR_D.BUILD** procedure to create the dictionary file. Answer a is incorrect because there is no **CREATE LOGMNR DICTIONARY** SQL command. Answer b is incorrect because the procedure used is not **DBMS_SYSTEM.LOGMNR_DICTIONARY_BUILD**. Answer d is incorrect because there is no creldict.sql script. Answer e is incorrect because you don't use RMAN to create the LogMiner dictionary file.

Question 31

Answers a and b are correct. With the Database Resource Manager, you can control the percentage of CPU resources and the degree of parallelism used by users. Answers c, d, and e are all incorrect because you cannot control these resources with the Database Resource Manager.

Question 32

Answer e is correct. There is no resconf.ora operating-system-level file to configure when you're setting up a resource plan for the Database Resource Manager. Answers a, b, c, and d are all necessary steps when you're setting up a resource plan for the Database Resource Manager.

Question 33

Answer a is correct. The **SET UNUSED COLUMN** clause of the **ALTER TABLE** command will cause the column in the table to be unavailable to users, yet it doesn't drop the data from the table (saving system resources). The data can be dropped later with the **DROP UNUSED COLUMNS** clause of the **ALTER TABLE** command. Answer b is incorrect because the **SET UNUSED COLUMN** clause doesn't remove data from the column but just makes the column unavailable. Answer c is incorrect because, to the user, the column will appear to not exist any longer. Answer d is incorrect because you cannot reverse a **SET UNUSED COLUMN** action.

Question 34

Answers b and d are correct. Only the current session can see data in temporary tables that were created by that session. Also, when a session ends, all temporary tables created by that session will have their data truncated. Answer a is incorrect because only the current session that created the temporary table can see the data in it. Answer c is incorrect because save-point and rollback operations are supported in temporary tables. Answer e is incorrect because you can create views and indexes on temporary tables.

Question 35

Answer a is correct. If you indicate that the materialized view should be updated using the ON DEMAND option, then you will need to use the warehouse refresh facility to update the view. Answer d is incorrect because the view would then be updated on each commit. Answers b, c, and e are all refresh options and not refresh modes and are therefore incorrect answers.

Question 36

Answer a is correct. You would use the **DISABLE VALIDATE** clause to validate records being inserted into a partitioned table without using the unique index modified in the **ALTER TABLE** clause. The index associated with the constraint will also be dropped. The data being inserted will be checked against the partition key of the table to ensure validity. Answers b, c, and d are incorrect because these don't perform this function.

Question 37

CUBE is correct. The **ROLLUP** operator creates simple cross-tab reports with multiple levels of subtotals and the grant total. The **CUBE** operator is similar to **ROLLUP** but it returns subtotals for all groupings in the result set.

Question 38

Answers b and c are correct. Parallel execution improves performance of large-table scans by using multiple query slave processes to scan the table. The same is true for index scans if the index is partitioned. If you set the init.ora parameter **PARALLEL_AUTOMATIC_TUNING=TRUE** and you are working in a multiprocessing environment, then the Oracle optimizer will consider a parallel execution plan when optimizing the SQL statement. Answer a is incorrect because OLTP transactions are usually small and discrete and generally don't require parallelism. Answers d and e are incorrect because these operations don't support parallelism.

Question 39

Answer a is correct. The **OUTLN.OL$** table contains the stored plans created when you issued the **CREATE OR REPLACE OUTLINE** command. Answer b is incorrect because the **OL$** table is owned by the **OUTLN** schema (by default). Answer c is incorrect because the **OUTLN.OL$HINTS** table contains hints for the stored outlines in **OL$**. Answers d and e are incorrect because they don't contain the stored plans and are incorrect table names.

Question 40

Answer b, **CURRENT_USER**, is correct. With invoker rights, the routine is called with the privileges of the caller, not of the definer. Tables that are not fully qualified are resolved in the schema of the caller. Answers a and d are incorrect because **CURRENT_ID** and **OWNER** are not valid options. Answer c is incorrect because **DEFINER** would cause the procedure to use the privileges of the user who owns the code.

Question 41

Answer a is correct. If you don't specify the **NATIONAL_CHARACTER_SET** when you create the database, it will default to the database character set. The only time that answer b is correct is when USASCII7 is the database character set; but this won't always be the case. Answers c and d are not valid answers.

Question 42

Answer c, **EXECUTE IMMEDIATE**, is correct. The PL/SQL command is used to execute dynamic SQL. It replaces the use of the **DBMS_SQL** package to execute dynamic SQL. Answers a, b, and d are not valid PL/SQL commands.

Question 43

Answer b is correct. You can set your PL/SQL code to gather statistics on your long-running operation by using **DBMS_APPLICATION_INFO.SET_SESSION_LONGOPS**. The procedure will populate the view **V$SESSION_LONGOPS**. Answers a, c, and d are not valid procedures.

Question 44

Answers b and d are correct. Because **DICTIONARY** is the default, no clause is required; however, if you choose to specify an extent management clause for a dictionary-managed tablespace, you'll need to make it answer b. Answer a is not valid. Answer c is incorrect because **SYSTEM** is not valid. Answer e is incorrect because **UNIFORM** doesn't apply to dictionary-managed tablespaces.

Question 45

Answer d is correct. The procedure **DBMS_TTS.TRANSPORT_SET_CHECK** is used to verify that a tablespace set is self-contained. If partitions are missing, this procedure will indicate the nature of the error in the **TRANSPORT_SET_VIOLATIONS** view. Answers a, b, c, and e are wrong because the operation will fail.

Question 46

Answer b is correct; you don't have to rebuild a secondary index on an IOT when you rebuild the IOT with the **ALTER TABLE MOVE** command. Answer a is incorrect because it is the opposite of answer b. Answer c is incorrect because you can build secondary performance indexes on an IOT. Answer d is incorrect because no special syntax is required to build a secondary performance index on an IOT.

Question 47

Answers c and d are correct. Descending-key indexes are implemented as function-based indexes, and they require statistics on the index and the base table before Oracle will use them. Answer a is incorrect because descending-key indexes were allowed but not accurate before Oracle8i. Answer b is incorrect because the query rewrite privileges are not required for descending-key indexes. Answer e is incorrect because descending-key indexes are supported in Oracle8i. Answer f is incorrect because you can't create descending-key bitmapped indexes.

Question 48

Answer c is correct. You can gather statistics for an index when you create it or rebuild it by adding the **COMPUTE STATISTICS** clause to your command. Each of the other answers is incorrect because **ESTIMATE STATISTICS** is not supported.

Question 49

Answer b is the only correct answer. The **INITIAL** extent can be set to a value other than the default, but in locally-managed tablespaces, **NEXT**, **PCTINCREASE**, **MAXEXTENTS**, **MINEXTENTS**, and **DEFAULT STORAGE** are not allowed. These storage parameters are not valid because the extent size and number are managed locally using a bitmap in each data file.

Question 50

Answer d is correct. Subpartitions are defined only when you create composite-partitioned tables. Answer a is incorrect because range-partitioned tables don't contain subpartitions. Answer b is incorrect because hash-partitioned tables don't contain subpartitions. Answer c is incorrect because nonpartitioned tables don't contain subpartitions. Answer e is incorrect because there is a correct answer given.

Question 51

Answer c is correct. All indexes on the table being loaded will be marked **UNUSABLE** and will need to be rebuilt. Answer a is incorrect; it is not the most correct answer because regular indexes are also going to be put in **DIRECT LOAD** state. Answer b is not the most correct answer because all indexes will be affected, not just the partitioned global indexes. Answer d is incorrect because Oracle won't rebuild indexes if the **SKIP_INDEX_MAINTENANCE=Y** flag is used. Answer d is incorrect because all indexes will be affected by the load.

Question 52

Answer a is correct. The **DBMS_OLAP.VALIDATE_DIMENSION** procedure is used to validate that a dimension is correct. Answers b, c, d, and e are not valid procedures and thus are incorrect.

Question 53

Answer d is correct. The **DBMS_MVIEW.REFRESH_ALL_MVIEWS** procedure is used to refresh all materialized views. Answers a, b, c, and e are all invalid procedure names and are thus incorrect.

Question 54

Answer e is correct. The silent mode allows you to do Oracle installations, and even database installations, without any user interaction required. Answers a, b, c, and d are all incorrect.

Question 55

Answer d is correct. The Oracle Database Migration Assistant will upgrade or migrate your existing Oracle database. Answers a, b, and c are all incorrect because these actions are performed by the Database Configuration Assistant. Answer e is incorrect because we have a correct answer here.

Question 56

HASH is correct. From looking at the entire SQL statement, you can deduce that this is a hash-partitioned table and that you need to add the keyword **HASH** to complete the SQL statement.

Question 57

Answer f is correct. All of the statements shown will cause one or more partitions of a global index to be marked **UNUSABLE**.

Question 58

Answer e is correct. SQL*Loader conventional operations cannot be done in **NOLOGGING** mode. Answers a, b, c, and d are all incorrect because these operations do support **NOLOGGING** mode.

Question 59

Answer c is correct. You use the **ALTER INDEX...SPLIT PARTITION** command to create a new partition in a global index. Answer a is incorrect because you can't add an index as such; rather, you must split an existing partition into two different indexes, resulting in the creation of an additional partition. Answers b, d, and e are all incorrect because they are not valid statements.

Question 60

Answer a is correct. An event logon trigger, a new Oracle8i feature, is very useful to have when you need to establish user-session context settings upon sign-on. Answers b and c are not valid parameters or commands. Answer d, though the **CREATE PROCEDURE** command is nice to have, is not the most correct answer. Answer e is almost correct, but the **DBMS_RLS** package is used—sometime after the user has already logged onto the system—to control the user's access to specific objects. It doesn't help establish context settings.

Glossary

Absolute data-file number

Used as a part of the ROWID in Oracle7, and also known as a restricted ROWID. This is the file number where the row is located. This number is relative to the entire database.

Analyze

The process of gathering statistics on a table and/or indexes in Oracle. This is required in order to use the cost-based optimizer.

Architecture

The logical design of a system.

ARCHIVELOGmode

Mode in which an Oracle database must be set in order to facilitate hot backups. Causes the archival of online redo logs to offline redo-log storage locations.

ASCII (American Standard Code for Information Interchange)

An eight-bit character system that's standard for transferring data between systems.

Automated instance registration

Ability of the Oracle8i database to register itself with the default listener service.

Automatic parallel execution

By setting the init.ora parameter PARALLEL_AUTOMATIC_EXECUTION=TRUE, you instruct Oracle to control values for all parameters related to parallel execution. Degree of parallelism, the adaptive multi-user feature, and memory sizing are affected.

Backup piece

In RMAN, a backup set can consist of one or more backup pieces.

Backup set

In RMAN, a backup set is the set of backup pieces making a single complete backup. The backup can be a full, incremental, or archive log backup.

Block

The most granular unit of measurement of storage within Oracle. All

Oracle segments consist of multiple blocks. Once defined for an Oracle database, the block size cannot be changed without re-creating the database.

Block number

Used in both the Oracle7 restricted **ROWID** and the Oracle8 extended **ROWID**. This number identifies each block within a given data file.

Bulk binds

The process of binding (assigning values to PL/SQL variables in SQL statements) an entire collection (varrays, nested tables, index-by tables, and/or host arrays) at once.

Channel

Used in RMAN to facilitate communications between the operating system and the backup process.

Client failover

Feature provided by Oracle8i and Net8 that allows connect time failover should a database not be available.

Client-side cache

Cache established on the client in association with the use of the Oracle Names Server. Allows the client to quickly resolve name-lookup requests in a local cache, thus reducing network traffic to the names server that might be required for this activity.

Client and connection load balancing

Features provided with Net8 and Oracle8i that allow you to balance client loads among different instances or databases.

Cold backup

The process of backing up an entire Oracle database; this process requires shutting the database down, so the database is cold (not running) during the backup.

Composite-partitioned table

A table partitioned using both hash and range methodology. The underlying table is physically created as a hash table, and an overlying logical range partition is created.

Context

Holding area for information that is useful to have easily available. The context is created at login time, exists for the life of the session, and is accessible only to the session that created it.

CUBE operator

An operator that enables a **SELECT** statement to calculate subtotals for all possible combinations of a group of dimensions.

Database buffer cache

Area of shared memory that is part of the SGA of an instance and that is created at database startup. Used to store blocks of database data in memory to reduce disk I/O requirements for frequently used database blocks. Renamed **DEFAULT** buffer pool in Oracle8.

Database migration

The process of moving a database from Oracle7 to Oracle8.

Database recovery

The process of restoring a database after the loss of one or more database-related datafiles. This can include instance recovery, which requires no administrative action, or media recovery, which requires administrative action.

Database upgrade

The process of moving a database from a version of Oracle8 or Oracle8i to a later version of Oracle8i.

DBMS_PROFILER

Package that is used to profile existing PL/SQL applications and to identify performance bottlenecks.

DBMS_STATS

Package that is used to view and modify optimizer statistics gathered for database objects.

DBMS_TRACE

Package that is used to trace the execution of PL/SQL functions, procedures, and exceptions on the server.

DBMS_TTS

Package that is used to check whether the transportable set is self-contained.

DDL (Data Definition Language)

Statements in Oracle used to create, drop, and alter objects.

Deferred constraint

A constraint that can optionally be checked at the end of a transaction rather than after the completion of a statement executed against the object the constraint is associated with.

Definer-rights routines

Routines that are bound to the schema in which they reside.

Degree of parallelism

The requested number of parallel processes to be used in the execution of a SQL statement. Can be defined using several methods, including default settings on objects, hints, and directives in SQL statements.

Descending-key index

An index in which the key values are sorted from highest value to lowest value; the opposite of an ascending-key index.

Dictionary-managed tablespace

A tablespace for which Oracle updates the appropriate tables in the data dictionary whenever an extent is allocated or freed for reuse. Storage management is handled by the data dictionary.

Dimension

An Oracle object that stores hierarchical information about data.

Direct load

The process of inserting data into a table by circumventing the standard Oracle insert processes (i.e., use of the database buffer cache) and instead inserting data directly into the Oracle table.

DLL (dynamic link libraries)

Used when creating external procedures to be called from Oracle.

DML (Data Manipulation Language)
SQL statements used to manipulate data within Oracle objects. DML includes INSERT, UPDATE, and DELETE statements.

Duplexed archived redo logs
Archived redo logs that are written to two destinations. (See also *multiplexed archived redo logs*.)

Enforced constraint
An option, new in Oracle8, that allows a constraint to be enabled without checking the existing records in the relationship.

Equipartitioned
The state of two Oracle partitioned objects where the partition range of one object corresponds to the partition range of the other.

EXPLAIN_PLAN
Oracle command used to determine the access path that will be used by a SQL query. Results can be used for query performance tuning.

Export (EXP)
Oracle utility used to export part or all of an Oracle database. There are several restrictions on the Oracle objects that can be exported successfully.

Extended ROWID
ROWID format used in Oracle8. The format of the extended ROWID contains four elements: the data object number, the relative file number, the block number, and the row number.

Fast-start fault recovery
A process that consists of fast-start checkpointing and fast-start rollback, both of which contribute to faster recovery from a system fault. Fast-start checkpointing occurs continuously, advancing the checkpoint as Oracle writes blocks. Fast-start rollback rolls back only the blocks necessary to complete a new transaction.

Fine-grained access control
Oracle8i feature allowing for database-controlled row-level security on tables and views.

Full backup
A complete database backup consisting of all database datafiles. If doing a cold backup, the control and redo log files would also be included.

Function
Stored PL/SQL code that returns a value.

Function-based index
An index used to facilitate queries that qualify a value returned by a function or expression. The value of the function or expression is precomputed and stored in the index.

Global index
An index that can be partitioned and that is not related directly to the table the index is created on. A global index allows an index to be nonequipartitioned with the table it is created against. Oracle does not recognize the relationship of the index and the table partitions.

Hash-partitioned table
A table partitioned on a derived hash value of a given column.

Hint
Method in a SQL statement of tailoring the way the optimizer will create the execution path for that statement. Hints can include suggested indexes to use, parallelism requests, and other custom access paths to the data.

Hot backup
The process of backing up a database while the database is still running.

Image copy
In RMAN, an image copy is an exact copy of a data file copied somewhere else. This copy can be used to create another database or to recover an existing database manually.

Import (IMP)
Oracle utility that allows the DBA to take a file created by the export utility and import that file into another database.

Incremental backup
RMAN feature that allows the DBA to back up only the data blocks that have changed.

Index fast full scan
Method of creating an index with columns; allows a query to scan only the index and return the data set requested.

Init.ora
Oracle parameter file that controls many characteristics of the database. This file must be present to start the instance (**NOMOUNT** mode).

Instance
Collection of started Oracle processes and the allocated SGA.

Instance recovery
An automatic Oracle process that is executed upon startup of the Oracle instance after an instance failure. Processing includes rollback of uncommitted transactions, freeing locks and SGA resources.

Invoker-rights routines
Routines that are not bound to the schema in which they reside. Rights are associated with the user that calls the routine.

Java stored procedure
A program you write in Java to execute in the Oracle database server, just like a PL/SQL stored procedure.

Java virtual machine (JVM)
The program that resides on a computer and runs the Java bytecode. This is synonymous with an interpreter.

JServer
Oracle's implementation of the JVM in the database server.

Local index
An index created that is equipartitioned with the related partitioned table. The index's partition equivalency is known to the database.

Locally-managed tablespace
A tablespace in which extent management is accomplished by maintaining a bitmap in each data file.

Logical ROWID
Used by secondary indexes on index-organized tables and based on the primary key value, this is used in the place of the physical ROWID to determine the physical location of a row.

Materialized view
New object type in Oracle8i. Unlike a conventional view, a materialized view actually physically stores rows and thus requires storage space. The view can be built on one table, or on several table joins, and can contain aggregate expressions. Based on the way the view is created, it can be updated either on commit of the base table or through the use of the data warehouse refresh facility. In Oracle8i, Oracle has also renamed replicated snapshots as materialized views.

Materialized view log
New Oracle8i object type that is associated with a given Oracle table and that records all changes to that table. Used to maintain materialized views. (It is much like a snapshot log, and snapshot logs are now called materialized view logs.)

Migration Preparation utility (MIGPREP)
New Oracle8i software that allows you to copy the Oracle Migration utility to the Oracle7 ORACLE_HOME directories that are to be migrated.

Multiplexed archived redo logs
Multiple archive-log destinations (up to five) are used to ensure recoverability in case of a crash. One of the destinations can be on a remote server.

Multiplexing
A feature of the Oracle Connection Manager that allows many user connections to use a single transport to access a database.

Names server
A feature of Net8 that allows for remote resolution of a database alias for clients.

Native dynamic SQL
A feature that allows you to place dynamic SQL statements directly into PL/SQL blocks.

Nested table
An Oracle collection type that allows the storage of more than one value in a column in a single row.

Net8
Oracle networking software that provides networking facilities between the Oracle database and clients.

NOLOGGING
Option for various objects in Oracle that prevents the creation of redo when DML is executed against those objects.

Nonequipartitioned
The state of two Oracle partitioned objects where the partition of one object does not correspond to the partition of the other.

Nonprefixed index
An index in which the leading edge does not match the partition key of the table associated with that index.

Object
A structure composed of attributes and methods.

Object reference
A reference in an object table or relational table to a row in an object table.

Object table
A nonrelational table that is a collection of objects and stored row object instances. Every row stored in an object table is an object itself.

OCP (Oracle Certified Professional)
One who has passed a battery of tests and has received official certification from Oracle of this status.

OID (object identifier)
A 16-byte number that is assigned to each object to make it unique throughout the entire database. Not used with relational tables.

Oracle Advanced Security Option (ASO)
Successor to Oracle's Advanced Networking Option, ASO is a Net8 networking option that allows the encryption of network traffic.

Oracle Data Migration Assistant
A wizard-like interface provided by Oracle that automates the migration and upgrade processes.

Oracle Database Configuration Assistant
Product supplied by Oracle that assists the DBA in the creation of Oracle databases.

Oracle Migration utility
An Oracle-provided utility designed to ease the migration of the Oracle7 database to an Oracle8i database.

Oracle Software Packager
Used to package applications into components. These components can then be run by the Oracle Universal Installer.

OUTLN_PKG package
Contains the subprograms used to manage stored outlines and achieve execution plan stability.

Package
Oracle programmatic construct that contains a collection of procedures and functions.

Partition key
The column or columns that a partitioned table is partitioned on.

Partition pruning
The process of removing a partition from consideration in a query based on its partition key's relation to the WHERE clause of the query.

Partitioning
The ability to split Oracle tables and indexes into different objects based on one or more partitioning criteria.

Pending area
The work area for changes to Database Resource Manager objects.

Plan stability
The ability to use stored outlines to maintain a consistent execution plan

so that Oracle is forced to use an optimal plan each time a query executes even if the environment or statistics change.

Prefixed index
An index that is created using the same key column(s) as the partition key.

Procedure
Oracle programmatic construct that is stored in the database and does not return a value.

Query rewrite
The ability of the Oracle database optimizer to modify a given SQL statement containing tables or views into a statement that uses a materialized view. This statement would not, when issued, have a materialized view in its **FROM** clause. Oracle can determine if the statement would likely benefit from accessing the materialized view, and modify the statement such that it uses the materialized view instead of the base table.

Range-partitioned table
A table partitioned on the range of values contained in a given column or columns.

Read-only database
A standby database that has been placed in read-only mode, allowing user queries; but the only writes allowed are to temp segments.

Read-only tablespace
A tablespace that has been placed in read-only mode, allowing no writes to the tablespace.

Recovery catalog
Schema in a database that stores RMAN backup data.

Redo
Records generated in the online redo logs that record all changes to the database. If the database is in **ARCHIVELOG** mode, once filled, online redo logs are copied to the archive log directory and become archived redo logs. These archived redo logs are used in recovery of Oracle databases.

Relative data-file number
Used in the new Oracle8 extended **ROWID** format, the relative data-file number is relative to the tablespace the data-file is associated with.

Resource allocation method
In the Database Resource Manager, a policy to use when you're allocating space for any particular resource. Resource allocation methods are used by both plans and consumer groups.

Resource consumer group
A means of grouping user sessions that have similar processing and resource usage requirements.

Resource plan
A means of allocating resources among the consumer groups.

Resource plan directives
A means of assigning consumer groups or subplans to resource plans, and allocating resources among consumer groups in the plan by specifying parameters for each resource allocation method.

Restricted ROWID
The ROWID format used in Oracle7. Contains three elements: the block number, the row number, and the absolute file number.

Reverse-key index
An index in which key values are reversed in an effort to balance the index.

RMAN (Recovery Manager)
Oracle8 and Oracle8i utility that facilitates backup and recovery of Oracle databases.

ROLLUP operator
An operator that enables a SELECT statement to calculate multiple levels of subtotals across a specified group of dimensions.

Row number
Used in both the Oracle7 restricted ROWID and the Oracle8 extended ROWID, the row number defines a unique row within a data block.

ROWID
Used in an Oracle database to uniquely identify an individual row in a database. Every row has a ROWID that is unique.

Schema
Collection of Oracle objects (tables, indexes, and so on).

Server Manager
Interface with Oracle that allows the DBA to manage the database.

Server pool
A pool of parallel server processes to be called upon when parallel processing servers are needed.

SGA (System Global Area)
An area of shared memory that consists of the shared pool, the default buffer cache, and the redo log buffer. It can also consist of optional structures, including the large pool, the KEEP buffer pool, and the RECYCLE buffer pool.

Shared pool
Part of the Oracle SGA; used to store the data dictionary cache, the library cache, and other memory structures.

Silent-mode install
Installation of one or more products through the Oracle Universal Installer by using a method that does not require user interaction. This is facilitated through the creation of a "response" file, which contains the proper selections to required and optional installation parameters.

Source database
In an Oracle migration from Oracle7 to Oracle8i, the source database is the Oracle7 database.

SQL (Structured Query Language)
Used to access data within an Oracle database.

SQLJ
Embedded SQL in Java that allows applications programmers to embed static SQL operations in Java code in a way that is compatible with the Java design philosophy.

SQL*Loader
Oracle utility used to load raw data into an Oracle database. This data can be in various formats, such as reports or other formats.

Standby Database managed recovery mode
When the standby database is kept in managed recovery mode, archive logs received from the primary database are applied automatically. The database cannot be used while in managed recovery mode.

Summary management
New Oracle8i feature that allows the storage of aggregate and summary data from both fact tables and dimension tables in an object called a materialized view. This data can be accessed much faster and is kept current by the database either through on-commit refresh or by using warehouse refresh procedures contained in Oracle-supplied packages.

Tablespace
A logical database storage unit for segments that is made up of one or more physical data files.

Tablespace point-in-time recovery (TSPITR)
A feature that enables you to quickly recover one or more non-SYSTEM tablespaces to a time that is different from that of the rest of the database.

Temporary table
A table that is used to hold session-private data that exists only for the duration of a transaction or session.

TNS layer (Transparent Network Substrate)
Networking layer provided by Net8 that provides a client and a server (nodes) with common application programming interfaces (APIs), allowing a persistent pathway to transmit data between the two nodes.

Top-N SQL queries
Queries designed to return the *n*-largest or *n*-smallest values of a column. This is accomplished by generating a sorted list of data from an inner query and limiting the number of rows with an outer query.

Transportable tablespaces
The concept of exporting data-dictionary metadata about a tablespace set along with the data files associated with the tablespaces in the set, and importing the tablespace metadata and tablespaces into a target database.

Trigger
Stored PL/SQL program that executes based on a DML statement (i.e., INSERT, UPDATE, or DELETE) being executed.

Universal Installer
New Java-based installer released with Oracle8i. This installer replaces the previous character and motif mode installers previously used with Oracle. The Universal Installer provides a common graphical front end for Oracle database software installations and other products packaged by the Oracle Software Packager.

Index

Bold page numbers indicate sample exam questions.

A

D

E

F

N

O

Q

R

V